P9-EEU-755

THE WRITER'S CRAFT

THE WRITER'S CRAFT

A Process Reader

THIRD EDITION

Sheena Gillespie   Robert Becker   Robert Singleton

Queensborough Community College
City University of New York

HarperCollins*CollegePublishers*

Acquisitions Editor: Patricia Rossi
Project Editor: Thomas R. Farrell
Design Supervisor and Cover Design: Wendy Ann Fredericks
Cover Photo: Hans Neleman/The Image Bank
Production Administrator: Valerie Sawyer
Compositor: The Clarinda Company
Printer and Binder: R. R. Donnelley & Sons Company
Cover Printer: The Lehigh Press, Inc.

For permission to use copyright material, grateful acknowledgment is made to the copyright holders on pp. 389–392, which are hereby made part of this copyright page.

The Writer's Craft, Third Edition

Copyright © 1993 by HarperCollins College Publishers

All rights reserved. Printed in the United States of America. No part of this book may be used or reproduced in any manner whatsoever without written permission, except in the case of brief quotations embodied in critical articles and reviews. For information address HarperCollins College Publishers, 10 East 53rd Street, New York, NY 10022.

Library of Congress Cataloging-in-Publication Data

Gillespie, Sheena, (date)–
    The writer's craft : a process reader / Sheena Gillespie, Robert
Becker, Robert Singleton. — 3rd ed.
    p.   cm.
    ISBN 0-673-46650-7
    1. College readers.   2. English language—Rhetoric.
    I. Becker, Robert (Robert J.)   II. Singleton, Robert.   III. Title.
    PE1417.G54   1993
    808'.0427—dc20   92-27987
                                                     CIP

92 93 94 95   9 8 7 6 5 4 3 2 1

AUSTIN COMMUNITY COLLEGE
LEARNING RESOURCE SERVICES

To Scheherazade Bonnie Sheelin (1976–1991).
To Zina, Ariela, and Benjamin.
To Ruth, Clifford, and Claude.

Contents

PREFACE   *xv*

1 GENERATING IDEAS: FREEWRITING, BRAINSTORMING, JOURNAL-KEEPING   *1*

Peter Elbow   FREEWRITING   *3*

William Stafford   A WAY OF WRITING   *5*

Pete Hamill   ESSAY WITH DRAFT 6/6/44   *10*

> "I carry around index cards, which lie flat in the jacket pocket, and if I hear language, gossip, a story, a mood, I write it down on an index card. . . . Then about once a week I lay out all the index cards and see if there are stories in them worth entering in the notebook; entering them is the first stage in the notes becoming stories."

Anne Frank   *from* THE DIARY OF A YOUNG GIRL   *18*

John Coleman   *from* BLUE COLLAR JOURNAL: A COLLEGE PROFESSOR'S SABBATICAL   *21*

William Safire   ON KEEPING A DIARY   *23*

Michael Herr   *from* DISPATCHES   *25*

Warm-up Exercises   *29*

2 CLARIFYING PURPOSE   *31*

Essay with Draft
Julia Alvarez   SNOW   *40*

> "I think of my first draft as a beautiful piece of marble. That is what is given; it is the gift that is given. But the hard work—how I earn the gift—is what I make out of it."

Essay with Draft
Linda Bird Francke   THE AMBIVALENCE OF ABORTION   *44*

"In the peace and quiet of Bermuda, I decided to put my thoughts on paper. It has always been easier for me to sort out my feelings on paper than to try to arrange them neatly in the serendipity of my mind."

Adam Liptak PLAYING AIR GUITAR 52

Lynne Sharon Schwartz THE SPOILS OF WAR 54

Pham Thanh MY TWO COUNTRIES, MY FLESH AND BLOOD 57

Margaret Zeman WAR'S AFTERMATH (Student Essay) 59

Guidelines for Clarifying Purpose 61
Warm-up Exercises 62
Writing/Revising Topics 62

3 ESTABLISHING MEANING: CREATING A DRAFT 64

Essay with Draft
Patrick Fenton NOTES ON THE WRITING OF "CONFESSIONS OF A WORKING STIFF" 70

"When I first started writing I thought I was doing something wrong. I would look at the first drafts with all the cross-outs, write-ins, and notes to myself, and I would think that it should come more easily to me. I would worry that I was working too hard at it. Then one day I was up in the Great Books section of the New York Public Library on Fifth Avenue and I saw something that amazed me. I looked at the actual rough drafts of the poet Walt Whitman's *Leaves of Grass,* and I saw that it was filled with the same false starts, the same cross-outs, and same write-ins that covered my own writing."

Essay with Draft
Joyce Maynard A PERILOUS JOURNEY 79

"Because this was an emotionally written piece, I hadn't known where it was going until I got there. . . . So I essentially reversed the parts of the essay, beginning with what had initially come at the end: thoughts about my life, threats to my children's happiness and safety. Then I moved on to my friend's story."

Patrick Fenton CONFESSIONS OF A WORKING STIFF 88

Anna Quindlen I AM A CATHOLIC 94

Anne Taylor Fleming LOSING PEOPLE 97

Guidelines for Establishing Meaning 99
Warm-up Exercises 100
Writing/Revising Topics 101

4 ADDRESSING AUDIENCE 104

Essay with Draft
Marshall Glickman MONEY AND FREEDOM 107

"I try to write my first draft as quickly as possible. Even if I change 95 percent of it, getting words on the page gives me something to work with and makes continuing less intimidating."

Essay with Draft
Hana Wehle   JANUSHINKA   115

"My first draft is unorganized thoughts about what I have to write. . . . In revising, I reorganize first by checking chronology. Then I rearrange materials as I would in making a collage."

Adrienne Rich   CLAIMING AN EDUCATION   123

Daniel Meier   ONE MAN'S KIDS   127

Guidelines for Addressing Audience   130
Warm-up Exercises   131
Writing/Revising Topics   132

5   SETTING TONE   134

Essay with Draft
Rachel L. Jones   JUDGING A BOOK BY ITS COVER   139

". . . I've essentially tried to write about what I've believed in, and that holds true with this essay. . . . . As you can see from the draft, I started it off with a 'memory'—relating the subject from something that had happened to me several years earlier. I've often found that to be a good way to pull people into your topic, by not just spouting facts and figures."

Student Essay with Draft
Margaret Cardello   I WISH   147

"Writing offers me a vehicle for self-expression. I learn so much about myself in my writing. I worry about my audience enjoying my writing, as it consists so much of my own feelings. . . . I do not believe there is a set formula to writing—nor do I believe there needs to be."

H. L. Mencken   THE PENALTY OF DEATH   154

Susan Jacoby   UNFAIR GAME   157

Anna Quindlen   GOING TO THE GYM   160

Linda Weltner   EVERY 23 MINUTES. . .   164

Guidelines for Setting Tone   166
Warm-up Exercises   166
Writing/Revising Topics   168

6   COMPOSING INTRODUCTIONS AND CONCLUSIONS   170

Essay with Draft
Richard Selzer   MERCY   174

"Revision is the act of pushing words around on a page until you like the way they look. This piece dawned with the incident of the dying flies. I was then put in mind of the patient with whom I shared the experience recounted. Obviously, the horror, guilt and the dilemma had accompanied me to Italy. And beyond, into the imagination."

Essay with Draft
Myra Miller   FAREWELL TO THE BIRD   182

"Some people love cars; others don't. As a firmly entrenched member of the second group, I'm a little surprised to realize that a car touched my life and will remain in my memory long after I last saw it."

Maya Angelou   STEP FORWARD IN THE CAR, PLEASE   188

Peter Steinhart   NOSES, NATURALLY   193

Brent Staples   A BROTHER'S MURDER   198

Guidelines for Introductions and Conclusions   201
Warm-up Exercises   201
Writing/Revising Topics   203

7 COMPOSING NARRATIVE AND DESCRIPTIVE ESSAYS   205

Essay with Draft
Julia Alvarez   DAUGHTER OF INVENTION   210

"Revision is how I pay for the fantasy of being a good writer."

Student Essay with Draft
Christine Donaghy   A SECOND CHANCE   223

"When I start a new paper, the individual topics are in my mind but not in any particular order. I find that jotting them down quickly and briefly, before any of them are forgotten, and sorting them out later to elaborate on them is the easiest system. I assign the ideas a numerical order, according to the way I want the story to flow, and then build on them one by one. The principle is similar to an outline but not as structured."

Student Essay with Draft
Louis J. Russo III   A SHOT AT DREAMS   231

"When the idea of revision came about I knew it had to be done. . . . I really wasn't sure what I wanted to get across. The one thing that I did know is that no matter what I did it couldn't lose the feeling that the piece originally had. The key was length. I knew that by shortening it I would be able to go for the knockout instead of throwing a series of jabs."

Eudora Welty   MISS DULING   237

Loren Eiseley   HOW FLOWERS CHANGED THE WORLD   240

Christopher Hallowell   MAN TALK   245

Joan Ackermann   IN NEW MEXICO: A FAMILY LIVES IN
ITS OWN WORLD   248

Guidelines for Narrative and Descriptive Essays   251
Warm-up Exercises   252
Writing/Revising Topics   252

8 COMPOSING EXPOSITORY ESSAYS   255

Essay with Draft
Edward Hoagland   HAIL THE ANHINGA   259

"I seem to write anything somewhere between three and six times, and so during the first draft I just try to put down everything that I have in mind and see at a glance how it looks, sounds and stands. Then it tends to grow, not shrink, until the last go-round."

Student Essay with Draft
Wendy C. Modeste   ARE YOU REALLY A FAILURE?   264

"I wrote, started over, wrote again. I would think about the piece, walk away for a while, and then come back. . . . I wanted to give some guidelines about how to deal with failure. . . . My hope is that someone will read this article and be encouraged and realize that failing at a task does not necessarily make him or her a failure."

Marcus Mabry   LIVING IN TWO WORLDS   278

Aristotle   YOUTH AND OLD AGE   280

George Orwell   POVERTY   284

Guidelines for Expository Essays   286
Warm-up Exercises   287
Writing/Revising Topics   288

9 COMPOSING PERSUASIVE ESSAYS   290

Essay with Draft
Jim Fusilli   CRITICIZING ROCK MUSIC CRITICS   295

"When I have an idea for a piece, I spend an inordinate amount of time thinking about, refining it, studying its angles, before I commit an outline to paper. In some cases, I've ruminated on pieces of fiction for years. This process, I think, is my journal."

Student Essay with Draft
Tekla Devai   WHY I DON'T READ THE NEWS ANYMORE   304

"Usually I do not have the work ready in my mind when I put my pen to the paper or turn on the word processor. As I write on, my thoughts become visible, and I can examine them, weigh them, and see whether they can withstand criticism."

Student Essay with Draft
George Kormos   GIVING THE DEATH PENALTY TO DRUG DEALERS   310

"I feel my style is very direct and to the point. When given a topic, I like to build my paper on the first impression I get from the piece. . . . I like to choose a topic that I can have fun with, a topic that I am fairly knowledgeable in. This gives me a chance to voice my opinions on certain issues and feelings I have."

Rachel L. Jones   WHAT'S WRONG WITH BLACK ENGLISH   316

Martin Luther King, Jr.   I HAVE A DREAM   319

Joseph Wood Krutch   THE VANDAL AND THE SPORTSMAN   324

Barbara Lazear Ascher   ON COMPASSION   326

Sydney H. Schanberg   HOW SHOULD REPORTERS COVER DEATH?   329

Louise Montague   STRAIGHT TALK ABOUT THE LIVING-TOGETHER ARRANGEMENT   332

Guidelines for Persuasive Essays   336
Warm-up Exercises   336
Writing/Revising Topics   337

10 POLISHING FOR PRESENTATION   340

Essay with Draft
E. B. White   DEATH OF A PIG   345

"I always write a thing first and think about it afterward, which is not a bad procedure because the easiest way to have consequential thoughts is to start putting them down."

Essay with Draft
Russell Baker   HERE TO STAY   356

"I have always thought journalism ought to be at least slightly imperfect, so my first drafts are almost always the final drafts. After a few minutes of pencil revision, the first draft goes to the printer. If it's not so hot I say, 'It's only daily journalism.' In the next forty-eight hours I'll have another chance to do better. Books are different. My last book has passages I rewrote fifty times."

William Zinsser   WORDS   364

Joan Didion   MARRYING ABSURD   369

Anne Morrow Lindbergh   A FEW SHELLS   372

Guidelines for Polishing for Presentation   376
Warm-up Exercises   376
Writing/Revising Topics   379

GLOSSARY   *381*

ACKNOWLEDGMENTS   *389*

Preface

It is often only in the process of writing that I really discover what it is I am trying to write about.

—David Updike

I think of my first draft as a beautiful piece of marble. That is what is given. . . . But the hard work—how I earn the gift—is what I make out of it.

—Julia Alvarez

I looked at the actual, rough drafts of the poet Walt Whitman's Leaves of Grass, *and I saw that is was filled with the same false starts, the same cross-outs, and the same write-ins that covered my own writing.*

—Patrick Fenton

These quotations capture the major themes of *The Writer's Craft*: discovery, rewriting, technique. Writing is discovery; revision is necessary; the "how-to" of writing can and must be learned—through writing.

The Drafts

Because student writers should learn to revise their work effectively, we have sought to emphasize what most inexperienced writers overlook—that revising is not a touch-up or correction phase of writing but that it is an instrumental, inseparable part of the overall writing process. Revising is not simply recopying. And since students often believe that experienced writers create essays without any of the mess or fuss that they themselves experience, the necessity of revising is best demonstrated by showing that professional writers also create drafts of their work. We wrote to established contemporary writers requesting their participation in our project and were surprised and overjoyed by their responses. The diversity of manuscripts we received confirms our belief in the importance of revision. Some drafts are almost illegible because of massive changes; others show signs of only scanty editing. Some are written and revised in longhand while others are mechanically reproduced with handwritten changes. Some, obscured by coffee stains, reflect long hours of labor but are transformed three or four or six or ten versions later into fresh typewritten copy. Whatever the author's personal style, the message is clear: Revision is indispensable. *The Writer's Craft* contains 18 original photographic reproductions of draft essays by professional writers. Students can witness in a textbook in-depth revising as it occurs from draft to finished product.

By examining the drafts, students will learn three essential concepts about writing and revising. First, they will no longer feel that professional authors are a breed apart, that their talents enable them to write flawlessly and without using processes common to all writers. Second, students will see the diversity of approaches to revising, a diversity that reinforces the personal nature of writing but that establishes beyond any doubt that revising—no matter *how* it is done—must be done. Third, by learning the vocabulary and techniques of revising, students will be able to understand and apply revision to their own writing.

The drafts included in this edition that have been created by students confirm these goals and purposes. These student writers, by using revision to make their essays more effective, exercise the same control over their drafts that is demonstrated by the professional writers. Again, the message we seek to convey is that *all* writers benefit from revising their work.

To help students and instructors use the drafts in this book we have developed special supporting materials. Each draft is preceded by an introduction that explains both how the authors applied that phase of the writing process to their work and then how they revised that work. Questions and commentary comparing draft and published versions focus on how and why specific revisions were made. Screened pages ensure easy access to the drafts; use of a second color helps readers work back and forth between drafts and published essays.

Arrangement and Organization

How does the organization of *The Writer's Craft* help students to improve the quality of their finished essays? The first five chapters discuss ways to generate ideas and to improve the writer's rhetorical stance by examining relationships among purpose, meaning, audience, and tone. Chapter 6 presents the special problems of beginning and ending an essay. Chapters 7, 8, and 9 present traditional—modal—ways to develop the body of an essay. Chapter 10 relates diction and sentence variety to the processes of revising and polishing. The ten chapters are thus organized as one would approach a writing project, beginning by choosing a topic and ending with editing. Throughout the text, students are reminded of the necessary interplay of creating/inventing, composing, and revising—a strategy that helps them to view themselves as writers in control of their writing.

In this edition, we have expanded the strategies for revision in Chapter 2, and draft paragraphs from professional writers illustrate the revision strategies. Chapter 3 has been revised radically to give new emphasis to the drafting process in establishing meaning. Chapter 10 has been reworked and highlights the relationship of diction and sentence variety to the process of editing and proofreading. These discussions help students distinguish these processes from the larger revision strategies discussed in earlier chapters.

Essays and Headnotes

The text presents fifty-nine classic and contemporary essays and journal entries chosen for their appeal to a college audience, their lively and varied styles, and their ability to illustrate an aspect of the writing process. Each author is introduced with a headnote, twenty-four of which contain original statements on prewriting or revision from such contributors as Edward Hoagland, Richard Selzer, Joyce Maynard, Pete Hamill, and Russell Baker.

The third edition contains twenty-five new selections by classic and contemporary authors highlighting topics of interest to students, including Adrienne Rich and Daniel Meier on gender issues in education, Christine Donaghy and Wendy Modeste on returning to college, Tekla Devai on rape, and George Kormos on drug dealers and the death penalty.

Apparatus

Within each chapter, introductions and questions direct students' attention to how the professional writers have used revision and other techniques to improve their writing. Each draft has its own introduction and questions. Each additional essay is followed by sets of questions on content and process. Each chapter has a set of warm-up exercises that grow out of the chapter's readings and phase of the writing process and provide continued practice in freewriting, brainstorming, journal-keeping, observing, and interviewing. Each chapter ends with a set of writing/revising topics that incorporate the subjects, process, and revision strategies demonstrated in the professional drafts. A glossary of rhetorical terms is also included at the end of the text.

In this edition, the warm-up exercises and writing/revising topics are more closely correlated with chapter readings. Also, the process questions that follow each essay are more recursive, catching up and reinforcing craft discussions from earlier chapters as well as providing exercises on the current chapter.

Guidelines

Guidelines at the end of each chapter provide "hands on," step-by-step instructions for students to follow when writing on their own. Arranged to summarize the phase of the process highlighted in the chapter, the guidelines are easy to read and apply.

Instructor's Manual

In addition to answering questions accompanying the drafts and essays, the Instructor's Manual contains additional suggestions for using the drafts and original quotes from authors, additional questions and writing topics, as well as a rhetorical and thematic table of contents. It also includes more quotes on the writing process from the authors of the draft selections. Our ideas and suggestions in the manual have grown out of "road testing" this book in our classes.

Acknowledgments

The third edition of *The Writer's Craft* would not have been possible without the enthusiasm, cooperation, and contributions of professional writers who were willing not only to submit drafts but also to share their prewriting and revision strategies. We are most grateful to Julia Alvarez, Russell Baker, Patrick Fenton, Linda Bird Francke, Jim Fusilli, Marshall Glickman, Pete Hamill, Edward Hoagland, Rachel L. Jones, Joyce Maynard, Myra Miller, Anna Quindlen, Sydney H. Schanberg, Richard Selzer, Brent Staples, Peter Steinhart, Hana Wehle, and the late E. B. White.

Our thanks also to student writers Miriam Vento and Steve Hirschfeld for sharing their journal entries and to Margaret Cardello, Tekla Devai, Christine Donaghy, George Kormos, Wendy C. Modeste, Louis J. Russo III, and Margaret Zeman for submitting drafts and essays.

Linda C. Stanley, Director of the English Department's Writing Program at Queensborough Community College, supported us with pertinent resource material, and Margaret Cavanaugh, Marge Caronna, and Kathy Howard assisted in preparation of the manuscript.

We have also received invaluable criticism from our reviewers:

Patricia A. Bridges, Grand Valley State University

Diane Thomas Christian, Angelo State University

Nicole H. M. Greene, University of Southwestern Louisiana

Finally, we would like to thank our acquisitions editor, Patricia Rossi, and our developmental editor, Marisa L. L'Heureux, for critiquing the manuscript and for insightful and meticulous editing; and our designers.

SHEENA GILLESPIE
ROBERT BECKER
ROBERT SINGLETON

THE WRITER'S CRAFT

Generating Ideas: Freewriting, Brainstorming, Journal-Keeping

As with any other craft, writing takes time and practice to master. As with any other craft, the practitioner must become familiar with the methods and tools of the trade. The tools that writers use are words and ideas, and you have already been using an abundant supply of these for many years. Yet in mastering the craft of writing, all writers need to use these tools *in certain ways* that assure effective communication with readers. Understanding the *process* of writing will help you to become more skilled in the craft.

Getting started is usually the trickiest part of writing. At one time or another, when faced with having to write something, you might have experienced these feelings:

- a suspicion that you have nothing of interest to say
- a belief that nothing you write will be good enough
- a fear of making mistakes

Any one of these conditions is enough to trigger writer's block. Obviously, blocked writers would welcome a successful formula for getting started, but even those who generally do not experience writer's block may benefit from a way to get started that will make them more comfortable with writing and better able to generate ideas.

Freewriting is one way of getting started. In his essay in this chapter Peter Elbow defines *freewriting* as the undelayed, uncensored writing down of whatever occurs to you about a subject. Without calling his method by that name, poet William Stafford instead describes his way of getting started as a kind of "fishing." In his essay in this chapter, he describes how he takes a pen and paper in hand and waits to catch some idea or impression, which then serves as a starting point for other ideas. Whether they wait (like Stafford) or write continuously (like Elbow), many experienced writers and other beginning writers have found it valuable to get something on paper—a thought, a feeling, or an impression—whenever they must fulfill a writing assignment.

Another technique that you might find helpful in getting started is *brainstorming*. Brainstorming is a *listing* of specific ideas. It is like freewriting in that it usually is done rapidly for a specified amount of time as a means of gathering thoughts about a subject, but whereas freewriting uses phrases and sentences, brainstorming records only isolated words in an effort to focus more specifically on the subject. Brainstorming is a machine-gun approach; freewriting meanders like a bird on a summer's day. When you write in list form you should not be tempted to criticize or correct the mechanics—new ideas, images, parts and subparts of the subject get all your attention. One item leads to another, and when your time is up, you can read over your list and eliminate or rearrange your ideas.

Keeping a journal provides another way of getting started. People have been recording their daily thoughts and activities in diaries, journals, and notebooks since writing first began. Journals are kept by the old and the young, by professionals and amateurs, by the famous and the forgotten. The diarists and journal writers in this chapter pay tribute to the diary or journal for serving them in several ways: helping them mature, storing their ideas for writing, recording their thoughts for posterity. Whereas a diary is usually a record of daily thoughts and actions, the journal may take off on meditative flights far from the day's occupations. It may mix the record of the day's activities with older memories, speculations, original or not-so-original thoughts. It can be like a letter to yourself that the world will probably never see, but that you can later mine for ideas for the essays you will be writing in your English composition course.

What does journal-writing consist of? Thoughts, feelings, experiences, and reactions to reading are often the subject matter of journals. The format is as varied as the content: short notes, stories, essays, drawings, poems, book and movie reviews, letters, quotations, songs—everything that interests or intrigues. Basically, your journal is *you*. It will express your interests, likes and dislikes, your ambitions, desires, and fears. What is written and how it is written are your own private concerns.

Most journal-keepers write intensely personal matter for their eyes alone. Anne Frank could have had no idea at all of the millions of people who would read, in many languages, the diary she kept during her days of hiding from the Nazis. On the other hand, some writers keep journals that they intend to publish. Some of the entries in this chapter are by writers like John Coleman, who wanted their journals to be read by others.

As you can see, there are many strategies for generating ideas for writing. While freewriting and brainstorming are effective techniques for rapidly gathering ideas for a short term, keeping a journal allows a writer to harness thoughts for future or long-term use. Whichever methods you find most suitable—and you will probably find yourself using all the techniques discussed—should help you to get started whenever you write. Once you are able to solve the problem of getting started, you may even begin to enjoy writing down your ideas, and writing itself will become more natural to you.

Getting Started by Freewriting

In the following essays, Peter Elbow and William Stafford describe their strategies for getting started. Read these essays carefully and think about how freewriting could help you generate ideas or overcome the problem of writer's block.

Peter Elbow

Peter Elbow (b. 1935) is director of the writing program at the University of Massachusetts at Amherst. He achieved national attention with his book *Writing Without Teachers* (1973). In *Writing with Power* (1981), Elbow describes the benefits of freewriting. His latest book is *What Is English?* (1990).

> Freewriting is the best way to learn—in practice, not just in theory—to separate the producing process from the revising process. Freewriting exercises are push-ups in withholding judgment as you produce so that afterwards you can judge better.

Freewriting

1   The most effective way I know to improve your writing is to do freewriting exercises regularly. At least three times a week. They are sometimes called "automatic writing," "babbling," or "jabbering" exercises. The idea is simply to write for ten minutes (later on, perhaps fifteen or twenty). Don't stop for anything. Go quickly without rushing. Never stop to look back, to cross something out, to wonder how to spell something, to wonder what word or thought to use, or to think about what you are doing. If you can't think of a word or a spelling, just use a squiggle or else write, "I can't think of it." Just put down something. The easiest thing is just to put down whatever is in your mind. If you get stuck it's fine to write "I can't think what to say, I can't think what to say" as many times as you want; or repeat the last word you wrote over and over again; or anything else. The only requirement is that you *never* stop.

2   What happens to a freewriting exercise is important. It must be a piece of writing which, even if someone reads it, doesn't send any ripples back to you. It is like writing something and putting it in a bottle in the sea. . . . Freewritings help you by providing no feedback at all. When I assign one, I invite the writer to let me read it. But also tell him to keep it if he prefers. I read it quickly and make no comments at all and I do not speak with him about it. The main thing

is that a freewriting must never be evaluated in any way; in fact there must be no discussion or comment at all.

3   Here is an example of a fairly coherent exercise (sometimes they are very incoherent, which is fine):

> I think I'll write what's on my mind, but the only thing on my mind right now is what to write for ten minutes. I've never done this before and I'm not prepared in any way—the sky is cloudy today, how's that? now I'm afraid I won't be able to think of what to write when I get to the end of the sentence—well, here I am at the end of the sentence—here I am again, again, again, again, at least I'm still writing—Now I ask is there some reason to be happy that I'm still writing—ah yes! Here comes the question again— What am I getting out of this? What point is there in it? It's almost obscene to always ask it but I seem to question everything that way and I was gonna say something else pertaining to that but I got so busy writing down the first part that I forgot what I was leading into. This is kind of fun oh don't stop writing—cars and trucks speeding by somewhere out the window, pens clittering across peoples' papers. The sky is still cloudy—is it symbolic that I should be mentioning it? Huh? I dunno. Maybe I should try colors, blue, red, dirty words—wait a minute—no can't do that, orange, yellow, arm tired, green pink violet magenta lavender red brown black green—now that I can't think of any more colors—just about done—relief? maybe.

4   Freewriting may seem crazy but actually it makes simple sense. Think of the difference between speaking and writing. Writing has the advantage of permitting more editing. But that's its downfall too. Almost everybody interposes a massive and complicated series of editings between the time words start to be born into consciousness and when they finally come off the end of the pencil or typewriter onto the page. This is partly because schooling makes us obsessed with the "mistakes" we make in writing. Many people are constantly thinking about spelling and grammar as they try to write. I am always thinking about the awkwardness, wordiness, and general mushiness of my natural verbal product as I try to write down words.

5   But it's not just "mistakes" or "bad writing" we edit as we write. We also edit unacceptable thoughts and feelings, as we do in speaking. In writing there is more time to do it so the editing is heavier: when speaking, there's someone right there waiting for a reply and he'll get bored or think we're crazy if we don't come out with *something*. Most of the time in speaking, we settle for the catch-as-catch-can way in which the words tumble out. In writing, however, there's a chance to try to get them right. But the opportunity to get them right is a terrible burden: you can work for two hours trying to get a paragraph "right" and discover it's not right at all. And then give up.

6   Editing, *in itself,* is not the problem. Editing is usually necessary if we want to end up with something satisfactory. The problem is that editing goes on *at the same time* as producing. The editor is, as it were, constantly looking over the shoulder of the producer and constantly fiddling with what he's doing while he's

in the middle of trying to do it. No wonder the producer gets nervous, jumpy, inhibited, and finally can't be coherent. It's an unnecessary burden to try to think of words and also worry at the same time whether they're the right words.

7   The main thing about freewriting is that it is *nonediting*. It is an exercise in bringing together the process of producing words and putting them down on the page. Practiced regularly, it undoes the ingrained habit of editing at the same time you are trying to produce. It will make writing less blocked because words will come more easily. You will use up more paper, but chew up fewer pencils.

8   Next time you write, notice how often you stop yourself from writing down something you were going to write down. Or else cross it out after it's written. "Naturally," you say, "it wasn't any good." But think for a moment about the occasions when you spoke well. Seldom was it because you first got the beginning just right. Usually it was a matter of a halting or even garbled beginning, but you kept going and your speech finally became coherent and even powerful. There is a lesson here for writing: trying to get the beginning just right is a formula for failure—and probably a secret tactic to make yourself give up writing. Make some words, whatever they are, and then grab hold of that line and reel in as hard as you can. Afterwards you can throw away lousy beginnings and make new ones. This is the quickest way to get into good writing.

9   The habit of compulsive, premature editing doesn't just make writing hard. It also makes writing dead. Your voice is damped out by all the interruptions, changes, and hesitations between the consciousness and the page. In your natural way of producing words there is a sound, a texture, a rhythm—a voice—which is the main source of power in your writing. I don't know how it works, but this voice is the force that will make a reader listen to you, the energy that drives the meanings through his thick skull. Maybe you don't *like* your voice; maybe people have made fun of it. But it's the only voice you've got. It's your only source of power. You better get back into it, no matter what you think of it. If you keep writing in it, it may change into something you like better. But if you abandon it, you'll likely never have a voice and never be heard.

10   Freewritings are vacuums. Gradually you will begin to carry over into your regular writing some of the voice, force, and connectedness that creep into those vacuums.

William Stafford

William Stafford (b. 1914) is an American poet and teacher who was a conscientious objector during World War II and has been active since in pacifist movements. He has published poetry in many journals, including *Harper's* and the *New Yorker,* and his collections of poetry include *Traveling Through the Dark* (1963), for which he received the National Book Award. Stafford defines the role of the poet as "finding out what the world is trying to be." He also writes extensively about his craft and in the following essay, "A Way of Writing," from his book *Writing the Australian Crawl* (1978), he describes how he usually gets started. As you read his essay, compare his approach to that of Elbow.

A Way of Writing

1   A writer is not so much someone who has something to say as he is someone who has found a process that will bring about new things he would not have thought of if he had not started to say them. That is, he does not draw on a reservoir; instead, he engages in an activity that brings to him a whole succession of unforeseen stories, poems, essays, plays, laws, philosophies, religions, or—but wait!

2   Back in school, from the first when I began to try to write things, I felt this richness. One thing would lead to another; the world would give and give. Now, after twenty years or so of trying, I live by that certain richness, an idea hard to pin, difficult to say, and perhaps offensive to some. For there are strange implications in it.

3   One implication is the importance of just plain receptivity. When I write, I like to have an interval before me when I am not likely to be interrupted. For me, this means usually the early morning, before others are awake. I get pen and paper, take a glance out the window (often it is dark out there), and wait. It is like fishing. But I do not wait very long, for there is always a nibble—and this is where receptivity comes in. To get started I will accept anything that occurs to me. Something always occurs, of course, to any of us. We can't keep from thinking. Maybe I have to settle for an immediate impression: it's cold, or hot, or dark, or bright, or in between! Or—well, the possibilities are endless. If I put down something, that thing will help the next thing come, and I'm off. If I let the process go on, things will occur to me that were not at all in my mind when I started. These things, odd or trivial as they may be, are somehow connected. And if I let them string out, surprising things will happen.

4   If I let them string out. . . . Along with initial receptivity, then, there is another readiness: I must be willing to fail. If I am to keep on writing, I cannot bother to insist on high standards. I must get into actions and not let anything stop me, or even slow me much. By "standards" I do not mean "correctness"— spelling, punctuation, and so on. These details become mechanical for anyone who writes for a while. I am thinking about what many people would consider "important" standards, such matters as social significance, positive values, consistency, etc. I resolutely disregard these. Something better, greater, is happening! I am following a process that leads so wildly and originally into new territory that no judgment can at the moment be made about values, significance, and so on. I am making something new, something that has not been judged before. Later others—and maybe I myself—will make judgments. Now, I am headlong to discover. Any distraction may harm the creating.

5   So, receptive, careless of failure, I spin out things on the page. And a wonderful freedom comes. If something occurs to me, it is all right to accept it. It has one justification: it occurs to me. No one else can guide me. I must follow my own weak, wandering, diffident impulses.

6   A strange bonus happens. At times, without my insisting on it, my writings become coherent; the successive elements that occur to me are clearly related. They lead by themselves to new connections. Sometimes the language, even the

syllables that happen along, may start a trend. Sometimes the materials alert me to something waiting in my mind, ready for sustained attention. At such times, I allow myself to be eloquent, or intentional, or for great swoops (treacherous! not to be trusted!) reasonable. But I do not insist on any of that; for I know that back of my activity there will be the coherence of my self, and that indulgence of my impulses will bring recurrent patterns and meanings again.

7   This attitude toward the process of writing creatively suggests a problem for me, in terms of what others say. They talk about "skills" in writing. Without denying that I do have experience, wide reading, automatic orthodoxies and maneuvers of various kinds, I still must insist that I am often baffled about what "skill" has to do with the precious little area of confusion when I do not know what I am going to say and then I find out what I am going to say. That precious interval I am unable to bridge by skill. What can I witness about it? It remains mysterious, just as all of us must feel puzzled about how we are so inventive as to be able to talk along through complexities with our friends, not needing to plan what we are going to say, but never stalled for long in our confident forward progress. Skill? If so, it is the skill we all have, something we must have learned before the age of three or four.

8   A writer is one who has become accustomed to trusting that grace, or luck, or—skill.

9   Yet another attitude I find necessary: most of what I write, like most of what I say in casual conversation, will not amount to much. Even I will realize, and even at the time, that it is not negotiable. It will be like practice. In conversation I allow myself random remarks—in fact, as I recall, that is the way I learned to talk—so in writing I launch many expendable efforts. A result of this free way of writing is that I am not writing for others, mostly; they will not see the product at all unless the activity eventuates in something that later appears to be worthy. My guide is the self, and its adventuring in the language brings about communication.

10   This process-rather-than-substance view of writing invites a final, dual reflection:

11   1. Writers may not be special—sensitive or talented in any usual sense. They are simply engaged in sustained use of a language skill we all have. Their "creations" come about through confident reliance on stray impulses that will, with trust, find occasional patterns that are satisfying.

12   2. But writing itself is one of the great, free human activities. There is scope for individuality, and elation, and discovery, in writing. For the person who follows with trust and forgiveness what occurs to him, the world remains always ready and deep, an inexhaustible environment, with the combined vividness of an actuality and flexibility of a dream. Working back and forth between experience and thought, writers have more than space and time can offer. They have the whole unexplored realm of human vision.

As Stafford observed in "A Way of Writing," he allows himself to wait, while Elbow is afraid that waiting will bring the whole delicate beginning to a stop. See which way works for you. If you find that you want constantly to go back and correct nonsense or incomplete sentences or misspelled words, then Elbow's ceaseless freewriting might be the better way for you to get started. As you will see from the roughness of some of the early drafts in this book, the first draft is no time to worry about spelling or punctuation errors.

According to Elbow, when you freewrite you are writing as rapidly as possible and ignoring organization, punctuation, grammar, and spelling. Essentially, you are trying to take dictation from your brain. You are following your mind wherever it leads you, regardless of logic or content. Elbow's method is the freest type of freewriting, but you might experiment with these also:

1. Freewrite for five minutes. Next read over what you have written. When you are finished, select only one idea of the many that cropped up in your freewriting and write about it for five more minutes. Use the techniques you learned for freewriting, but this time stick to your single topic as closely as possible.
2. Sit quietly with your eyes closed for three to five minutes. After the time is up, freewrite for fifteen minutes. How did you feel this time when you began writing? Was it helpful to concentrate before beginning to write?

These freewriting methods all have one important thing in common—they will help you to generate ideas. Some of the ideas that you have generated in your freewriting may serve as the basis for the more structured kinds of writing you will be doing throughout the semester. In addition, freewriting will allow you to become used to writing. Remember that exercising writing "muscles" is like any form of exercise: the more you do it, the easier the process becomes and the more confident you become.

Getting Started by Brainstorming

As mentioned earlier, brainstorming is the rapid listing of ideas. For a recent short story commemorating the fortieth anniversary of D-Day, journalist and essayist Pete Hamill used brainstorming to generate ideas for his assignment. Hamill simply wrote down associations with D-Day, which later became the basis for his story. He describes the process this way:

> A scrap of language, a suggestion of a mood, a face, a smell might set me off. I then allow it to expand in my imagination, to suggest other images, much in the same way that music works. I make notes then. If the story is in a specific place, and I need detail to support it, I go to the books (my own, the library's, etc.).

Note how Hamill's brainstorming list contributes to his final draft. The author uses certain "scrap[s] of language" in the brainstorming list to suggest details that need expanding; for example, only in the story do we learn that the "bundles" are soldiers' bodies. A "suggestion of a mood" is also contained in the brainstorming list: the war action present in the list of details is the dominant feature of the italicized sections of the story. Also important are the sensations mentioned in the brainstorming list: smells, sights, and sounds abound. These same descriptive details are preserved in the completed story.

With his brainstorming list, Hamill captures important details that he does not want to lose, details that are essential to the essay he wants to write. Note that all the items on the list do not appear in the final draft: this is the result of the author's careful selection of only those ideas that are essential to his story. In any brainstorming list, some details will not fit into the essay and must be discarded. While this process of selection entails some hard choices for any writer, take comfort in the fact that such sacrifices will be offset by the important details you have preserved.

Just as Hamill uses his brainstorming list to generate and fix ideas about a topic, you might use your own list to help prepare a first draft. In this way, the vividness of detail that you capture initially in your list can be carried over into the final product.

Pete Hamill

Pete Hamill (b. 1935) is the author of several books, including the screenplay "Doc," the novels *Flesh and Blood* (1977) and *The Guns of Heaven* (1983), and the essay collection *The Invisible City* (1980). Over a 20-year newspaper career, Hamill was also a columnist and reporter for the *New York Post* and the *New York Daily News.* When asked how he usually generates ideas for a story, Hamill replied:

> I keep a notebook, no journal. I carry around index cards, which lie flat in the jacket pocket, and if I hear language, gossip, a story, a mood, I write it down on an index card; sometimes this means heading for the men's room (if in a restaurant) or the other end of an apartment when I'm at a dinner party. Then about once a week I lay out all the index cards and see if there are stories in them worth entering in the notebook; entering them is the first stage in the notes becoming stories. Some might never be used, but there are always 20 or 30 just waiting there to be realized.

Brainstorming List

They were supposed to land at Fox Green, but the
LCV was slapped around and they went too far.

Rising up, then pounding hard into the troughs, the coxswain's
eyes panicky, the officer unsure where he was;

They could see a church steeple, which he learned later
was Colleville.

Tanks burning, thick black smoke, along the tideline.
There was a hard wind: the smoke blew flat along the beach.

The roar of the engines; mouths moving without words.

The elegy.

The bundles on the shore: the 1st 2d 3d waves.

Mines on stairs. Swerving away,

Men throwing up over the side.

Then an .88 came right through the armor,
and they were screaming, and the water came
over the sides and through the hole.

Two cans came in, blasting at pill boxes and
machine gun nests, so close, they must have scraped bottom.

The mines like pie plates. Contact mines.

Stakes under the tide. Mortar fire.

They were supposed to land at Fox Green, but the
LCV was slapped around and they went too far

Rising up, then pounding hard into the troughs, the coxswain's
eyes panicky, the officer unsure where he was;

They could see a church steeple, which he learned later
was Colleville.

Tanks burning, thick black smoke, along the tideline.
There was a hard wind: the smoke blew flat along the beach.

The roar of the engines; working moving without words.

The the elegy.

The bundles on the shore: the 1st 2d 3d waves.

Bombs on stones. Swerving arm,

Men throwing up over the side

Then an .88 came right through the armor,
and they were screaming, and the water came
over the sides and through the hole.

Two cans came in, blasting at pill boxes and
machine gun nests, so close they must have scraped bottom

The mines like pie plates. Contact mines.

Stakes under the tide. Mortar fire.

6/6/44

1   Drum and Keegan, old now, steel-haired, their skins freckled, shirts too tight, sat together in the warm June sunshine on a bench across from the playground. Prospect Park smelled of new-mown grass. There was no breeze. Keegan smoked a cigaret and glanced at the newspaper on his knee. Drum watched young mothers pushing children on swings.

2   "I don't even give a hill a beans what's in the paper," Keegan was saying. "I carry it around because you gotta have sumpthin' to do. Old guy sits on a park bench nowadays, they think you're a degenerate."

3   "I know what you mean."

4   "But lookit this stuff." He tapped the newspaper. "Nicaragua. El Salvador. We're mining harbors in a country we ain't at war with, Harry. We pay all these el creepos to fight for us. These people kill nuns, Harry. I don't get it anymore, Harry."

5   Drum smiled. "It's no concern of ours anymore, Charlie."

6   "Yeah? Well, we didn't pull crap like this when I was a kid, when you was a kid."

7   Drum leaned forward, his elbows on his knees. "That woman in the dungarees. With the yellow blouse. Reminds you of Helen, doesn't she?"

8   Keegan looked at Drum. "I thought you weren't gonta talk about her anymore."

9   "I'm not talkin' about her. I'm just sayin', that woman looks like her. A statement of fact. Look at me. You see a tear? You see me upset?"

10   "No, but I don't want to neither. Every time you talk about Helen, you get weepy."

11   "I was married to her f' 32 years, Charlie."

12   Keegan opened the newspaper, "Hey, lookit this! Forty years! The anniversary. Forty years since D-Day. Can you believe it?"

13   "Yeah."

14   "Jeez, I forgot, Harry. You was there, right?"

15   Drum shrugged and stood up. "Let's take a walk."

16   *They loaded us on the LCVs in the dark, 13 miles out, the waves rising and falling, bazookas and TNT piled on the deck, and all of us with full field packs, knowing everything came to this moment, this night, this day in the English Channel; all the training, the convoy across the Atlantic, the boredom and pubs and women of England. I wrote Helen 121 letters from England alone, crazy letters, mad nutty kid letters, the words just pouring out of me, nothing about the war, nothing about Nazis or democracy or freedom or any of that; just me crazy for her, crazy to be with her, crazy to come back alive, crazy to have kids with her, a house with her, crazy to live a life. And in the LCV, jammed in with Smitty and Ralph and Cappy and Max, that's all I thought about. If I could think about Helen, her face, her hair, the way she laughed, the smell of her in the park in summer, then I wouldn't have to think about what was at the other side of the Channel. I dozed and thought about her. I squatted*

there, and thought about her. I thought of her as we rose and fell and moved through the waves, and the big guns pounded the shore.

17   They came over a rise and looked down at the broad green sward of the meadow. The Parks Department had erected metal fences for ballplayers, and Drum hated them. Drum wanted the world to stay the same for all of his life.

18   "I see those fences," he said, "I want to blow them up."

19   "They put you in the can f' that," Keegan said, laughing in his wheezy way. "And I'm too old to come visit you."

20   "But do you blame me?"

21   "Everything's changed, Harry. You can stand here and pray for a week, you ain't gona see a trolley car, you ain't gonta go to Ebbetts Field, you ain't gonta go to Luna Park."

22   "I know."

23   *I never forgot the noise. The guns of the Texas and the engines of the assault craft, and planes bombing, and guys yelling with megaphones from one boat to another. The sky went from black to gray. Miller, the farm kid from South Carolina, got up and lurched to the side of the LCV and vomited over the side, and the wind blew it all around, and then another guy was puking, and then dozens of them, and next to me Max was stiff against the steel bulk-head, his teeth chattering, and all of us were wondering who would live and who would die. The boat rose on the crest of a wave and I could see LCVs everywhere, and right ahead of us was Omaha Beach.*

24   They strolled down to the marsh that used to be the Swan Lake. Keegan dropped the newspaper in a trash can. There were ugly chunks of dirty concrete where the boat-house used to be.

25   "There was a waterfall over there," Drum said. "Remember? And paddle boats shaped like swans, and a guy selling CrackerJacks, and everbody walking across the park to the ballgames."

26   "Yeah, and up there, past the waterfall, there was a stream. Cleanest water I ever seen."

27   "Devil's Cave was next to the stream."

28   "On the left," Keegan said. "I used to hide there when it rained." He looked at Drum, who was staring out at the dead lake. "It was nice, sitting there in the rain."

29   "It was."

30   *And then it was day and we were a thousand yards from shore and the coxswain's eyes were panicky and the lieutenant unsure of where he was, looking at this map, which was soaking wet, and peering out over the top and moving his mouth without making words. I could see the beach, two tanks with smoke pouring out of them, the wind blowing the smoke flat, and a church steeple, and high cliffs, and smoke everywhere. The dull thump of explosives got sharper, splitting the air. And then I saw tracers coming from the cliffs and rows of bundles on the beach. There were huge poles*

rising from the water with contact mines hanging from them like pie plates, and huge logs cantilevered out of the sand, and Belgian Gates, these huge steel frame doors leading to nowhere, and we were closer, and bullets were caroming off the steel bulkheads, and we were closer, and the surf was being chopped by the machine guns, and we were closer, and then I saw the bundles on the beach again, and they weren't bundles, they were men, the men of the first wave, and the second wave, and the third; and two tanks were burning, and there was no artillery, and we were closer, and the coxswain was screaming at the lieutenant, and then there was a grinding sound, and the engines idled, and then the ramp was lowered, and waves poured into the LCV, and we were moving into the water. It was over our heads. I saw Cappy go under and Ralph thrashing in the water and then Miller's head exploded and there was blood and bone and tissue all over us and the lieutenant was screaming and yelling and then Robert shoved him out ahead of us into the water and then it was my turn and I said, Helen. I said, Helen. I said, Helen, Helen, Helen.

31   They left the park at 11th Avenue.

32   "Come on over later, eat something, Harry," Keegan said. "I don't like it that you're living alone. You're what? Sixty? That's a young guy nowadays, Harry. You should—"

33   "I'll see you tomorrow, Charlie."

34   *I lay behind two bodies while the machine guns hammered. I could see two battleships and a couple of cruisers, and someone was screaming off to the left, and mortars exploded in the sand, and there was blood on my face and hands and carbine and none of it was mine. The noise was ferocious, shells screaming in from the Texas, metal and rocks breaking and splintering, rifle fire and machine guns hammering and mortars and my face in the sand, and then I turned and saw two cans racing in near the shore, unloading their five-inchers, and a whumping sound, and more screaming, and one of the guys I was huddled behind was whimpering. And then someone shouted that we better get up or we'd die on the damned beach, and I waited, and then got up, and started to run, and then I was down and I could see planes overhead and my leg burning and when I tried to move I couldn't and I looked at the sky again and thought, that's it, it's over, I won, that's my war. I thought, That's it, Helen. I thought, it's June 6, 1944, 6/6/44, and I just got my ticket home.*

Getting Started by Keeping a Journal

How do you begin a journal? Simply by obtaining a notebook (preferably separate from that used for class notes) and writing in it. The easiest way to start is to record an experience you had during the day and examine your feelings and thoughts about it, as many of the writers here do, or to react to something you read or overheard or saw on television or in a film.

Even though you may not be interested in keeping a journal, you might find through experimenting with writing in one that it becomes a means of communication, a vehicle for self-understanding, a record of your thoughts, or a source for formal writing. The following pages show a few typical journal entries, including some written by students like yourself, Miriam Vento and Steven Hirschfeld. You will notice that sometimes a journal entry may wander from one subject to another until the writer finds a subject that he or she feels is worth developing. At other times the writer sticks to one train of thought throughout. Written either way, your journal entries can be a valuable source of ideas and feelings that you may be able to develop into extended essays.

The following two entries are from student writer Miriam Vento's journal.

2/27/83

I like Sundays, they are nice and long. Every thing is nice and quiet. People are home reading their newspapers or catching a black and white film. I hate to waste a Sunday studying for an exam. or cleaning my room. I prefer to spend it with my friends or just relaxing around the house. I try to avoid all thoughts about school on a Sunday. If I start to think about school I get very nervous. After twelve years I still can't feel comfortable in a classroom. Perhaps I suffer from a mild case of claustrophobia. When the buses are very crowded sometimes I feel like running out of them. At home when the heat is on and all the windows are locked, I feel like I'm suffocating I immediately open up the windows or go outside. I love nature and I wish I could live in a place where the air is clean and where life isn't a rush. My sisters and I ~~Me and my little~~ talk before going to sleep each night. We were once talking about our dream world. I told them my dream world would be made up of poets, writers and artists. The flowers would grow wild. The weather will be just right, not too cold nor to hot. Animals will roam free and would not hurt anyone. Thank God for daydreams!

3/19/83

I just got back from the park, my ~~~ friend and I were playing puddle ball. We're terrible! I'm not an athletic person though I wish I was. When I was a child I was more active. I would run, ride a bicycle, jump rope, ride a skateboard and play softball. Sometimes my grandmother had a rough time ~~bringing~~ my sisters and me home. We just loved to play in the streets.

My childhood seems so long ago. And I'm only eighteen. I wonder how far away it will look when I'm fifty.

Childhood has to be the best time in one's life. It is that time in life when one does not have to worry about anything. There are no worries, no strong fears, no pressure. Everything is just fine.

The ~~~ II is due this coming Thursday and I still don't know what to write about. I'm afraid to begin. I really want to do well on this one.

Writing is strange. Sometimes it comes out so quick and naturally. Other times you have to really think. Right now I find it very hard to fill this page up. It's a nice feeling when it all flows out. It's even nicer when you are finished.

It's funny because last year when I finished high school I set out to write a book called "My High School memoirs." I wasn't planning to publish it or anything like that. The book only lasted two typed pages. I showed my sisters what I had written so far and they told me "Miriam, this stinks!"

So goes my writing career!

The following journal entry is by student writer Steven Hirschfeld.

MAY, 14, 1983

I don't think about writing in a journal as something I have to do. I like to think about the day and record it with a few thoughts about it. I also like the idea of having an endless, continued chronology of my adult life. There are times that I feel like contemplating about how things have changed this week or what was on my mind a certain date. At these times I look over past journal entries.

The days I don't have anything to write about or creative to brainstorm, I will often read the entire past week and have much material to write from.

The personal reason that a journal is too precious to me stems from the a past of myself that I want to keep as my conscience changes. The journal has a long-term advantage in having a reference from times when we were innocent. As experiences tend to harden our conscience as we grow older, the earlier entries will always be a record I can learn with.

There are times that I don't feel very well and have the journal as a self-healing record of happier times to always remind me that life does have its better moments even when I'm feeling down. It is this self-friendship that makes me strong by understanding myself like no one else does. Of course my journal is private, but my friendship can be shared by everybody.

Anne Frank

Anne Frank (1929–1944) hid with her family in Amsterdam during the Nazi occupation. They were arrested in 1944, and eight months later Anne Frank died in the concentration camp at Bergen-Belsen. Her diary was discovered by her friends in 1947 and was published in the United States by her father in 1952. Anne Frank never intended that her journal be published. She simply wrote about her experiences as an adolescent and regarded her diary as her best friend and confidante "Kitty."

From

The Diary of a Young Girl

Thursday, 11 May 1944

. . . You've known for a long time that my greatest wish is to become a journalist someday and later on a famous writer . . . Whether I shall succeed or not, I cannot say, but my diary will be a great help. . . .

Friday, 19 May 1944

. . . All goes well with Peter and me. The poor boy seems to need a little love even more than I do. He blushes every evening when he gets his good-night kiss and simply begs for another . . .

Friday, 9 June 1944

. . . The whole of the Secret Annexe except Van Daan and Peter have read the trilogy *Hungarian Rhapsody* . . . It is a very interesting book, but in my opinion there is a bit too much about women in it . . .

Wednesday, 14 June 1944

. . . Peter loves me not as a lover but as a friend and grows more affectionate every day . . . Peter is good and he's a darling, but still there's no denying that there's a lot about him that disappoints me . . . He lets me say a lot of things to him that he would never accept from his mother . . .

Both Peter and I have spent our most meditative years in the "Secret Annexe." We often discuss the future, the past, and the present, but . . . I still seem to miss the real thing and yet I know it's there.

Thursday, 6 July 1944

Dear Kitty,

It strikes fear to my heart when Peter talks of later being a criminal, or of gambling; although it's meant as a joke, of course, it gives me the feeling that he's afraid of his own weakness . . .

We all live with the object of being happy; our lives are all different and yet the same . . . You must work and do good, not be lazy and gamble, if you wish to earn happiness. Laziness may *appear* attractive, but work *gives* satisfaction.

Poor boy, he's never known what it feels like to make other people happy, and I can't teach him that either . . .

Saturday, 15 July 1944

. . . I have one outstanding trait in my character, which must strike anyone who knows me for any length of time, and that is my knowledge of myself. I can watch myself and my actions, just like an outsider. The Anne of every day I can face entirely without prejudice, without making excuses for her, and watch what's good and bad about her . . . I understand more and more how true Daddy's words were when he said: "All children must look after their own upbringing." Parents can only give good advice or put them on the right paths, but the final forming of a person's character lies in their own hands . . .

I ponder far more over Peter than Daddy. I know very well that I conquered him instead of him conquering me. I created an image of him in my mind, pictured him as a quiet, sensitive, lovable boy, who needed affection and friendship . . . I needed a living person to whom I could pour out my heart . . . it automatically developed into an intimacy which, on second thought, I don't think I ought to have allowed . . .

"For in its innermost depths youth is lonelier than old age." I read this saying in some book and I've always remembered it, and found it to be true . . .

Tuesday, 1 August 1944

Dear Kitty,
"Little bundle of contradictions." That's how I ended my last letter and that's how I'm going to begin this one . . . What does contradiction mean? Like so many words, it can mean two things, contradiction from without and contradiction from within . . .

. . . I have, as it were, a dual personality. One half embodies my exuberant cheerfulness, making fun of everything, my high-spiritedness, and above all, the way I take everything lightly. This includes not taking offense at a flirtation, a kiss, an embrace, a dirty joke. This side is usually lying in wait and pushes away the other which is much better, deeper and purer. You must realize that no one knows Anne's better side and that's why most people find me so insufferable . . .

I'm awfully scared that everyone who knows me as I always am will discover that I have another side, a finer and better side. I'm afraid they'll laugh at me, think I'm ridiculous and sentimental, not take me seriously . . . Sometimes, if I really compel the good Anne to take the stage for a quarter of an hour, she simply shrivels up as soon as she has to speak, and lets Anne number one take over, and before I realize it, she has disappeared . . .

A voice sobs within me: "There you are, that's what's become of you: you're uncharitable, you look supercilious and peevish, people dislike you and all because you won't listen . . ." Oh, I would like to listen, but it doesn't work; if I'm quiet and serious, everyone thinks it's a new comedy and then I have to get out of it by turning it into a joke, not to mention my own family, who are sure to think I'm ill, make me swallow pills for headaches and nerves, feel my neck and my head to see whether I'm running a temperature, ask if I'm constipated and criticize me for being in a bad mood. I can't keep that up: if I'm watched to that extent, I start by getting snappy, then unhappy, and finally I twist my heart round again, so that the bad is on the outside and the good is on the inside and keep on trying to find a way of becoming what I would so like to be, and I could be, if . . . there weren't any other people living in the world.

Yours, Anne

[This is the last entry. Three days later the occupants of the "Secret Annex" were arrested. Several months later Anne died in the concentration camp at Bergen-Belsen.]

John Coleman was born in Canada in 1921. He received his Ph.D. from the University of Chicago and has published several books on labor and economics. While President of Haverford College, Coleman took a sabbatical leave in the spring of 1973 and worked at several blue-collar jobs, including ditch digging. He is currently an innkeeper in New England. As you read this excerpt from *Blue Collar Journal: A College President's Sabbatical* (1974) explaining his experiences while on leave, jot down your ideas about a job change that you would like to try.

From

Blue Collar Journal: A College President's Sabbatical

Tuesday, March 27

1   One of the waitresses I find hard to take asked me at one point today, "Are you the boy who cuts the lemons?"

2   "I'm the man who does," I replied.

3   "Well, there are none cut." There wasn't a hint that she heard my point.

4   Dana, who has cooked here for twelve years or so, heard that exchange.

5   "It's no use, Jack," he said when she was gone. "If she doesn't know now, she never will." There was a trace of a smile on his face, but it was a sad look all the same.

6   In that moment, I learned the full thrust of those billboard ads of a few years ago that said "BOY. Drop out of school and that's what they'll call you the rest of your life." I had read those ads before with a certain feeling of pride; education matters, they said, and that gave a lift to my field. Today I saw them saying something else. They were untrue in part; it turns out that you'll get called "boy" if you do work that others don't respect even if you have a Ph.D. It isn't education that counts, but the job in which you land. And the ads spoke too of a sad resignation about the world. They assumed that some people just won't learn respect for others, so you should adapt yourself to them. Don't try to change them. Get the right job and they won't call *you* boy any more. They'll save it for the next man.

7   It isn't just people like this one waitress who learn slowly, if at all. Haverford College has prided itself on being a caring, considerate community in the Quaker tradition for many long years. Yet when I came there I soon learned that the cleaning women in the dormitories were called "wombats" by all the students. No one seemed to know where the name came from or what connection, if any, it had with the dictionary definition. *The American College Dictionary* says a wombat is "any of three species of burrowing marsupials of Australia . . . somewhat resembling ground hogs." The name was just one of Haverford's unexamined ways of doing things.

8   It didn't take much persuasion to get the name dropped. Today there are few students who remember it at all. But I imagine the cleaning women remember it well.

9   Certainly I won't forget being called a boy today.

Wednesday, March 28

10   A day off once again.

11   I went into a restaurant downtown, the first time since I started work as a sandwich man. My curiosity won out. I ordered a club sandwich just to see how well it held together. It was noon, and I knew the man or woman in the kitchen must be having a rough time at that hour, but I ordered it just the same.

12   The sandwich looked fine, and its ingredients were fresh. I sent my compliments to the sandwich man, but I think the waitress thought I was nuts.

13   The place where I really wanted to eat was the Oyster House. I wanted to sit down at one of the tables and have someone—one of the many waitresses I like—bring me the menu. I wanted to order that stuffed fillet of sole, after some oysters at the bar. And I wanted the salad on the side, complete with cherry tomato and cucumber slice, and blue cheese dressing on top. I know some of the inside secrets of the place. I know, for example, that yesterday a customer got a thumbtack in his corn chowder (he was very nice about it). But I know too that the sanitation is generally good and that the people who work here care. I just wanted to see the whole meal come together as a production, fashioned by people whom I knew.

14   I'll eat there someday as a customer. And nothing that happens will escape my eye.

Sunday, April 1

15   It was hard, steady work all day long.

16   The rhythm of each day and even of each week is familiar enough that it should be getting boring by now. It doesn't seem that way yet. There is enough variety in the flow of orders and of people too that I seldom feel I have been through all this before. Cleaning up the aluminum trays, where my supplies are kept, at the end of each day is dull; I'd happily skip that if I could. But even in that there is a small element of suspense: the question each time is how far I can get with closing up for the night before the last waitress comes in with an order that requires getting the supplies out again.

17   I wonder how many loaves of bread and heads of lettuce I'd go through if I stuck at this job until retirement age.

Tuesday, April 3

18   The last day once again.

19   Joey's parting words to me were that I had been "more than just satisfactory." He said that, if I ever came back to Boston to work, I should try the Oyster House first. That's worth as much as getting an honorary degree any day.

20   Tonight I dropped my uniform in the dirty linen basket and punched the clock for the last time. The happy news is that Lonnie will be back from the hospital tomorrow and ready to take up his place once again. I looked at the salad bar as I walked out at 10:00. It had been mine for a while, but it was now Lonnie's once more.

Wednesday, April 4. Haverford, Pennsylvania

21   I drove back to Haverford today. There is a meeting of the Federal Reserve Bank's directors tomorrow morning. That meeting should end by noon. Then I can take off the director's disguise and put on the workman's again.

22   The time left is so short that I don't want to spend much of it looking for a job. I had enough of that in those three days of walking Boston's streets. So for the past week I have been buying whatever out-of-town papers I could get at a newsstand off Washington Street and studying want ads again. The area around Washington, D.C., looks most promising this time. Unless our directors' meeting is unusually long, I should be there by midafternoon. So I can start the next job hunt before dark.

23   Tonight I'm in my own home on the campus. There are lights and noises in the dormitories across the cricket field. A few recent issues of the students' newspaper are lying on the coffee table downstairs. The telephone is at my side. It's tempting to get back into Haverford affairs once again. A lot must be happening here.

24   Maybe one short visit to a dorm. Maybe just one issue of the *News*. Maybe just a couple of calls to colleagues to see how things are doing while I'm away.

25   But I don't feel ready to come back. Not yet. I went downstairs and turned out all the lights. The president isn't at home.

William Safire

William Safire (b. 1929) was born in New York City, attended Syracuse University, and began his career as a journalist with the *New York Herald Times*. After spending two decades in broadcast journalism with NBC News, he became a columnist with *The New York Times* in 1973. His many books include *Before the Fall* (1975), *On Language* (1980), and *Freedom* (1987). As you read "On Keeping a Diary" (1974), make a list of the points you find most convincing.

On Keeping a Diary

1   Diaries are no longer dear; as the invention of the telephone began the decline of letter writing, the invention of the tape recorder has led to the atrophy of the personal diary. Many of us record our words but few of us record our thoughts.

2   Why is a diary stereotyped today as the gushing of a schoolgirl or the muttering of a discontented politician, unworthy of the efforts of a busy person? Perhaps because we are out of the habit of writing, or have fallen into the habit of considering our lives humdrum, or have become fearful of committing our thoughts to paper. . . .

3   Diaries remind us of details that would otherwise fade from memory and make less vivid our recollection. Navy Secretary Gideon Welles, whose private journal is an invaluable source for Civil War historians, watched Abraham Lincoln die in a room across the street from Ford's Theater and later jotted down a detail that puts the reader in the room: "The giant sufferer lay extended diagonally across the bed, which was not long enough for him . . ."

4   Diaries can be written in psychic desperation, intended to be burned, as a hold on sanity: "I won't give up the diary again," wrote novelist Franz Kafka; "I must hold on here, it is the only place I can." Or written in physical desperation, intended to be read, as in the last entry in Arctic explorer Robert Scott's diary: "For God's sake look after our people."

5   But what of people who are neither on trial nor freezing to death, neither witnesses to great events nor participants in momentous undertakings? To most of us, a diary presents a terrible challenge: "Write down in me something worth remembering," the neatly dated page says; "prove that this day was not a waste of time."

6   For people intimidated by their own diaries, here are a handful of rules:

7   1. *You own the diary, the diary doesn't own you.* There are many days in all our lives about which the less written the better. If you are the sort of person who can only keep a diary on a regular schedule, filling up two pages just before you go to bed, become another sort of person.

8   2. *Write for yourself.* The central idea of a diary is that you are not writing for critics or for posterity but are writing a private letter to your future self. If you are petty, or wrongheaded, or hopelessly emotional, relax—if there is anybody who will understand and forgive, it is your future self.

9   3. *Put down what cannot be reconstructed.* You are not a newspaper of record, obligated to record every first time that man walks on the moon. Instead, remind yourself of the poignant personal moment, the remark you wish you had made, your predictions about the outcome of your own tribulations.

10   4. *Write legibly.* This sounds obvious, but I have pages of scribblings by a younger me who was infuriatingly illiterate. Worse, to protect the innocent, I had encoded certain names and then misplaced my Rosetta Stone; now I will never know who "JW" was in my freshman year at college, and she is a memory it might be nice to have.

11   Four rules are enough rules. Above all, *write about what got to you that day,* the way a parched John Barrymore did during a trip to Mexico in 1926 when he discovered a bar that to him was an oasis:

The beer arrived—*draft* beer—in a tall, thin, clean crystal of Grecian proportions, with a creamy head on it. I tasted it. . . . The planets seemed to pause a moment in their circling to breathe a benediction on that Mexican brewer's head. . . . Then the universe went on its wonted way again. Hot Dog! But that *was* a glass of beer!

12   That is the art of the diarist in its pure form, unafraid, intimate, important in its insignificance, ringingly free. Who can compare Barrymore's frothy recall with the insecure jottings-down of most of us on little expense ledgers?

13   Wish I still kept a diary. But you see, I get very tired at the end of the day, and besides, nothing interesting happens any more. And so to bed. . . .

Michael Herr

Michael Herr (b. 1940) is a frequent contributor to *Rolling Stone, Esquire,* and *American Review.* He also wrote the screenplays for "Apocalypse Now" (1979) and "Full Metal Jacket" (1987), and in 1977 published *Dispatches,* a documentary about the Vietnam War during the late sixties. Herr has noted that reporting the war was extremely difficult: "I went to cover the war and the war covered me." As you read his journal entry from *Dispatches,* speculate as to why Herr felt so overwhelmed by his Vietnam experience.

From

Dispatches

1   You could be in the most protected space in Vietnam and still know that your safety was provisional, that early death, blindness, loss of legs, arms or balls, major and lasting disfigurement—the whole rotten deal—could come in on the freaky-fluky as easily as in the so-called expected ways, you heard so many of those stories it was a wonder anyone was left alive to die in firefights and mortar-rocket attacks. After a few weeks, when the nickel had jarred loose and dropped and I saw that everyone around me was carrying a gun, I also saw that any one of them could go off at any time, putting you where it wouldn't matter whether it had been an accident or not. The roads were mined, the trails booby-trapped, satchel charges and grenades blew up jeeps and movie theaters, the VC[1] got work inside all the camps as shoeshine boys and laundresses and honey-dippers,[2] they'd starch your fatigues and burn your shit and then go home and mortar your area. Saigon and Cholon and Danang held such hostile vibes that you felt you were being dry-sniped every time someone looked at you, and

---

1. Vietcong.
2. Latrine cleaners.

choppers fell out of the sky like fat poisoned birds a hundred times a day. After a while I couldn't get on one without thinking that I must be out of my fucking mind.

2   Fear and motion, fear and standstill, no preferred cut there, no way even to be clear about which was really worse, the wait or the delivery. Combat spared far more men than it wasted, but everyone suffered the time between contact, especially when they were going out every day looking for it; bad going on foot, terrible in trucks and APC's,[3] awful in helicopters, the worst, traveling so fast toward something so frightening. I can remember times when I went half dead with my fear of the motion, the speed and direction already fixed and pointed one way. It was painful enough just flying "safe" hops between firebases and lz's; if you were ever on a helicopter that had been hit by ground fire your deep, perpetual chopper anxiety was guaranteed. At least actual contact when it was happening would draw long ragged strands of energy out of you, it was juicy, fast and refining, and traveling toward it was hollow, dry, cold and steady, it never let you alone. All you could do was look around at the other people on board and see if they were as scared and numbed out as you were. If it looked like they weren't you thought they were insane, if it looked like they were it made you feel a lot worse.

3   I went through that thing a number of times and only got a last return on my fear once, a too classic hot landing with the heat coming from the trees about 300 yards away, sweeping machine-gun fire that sent men head down into swampy water, running on their hands and knees toward the grass where it wasn't blown flat by the rotor blades, not much to be running for but better than nothing. The helicopter pulled up before we'd all gotten out, leaving the last few men to jump twenty feet down between the guns across the paddy and the gun on the chopper door. When we'd all reached the cover of the wall and the captain had made a check, we were amazed to see that no one had even been hurt, except for one man who'd sprained both his ankles jumping. Afterwards, I remembered that I'd been down in the muck worrying about leeches. I guess you could say that I was refusing to accept the situation.

4   "Boy, you sure get offered some shitty choices," a Marine once said to me, and I couldn't help but feel that what he really meant was that you didn't get offered any at all. Specifically, he was just talking about a couple of C-ration cans, "dinner," but considering his young life you couldn't blame him for thinking that if he knew one thing for sure, it was that there was no one anywhere who cared less about what *he* wanted. There wasn't anybody he wanted to thank for his food, but he was grateful that he was still alive to eat it, that the motherfucker hadn't scarfed him up first. He hadn't been anything but tired and scared for six months and he'd lost a lot, mostly people, and seen far too much, but he was breathing in and breathing out, some kind of choice all by itself.

3. Armored Personnel Carriers.

5   He had one of those faces, I saw that face at least a thousand times at a hundred bases and camps, all the youth sucked out of the eyes, the color drawn from the skin, cold white lips, you knew he wouldn't wait for any of it to come back. Life had made him old, he'd live it out old. All those faces, sometimes it was like looking into faces at a rock concert, locked in, the event had them; or like students who were very heavily advanced, serious beyond what you'd call their years if you didn't know for yourself what the minutes and hours of those years were made up of. Not just like all the ones you saw who looked like they couldn't drag their asses through another day of it. (How do you feel when a nineteen-year-old kid tells you from the bottom of his heart that he's gotten too old for this kind of shit?) Not like the faces of the dead or wounded either, they could look more released than overtaken. These were the faces of boys whose whole lives seemed to have backed up on them, they'd be a few feet away but they'd be looking back at you over a distance you knew you'd never really cross. We'd talk, sometimes fly together, guys going out on R & R,[4] guys escorting bodies, guys who'd flipped over into extremes of peace or violence. Once I flew with a kid who was going home, he looked back down once at the ground where he'd spent the year and spilled his whole load of tears. Sometimes you even flew with the dead.

6   Once I jumped on a chopper that was full of them. The kid in the Op shack had said that there would be a body on board, but he'd been given some wrong information. "How bad do you want to get to Danang?" he'd asked me, and I'd said, "Bad."

7   When I saw what was happening I didn't want to get on, but they'd made a divert and a special landing for me, I had to go with the chopper I'd drawn, I was afraid of looking squeamish. (I remember, too, thinking that a chopper full of dead men was far less likely to get shot down than one full of living.) They weren't even in bags. They'd been on a truck near one of the firebases in the DMZ[5] that was firing support for Khe Sanh, and the truck had hit a Command-detonated mine, then they'd been rocketed. The Marines were always running out of things, even food, ammo and medicine, it wasn't so strange that they'd run out of bags too. The men had been wrapped around in ponchos, some of them carelessly fastened with plastic straps, and loaded on board. There was a small space cleared for me between one of them and the door gunner, who looked pale and so tremendously furious that I thought he was angry with me and I couldn't look at him for a while. When we went up the wind blew through the ship and made the ponchos shake and tremble until the one next to me blew back in a fast brutal flap, uncovering the face. They hadn't even closed his eyes for him.

8   The gunner started hollering as loud as he could, "Fix it! Fix it!," maybe he thought the eyes were looking at him, but there wasn't anything I could do. My hand went there a couple of times and I couldn't, and then I did. I pulled the

4. Rest and recreation.
5. Demilitarized zone.

poncho tight, lifted his head carefully and tucked the poncho under it, and then I couldn't believe that I'd done it. All during the ride the gunner kept trying to smile, and when we landed at Dong Ha he thanked me and ran off to get a detail. The pilots jumped down and walked away without looking back once, like they'd never seen that chopper before in their lives. I flew the rest of the way to Danang in a general's plane.

Guidelines for Generating Ideas

Freewriting

1. Sit down in a quiet place where you will not be interrupted.

2. Be prepared to write for a predetermined amount of time.

3. After you begin to write, do not stop! If you run out of ideas, write that down, too. If your hand begins to ache, write about the pain you are experiencing.

4. Try to write as quickly as you can. Remember, you are trying to take dictation from your brain. See if you can keep up with it.

5. Keep yourself open to all ideas and sensations that occur while freewriting. Try to use all five senses (smell, taste, touch, hearing, sight). Also, try to avoid censoring any ideas. This may be difficult to do if you think that someone may read your freewriting.

6. Finally, while you are writing, do not worry about the rules and regulations of *formal* writing—spelling, punctuation, and grammar.

Brainstorming

1. Find a quiet place where you will not be interrupted.

2. At the top of a blank sheet of paper, write down the idea that will be the focus of your brainstorming.

3. Take a few moments to sit and think about your general topic before you begin to write.

4. Quickly write down in list form the specific ideas you are generating about your topic. As with *freewriting*, you do not need to pay attention to grammar, punctuation, or spelling. If you are brainstorming with a group of people, each of you can contribute to a master list the contents of your separate lists.

Keeping a Journal

1. Purchase a notebook or diary.

2. Write in it for at least fifteen minutes five times a week.

3. Write about anything that comes into your mind, the events of your day, your emotional response to a person or incident, or your thoughts about something you said, read, or saw.

4. Try to vary the form of your entries (diary, poem, essay, short story, dialogue, letter).

5. Do not rewrite or correct your journal unless you want to.

Warm-up Exercises

Freewriting

1. Choose one of the following topics and freewrite about it for fifteen minutes:

   last Saturday night   your dream come true
   starting your own business

2. Quickly write down a color. Now close your eyes and try to see the color you have chosen. As you keep this color before you, allow images and associations concerning it to enter your mind. After five minutes of this color meditation, use freewriting to capture all that you have seen. (Try to freewrite for ten minutes.)

3. Freewrite about either of these ideas that Anne Frank expressed in her journal:

   Parents can only give good advice or put them [their children] on the right paths, but the final forming of a person's character lies in their own hands . . .

   For in its innermost depths youth is lonelier than old age. I found this saying in some book and I've always remembered it, and found it to be true . . .

Brainstorming

1. Choose one of the following and list your feelings and thoughts about it. Do not attempt to organize, but try to free-associate for ten minutes:

family albums	prejudice
fast food	stereotypes
social class	blue collar jobs
success	computers
parents	cities
happiness	

2. Imagine yourself at a place that you like especially well, such as a lake, a beach, a mountaintop, or a meadow. Close your eyes, relax, and remain there for five minutes. While you are at this place, be sure to use all your senses to experience your environment fully: note smells, sounds, sensations, tastes, and sights. When this thinking period is over, create a brainstorming list of your visit in the following way. Begin each item of your list with the word *I* and a sense word:

		see
		hear
I	+	feel
		taste
		smell

For example, after visiting a city, your abbreviated list might look like this:

I *see* glass and concrete skyscrapers.
I *see* yellow taxicabs.
I *hear* car horns.
I *smell* sausages cooking.
I *feel* the heat of the pavement.
I *taste* soot.
I *hear* people talking.
I *feel* a crowd of people pushing me.
I *hear* the rumble of a subway.
I *hear* a street musician playing a saxophone.

3. Memory can be one of your richest sources for writing. You may see someone who reminds you of a person in your past; a perfume may lead you to remember an experience; a young boy playing basketball may remind you of your first game. Use your memory as your source to make a list of your associations with one of the following:

a special childhood friend	your first date
your first night away from home	your first case of stage fright

Keeping a Journal

1. Write a journal entry, using an experience you had during the day as the catalyst for evaluating your feelings and thoughts about a subject.

2. Write a journal entry about insights you had while visiting an unfamiliar town or city.

3. Select a quotation or saying with which you either agree or disagree. In your journal, write down the reasons for your beliefs.

4. Write a journal entry on any of the following:

a role model in sports, fashion, your expected career	playing on a team
	your reactions to a professor
your attempt to stop smoking	your favorite season of the year
learning to drive	feeling lonely
your first job	a vivid dream

5. Write a journal entry on (a) your reaction to taking a blue collar job or (b) your impressions about war after reading Hamill's "6/6/44" or the selection from Herr's *Dispatches* or both.

Clarifying Purpose

The strategies presented in Chapter 1 will allow you to begin writing with greater ease. Just as athletes need to warm up their bodies before engaging in activity, writers need to use warm-up exercises like freewriting, journal-keeping, and brainstorming before writing a first draft. Yet every time you sit down to write, you need to engage in another prewriting activity—*thinking*. Of course, you think about writing before, during, and after writing; however, if you step back from the process and examine it carefully, you will see how much you take for granted in the thinking stage and how complex it really is.

Writers need to think about many things before they begin. One of these is their *purpose*—the reason for writing. For you, and for every writer, the question of purpose can be stated as "*Why* am I writing?" You will probably give one or more of these traditional answers:

- to inform
- to explain
- to express
- to evaluate
- to entertain
- to persuade
- to comfort
- to illustrate

Or perhaps you will answer:

- to complete an assignment
- to get a good grade
- to publish

In the latter case you are really talking about the motive for writing. Purpose is such a large concept that it can include both these kinds of answers and more. Chances are that you cannot explain your reason for writing with just one statement; frequently, writers have several related purposes in mind. Although you should try to identify your purpose as soon as possible, don't expect it to be as clear as it will become when you have moved into the writing and revising of your essay. Also, there are times when you might not know for certain your reason for writing. In such instances the writing itself will help you to clarify *why* you are writing.

For example, one step in clarifying your purpose is to ask what form your writing will take. In a journal entry you may simply need to communicate with yourself—to clarify your thoughts or understand your reaction to an experience. In a personal letter you may wish to communicate your thoughts and feelings in a more polished form to someone important in your life. And in a letter of application for a job, you will try to present your qualifications for the position as effectively as possible. Writing you are asked to do in school, such as essays or term papers, will be more formal and complex, making the clarification of purpose more important and perhaps more difficult.

Depending on the nature of your assignment and topic, you may need to inform, explain, express, evaluate, entertain, or persuade. Think about the kind of information you will need: facts, examples, evidence, reasons. Careful thinking in this prewriting stage will lead to sharper, clearer writing whether you are producing a letter, memorandum, or essay.

At this point, you know how to use prewriting to generate ideas and clarify purpose. Now, and throughout this textbook, you will learn how to apply the *revision* stage of writing (what comes after something is on paper). Most inexperienced writers, however, look upon revising as correcting and recopying, as changing, for example, only a comma or a word or two. This type of revision is called *editing* (see Chapter 10), but to use revision only in this way severely limits your effectiveness: editing does not make use of the ways to reform and restructure that occur to you as you are writing. Here are the fundamental revising strategies you should begin using consciously.

Revising Strategies

Addition   Adding new information to an essay. Use addition when you want to tell more about your topic or when you wish to clarify something that you have already written by including more information. Words, phrases, sentences, or entire paragraphs may be added to a work to clarify ideas or feelings. When you want to *develop* your ideas, you will always be using addition. Some common ways of adding information include giving an example, citing an expert, offering an anecdote, providing a description, and making an analysis. In manuscripts, a writer's use of a caret ∧ indicates an addition. Just as frequently, additions may be crammed into margins or between lines of text.

The scheme of buying a spring pig in blossom time, feeding
it through summer and fall, and butchering it when the solid cold
weather arrives, is a familiar scheme to me and simply follows a
pattern centuries old. It is a tragedy enacted on most farms with
perfect ~~devotion~~ *fidelity* to the original script. The murder is in the first
degree but is quick and skilful; and the smoked bacon and ham provide
a ceremonial ending whose fitness is seldom questioned, Once in a
while something goes wrong---one of the actors ~~drops a line~~ *goes up in his lines* and the
whole performance stumbles and halts. My pig failed to show up for a *one day*
meal. The alarm spread rapidly. The classic form of the tragedy was
lost; I found myself suddenly cast in the role of a pig's friend and *outline*
physician, a farcical ~~business~~ *character* with an enema bag for a prop. I had a
presentiment hunch, the very first afternoon, that the play would never regain its
balance and that my sympathies were now wholly with the pig. This was
slapstick---the sort of *dramatic* treatment which instantly appealed to my old
dachshund, who joined the vigil, held the bag, and, when all was over,
presided at the interment. When we slid the body into the grave, we
both ~~xxxxxxxxxx~~ were shaken to the core, ~~and not from any~~
~~hunger~~ *The loss we felt was not the loss of ham - but the*
to me, ~~not that~~ he represented a distant nourishment in
He had become precious because he had a hungry time.
flopped in a suffering world
loss of pig. But I'm running ahead of my *story, and will* have to go back.

—Draft paragraph from
E. B. White's "Death of a Pig"

blackish
The anhinga is a snake-necked, spear-billed,/bird/~~xxxxxxx~~
on its wings, and   Florida's Everglades or
with silver//all but nonpareil at catching fish in swamps like/Georgia's
for action/   a picturesque ~~xxxxx~~
Okefinokee. It doesn't wait/like ~~an~~ egret or statuesque heron,
swims about, tucking
but ~~tucks~~ its wings against its sides and swims fast underwater
its ~~the~~ tail a rudder. Then it
with its feet, ~~ruddering/then~~ emerges to flourish and swallow

whole a piscatorial prize, or crayfish, baby turtle, baby alligator.

> Yet to complement such mastery underwater, you ~~will~~ *may* see it soaring
> ~~in/Hawklike~~ *in towering* circles on the southern thermals like a hawk to
> *slowly*
> entertain itself

> —Draft paragraph from
> Edward Hoagland's "Hail the Anhinga"

Deletion   Removing information from an essay. Deletion is the opposite of addition and requires you to remove words, phrases, sentences, or paragraphs from your draft. Deletion is used to sharpen the focus of your essay when you have cluttered it by providing too much information about its topic or when you have strayed from it. Deleting enables you to exert control over the amount of information contained in your essay, and condensing your ideas will help you to prevent a reader from becoming confused or bored. When deleting, keep only those details that are most interesting and informative. In drafts, the most common indication of deletion is the crossing out of text. Sometimes, however, a writer will draw a box around a large section of a draft and show a deletion by drawing a large X over it.

In the summer of 1960 my family emigrated to New York City, fleeing the tyrant Trujillo. It was an active Caribbean in those days: in nearby ~~Cuba~~, Russian missiles were being assembled, trained ~~supposedly~~ at New York City. Trujillo was completing his thirty-~~first~~ year as dictator, and a small band of men were charting his ~~ambush~~ and assassination on a highway outside the capitol. In New York we found a small apartment on the upper east side, too upper to be posh. "A sublet," it was called, full of sturdy furniture that seemed fragile because it was not ours. We were always scolded to be extra careful pulling a drawer open or clicking a cabinet shut. My three sisters and I were enrolled in a Catholic school about ten blocks downtown from our apartment, taught by the Sisters of Charity, buxom women in long black dresses with black bonnets that made them look peculiar like dolls in mourning. I liked them a lot, especially my grandmotherly teacher, Sister Zoe, who was tutoring me in English and smiling good humoredly at my many mistakes. There were not that many Hispanics those days in the city, and as the only foreign youngster (Nowadays I would no doubt be called a minority student) in my classroom, I had a special, pampered place in Sister Zoe's heart. and a special seat in the first row by the window, apart from the other children so that when their forty heads bent over their vocabulary books, Sister Zoe could come over and tutor me without disturbing them.

Slowly, she enunciated the new words I was to repeat: <u>laundromat</u>, <u>cornflakes</u>, <u>snow</u>, <u>subway</u>, and soon, bomb, nuclear war, radioactive fallout.

—Draft paragraph from
Julia Alvarez's "Snow"

It all began when I was ten.
I decided to take up a sport called Hockey.
I began to purchase the equipment for
the sport hoping that I will ~~thoroughly~~ thoroughly
enjoy the game. Well, I did. I enjoyed
the game so much, I began to play it
everyday untill I got good at it.
Then, when I felt, I was good enough
I joined a team. ~~the most fun I ever
had was when I started playing for
this team. We were named the Bruins.
We weren't such a good team, but I
was having fun and I guess thats
all that counts.~~

When I turned fourteen I was
asked to play for a team on the
island called the Flames. They
were a really good team, and I was
excited to play for them. I was invited
on a one year tryout basis, ~~so this
made me work harder then ever
before.~~ The coach told me that at times

proffesional scouts Come and see Scout his
team. I was virtually anobody, bieng a rookie
and all. at the end of the season .

—Draft paragraphs from
Louis J. Russo III's "A Shot at Dreams"

Substitution   Replacing information with other information. Substitution is a
revision strategy that helps you to say *exactly* what you want to say. A combination
of addition and deletion, substitution requires a writer to replace ineffective or
undesirable words, phrases, sentences, or paragraphs with more satisfactory ones.
By replacing what you already have written with the exact word, phrase, or sentence
that you need, you will make your writing more clear, understandable, and
enjoyable. Substitutions are recognizable because they combine the methods for
indicating additions and deletions. Sometimes in a draft a word will be written above
one that is crossed out, or a marginal notation will appear alongside a block of text
marked for deletion.

```
                        mistaking
     Yet there was no  escaping the blanched expression on
the face of the woman who'd hired me, nor the confused stares
                            when I started work.
of some of the other editors. "Oh, you got your hair braided,"
my benefactor  gulped. "It's so...different."
     That episode comes to mind because, once again, I've
come across that journalistic catch prhase of the 90's,
                                     y
that red flag that invariable makes me furious. Yet another
big newspaper recently was affirming its commitment to "cultural
diversity" in the newsroom, but explained that they were
                            lack
stymied because of the dearth of "qualified minorities,"
                                               stop using
  I wish Newspaper editors and publishers should find the
guts to drop that term and say what they really mean. They
               ACCEPTABLE
are looking for ACCEPTABLE MINORITIES, AND NOTHING ELSE.
No dreadlocks, or braids, no social consciences, dashikis,
political activism, cornrows, militant posturing, innercity
sensibilities, or any of that other messy stuff. They want
minorities so non-threatening you'd almost think they were
                                    S
some of the good old boys with a Mouth Florida suntan.
```

—Draft paragraphs from
Rachel L. Jones' "Judging a Book by Its Cover"

I DETECT

Behind this argument ~~there lies~~ a queasy sense of

(IN THE COMPUTER BUSINESS)

uncertainty, I have noticed it often in persons who ~~have are~~   WORK

IN

devoted ~~to~~ the computer industry and even among those who ~~aren't~~   DON'T

NEW

but have bought ~~their~~ machines, ~~anyhow.~~ When they meet somebody

CANNOT   WARNING

who still hasn't taken the plunge they ~~can't~~ resist ~~telling~~

WILL SOON

you that ~~you are going to~~ be obsolete if you don't buy ~~in,~~   FAST

because, like it or not, ~~maybe~~ the computer is here to stay.

—Draft paragraph from
Russell Baker's "Here to Stay"

Rearrangement   Reorganizing information in an essay by *moving, combining,* or *redistributing*. Rearrangement enables you to control the flow and pattern of an essay by changing the location of information. You may have noticed the increasing power of a clearly written argument. On the other hand, when essay parts are out of place, or when sentences or paragraphs appear where they do not belong, the reader becomes confused or distracted. These effects are largely achieved by the *organization* of the essay, and rearrangement helps you to exert great power over your writing because it allows you to control organization. While rearrangement may be a time-consuming and occasionally difficult revision strategy to use, it is invaluable in increasing the effectiveness of an essay. In their drafts, most writers indicate rearrangement with lines and arrows, usually drawing boxes around the sections of text they want to move and showing where they will then be placed.

Moving   Taking information from one place in an essay and placing it somewhere else. No information is gained or lost, but reorganizing makes the essay clearer and more effective.

Combining   Taking pieces of information from two or more locations in an essay and placing them together. This rearrangement may be moved to yet another location, and it may form part of a paragraph, a whole new paragraph, or even a whole new section of an essay. Whatever the final form, the result of concentrating information is an essay with greater power.

Redistributing   Taking a block of information and breaking it up into smaller units which are placed in other locations in the essay (the opposite of combining). Like the other rearrangement techniques, redistribution helps to organize an essay by reorganizing information.

There's a view among some folks that rock can't be

critically analyzed, that the difference between the blatantly

commercial and the artistic is virtually indistinguishable in a

musical form that, by its inherent nature, is simple.   I

disagree; in fact, it's rock's simplicity that makes it easy to

find its best work. Passion is the key; the difference between

something calculated for its sales potential and the heartfelt.

Record company executives are beating the bushes looking for a

group that can emulate the fervor delivered by Ireland's U2 but

the depth of passion in Bono's earthy tenor can't be faked.

Another example: Compare singer Rod Stewart's 1971 release

"Every Picture Tells a Story" and the junk he dashes off today.

The voice may sound the same but the difference is apparent.

Rock's art strikes at the heart. Examine it in a critical

context and the truth will out.

—Draft paragraph from
Jim Fusilli's "Criticizing Rock Music Critics"

                          genuinely tried and
     How does it feel when you have failed over & over & over

again. Well, it's very painful   There are no words to

describe the inner feelings...   it's very painful   pain,

that you feel. In a few words it hurts, and hurts and

hurts...!

In a few words it hurts! it's embarrassing! It's and

at times it's devastating, but life goes on. Failure is not

a thing an experience that we seek.

     Looking at the _____ and knowing that it's not difficult

but in a few words, It hurts, because deep down on the inside

you know "I am not a failure." It's embarrassing because you

```
are sitting in front of this professor for the fourth time
                    over
taking this classₐ again (forever).  It's also devastating
to your ego
ₐbecause your records show that you are a failure.  How can

you feel good about yourself when  how can you keep on

smiling,  how can  and you walk with your head up knowing

that you are labeled as a failure.
```

—Draft paragraphs from
Wendy Modeste's "Are You Really a Failure?"

In terms of purpose, particularly, revision should be used to confirm *why* you are writing. Your success as a reviser may depend largely on your ability to remove yourself from what you have written and to view it anew as a reader. After completing a writing project, step back from it, maybe for a day or two. When you read it again, ask at every stage what your real purpose is and whether this paragraph or passage is saying what you expected when you wrote it. This shift from writer-self to reader-self is not easy, but the more frequently you write and the more you force yourself to view *consciously* what you have taken for granted, the easier it will become and the better you will become at revising your own work.

Julia Alvarez

Julia Alvarez (b. 1950) was born in New York City. Soon after her birth her family moved to the Dominican Republic, returning to the United States ten years later. She has published poetry, essays, and short fiction. Her most recent collection, *How the Garcia Girls Lost Their Accents,* was published in 1991. She is currently teaching creative writing at Middlebury College in Vermont. You may be surprised to learn that one of her main reasons for revising is her respect for her readers.

> In asking people to read what I've written, I'm aware that I'm taking them away from sunsets, a shared glass of cold wine with a friend, a walk through a snowy field—some first rate experiences. I better not waste their time. I've got to earn the right to their attention: Revise, revise, revise!
>
> Revision is how I pay for the fantasy of being a good writer.

Snow

Introduction to the Essay and Draft

In response to the question "Why write?" Julia Alvarez provides the following explanation of her purpose:

> *I wrote "Snow" on request, really. An editor I know was putting together a collection of pieces on "the Nuclear Age," and rather than becoming polemical or railing against nuclear weapons, I thought I might best "prove" the destructiveness of nuclear weapons if I showed how a simple, poignant, and "natural" moment becomes in this nuclear age a moment of possible holocaust for a child.*

For Alvarez, then, the question "Why write?" is answered by these multiple purposes: to express her opinion, to make people aware of an issue, and to convince readers of the seriousness of a problem. These purposes seem straightforward, but Alvarez fulfills them in an indirect fashion. Her desire to avoid a "polemical" piece of writing and instead create a "simple, poignant, and 'natural' moment" is not immediately fulfilled—her purpose is realized only after the thorough, careful revision of her first draft.

Speaking of her use of revision to achieve her purpose in "Snow" and of revising in general, Alvarez states:

> *I hate revision, but revising is when I find out what I say. Inspiration is a huge basket of stuff—it is all in there—and revision is how I find out what is there. Revision is discarding treasures sometimes. . . . I don't think writing is what happens in the first draft. I think of my first draft as a beautiful piece of marble. That is what is given;*

it is the gift that is given. But the hard work—how I earn the gift—is what I make out of it. My first draft is my stone.

The way a sculptor carves a piece of stone into a work of art is similar to the way that Alvarez works her essay. The early draft that is reproduced here has been looked over by an editor (Alvarez herself notes: "It's not just teachers who mark up papers!"), but it is the author who has decided to accept the recommendations. In this way another reader—and this may be a friend, a classmate, or a teacher who acts as an editor—helps the writer to carve and polish an initial draft so that it becomes clear, enjoyable prose. Although tedious at times, revision is needed to transform a rough stone into a finished piece.

As you see when you compare Alvarez's draft with the completed work, one main area that has benefited from thoughtful and detailed revision is the author's clarification of her purpose.

Published Essay

1   In the summer of 1960 my family emigrated to the United States, fleeing the tyrant Trujillo. In New York we found a small apartment with a Catholic school nearby, taught by the Sisters of Charity, hefty women in long black gowns and bonnets that made them look like peculiar dolls in mourning. I liked them a lot, especially my grandmotherly fifth grade teacher, Sister Zoe.

2   As the only immigrant in my class, I was put in a special seat in the first row by the window, apart from the other children, so that Sister Zoe could tutor me without disturbing them. Slowly, she enunciated the new words I was to repeat: *laundromat, corn flakes, subway, snow.*

3   Soon I picked up enough English to understand holocaust was in the air. Sister Zoe explained to a wide-eyed classroom what was happening in Cuba. Russian missiles were being assembled, trained supposedly on New York City. Kennedy, looking worried too, was on the television at home, explaining we might have to go to war.

4   At school, we had air raid drills. An ominous bell would go off and we'd file into the hall, fall to the floor, cover our heads with our coats, and imagine our hair falling out, the bones in our arms going soft. At home, Mother and I said a rosary every night for world peace. I heard new vocabulary: nuclear bomb, radioactive, Third World War. Sister Zoe explained how it would happen. She drew a picture of a mushroom on the blackboard and dotted a flurry of chalk marks for the dusty fallout that would kill us all.

5   The months grew cold, November, December. It was dark when I got up in the morning, frosty when I stepped outside. One morning as I sat daydreaming out the window I saw dots in the air like the ones Sister Zoe had drawn—random at first, and then lots and lots. I shrieked, "The bomb, the bomb!"

6   Sister Zoe jerked around, her full black skirt ballooning as she hurried to my side. A few girls began to cry.

7   But suddenly, Sister's shocked look faded. "Why, dear child, that's snow!" she laughed.

8   "Snow," I repeated. I looked out the window warily. All my life I had heard about the white crystals that fell out of American skies in the winter. From my desk I watched the fine powder dust the sidewalk and parked cars below. Each flake was different, Sister Zoe had said, like a person, irreplaceable and beautiful.

Draft

1   In the summer of 1960 my family emigrated to New York City, fleeing the tyrant Trujillo. It was an active Caribbean in those days: in nearby Cuba, Russian missiles were being assembled, trained supposedly at New York City. Trujillo was completing his thirty-first year as dictator, and a small band of men were charting his ambush and assassination on a highway outside the capitol. In New York we found a small apartment on the upper east side, too upper to be posh. "A sublet," it was called, full of sturdy furniture that seemed fragile because it was not ours. We were always scolded to be extra careful pulling a drawer open or clicking a cabinet shut. My three sisters and I were enrolled in a Catholic school about ten blocks downtown from our apartment, taught by the Sisters of Charity, buxom women in long black dresses with black bonnets that made them look peculiar, like dolls in mourning. I liked them a lot, especially my grandmotherly teacher, Sister Zoe, who was tutoring me in English and smiling good humoredly at my many mistakes. There were not that many Hispanics those days in the city, and as the only foreign youngster (Nowadays I would no doubt be called a minority student) in my classroom, I had a special, pampered place in Sister Zoe's heart and a special seat in the first row by the window, apart from the other children, so that when their fourty heads bent over their vocabulary books, Sister Zoe could come over and tutor me without disturbing them. Slowly, she enunciated the new words I was to repeat: laundromat, cornflakes, snow, subway, and soon bomb, nuclear war, radioactive fallout.

2   That fall my mother took us to Macys for our first winter coats ever. We had never been in the cold, never seen snow. My mother and the saleslady who sold her four different sizes of the same maroon coat with a velvet maroon collar, chatted about the pros and cons of snow. "It sure is beautiful but it's awful to shovel!" The lady rolled her eyes. I wanted a pillbox hat like Jacqueline Kennedy or a little pony like Caroline, and I was told by my mother that if I behaved myself, Santa might surprise me when Christmas came around.

3   At school, I picked up enough English to understand holocaust was in
the air. A worried Sister Zoe explained to a wide-eyed classroom what was
happening in Cuba, *where Russian missiles were being assembled, trained supposedly at* Kennedy, looking worried too, was on the television at *NYC.*
home, explaining we might have to go to war. At school, we had air raid *(line #3)*
drills, an ominous bell would go off and we'd file into the hall, fall to the
floor, cover our heads with our coats and imagine our hair falling out, the
bones in our arms going soft. At home, mother and the four girls said a rosary ever
night   for world peace. I heard my new vocabulary used *so often* in fearful,
concerned tones: nuclear bomb, radioactive fallout. Sister Zoe explained what
could happen. She drew a picture of a mushroom on the blackboard and dotted
a flurry of chalkmarks for the dusty fallout that would kill us all.

4   The months grew cold, November, December. It was dark when I got up
in the morning, frosty when I stepped outside. One morning as I sat daydreaming out the window of our sixth grade classroom, I thought--no, I was
sure-- I saw dots in the air like the ones Sister Zoe had drawn, random ones at firs
and then lots and lots! A deadly dust was falling out of the sky. I shrieked
and stood up. "The bomb! The bomb!" I cried. Sister Zoe jerked around, her
full black skirt ballooning and twisting around her legs as she hurried to my
side by the window. A few girls began to cry. One wailed her way to Sister
Zoe and clutched at the nun's skirt.

5   Sister Zoe's shocked look faded, her lips turned up, her blue eyes
twinkled. "Oh, dear child, why that's snow!" she laughed. "Snow."

6   "Snow," I repeated. I looked out the window warily. All my life I
had heard about the pretty white crystals that fell out of American skies
in the winter. All day from my desk by the window I watched the fine powder
dust the sidewalk and parked cars below. Each flake was different, Sister
Zoe had said, like a person, irreplaceable and beautiful.

Comparing Draft and Essay

Draft Paragraph 1

1. Alvarez refers to her first draft as a "beautiful piece of marble" that needs to be worked on. Compare this opening paragraph of "Snow" with the published version. How has she sculpted her opening paragraph? What has she omitted? What purpose do these omissions serve?

2. Why do you think that Alvarez rearranges this paragraph by splitting it up? How does this revision affect your ability to focus on details?

3. The author chooses to remove the phrase *"bomb, nuclear war, radioactive fallout"* from this paragraph. How does this deletion make the overall essay more "simple, poignant, and 'natural' "?

Draft Paragraph 2

4. There are times when details do not support an essay's purpose and need to be omitted. Note, for example, how the information contained in this paragraph draws your attention away from the author's primary purpose. Therefore, in this paragraph, like the previous one, Alvarez uses deletion as her main revising technique. Even though the draft loses many details, the resulting essay is clearer and stronger.

Draft Paragraph 3

5. Compare this paragraph with published paragraphs 3 and 4. How do the changes reaffirm Alvarez's purpose? What kinds of revisions can you identify? (See pages 32–39.)

Draft Paragraph 4

6. When she revises, Alvarez fine-tunes her work—she concentrates her ideas so that they are forceful and clear. In doing this, she also maintains the focus of her purpose. Note the changes in this paragraph (see also published paragraph 5). How do the author's revisions affect your understanding of her purpose?

Draft Paragraphs 4 and 5

7. Alvarez has stated that "revision is discarding treasures sometimes." Note how some of the concrete details in this paragraph are sacrificed so that published paragraphs 6 and 7 may achieve their subtle purpose.

Draft Paragraph 6

8. Did you anticipate how the essay would end? Does the simplicity of the conclusion fulfill the author's main purpose?

Linda Bird Francke

Linda Bird Francke (b. 1939) was born in New York City and attended Bradford Junior College. She is a nonfiction writer who focuses on issues related to women. Her writings include *The Ambivalence of Abortion* (1976) and *Growing Up Divorced* (1983). She collaborated with Rosalynn Carter on *First Lady of Plains* (1984) and most recently with Jehan Sadat on *An Egyptian Woman* (1987).

In response to our inquiry about the existence of a previous draft of her essay on abortion, Francke wrote:

> Your textbook idea of showing the real world to would-be writers among college students is a wonderful one. To submit material for such a book from writers, however, smacks of masochism. The agony and drudgery of rewriting is one of the heaviest crosses a writer has to bear, and I for one, throw out previous drafts to repress the memories. Using a word processor makes it a downright cinch to send away failed pieces. The greatest invention in my writer's life is that magic button which says "erase." And away it all goes.

The idea of the book, however, appealed to her, and as a result she wrote the purpose statement on her essay on abortion especially for it. She felt "the story around the writing may make it pertinent to your students." As you read "The Ambivalence of Abortion," which first appeared in *The New York Times* in May 1976, speculate as to the response Francke received from her readers.

The Ambivalence of Abortion

Introduction to the Essay and Purpose Statement

The following essay by Linda Bird Francke is a rarity. As she mentions in her statement of purpose, the published essay that you see is also her first draft! It is unusual for any author to get everything "right" the first time; the best anyone can hope for is to need to make only surface changes in the draft, that is, alterations of punctuation, grammar, and diction (the choice of words).

Sometimes if a writer thinks about an essay for a long time before writing it, the draft will reflect all of that conscious and subconscious thinking. In this case, the "first" draft is hardly that at all: innumerable drafts have been written and revised within the writer's mind during the weeks of the prewriting period. While it cannot be said that extensive prewriting will result in a clean first draft, it is true that careful planning will affect revision. In general, the more you think about your topic before you write, the better prepared you are to revise in accordance with your objectives.

Why she wrote the piece is the focus of Francke's statement.

1   Though this essay on my abortion was very painful to write, it was not difficult to write. Several weeks after the abortion my husband and I went to Bermuda where he had work to do and I could have a few days of rest from my job and our three children. But the conflicting feelings I had about the abortion

continued to churn. Was there something the matter with me, I remember thinking, that I continued to dwell on the abortion weeks after the fact. In the peace and quiet of Bermuda, I decided to put my thoughts on paper. It has always been easier for me to sort out my feelings on paper than to try to arrange them neatly in the serendipity of my mind. And besides, You can't lie to yourself on paper, nor forget whatever spontaneous insight flashed through your mind only to be forgotten. So I called a business equipment store, rented a typewriter, and set myself up on the bouganvillaed terrace in the sun. What resulted is this first and final draft. I had no intention of publishing it. This essay was written for me, to better understand my conflict, to admit privately what would have been a very unpopular feminist notion, that abortion was not as simple as we had been lead to believe. Abortion was - and is - not political. The decision It is personal. And for three hours or so, I put my recollections and feelings on the hotel stationary from the drawer in our room. When I was through, I felt greatly relieved. The abortion was finally behind me.

2   It was not until three years later that I sent the essay to the Op-Ed page at the New York Times. In the interim, abortion had become an even more polarized political issue and I thought it was important to tell the human side of the issue - to allow women who had never doubted that they had made the right decision but who had suffered nonetheless, to discover they were not alone. I did not change any of the words I had written three years before. Those were my feelings at the time, fresh from the abortion, and therefore more valid than they would have been with hindsight. And the response was

overwhelming. By expressing my own conflict, hundreds and
hundreds of other women followed suit in letters sent to me.
Did they all feel better for it? I hope so. Writing from the
heart may not be easy. But often such a deeply personal form of
writing provides the universal chord that not only bonds, but
heals.

Published Essay

1   We were sitting in a bar on Lexington Avenue when I told my husband I
was pregnant. It is not a memory I like to dwell on. Instead of the champagne
and hope which had heralded the impending births of the first, second and third
child, the news of this one was greeted with shocked silence and Scotch. "Jesus,"
my husband kept saying to himself, stirring the ice cubes around and around.
"Oh, Jesus."

2   Oh, how we tried to rationalize it that night as the starting time for the
movie came and went. My husband talked about his plans for a career change in
the next year, to stem the staleness that fourteen years with the same investment-
banking firm had brought him. A new baby would preclude that option.

3   The timing wasn't right for me either. Having juggled pregnancies and child
care with what freelance jobs I could fit in between feedings, I had just taken on
a full-time job. A new baby would put me right back in the nursery just when
our youngest child was finally school age. It was time for *us*, we tried to
rationalize. There just wasn't room in our lives now for another baby. We both
agreed. And agreed. And agreed.

4   How very considerate they are at the Women's Services, known formally as
the Center for Reproductive and Sexual Health. Yes, indeed, I could have an
abortion that very Saturday morning and be out in time to drive to the country
that afternoon. Bring a first morning urine specimen, a sanitary belt and napkins,
a money order or $125 cash—and a friend.

5   My friend turned out to be my husband, standing awkwardly and ill at ease
as men always do in places that are exclusively for women, as I checked in at
nine A.M. Other men hovered around just as anxiously; knowing they had to be
there, wishing they weren't. No one spoke to each other. When I would be
cycled out of there four hours later, the same men would be slumped in their
same seats, locked downcast in their cells of embarrassment.

6   The Saturday morning women's group was more dispirited than the men in
the waiting room. There were around fifteen of us, a mixture of races, ages and
backgrounds. Three didn't speak English at all and a fourth, a pregnant Puerto
Rican girl around eighteen, translated for them.

7   There were six black women and a hodge-podge of whites, among them a T-shirted teenager who kept leaving the room to throw up and a puzzled middle-aged woman from Queens with three grown children.

8   "What form of birth control were you using?" the volunteer asked each one of us. The answer was inevitably "none." She then went on to describe the various forms of birth control available at the clinic, and offered them to each of us.

9   The youngest Puerto Rican girl was asked through the interpreter which she'd like to use: the loop, diaphragm, or pill. She shook her head "no" three times. "You don't want to come back here again, do you?" the volunteer pressed. The girl's head was so low her chin rested on her breastbone. *"Sí,"* she whispered.

10   We had been there two hours by that time, filling out endless forms, giving blood and urine, receiving lectures. But unlike any other group of women I've been in, we didn't talk. Our common denominator, the one which usually floods across language and economic barriers into familiarity, today was one of shame. We were losing life that day, not giving it.

11   The group kept getting cut back to smaller, more workable units, and finally I was put in a small waiting room with just two other women. We changed into paper bathrobes and paper slippers, and we rustled whenever we moved. One of the women in my room was shivering and an aide brought her a blanket.

12   "What's the matter?" the aide asked her. "I'm scared," the woman said. "How much will it hurt?" The aide smiled. "Oh, nothing worse than a couple of bad cramps," she said. "This afternoon you'll be dancing a jig."

13   I began to panic. Suddenly the rhetoric, the abortion marches I'd walked in, the telegrams sent to Albany to counteract the Friends of the Fetus, the Zero Population Growth buttons I'd worn, peeled away, and I was all alone with my microscopic baby. There were just the two of us there, and soon, because it was more convenient for me and my husband, there would be one again.

14   How could it be that I, who am so neurotic about life that I step over bugs rather than on them, who spend hours planting flowers and vegetables in the spring even though we rent out the house and never see them, who make sure the children are vaccinated and inoculated and filled with vitamin C, could so arbitrarily decide that this life shouldn't be?

15   "It's not a life," my husband had argued, more to convince himself than me. "It's a bunch of cells smaller than my fingernail."

16   But any woman who has had children knows that certain feeling in her taut, swollen breasts, and the slight but constant ache in her uterus that signals the arrival of a life. Though I would march myself into blisters for a woman's right to exercise the option of motherhood, I discovered there in the waiting room that I was not the modern woman I thought I was.

17   When my name was called, my body felt so heavy the nurse had to help me into the examining room. I waited for my husband to burst through the door and yell "stop," but of course he didn't. I concentrated on three black spots in

the acoustic ceiling until they grew in size to the shape of saucers, while the doctor swabbed my insides with antiseptic.

18   "You're going to feel a burning sensation now," he said, injecting Novocaine into the neck of the womb. The pain was swift and severe, and I twisted to get away from him. He was hurting my baby, I reasoned, and the black saucers quivered in the air. "Stop," I cried. "Please stop." He shook his head, busy with his equipment. "It's too late to stop now," he said. "It'll just take a few more seconds."

19   What good sports we women are. And how obedient. Physically the pain passed even before the hum of the machine signaled that the vacuuming of my uterus was completed, my baby sucked up like ashes after a cocktail party. Ten minutes start to finish. And I was back on the arm of the nurse.

20   There were twelve beds in the recovery room. Each one had a gaily flowered draw sheet and a soft green or blue thermal blanket. It was all very feminine. Lying on these beds for an hour or more were the shocked victims of their sex, their full wombs now stripped clean, their futures less encumbered.

21   It was very quiet in that room. The only voice was that of the nurse, locating the new women who had just come in so she could monitor their blood pressure, and checking out the recovered women who were free to leave.

22   Juice was being passed about, and I found myself sipping a Dixie cup of Hawaiian Punch. An older woman with tightly curled bleached hair was just getting up from the next bed. "That was no goddamn snap," she said, resting before putting on her miniskirt and high white boots. Other women came and went, some walking out as dazed as they had entered, others with a bounce that signaled they were going right back to Bloomingdale's.

23   Finally then, it was time for me to leave. I checked out, making an appointment to return in two weeks for an IUD insertion. My husband was slumped in the waiting room, clutching a single yellow rose wrapped in a wet paper towel and stuffed into a baggie.

24   We didn't talk the whole way home, but just held hands very tightly. At home there were more yellow roses and a tray in bed for me and the children's curiosity to divert.

25   It had certainly been a successful operation. I didn't bleed at all for two days just as they had predicted, and then I bled only moderately for another four days. Within a week my breasts had subsided and the tenderness vanished, and my body felt mine again instead of the eggshell it becomes when it's protecting someone else.

26   My husband and I are back to planning our summer vacation and his career switch.

27   And it certainly does make more sense not to be having a baby right now— we say that to each other all the time. But I have this ghost now. A very little ghost that only appears when I'm seeing something beautiful, like the full moon on the ocean last weekend. And the baby waves at me. And I wave at the baby. "Of course, we have room," I cry to the ghost. "Of course, we do."

Comparing Purpose Statement and Essay

As mentioned earlier, the answer to the question "Why write?" is often specific to the writer and/or the project at hand. For Francke, both of these observations are true. Note the author's explanation of her purpose in the first paragraph of her statement. The prewriting stage, which has lasted "several weeks," has also settled Francke's purpose: she wants to write down her "recollections and feelings" so that she can better understand them and eventually settle those conflicts that "continued to churn." Francke's purpose here is quite personal: she "had no intention" of publishing her thoughts. Rather, she desired the privacy of writing to sort out her ideas and unburden her soul. In this context of *purpose,* she was successful. Surely, she does get her thoughts and emotions down on paper. Her feeling "greatly relieved" at having done so leaves little doubt that she has realized her intended purpose.

The second paragraph of the author's statement introduces a new purpose. Three years have passed, and Francke now wants to "go public" with her essay. She wants to "tell the human side of the issue," and she also wishes women who have had abortions to know that "they were not alone." The "overwhelming" response to the publication of her essay, the "hundreds and hundreds" of letters from women in similar circumstances, testifies to Francke's attainment of her new objectives.

The merging of Francke's private purpose (self-expression, self-realization) with her public purpose (help and empathy for others) is expressed in the last sentences of her statement. That is, the author's hope that women who read the essay will feel better—as she felt better by writing it—reflects not only a general unification of her purposes but also reveals how purpose may create a bond—a "universal chord"—between writer and reader. As you answer the following questions, note how your awareness of Francke's purposes in writing affects your own reactions.

Published Paragraphs 1 through 3

1. In her purpose statement, Francke mentions the "conflicting feelings" that she has about her abortion. What indications of this conflict are present in the opening paragraphs? How does Francke's use of the word "rationalize" express conflict? What is the purpose of repeating the word "agree"?

Published Paragraphs 4 through 9

2. Does the clinic seem like a warm and comforting place to you? How could writing down these details benefit the author? What purpose could be served by writing about an unpleasant situation?

Published Paragraph 10

3. "But unlike any other group of women I've been in, we didn't talk." Why do you think that the author includes this statement? What part of her overall purpose

is served by it? How does the last sentence of the paragraph emphasize this purpose?

Published Paragraphs 11 and 12, 17 through 21

4. In the second paragraph of her purpose statement, Francke expresses a desire to reach out to other women, to let them know that "they were not alone." How do you think these paragraphs achieve this purpose? How do you think that women who have shared this experience will react to them?

Published Paragraphs 13 through 16

5. Francke notes in her purpose statement that "abortion was not as simple as we had been led to believe." How do these paragraphs support this idea?

Published Paragraphs 23 through 27

6. These paragraphs restate the author's desire to explore and settle an inner conflict. How do the shifts in subject accomplish this purpose?

Adam Liptak

Adam Liptak (b. 1960) is from Stamford, Connecticut, and studied at Columbia University and Yale Law School. His many articles have appeared in several magazines, including *Vanity Fair* and *Rolling Stone*. "Playing Air Guitar" is an essay in the "About Men" series in *The New York Times Magazine*. As you read about his experiences as a teenager playing air guitar, compare your associations with rock musicians to Liptak's.

Playing Air Guitar

1   When I hear a song on the radio that I really like, or that used to be a favorite, I sometimes dance around a little bit and pretend to play guitar. I play air guitar. It probably looks dumb to an outsider, but to the man who plays, it is quite serious—a primal and private dance. Men identify with the great rock guitarists the way they do with sports legends, and we mimic their gestures and attitudes in an instinctive quest for grace.

2   What you do is: extend your left arm sort of crookedly, faking chord changes on the neck of an invisible electric guitar, rhythmically. Your right hand strums. Your head bobs. Your hips twitch. A nearby mirror reflects your grimaces. There is loud music on.

3   When I was a teen-ager, I used to play all the time. The impulse arose at odd moments. Just walking around, in an empty, late-afternoon school hallway, say, I might be seized by the inner music, drop to a crouch and let loose a devastating solo, the whole thing over in 10 seconds. A favorite song on the car radio, I am embarrassed to recount, could make me take my hands from the wheel and imitate a Stones riff—stopping only to keep my father's car from drifting into the next lane.

4   Certainly air guitar was handy at parties, where by stiffening and lowering the arms a little it passed for dancing. Countless men still dance this way.

5   But the true essence of air guitar is intensely personal and a little embarrassing, a strange conflation of fantasy and desire. I remember summer dusks in anticipation of parties—this at a time when a party was a promise of wonder, of a life transformed—climbing out of the shower, the evening's first beer lodged precariously on the soap tray, and hearing the perfect song. Here was pleasure: a long swig, a half-turn on the volume knob, the hallucinatory rush of adrenaline, followed by mindless dancing around in front of the fogged-up mirror.

6   As with anything, it is possible to play air guitar well or poorly, but it has nothing at all to do with being able to play guitar, which is in fact a drawback. One is after an image, a look; technical proficiency is distracting. The choice of role model is important, but what one copies is stance, attitude and character. Virtuosity is for the most part irrelevant. Only the electric guitar counts; there is no such thing as playing acoustic air guitar. Years of practice help, and so does an appreciation for loud, dumb music.

7   I am certain that the success of the movie "Risky Business" had a great deal to do with the scene in which Tom Cruise bounds about the living room in a shirt, socks and underpants. His parents are out of town, of course. He turns up the stereo and indulges in a whole array of rock-star moves and prancing.

8   Talking with friends afterward, I discovered that our enjoyment of the scene—of its celebratory tone—was tempered by an uneasy feeling of having somehow been found out. A kind of reverse identification had taken place, and we saw ourselves not as guitar heroes but as slightly absurd kids from the suburbs. This shock of recognition was followed by a shudder.

9   In college, I played less often but more openly. Sometimes, at the end of a beery night, my friends and I would put together a whole band—it was always the Stones, and I always wanted to be Keith Richards—and clamber up onto the furniture and play, each of us with his eyes closed, in a way alone. It sounds like a silly and slightly aggressive scene, and it was.

10   At the same time, this was a way men could dance with other men without compromising their version of masculinity. At parties, dancing with women, my best friend and I might step away and take a moment to jam, leaning on each other this way and that, falling over and playing incredible dual solos on our invisible Fenders. The women we abandoned were generally not amused.

11   We joked about it, air guitar being a perfect subject for my generation's mode of discourse, which is a mix of the intimate and the ironic. Here we could say just what we meant, confessing to the odd habit in a deadpan way, so that no listener could be quite sure if we really meant it. Or we could go beyond our own experience—admit to playing naked on city rooftops, say—and then double back and make fun of anyone taken in or, worse, who admitted to doing the same thing.

12   I have noticed lately the attempt to institutionalize air guitar, in the form of "concerts" at colleges, "lip-sync" contests at certain nightclubs in the boroughs of New York and on television shows. There is something peculiarly American about making the intimate public and competitive, something reassuring at first but in the long run repulsive.

13   This is not to say that an air guitar contest is without humor. To see four or five people aping the movements of an entire band with the appropriate music in the background can be hilarious. An ensemble called Men Without Instruments, at Princeton University, is funny even to contemplate.

14   I don't know if teen-agers today find in Prince and Bruce Springsteen adequate idols. I suspect they do. And I suppose they know the moves better than we ever did, thanks to music videos.

15   These days, I find myself at some emotional distance from most of the popular music I hear, and going to rock concerts has lost its appeal. I still put on loud music first thing in the morning, though, loud enough to hear in the shower, which is down the hall from my stereo. And sometimes, as I start to dress, barefoot, my shirt unbuttoned and my tie loose around my neck, I play a couple of notes if it feels right. And then, refreshed, I finish dressing and go to work.

Considering Content

1. Liptak obviously had great enthusiasm for playing air guitar. What makes it appealing? What examples did you find most convincing?

2. What profile of Liptak and his college friends emerges from the essay? How does he portray male friendships? How are their activities and musical tastes similar to or different from those of today's students?

3. Explain the meaning of the comment that playing air guitar is "a perfect subject for my generation's mode of discourse, which is a mix of the intimate and the ironic"? How would you describe your generation's "mode of discourse"?

Considering Craft

1. Liptak's primary purpose is to inform his readers about his passionate relationship with air guitar. Do you also find evidence that he is trying to clarify this experience for himself? What is it?

2. In paragraph 1 Liptak included the subject of his essay. Where does his thesis statement appear? How does he support it later in the essay?

3. Read over Liptak's introduction and conclusion. How do they enhance his purpose and meaning? Did you find them effective? Why or why not?

Lynne Sharon Schwartz

Lynne Sharon Schwartz (b. 1939) was born in Brooklyn, New York, and educated at Barnard College. She has published several novels, two collections of short stories, and a children's book. During a recent interview on the publication of her new novel, *Leaving Brooklyn* (1991), she commented, "I really wrote all my life. I started writing at six, and I wrote my first novel at eleven." As you read her account of a teaching experience after the Vietnam War (1980), which first appeared in *The New York Times,* speculate on her purpose in writing this piece.

The Spoils of War

1   He always sat in the back row, as far away as he could get: long skinny body and long face, thin curly hair, dark mustache. Sometimes his bony shoulders were hunched as he peered down at his notebook lying open on that bizarre prehensile arm that grows out of college classroom chairs. Or else he leaned way back, the lopsided chair balanced on two legs and propped against the rear wall, his chest appearing slightly concave beneath his white shirt, and one narrow leg, in jeans, elegantly stretched out to rest on a nearby empty chair.

2   Casual but tense, rather like a male fashion model. Volatile beneath the calm: someone you would not want to meet on a dark street. His face was severely impassive in a way that suggested arrogance and scorn.

3   He must have been about twenty-seven years old, an extremely thin young man—ascetic, stripped down to the essentials. His body looked so brittle and so electrically charged that I almost expected crackling noises when he moved, but in fact he slipped in and out silently, in the wink of an eye. His whole lanky, scrutinizing demeanor was intimidating. He would have no patience with anything phony, I imagined; would not suffer fools gladly.

4   About every fourth or fifth class he was absent, common enough for evening-session students, who had jobs, families, grown-up lives and responsibilities. I was a trifle relieved at his absences—I could relax—yet I missed him, too. His presence made a definite and compelling statement, but in an unintelligible language. I couldn't interpret him as readily as I could the books on the reading list.

5   I was hired in the spring of 1970. It was wartime. Students were enraged. When I went for my interview at Hunter College I had to walk past pickets into a building where black flags hung from the windows. I would use the Socratic method, I earnestly told the interviewer, since I believed in the students' innate intelligence. To myself, I vowed I would win their confidence. After all, I was scarcely older than they were and I shared their mood of protest. I would wear jeans to show I was one of them, and even though I had passed thirty and was married and had two children, I would prove that I could be trusted. I was prepared—even eager—for youthful, strident, moral indignation.

6   Far from strident, he was totally silent, never speaking in class discussions, and I was reluctant to call on him. Since he had a Spanish name, I wondered whether he might have trouble with English. Bureaucratic chaos was the order of the day, with the City University enacting in microcosm the confusion in the nation at large; it was not unusual for barely literate or barely English-speaking students to wind up in an Introduction to Literature class. His silence and his blank arrogant look could simply mean bewilderment. I ought to find out, but I waited.

7   His first paper was a shocker. I was surprised to receive it at all—I had him pegged as the sullen type who would give up at the first difficult assignment, then complain that college was irrelevant. On the contrary, the paper, formidably intelligent, jarred my view of the fitness of things. It didn't seem possible—no, it didn't seem *right*—that a person so sullen and mute should be so eloquent. Someone must have helped him. The truth would come out in impromptu class papers, and then I would confront him. I bided my time.

8   After the first exam he tossed his blue book onto my desk, not meeting my eyes, and, wary and feline, glided away, withdrawing into his body as if attempting a disappearing act. The topic he had chosen was the meaning of "the horror" in Joseph Conrad's *Heart of Darkness,* the novella we had spent the first few sessions on.

9   He compared it to Faulkner's *Intruder in the Dust.* He wrote at length about racial hatred and war and their connection in the dark, unspeakable places in the

soul from which both spring, without sentimentality but with a sort of matter-of-fact, old knowledge. He knew Faulkner better than I did; I had to go back and skim *Intruder in the Dust* to understand his exam. I do know that I had never before sat transfixed in disbelief over a student paper.

10   The next day I called him over after class and asked if he was aware that he had an extraordinary mind. He said, yes, he was. Close up, there was nothing arrogant about him. A bit awkward and shy, yet gracious, with something antique and courtly in his manner.

11   Why did he never speak in class, I asked.

12   He didn't like to speak in front of people. His voice and his eye turned evasive, like an adolescent's, as he told me this. Couldn't, in fact. Couldn't speak.

13   What do you mean, I said. You're not a kid. You have a lot to say. You write like this and you sit in class like a statue? What's it all about?

14   He was in the war, he said, and he finally looked at my face and spoke like the adult that he was. He was lost for a long time in the jungles of Vietnam, he explained patiently, as if I might not know what Vietnam was, or what a jungle was, or what it was to be lost. And after that, he said, he couldn't. He just found it hard to be with people. To speak to people.

15   But you're so smart. You could do so much.

16   I know. He shrugged: a flesh-and-blood version of the rueful, devil-may-care, movie war-hero shrug. Can't be helped.

17   Anything can be helped, I insisted.

18   No, he insisted back, quietly. Not after that jungle.

19   Hunter had a counseling service, free. Go, I pleaded.

20   He had already gone. They keep asking me questions about my childhood, he said, my relationship with my parents, my toilet training. He grinned quickly, turning it on and off. But it doesn't help. It's none of that. It's from when I was lost in that jungle.

21   You must work, I said. Don't you have to talk to people when you work?

22   No, he was a meter man.

23   A what?

24   He went around checking on cars, to see if they had overstayed their time at the parking meters.

25   You can't do that forever, I said. With your brains!

26   Well, at least he didn't have to talk to people, he said sweetly. For now. Maybe later on he would get braver.

27   And what would he do if I called on him in class? If I made him talk?

28   Oh no, don't do that, he said, and flashed the wry grin again. If you did that I'd probably run out of the room.

29   I never called on him because I didn't want to risk seeing him run out of the room. But at least we stopped being afraid of each other. He gave up his blank look, and occasionally I would glance at his face, to see if I was still making sense or drifting off into some seductive, academic cloud of words.

30   I thought of him a lot this summer after I saw young men lined up at post offices to register for military service. I thought of him also when I heard Ronald

Reagan and John Anderson, on television, solemnly pledge themselves to the defense of this country's shores. No candidate has yet pledged himself to the defense of this country's young men, to "taking every measure necessary" to "insure" that their genius does not turn mute and their very lives become the spoils of war.

Considering Content

1. What portrait of Schwartz's student emerges in the first three paragraphs?

2. Characterize Schwartz's attitude toward her first teaching position. What does she hope to accomplish? Why does she find this unnamed student so unnerving?

3. To what does she attribute his silence in class? What does she discover after reading his first paper? What suspicions does she still harbor?

4. "It's from when I was lost in that jungle." Describe the effects of this experience. How do they relate to the essay's title? Characterize your response to their effects.

5. How does this student's experience in Vietnam compare with that of other veterans you may know. What new meaning about Vietnam did you discover through reading this essay?

Considering Craft

1. Schwartz's purpose is to inform her readers about the effects of the Vietnam War on one of her students. Is she also trying to persuade them about the human tragedies resulting from all wars? Explain your answer.

2. Review Schwartz's conversation with her student. Do his factual responses also evoke an emotional response in the reader? How?

3. Characterize Schwartz's attitude toward her subject. Is she angry, resigned, frustrated, sad? Explain your answer.

Pham Thanh

Pham Thanh (b. 1956) was born in Vietnam and brought to the United States for medical care in 1968. He currently lives and works in Berkeley, California. In April 1991, the unusual personal story of his two lives was shown on public television. As you read his essay first published in *The New York Times,* write a journal entry on your responses to his war experiences.

My Two Countries, My Flesh and Blood

1   We have been told repeatedly in recent weeks that the ghosts of Vietnam have been laid to rest in the Persian Gulf. But I still hear them in the night, and I bet I'm not alone.

2   In 1968, when I was 12 years old, I was injured and then saved by American soldiers during a battle in my village south of Da Nang. My father was beaten to death by South Vietnamese soldiers as he demonstrated outside an American base against the bombing and shelling of our village.

3   A few months later, my mother and grandmother were killed when a G.I. threw a grenade into our bomb shelter; the grenade severed my esophagus. An American medic found me, bandaged my wounds and sent me in a helicopter to the provincial hospital.

4   From there I was rescued some months later, near death, by the Committee of Responsibility, a private American group, which sent me to California for specialized surgery. At first, I resisted treatment, fearing I would be tortured or experimented on medically; but eventually the doctors won my trust. My physical wounds healed, and the committee found a foster family to take me in. I made a new home in California among a people I had considered my enemy.

5   In spite of my losses in Vietnam, I am deeply grateful for my foster family and for the blessings of my adopted country. An American citizen since 1982, I work at a high-tech company that makes artificial hearts. But I am also still Vietnamese, and since 1980 I have traveled as often as possible back to my village, Binh Phu, trying to rid myself of the ghosts that haunt my imaginings.

6   I tend my family's graves and listen as my surviving aunts sing grandchildren to sleep. The people of my village live constantly with remnants of the war—with bomb craters, and M-79 grenades that explode when struck by hoes in paddies. The war is part of the fabric of daily life in Binh Phu. In this atmosphere, my losses seem bearable. In the U.S., I find it harder to sleep at night. The roar of a helicopter can still leave me in tears. Vietnam becomes a nightmare here, and not for me alone.

7   For understandable reasons, most Americans want to forget the Vietnam War, and so it has taken on mythological dimensions. The very word "Vietnam" evokes feelings of frustration, failure and loss, no matter which side of the war you were on. To lay these memories to rest will take more than victory over Iraq and a Presidential pronouncement that the "Vietnam syndrome" is dead.

8   Americans must understand, not bury, the Vietnam experience. We need normal diplomatic relations and an end to the trade embargo so that the metaphor "Vietnam" loses its charge and the country Vietnam takes on reality. We need an accounting of the damage done to places like Binh Phu, so that aid, like medicines and prosthetics, can be sent.

9   Admittedly, I have a special interest in normalization. Last year, I wed a young woman from my village and had to leave her behind when I returned to California. Under U.S. law it is illegal for me, an American citizen, to do business in Vietnam, and it is almost impossible for my wife to visit to see if she wants to emigrate.

10   Our separation mirrors the gulf that must be bridged to heal each country's soul. I will return home, finally, to propitiate my ghosts. For others haunted by Vietnam, closer ties with it can do the same.

Considering Content

1. What evidence does Thanh offer to support the fact that he is still haunted by "the ghosts of Vietnam"?

2. To what extent do you agree that "Americans must try to understand, not bury, the Vietnam experience"? What associations, if any, do you have with the word "Vietnam"?

3. To what extent is Thanh, like the student in Schwartz's essay, a casualty of war?

Considering Craft

1. Thanh's purpose is to inform his readers of his experiences in Vietnam. Is he also trying to persuade his audience that "Vietnam is not a myth, a metaphor or a memory"? To what extent does he succeed?

2. Why does Thanh include his visits to the graves of his family members? What does this inclusion contribute to the essay's thesis?

3. Thanh's essay was published immediately after the Gulf War. What effect could that have had on his purpose for writing? How might it affect a reader's response? Your response?

Margaret Zeman

Margaret Zeman (b. 1973) graduated from Sacred Heart Academy, Hempstead, New York, in 1991 and is currently a freshman honors student at the University of Delaware, where she is an English major. Her purpose in writing this article stemmed from her disapproval of U.S. involvement in Kuwait and her conviction that war is never the answer.

War's Aftermath

1   Writing at a point when I should be feeling joy and jubilation at the war's end, my feelings are quite the contrary. Yes, I am glad our soldiers are coming home, but I feel as though America has learned nothing from the experience, and is only paving the way for other crises of this nature.

2   Victory for America, defeat for Iraq rings triumphantly in every newspaper and television show across the country, and most seem to be affirming that the ends of war justify the means used to obtain victory. If this is so, then I suppose that in another twenty years, I should become ready to send my son or daughter off to die, because we have learned absolutely nothing.

3   Wars take innocent lives, destroy cities, devastate families, and reduce human life to the market price of items such as oil. We have freed Kuwait, but what have we really accomplished, and, more importantly, what message have we sent to the rest of the world regarding aggression?

4   Saddam Hussein kills Kuwaitis and we turn around and kill Iraqis. I must commend Mr. Bush on this innovative approach to teaching morality. The time has come for people and leaders of nations to stop and consider what implications their actions are going to have.

5   War is a completely primitive and barbaric approach to problems that solves nothing. Nations send astronauts to explore space, yet still institute war in times of conflict.

6   With endless opportunities existing today in education and with so many intelligent individuals in society, why do we always choose war? Have we no confidence or hope for any other alternative?

7   The war has ended and our troops are coming home, but I feel not pride; I feel fear and trepidation as we close the chapter of a book that only keeps re-opening.

Considering Content

1. Zeman claims that America has learned nothing from the experience of the Gulf War. What evidence do you find most convincing? To what extent do you agree or disagree with her thesis?

2. "Nations send astronauts to explore space, yet still institute war in times of conflict." What is the purpose of this comparison? How does it affect the writer's thesis?

Considering Craft

1. Zeman's purpose is to persuade her readers to re-evaluate the issue of war. Is her presentation logical? Does she also appeal to readers' emotions? Explain your answer.

2. Review the first and last paragraphs of her essay. How do they reinforce her purpose?

3. Effective writing should be simple, clear, and concise. Choose two paragraphs that most effectively illustrate these qualities.

Guidelines for Clarifying Purpose

1. As you approach any writing task, consult the following list in order to answer the question "Why am I writing?" Check off any responses that you think apply, and add others you think necessary.

   - You want to write for your enjoyment.
   - You would like to unburden yourself of worries.
   - You want to convince someone of something.
   - You want to offer your opinions about a subject.
   - You want to amuse or entertain yourself or someone else.
   - You need to communicate information (sales figures, a complaint, an invitation).
   - You have to write as part of your job (a class assignment, an annual sales report).
   - You would like to make money.

   After you determine all your reasons for writing, look them over carefully. Which one is your main purpose? Which are secondary? Remember to separate motives from purposes. After all, your motive for completing a class assignment may be to receive a high grade, but your purpose may be to inform your reader about your topic.

2. While you are writing your essay, or letter, or assignment, keep your main purpose clearly in mind. If you find yourself drifting, make sure that you return to it. If, for example, your purpose is to entertain, be sure to present amusing stories or examples. If your overall purpose is to inform, include as many facts as you can about your subject.

3. When you have completed your writing project, read it over carefully. Try to read the essay as if you were not the writer so that you can approach it with the objective attitude that a new reader will have. Then, consult your list of major and minor purposes and answer the following questions:

   - What is the purpose of this essay?
   - Is there more than one purpose?
   - Which purposes are minor ones?
   - Do I stick to my main purpose?
   - Is my purpose unclear at any point?

4. Your revision of your essay will depend on your responses to the preceding questions. If you cannot find your main objective, if major and minor purposes compete for attention, or if your purpose becomes vague or confused, you will have to make substantial alterations in your essay to ensure that the purpose is made clear in later drafts.

5. Review the revising strategies on pages 32–39 and remember how each one can help to clarify the purpose of your essay. In general, revision is needed whenever your purpose is not clear to a reader.

6. Revise the essay so that your purpose is unmistakable. For each new draft you create, repeat steps 3 and 4 of these guidelines.

Warm-up Exercises

1. Freewrite for 15 minutes about your parents, grandparents, aunts, or uncles. Read over what you have written. Is there any pattern to your memories? Now write several paragraphs to be used as a speech at the next birthday party for one of these older relatives. Your purpose is partly to honor and partly to entertain.

2. Brainstorm about your associations with one of the following:

   class participation   Vietnam
   war wounds   leaving home
   rock music   Persian Gulf War

3. Write a journal entry on a decision you made about which you feel ambivalent. Evaluate what you have written. Has the process of expressing it helped you think about it more clearly? If so, write about it with the specific purpose of explaining the decision to a specific person or group.

4. Select a possible purpose in writing on the following:

   soap operas   abortion
   pregnancy among teenagers   choosing a career
   nuclear war   physical labor
   today's music   commercials

   Is there one on which you can expand for an essay?

Writing/Revising Topics

1. Rewrite "The Ambivalence of Abortion" from the point of view of Linda Bird Francke's husband. What changes in purpose might you have to make? In revising your draft, focus on purpose. Can you state yours clearly based on what you have written?

2. In the purpose statement that precedes her essay, Linda Bird Francke writes the following:

   It has always been easier for me to sort out my feelings on paper than to try to arrange them neatly in the serendipity of my mind. And besides, you can't lie to yourself on paper, nor forget whatever spontaneous insight flashed through your mind only to be forgotten.

   In fact, according to Francke, her essay is essentially a journal entry that has been made public. (You might recall that her objective in writing encompasses both private and public purposes.) With this possibility in mind, select from your journal an entry that is important to you. Revise this entry—with emphasis perhaps on addition and rearrangement—into an essay for the general public, or at least for your English class and instructor.

3. Julia Alvarez makes good use of her unfamiliarity with snow. Write about the first time you came face to face with something you didn't know existed, or something you had been aware of only vaguely, making sure your purpose is clear to your reader.

4. Using one of the topics in Warm-up Exercise 4 as the basis, write an essay, making sure that you have a definite purpose in mind. Then let your reader-self take over. Now rewrite the essay using such revision strategies as deletion or addition to make your purpose clearer.

5. According to Thanh, "Americans must understand, not bury, the Vietnam experience." Write an essay about the first time you became aware of the Vietnam War and its many consequences. How did this experience help you better understand the war?

6. "Men identify with the great rock guitarists the way they do with sports legends, and we mimic their gestures and attitudes in an instinctive quest for grace." How does Liptak's thesis apply to your generation's attitudes toward rock stars? Write an essay that supports or contradicts Liptak's point of view. Clarify your purpose before you begin to write.

7. Herr (Chapter 1) and Schwartz and Thanh in this chapter discuss aspects of the Vietnam experience. Write an analysis of your impressions of the Vietnam War as a result of reading about it from their perspectives.

*E*stablishing Meaning: Creating a Draft

The relationship between *purpose* and *meaning* is a close one since an answer to the question "Why write?" implies that you have something to say, that there is something you want to communicate. Therefore, after you answer the question *"Why am I writing?"* the next step is to seek out *what* you want to write. Your search for *what* you want to communicate is your attempt to establish *meaning*. Practically speaking, establishing meaning involves

1. generating ideas by freewriting, brainstorming, or writing in your journal,
2. narrowing your topic,
3. writing a thesis statement, and
4. drafting an essay that supports and develops that statement.

Narrowing your topic and writing a thesis statement are closely related steps. To some extent they occur simultaneously. *What you want to say* is your whole essay; your thesis statement is what you want to say expressed in a single sentence. It is thus your main point, a general statement of the essay's contents, a summary that points the reader's way through the details, examples, or illustrations of the rest of the paper. It is important that it is a sentence, and not just a phrase or label or headline, because it must state the topic and go on to make an assertion or a prediction about that topic. (It may even be a kind of mini-outline, indicating the organization of the paper.) Probably the best place to put this summary sentence is at the end of the introduction, where it will tell in general what readers will find developed in the rest of the essay.

Whether you choose your own topic or are assigned one, you will have to match the size of your topic to the size of your writing project. If you are asked to write, for instance, three to five pages, you will need to check whether your topic can be reasonably covered in a paper of that length. If your topic is too big for your paper, you will need to choose a narrower area or aspect so that you can cover it.

Most topics, as they first occur or are assigned to you, are too broad (for example, nuclear energy, religious sects, women's rights, company improvements, shop safety, sales trends), and you must find the specific area that you want to write about (the benefits of nuclear energy, why young people join religious sects, women's rights to equal pay, incorporating a company merit system, maintaining clean air in the plant, the effects of high unemployment on sales). A narrow topic is easier to write about simply because it is more manageable.

Narrowing a topic is similar to brainstorming and other techniques for generating ideas: you must be willing to consider the topic from all sides, jotting down notes of what you know and what you might need to learn and pondering where various aspects of the topic might lead. At this time you should try to decide on a specific issue you want to make the subject of your essay.

At the same time you are narrowing your topic, you will be looking for its main point or thesis. Try writing a thesis statement, but be prepared to change it. Be ready to change direction, to consider other possibilities, to step back and take the measure of your subject. A trial statement may provide you with a working guide at this early stage, but you probably won't be sure of your thesis until you are much further along and have written a draft or two.

A good thesis statement is narrow enough to fit your narrowed topic, but not so narrow as to lead nowhere. (You will have a chance to practice writing thesis statements in the Warm-up Exercises at the end of this chapter.) Consider the following statement:

On Monday, March 16, 1992, WNNC was bought by Big Cities Communications for $3.5 billion.

This sentence would not work as a thesis statement. It is a statement of fact; it leads nowhere. A thesis statement is a sentence in need of defense or development or both, a generalization in search of its specifics. A mere statement of fact is already too specific to need developing; it may, however, be used to develop some other—general—statement. Now consider this sentence:

The sale of WNNC to Big Cities Communications is a threat to media independence.

Now, with the assertion of a position, opinion, attitude, or value judgment, the essay has found its thesis, a statement that can and must be defended and supported. The best thesis will probably be controversial; at a minimum it will be general enough to need detailed support.

As you brainstormed, narrowed your topic, and decided on a thesis, many ideas about your topic occurred to you. If it helps you to focus or organize your thoughts at this stage, make a rough outline of the points you expect to cover. Essentially, an outline is a diagram of all an essay's points. Using an outline will almost always help you to adhere to your meaning, but the type of outline will vary with personal requirements and the purpose of a particular writing project. For example, Patrick Fenton used the following informal outline to help him organize his essay "Notes on the Writing of 'Confessions of a Working Stiff,'" which appears later in this chapter.

Written on the Nassau
County line bus: 8:45 A.M.
6/2/87

Confessions of a Working Stiff #2
    Reflections of going up to
New York Magazine (1973) to
meet with editor, Byron Dobell.
"You're a writer." These words
opened up doors of my mind.

    Tell about 3 cent show.
For 3 cent deposit on old
glass milk bottle—have
price for admission to
kid's show—movies at Public
School #10—(after school.)
Winter. Walking home to
tenement for stew.

    Place of kid's dreams—
place where dreams started.
Milk bottles—kid's dreams.

    First piece published
Park Slope News—weekly
paper $15. Long, over
long, but had promise. Marian
Leifsen pushes me to keep
writing.

    Mention how some stories
write themselves, Hemingway
in cafe writing. (Trying to
keep up with story.) I've
known that. Confessions of

a Working Stiff was a story
that wrote itself.

    Mention hard work at
airport—sometimes I
thought I'd be there
forever.

A WORKING STIFF WAS A STORY THAT WROTE ITSELF.

MENTION HARD WORK AT AIRPORT - SOMETIMES I THOUGHT I'D BE THERE FOREVER.

You will note that this outline is a bare list of some ideas the author will incorporate into his work and more resembles Pete Hamill's brainstorming (see pages 10–11) than a formal outline.

If you are ready to write a more formal outline, which shows the order and relationship of all your points, you may want to set it up in the following traditional format so that your thesis and main supporting arguments stand out:

Title

  I. Introduction—brief, eye-catching explanation of purpose, ending with statement of thesis
 II. Body—develop thesis, fully explain idea
    A. Main supporting point
      1. Subsidiary point
      2. Subsidiary point
    B. Main supporting point
      1. Subsidiary point
      2. Subsidiary point
    C. Main supporting point
      1. Subsidiary point
      2. Subsidiary point
III. Conclusion—brief, general summary with restatement of thesis

Whether or not you have produced an outline, once you have generated ideas about your topic you are ready to create a draft. *Drafting* is the composing part of the process; in drafting you actually write out your paragraphs. At this stage you will discover the value of prewriting activities. The more that you think about your topic, the more diligently that you apply the Guidelines to your work (see pages 29 and 60), and the more effort that you put into creating an outline, the easier drafting will be.

Drafting, the writing out of your ideas, is in some ways a different process for every writer. You have your own style for creating drafts, and you may note that this style changes when you approach different writing tasks. Yet many aspects of drafting are similar for all writers. For example, when you are composing your essay, you may note how you stop to look over what you have written to see what should come next. Or you might go back to a paragraph you have just written to see whether or not you should include an idea that has just occurred to you. Or you might stop right in the middle of a paragraph because you have run out of ideas and need to think about what other thoughts you want to include. These actions, all parts of drafting, generally occur with all writers. You can also see that composing is more than a single process; in fact, it encompasses all writing processes. Prewriting (stopping to think about new ideas) and revising (changing what you have written almost immediately after writing it) are always occurring when you are drafting!

When you write the first draft of an essay, remember that it is only the first of many that you should create in the course of discovering and accurately conveying your meaning to a reader. This way, you will not feel compelled to "get it right" the first time. Indeed, by eliminating this pressure, you will free yourself to travel wherever your composer's imagination takes you: you are freeing yourself to discover your meaning. Of course, you may not want your first draft to resemble a freewriting exercise, where seemingly dissociated ideas rapidly succeed each other. Yet, by engaging in prewriting activities, you have already greatly decreased this possibility. Then, in narrowing your topic and in selecting a thesis, you have further reduced the chances of this occurring. The freedom of creation that exists in a first draft is the freedom to discover meaning in a more selective way. Chances are that the new ideas that crop up in your first draft are closely related to your intended topic. Try not to limit the range of your discoveries in your first draft; it is the purpose of future drafts to judge the value of what you have created in the first one.

If you have elected to construct an outline as part of your prewriting, you can use it to keep your essay more on track. Since it is difficult to keep in mind all the main points and supporting details that you intend to use in the exact order you wish to use them, an outline with these ideas written out will save you the trouble of juggling these ideas in your head while you are concentrating on other aspects of composing. Following your outline is like using a road map, recipe, or blueprint: it helps you to know where you are and where you are going.

On the other hand, you might wait to do your outline until after your first draft, using it to determine which ideas you want to highlight or downplay. By seeing your ideas in writing, you may then discover the essential meaning that you want to convey with more precision in your next draft. Some writers find it more effective to begin such a draft before attempting an outline.

When you write you attempt to support your thesis at every stage, but the last chance to do that is when you revise. Once again you need to separate yourself from your essay, to create a reader-self who can look with an open and discerning eye at what your writer-self has written. It is the obligation of this reader-self to inform your writer-self of any problems in the work. If the reader-self says, "I don't understand this," or asks, "Why is this included?" or "How does this idea support your main point?" or "What finally does this essay say?" the writer-self must respond with a revision that answers these criticisms. Be ready to make major changes in your first draft. Careful questioning and rereading of the draft should not only pinpoint problem areas but also suggest ways to make the essay better. You may want to refer again to the Revising Strategies discussed in Chapter 2 (pages 32–39).

As you have observed in Chapter 1, a product of journal writing is self-discovery. Writers gain awareness of themselves through writing. This kind of learning is not restricted to journals; rather, it is common for a writer, in the course of composing a formal essay, to uncover his or her real feelings about an issue or his or her interpretation of an event. Thus on certain occasions a writer may not discover his or her meaning until an entire draft has been written. In these cases, the first drafts serve as vehicles for discovering one's thesis, and revising ensures that one's newly discovered meaning is conveyed to the reader.

Later in this chapter you will see how Patrick Fenton makes substantial changes in his essay to establish his meaning and you will also learn how Joyce Maynard rearranges her entire essay to change her emphasis. In both cases these experienced writers make many modifications in many drafts to ensure that *what* they say is what they *want* to say.

Patrick Fenton

Patrick Fenton (b. 1944) is a freelance writer who is largely self-taught. A high-school dropout, Fenton worked in factories and on loading docks, and some years ago discovered writing as an unexpected source of self-expression. He explains why he has continued to write:

> I kept on writing because it made me feel more alive. It gave me the opportunity to be myself, to express a personal part of me that was almost smothered when I was young and worked in the factories of Brooklyn. I probably had more reasons than the average person to give up writing. After quitting high school at the age of 16 it looked like I was headed for a life of factory work.
>
> . . . I owe a lot to Pete Hamill, the New York journalist, who gave me the encouragement I needed to keep on writing. In 1968, I sent him a long letter about an article he wrote for the *Village Voice* about our old neighborhood. He sent me back an answer saying: "it's obvious from your letter that you can write like hell yourself. Why don't you do something with it? . . . Just write naturally, the way you wrote that letter." It was the best advice I ever received.

For this edition of *The Writer's Craft* Patrick Fenton reconstructed the process that led to the publication of his first essay "Confessions of a Working Stiff," in *New York* magazine in 1975. He responded with the following notes, draft, and essay, as well as the outline discussed in the introduction to this chapter. "Confessions of a Working Stiff" appears on page 88.

Notes on the Writing of "Confessions of a Working Stiff"

Introduction to the Essay and Draft

In the following essay and draft, Patrick Fenton explains to readers how he became a writer. In particular, the author traces some landmark events leading up to the publication of his essay, "Confessions of a Working Stiff," which appears later in this chapter. As you read over the draft and essay, try to discover how Fenton progressed from his outline (see pages 66–67) to his final version. Try to imagine the mind of the writer *in process* as it drafts its thoughts into words and sentences that convey meaning.

One way to understand how Fenton has used drafting to establish meaning is to examine multiple versions of a single paragraph as it is transformed from a rough idea to a more polished one. Note the changes in meaning in the following:

From his outline:

Mention hard work at
airport—sometimes I
thought I'd be there
forever.

From his first draft: The following is taken from Fenton's first draft on page 77–78, represented by the typewritten copy before it was removed from the typewriter and revised by hand. Some revisions—those changes and false starts that the author made at the time of drafting—are shown.

When I got older I dreamed of leaving a job I felt trapped
in. I remember looking out at the oil slicked ramp of Seaboard
World Airlines one rainy morning and thinking, I'll be here forever.
By now the endless reading, the writing over and over again, was
starting to take some form
By now, after read endless reading of other writers on writing, the
reading of textbooks, my own ~~write~~ writing started to take form.
By now, after doing it over and over again, my own writing started
to take form. Sometimes I would write until 3 in the morning,
tearing up maybe 30 sheets of paper to get 5 finished pages.
~~Still, I couldn't type, so I would have to~~ I didn't know how to
type, and it would annoy me that I had this new problem to deal
with.

From his second draft:

When I got older I dreamed of leaving a job I felt trapped
in. I remember looking out at the oil slicked ramp of Seaboard
World Airlines one rainy morning and thinking, I'll be here forever.
~~By now the endless reading, the writing over and over again, was~~
~~starting to take some form~~
~~By now, after read endless reading of other writers on writing, the~~
~~reading of textbooks, my own write writing started to take form.~~

By now, after doing it over and over again, my own writing started
to take form. Sometimes I would write until 3 in the morning,
tearing up maybe 30 sheets of paper to get 5 finished pages.
~~Still, I couldn't type, so I would have to~~ I didn't know how to
type, and it would annoy me that I had this new problem to deal
with.

From his finished essay:

When I got older, I dreamed of leaving a job that I felt trapped in. I
remember looking out at the oil-slicked ramp of Seaboard World Airlines
one rainy morning and hopelessly thinking, I'll be here forever. There were
few smiles on the faces of the cargo handlers who worked the ramp. There

was the heat in the summer and bone chilling winters. Each day was the same as the last, pushing and pulling, heaving and straining with our backs. There was never talk of books or poems, or anything that would make the mind wander from the routine of the airline.

Note how Fenton struggles with the central ideas that he wants to get across in the paragraph, that he was working a dead-end job and that writing was becoming increasingly important to him. His attempts to convey these ideas become more successful as he moves from draft to draft.

In his first draft, the important ideas about working that are noted in the outline are nearly lost among those concerning reading and writing. In the second draft, however, the author makes major revisions to recapture his meaning and convey it clearly. He realizes, it seems, that he must give more details about his job to create a mental image the reader can hold onto and use to understand Fenton's situation. It also appears that Fenton realizes that he cannot include all the necessary information about the job and about writing in the same paragraph. Consequently, in the revision that appears as his final version, he has redistributed the original paragraph into two—one reserved for a description of the job and one for a discussion of his progress as a writer (see paragraph 11 of the finished essay).

By using drafting to discover what he really wants to say, and by using revising to shape his meaning, Fenton crafts his initial outline into a finished essay. As you read through the complete draft and published versions of "Notes on the Writing of 'Confessions of a Working Stiff,' " you will discover other places where the author has forged meaning. Keep in mind the revising processes that he uses to establish meaning, and try to apply these same processes to your drafts when you write.

Essay

1   "You're a writer," Bryon Dobell said as we sat in the offices of *New York* Magazine one wintry afternoon in 1973. The old building, which used to be located at 207 East 32d Street in Manhattan, had no elevator in it. I remember walking up what seemed like endless flights of stairs to get to the top floor. Then I walked into his office and a part of my life changed forever. Byron bought my first story for a major New York magazine. Four weeks later I would get a book offer from Atheneum (one of the best publishers in New York), appear on the David Susskind Show, and for the next 14 years "Confessions of a Working Stiff" would be anthologized in college writing textbooks all across the country.

2   In the beginning it seemed so impossible. There were so many obstacles; grammar and spelling not being the least of them. But if one can get the body in shape to play tennis, to run down a baseball in the high sun, why can't he get his mind in shape to write? In the beginning I approached the task of writing this way. I still do. Like the athlete adding miles each day as he pushes his body

for the long distance run, I added books each day as I pushed my mind for writing.

3   First, there were the reference books, the running shoes of writing that help make the mind feel comfortable and surefooted. I dropped out of high school when I was 16; so I had a lot to get in shape. I started by buying an *Instant Spelling Dictionary*. (A spelling dictionary is a quick way of finding the correct spelling of words that you already know the definition of.) Then I carefully read some books on grammar: *The Elements of Style* by Strunk and White; later on *A Handbook for Writers,* by Celia Millward of Boston University, would find its way to my book shelf.

4   Over the years I educated myself by reading books on the craft of writing. (I have never attended a college course on writing.) I learned about revision by reading William Zinsser's *On Writing Well.* I learned to read carefully by studying Mortimer J. Adler's *How to Read a Book.* But the book that influenced me to keep on writing was a book by Donald Hall called *Writing Well.* It was Hall who brought me close to what Hemingway was doing with the short sentence. His book was the first college textbook on writing that I ever read. I still keep my first copy of it above the desk where I write: its back cover missing, its pages all rumpled.

5   But of course, learning the craft of writing takes more than just reading books on the subject. It takes a desire to try to say something differently, to try to see something differently—as if you saw it for the first time. Whenever I wonder how the desire to write started in me, my mind drifts back to the Three Cent Show in the vast auditorium of Public School #10 in my old neighborhood in Brooklyn. It was here that my mind was left free to dream, free to imagine.

6   The Three Cent Show was one of those great American events that took place in one form or another all across the country in the hard times of the late '40s. It was a cheap form of entertainment where cartoons and movies were played for kids in the back rooms of barber shops, or in the auditoriums of public schools, for little or no admission. In the days when not everyone owned a television, the Three Cent Show brought much excitement. On gray wintry afternoons, hordes of kids would leave the tenements of 17th Street and head down the hill to Public School #10. In our pockets would be the admission price—three cents that we received from the deposit of a milk bottle at Jack The Wonder Dairy's store.

7   The Three Cent Show. A place of first dreams. One hundred kids, maybe even more, all gathered in the dark of a public school auditorium in winter's evening. That great stretch of curtain, all patterned in what looked like the finest silk from where we sat. Its ragged ends reaching endlessly until it disappeared in the shadows of the high ceiling of P.S. #10. Outside, cold winds would coat the tall windows of the school with sheets of ice as we waited warmly in the dark for the show to start. And as the great curtains slowly drew open a roar would go up, and for a few magical hours we would be lost in a world of children's dreams.

8   For three straight hours, cartoons would play, followed by short movies called chapters which continued all through the winter. Then finally the lights

would come up and a hush would come over the crowd as a man in a suit would announce that the raffle was starting. "Please have your tickets ready," he would say. And we all would look down at the numbers on our door tickets. Then, for what seemed like another three hours, there would be the calling out of numbers, and hoots from the crowd of kids as wooden glider planes were won, comic books, puzzles with 300 pieces, and daggers and dolls were pulled out of a great sack. It was here that I learned to dream, to see things differently.

9   I suppose all good writing starts out from dreaming. It starts out from the sorting of bits and pieces of dreams that make us what we are. I was always a dreamer. When I was young I used to dream of the places illustrated in the Sunday comics each week. I used to dream of the comic book small towns that were somewhere across America. Small towns where kids used to beat dust from great patches of Oriental rugs in their yards. Towns where kids took short cuts through fences that always had one slat that would swing up as if it was on a hinge. Towns where kids had dogs with a black circle around one eye. Towns where fathers smoked pipes as they raked leaves, and apple pies cooled on window sills.

10   When I got older, I dreamed of leaving a job that I felt trapped in. I remember looking out at the oil-slicked ramp of Seaboard World Airlines one rainy morning and hopelessly thinking, I'll be here forever. There were few smiles on the faces of the cargo handlers who worked the ramp. There was the heat in the summer and bone chilling winters. Each day was the same as the last, pushing and pulling, heaving and straining with our backs. There was never talk of books or poems, or anything that would make the mind wander from the routine of the airline.

11   By day I would work the airline, and at night I would write. Sometimes I would write until three in the morning, tearing up maybe 30 sheets of paper to get five finished pages of good writing. After awhile the writing came a little easier, but I didn't know how to type, and it would annoy me that I had this new obstacle to deal with before I became a published writer. I would feed reams of paper into a Smith Corona that I had bought until I taught myself how to type. Eventually I had enough confidence to send a story down to a weekly paper called the *Park Slope News*. The story was picked up and I was told by the editor, Marian Leifsen, that I would receive $15 for any future stories. For the next three years, with the help of Marian Leifsen, I learned how to write.

12   Then one night in 1973, I sat down and started to write a story called "Confessions of a Working Stiff." It was about Seaboard World Airlines and a job that I hated. I don't remember exactly how long it took me, but I know it was no more than a few days. The story just wrote itself. I sat at the kitchen table and it kept coming and coming. I remember walking up the long flights of stairs of *New York* Magazine to talk to the editors about it. I remember stopping to get my breath at each floor. I remember my work boots all covered with ramp oil as I passed men in neat suits. I remember passing elegant women that smelled of fine scents. I remember Byron Dobell saying, "You're a writer."

Rough Draft

1   "you're a writer" Byron Dobell said as we sat in the offices
of New York-- his office one winter afternoon in 1973.

"You're a writer," Byron Dobell said as we sat in the old offices
of New York Magazine that used to be located at 207 E.32d Street. *until*

2   "You're a writer", Byron Dobell said as we sat in his office
IN THE OFFICES OR NEW YORK MAGAZINE
one wintry afternoon in 1973. I remember walking up what seemed to
be endless flights of stairs to get to the editorial offices of *TOP FLOOR*
the magazine. The old building,which used to be located at 207
E.32d Street had no elevator in it. Then I walked into his office
and a part of my life was changed forever. Byron bought my first
MAJOR
major story for a New York magazine and two weeks later I would *4*
get a book offer,appear on the David Susskind Show,and for the *FROM ATHENEUM (ONE OF THE BEST PUBLISHERS IN THE CITY)*
CONFESSIONS OF A WELFARE STIFF
next 14 years,the story would be anthologized in college writing
ALL ACROSS THE COUNTRY
textbooks at least once a year.
MENTION AT END OF STORY
HOW YOU NOW LECTURE ON
WRITING AT SCHOOL).
3   In the beginning it seemed so impossible. There were so many
obstacles;grammar and spelling not being the least of them. But if
one can get the body in shape to play tennis,to run down a baseball
in the high sun,why can't they get their mind in shape to write ?
Not so,you say. I approached In the beginning I approached the
task of writing that way. I still do. Like an athlete pushing

Like the athlete pushing himself for the long distance run,I pushed
my mind
HIT BODY
HIS BODY
Like the athlete adding miles each day as he pushes himself for
the long distance run,I added books each day as I pushed my mind *EACH*
for writing.

4   First,there were the textbooks,the running shoes of writing
REFERENCE
that would make the mind feel comfortable and sure. I had dropped *HELP* *FOOTED*
out of school when I was 16,so I had a lot to get in shape. I
started when I was 27 by buying an "Instant spelling Dictionary"
(A spelling Dictionary lets you look up words is a quick way of
finding the correct spelling of words that you already know the
definition of.) Then I carefully read some books on grammar:THE
ELEMENTS OF STYLE by Strunk and White,HANDBOOK FOR WRITERS,by
LATER ON A
Celia Celia Millward of Boston University. *FOUND ITS WAY TO MY*
BOOK SHELF. SHELF.

5   ~~(Over the years, education will the years)~~

Over the years, educating myself, I read many ~~books on the art~~
OVER THE YEARS I EDUCATED MYSELF BY READING BOOKS ON
~~of writing. I learned much from William Zinsser~~ about style
THE ~~ART~~ CRAFT OF WRITING. I LEARNED ABOUT REVISION
~~and revision from William Zinsser's, ON WRITING WELL.~~ But the
BY READING WILLIAM ZINSSER'S, ON WRITING WELL, ~~WITH MY READING~~

book that gave me the most hope the- ~~that I could to a writer~~   HOW TO
I LEARNED TO READ CAREFULLY BY READING MORTIMER J. ADLER'S,   READ A
was a ~~textbook~~ book by Donald Hall called WRITING WELL. It was   BOOK
COLLEGE   BUT THE ~~FIRST~~ BOOK THAT INFLUENCED ME
the first ~~book I ever~~ textbook ~~ix~~ on writing that I ever read~~)~~   TO KEEP FROM QUITTING AGAIN WAS
EVER HELD IN MY HAND,   A BOOK
and to this day I still keep ~~a rumpled~~ my first copy of it above   BY DONALD CALLED,
                                                              WRITING WELL.
the desk where I write, it's back ~~covered~~ cover long missing and

its pages all rumpled. It was Hall who ~~first~~ brought me close
TO WHAT HEMINGWAY WAS DOING WITH THE SHORT SENTENCE.
to ~~what Ernest Hemingway was doing with his short sentences.~~
the beauty that Ernest ~~Hemingway~~ achieved in his short sentences.
~~It was Hall who~~
~~IT WAS HALL WHO BROUGHT ME~~
~~BROUGHT ME CLOSE TO WHAT HEMINGWAY~~

6   But of course, learning the craft of writing takes more than
just reading books on the subject. ~~Like the jockey coming out~~
~~of the starting on the fastest horse, unless~~

It takes a desire ~~in yourself~~ to want to say something different
to want to see something different, as if you saw it for the first
                      THE
time. Whenever I wonder how ~~that~~ desire to write started in me, I
think back to the Three Cent Show in the vast auditorium of Public
                   IN MY OLD BROWN NEIGHBORHOOD.
School # 10 ~~where~~ my mind was left free to dream, free to imagine.
        IT WAS HERE THAT

7   The Three Cent Show was one of those great American events
that took place in one form or another all across the country
in the hard times of the late '40s. It was a cheap form of
entertainment where cartoons and movies were played for kids in
        BACK ROOMS   LIBRARIES
the backs of barber shops or ~~pubs~~ in the auditorium of public
      FOR
schools little or no admission. On gray wintry afternoons, hordes
of kids would head down from the "Hill", ~~the area I lived in~~ as
they made their way to P.S.10. In our pockets would be the
                                RECEIVED
admission price--three cents that we ~~got~~ from the deposit of
a milk bottle at Jack The Wonder Dairy's store.

8   The Three Cent Show. A place of first dreams.   150 OR THREE HUNDRED
         MORE
maybe even 150, all gathered in the dark of a public school
                        IN LATE EVENING   IN WINTERS EVENING
auditorium ~~after school~~. That great stretch of curtain, all
                                                       THE
patterned in what looked like the finest silk from where ~~we~~ sat,
reaching endlessly until it disappeared in the shadows of the
high ceiling of P.S.#10. Outside, the ~~force of~~ winter's winds
                               THE   OF THE SCHOOL
would coat tall windows with sheets of ice as we waited warmly
in the dark for the show to start. And as the great curtains

slowly drew open a roar would go up, and for a few magical hours
~~we~~ would be lost in a world of children's dreams.

9   For 3 straight hours, cartoons would play, followed by short
movies called chapters which continued ~~all~~ winter. *THROUGH* Then finally
the lights would come up and a hush would come over the crowd as
a man in a suit would announce that the raffle was starting.
IT WAS TIME TO LOOK DOWN AT THE NUMBERS ON OUR DOOR TICKETS.
Then, for what seemed like another 3 hours, there would be the
calling out of numbers and hoots from the crowd of kids as
wooden glider planes were won, comic books, puzzles with 200 ~~cardboard~~
pieces, and daggers and dolls were pulled out of a great sack.
It was here that I learned to dream, to see things differently.

10   I suppose all good writing ~~comes from a form of dreaming~~
starts out from dreaming. It starts out from the sorting of
bits and pieces of dreams that make us what we are. I was always
a dreamer. When I was young I used to dream of the places
illustrated in the Sunday comics each week, ~~the small towns that~~
THE SMALL TOWNS THAT
were somewhere across America. Small towns where kids used to
beat ~~rugs- great long rolls of Oriental great patches of Oriental~~
~~rugs-~~ dust from great patches of Oriental rugs in their yards.
Towns where kids ~~cut through-~~ took short cuts through fences
that always had one slat that would swing up as if it was on a hinge.
Towns where kids had ~~dogs with white~~ dogs with one black circle
around ~~their eye-~~ *ONE* an eye. Towns where fathers smoked pipes as
they raked leaves. And I ~~have no doubt, the small town kids were~~
~~dreaming of life in the big city.~~
I DOUBT THAT SMALL TOWN KIDS
and apple pies cooled on window sills.

11   When I got older, I dreamed of leaving a job I felt trapped *THAT*
in. I remember looking out at the oil slicked ramp of Seaboard
World Airlines one rainy morning and thinking, I'll be here forever.
~~By now the endless reading, the writing over and over again, was~~
~~starting to take some form~~
~~By now after read endless reading of other writers on writing, the~~
~~reading of textbooks, my own write writing started to take form.~~
THERE WERE FEW JOICES ON THE RACKS OR FOR MEN WHO
WORKED THE RAMP. EACH DAY WAS THE SAME AS THE LAST
ONE, ... AS PULLED NO PUSHED
WITH OUR BACKS, HEAVING AND STRAINING

12 *NEW →* *PAR ↓* By now, after doing it over and over again, my own writing started
to take form. Sometimes I would write until 3 in the morning,

tearing up maybe 30 sheets of paper to get 5 finished pages. ~~Still, I couldn't type, so I would have to~~ *AFTER AWHILE THE WRITING CAME A LITTLE EASIER, BUT* I didn't know how to type, and it would annoy me that I had this new problem to deal with.

13 *I would FEED REAMS OF PAPER INTO ~~THE~~ A* ~~Over and over again~~ I would feed paper ~~into my~~ a Smith *THERE WAS NEVER TALK OF BOOKS, OR IDEAS OR ANYTHING THAT WOULD MAKE THE MIND WANDER FROM THE ROUTINE OF THE AIRLINE.* Corona that I bought until I taught *just* myself how to type. After awhile I had enough confidence to send ~~some stories~~ *3 3 A STORY* down to a neighborhood paper called the Park Slope News. The story was picked up and I ~~received~~ was told by an editor named Marian Leifsen that from now on I would receive $15 for ~~future stories~~ any future stories ~~that I write, for the paper~~ *SAME PAR.*

~~I wrote for the Park Slope News for 3 years. With the help of Marian Leifsen~~ For the next 3 years, with the help of Marian Leifsen, I learned ~~how~~ how to write.

14 Then ~~in 1979, I sat down one night and started to write a~~ *WORKING AT* *THEN ONE NIGHT IN 1979 I SAT DOWN AND STARTED TO WRITE A STORY CALLED CONFESSIONS OF IT WAS ABOUT SEABOARD AIRLINES AND A STORY THAT I WATCH* ~~story called, CONFESSIONS OF A WORKING STIFF. I~~ don't remember *EXACTLY* ~~I~~ how long it took me, but I know it was no more than a few days. The story just wrote itself. I sat at the kitchen table and it kept coming and coming. ~~I just remember going up to New York Magazine and hearing Byron Doblee say,"you're a writer."~~ I remember walking up the long flights of stairs of New York *TO TALK TO THE EDITORS ABOUT IT.* Magazine. I remember stopping to get my breath at each floor. I remember ~~passing th~~ my work boots all covered with ~~dark~~ oil *RAMP ELEGANT* as I passed men in ~~smart~~ *SLICK* suits. I remember passing women ~~that~~ *THAT SMELLED OF* ~~with~~ fine scents. I remember Byron Dobell saying,"you're a writer."

Comparing Draft and Essay

Draft Paragraphs 1 and 2

Though Fenton has narrowed his topic and knows generally what he wants to say, note how he works at establishing the meaning of this opening paragraph. Again, getting started in drafting can be compared to taking the first step of a journey: it is sometimes difficult to overcome inertia and begin!

1. What revising strategies does Fenton employ in these paragraphs? How are they used to get the author's point across to the reader?

Draft Paragraph 3

2. In the space between paragraphs, Fenton has written "Mention at end of story how you now lecture on writing at schools." Do you think that he will listen to this suggestion? What evidence regarding narrowing a topic and establishing a thesis can you use to back up your prediction?

Draft Paragraphs 7 through 9

3. One aspect of meaning that Fenton wants to establish is a sense of place: he wants the reader to experience this re-created scene. What changes does he make in his draft to convey a feeling of place to you? Locate specific revisions that help you to understand the author's meaning more clearly.

Draft Paragraph 10

4. Toward the end of this paragraph, Fenton deletes the sentence "And I have no doubt, the small town kids were dreaming of life in the big city" and its subsequent revision "Now, I have no doubt that small town kids. . . ." What do you think influences the author's decision to omit this thought?

Draft Paragraphs 11 through 13

5. As mentioned in the introduction to the draft, Fenton has made many changes to draft paragraph 11 to convey his meaning more clearly. Compare this paragraph with paragraphs 10 and 11 in the finished essay and explain how specific revisions contribute to the sharpening of what he wants to say.

6. How does the author use rearrangement to change the structure of these paragraphs? What advantages does the new organization have over the old one?

Joyce Maynard

Joyce Maynard (b. 1954) lives in New Hampshire with her husband and two children. Her autobiography, written during her freshman year at Yale, *Looking Back: A Chronicle of Growing Old in the Sixties,* was published in 1973. She also published a novel, *Baby Love,* in 1981. She now writes frequently for the "Hers" column of *The New York Times,* a weekly feature written by and for women. This is Maynard's description of how she wrote "A Perilous Journey."

> Often I think for days about an essay I'm planning to write, and then struggle for hours over it. But this one came fast, all in one breath. It was, as I say in the piece, my response to the devastating news that a friend's son had been killed in a car crash. Ten minutes after getting off the phone, I sat down to write, and thirty minutes later, the draft you see below (with its considerable raggedness intact) was finished.

A Perilous Journey

Introduction to the Essay and Draft

After you read both the draft and the published version of Joyce Maynard's essay, you might wonder whether they are in fact versions of the same work. Although each essay affects you as a reader, the published one leaves a much greater impact. Maynard explains the changes she went through in writing about the event.

> First there was simply shock, a need to state the basic facts and to recount (for myself, as much as the reader) the few scraps of experience I'd had with my friend's son, and then, my experience with her. I had to work through those things to get to another place: which was, larger thoughts about parenthood and risk, and my own inability to completely protect my children. Because this was an emotionally written piece, I hadn't known where it was going until I got there.

Although these multiple meanings are present in the draft, they are never expressed impersonally; rather, Maynard reveals meaning in the context of a very personal essay. It is her purpose, remember, to explain her meaning in a way that will draw a reader into her particular world. Yet the author's ability to achieve her purpose results from the control she ultimately exerts over her meaning and her draft. Whereas there is no change in purpose from the draft to the published essay, the structure of the essay has been considerably altered, changing the reader's response to the piece.

The draft begins with an explanation of the friend's son's death and a recollection of his stormy life and concludes with a description of the author's own family and an expression of her fears and realizations regarding child-rearing. Because of this arrangement, a reader tends to focus on Maynard's life and her apprehensions about bringing up her daughter. Concern for the friend and for the son's tragic life is secondary. However, when Maynard reorganizes her essay she highlights her friend's story by placing it in the middle of the piece framed by her own story. In the following paragraph Maynard tells why it was necessary to rearrange the essay:

> The image I describe, in the piece, of my daughter walking down our driveway, really did come to mind as I thought about my friend's son. But to finish the essay with that—to jump from a boy's real and enormous tragedy to a child's small sorrow at the loss of her popcorn—seemed, in the end, to trivialize my friend's experience. So I essentially reversed the parts of the essay, beginning with what had initially come at the end: thoughts about my life, threats to my children's happiness and safety. Then I moved on to my friend's story.

Maynard's revision of the draft is major, and it is only because the author undertakes such a revision that readers are able to understand why a child's simple quarter-mile journey is indeed perilous.

Published Essay

1   People we know in the city, seeing the main street of the small town where we live, say what a wonderful place it must be to raise children. And of course, in many ways it is. This winter we built a snow fort covered with pine boughs, and we ski out our back door. More than one fundamentalist–survivalist religious group has settled in our particular valley of New Hampshire out of a conviction that we're situated in such a way as to escape the worst of a nuclear blast.

2   There are—I reassure my daughter, after a scary episode of "T. J. Hooker"—no bad guys around here. So the other day I let her, for the first time, walk off alone down our dirt road for a quarter-mile journey through what are mostly woods to visit our neighbors. I bundled her up warmly for the trip and gave her a plastic bag filled with popcorn to eat along the way. I stood at the window, watching the pompon on her hat bob off down the driveway. Then she dropped the popcorn, kernels scattering in all directions, and bent to pick them up—but with her mittens still on, which made the job difficult. A strong gust of wind came. She gathered up what she could that the wind hadn't blown away and set out again. I thought of how impatient I'd been with her before she left. How I'd complained that she was taking too long putting on her boots. The way I'd brushed her hair just roughly enough that she cried out.

3   I wanted, then, to run out and put my arms around her, take her hand and walk with her the rest of the way. It seemed suddenly as if the sky had darkened and there was a wolf behind every tree. Of course, what I really did was just stand there.

4   Word came this morning that my friend Janet's 17-year-old son was killed in a late-night car crash—one of two passengers in a car driving too fast down the wrong side of the highway. The three boys hit an old pickup truck whose occupants remain in intensive care. The boys are all dead.

5   I didn't know Janet's son, except as a skinny figure leaning out the passenger side of another friend's truck (he never learned to drive), trying to bum a cigarette from my husband. But I knew his story from his mother. There was no way to ask Janet how she was, how things were going in her life, without getting to "How's Sam?" And he was never fine, his life was never going well, and as long as it wasn't, of course, neither could hers.

6   Janet's son was known as a town bad boy. There were drugs involved, school suspensions, juvenile officers and later the police. Sam's father—divorced from Janet and living in another state—had broken off communication with the boy a few years back. There had been counselors and therapists and, for Janet, a parents' support group called Tough Love.

7   A while back Janet had found a residential drug-treatment program in another city—the kind of place a kid goes to when he has reached the end of the line. He agreed to try it; the town agreed to pay part of the enormous cost. I'd never seen Janet look so hopeful as she did in September, just after Sam left for Odyssey House. Two days after Christmas he was home for good. Kicked out

(and no one has to get kicked out of a program like that—you can leave any time) for plotting to break into the center's office, steal the operating cash and go on a spree.

8   My friend Janet is a wise, funny, loving but unsentimental woman— marvelous looking and beautiful-spirited. She's an artist and a lover of birds, which is how we came to meet her a couple of Septembers back on top of Pitcher Mountain watching for hawks. She was just 19 when her first child, her son, was born; he was 5 or 6 when she and her husband separated. I've heard her speak, full of regret, about not having handled carefully enough that hard time in her children's lives. I've heard her voice regrets over mistakes she felt she made. It's hard to find yourself living under the same roof with a person you'd have had nothing to do with (I've heard her say) if you hadn't happened to give birth to him.

9   Usually my children are around us—all over us—as we've talked about this. We'd be in my living room, surrounded by the tangible chaos an 18-month-old and a 5-year-old make of their parents' lives, Audrey begging for the chance to stay up an hour later and Charlie dancing his wild dervish dance to "The Big Chill" soundtrack with an uncapped felt-tip marker in his fist.

10   They are children of an age, still, to be picked up and put in another place when they're heading in the wrong direction. Children to whom one can still hold out the threat of no dessert and for whom that lyric about "You better watch out, better not pout, cause Santa Claus is coming to town" still carries a lot of power. My daughter will still sometimes say, "You're the best mommy in the entire universe." My son wakes in the night with my name on his lips. I try unsuccessfully to imagine my two round-faced offspring being teen-agers who will someday stop smiling, stop speaking to me. Going up to their rooms and closing the door, blasting me out of the house with their music. And worse.

11   Janet was, I know, a loving mother who did everything she could to save her son, and still he just didn't make it. New Year's Eve, the week before the crash, I saw Janet and the man who—if she were freer, and not bound up by attempts to make things O.K. for her children—she might happily have been living with. "Something terrible is going to happen," she said, powerless to change anything.

12   And it's true: if another friend's 17-year-old had been killed in a crash I'd be thinking about the senseless way car accidents have of altering a seemingly cloudless horizon. With Sam's death there is a different sort of grief—of having seen this coming as clearly as if the vehicles had been toys that were wound up and set on a track. Sam's feeling of emptiness—the inability of everyone who tried to give him excitement or hope or even interest in living—appeared bottomless. He seemed so bent on self-destruction that the shock at his death lay most strongly in the fact that he was a passenger in the car and not its driver.

13   Parents of older children, nodding in the direction of my two small ones, shake their heads and tell me: "Wait until they're teen-agers. They'll break your heart." Well, I don't feel the grip of terror. I have to believe that a person has some control over the way things turn out, and beyond that I have to trust my son and daughter. But I don't feel even close to immune, either, to Janet's kind

of disaster, the chaos an unhappy teen-ager can bring on a household. I don't believe I have the power to insure my children's survival. And there is no such thing as a safe place to bring up children, however much the landscape resembles a scene printed on a calendar. It's always a perilous journey through the woods. Not only for the child, but for the mother, back at home, who stands watching through the glass.

Draft

1   Word came ~~today~~ [this morning]. My friend's [Janet's] seventeen year old son killed ~~Friday night in a~~ in a car crash late Friday night. One of two passengers in a ~~truck~~ [car] driving too fast down the wrong side of the highway ~~one town over the line~~. The three boys hit a compact car whose occupants remain in intensive care. The three boys are all dead.

2   I didn't know Janet's son, except as a skinny figure leaning out the passenger side of another friend's truck (he never learned to drive), trying to bum a cigarette from my husband. ~~I remember how small he looked~~ But I knew his story ~~pretty well~~ from his mother. ~~It was an inescapable~~ There was no way to ask Janet how she was, how things were going, ~~but~~ [in her life except] to begin with "How's Sam?" And he was never fine, ~~the news was never good~~ [his life was never going well], and as long as it wasn't, of course, neither could hers. Inescapable fact of parenthood--the way a person's destiny comes to be controlled no longer simply by ~~one's~~ her own actions, but by the lives of however many satellites she ~~sends~~ [has sent] into orbit.

3   Janet's son was known ~~in~~ [as a] town, ~~never for any large offenses, just small ones.~~ [bad boy.] There were drugs involved, of course, school suspensions, juvenile offenses. Sam's father--living in another state--had broken off communication with his son a few years back. There had been counselors and therapists and, for ~~Janet~~ [support], a parent's group called Tough Love. A while back Janet had found a residential drug treatment program in another city-- the kind of place ~~you sent~~ a kid goes to when ~~it's~~ [he's reached] the end of the line. ~~She got him~~ He agreed to try it, the town agreed to pay ~~for~~ part of the enormous cost. ~~When I saw her in September,~~

looked
~~after-he'd-left,-she-seemed-more-hopeful~~ I'd never seen Janet

look so hopeful as she did in September, just after Sam had left

for Odyssey House. Two days after Christmas, he was home for

good. Kicked out (and nobody has to get himself kicked out of a

place like that. You can leave anytime.) for ~~stealing-something~~

breaking into an office and stealing something.

deeply-intelligent, wise
4   My friend Janet is a gentle, loving woman--beautiful-
just
looking, and lovely spirited. She was nineteen when her son was

born; he was five or six when she and her husband separated.

~~I've-heard-her~~ I've heard her talking, full of regret, about not
carefully enough
having handled that time in her children's lives. I've heard her

voice a hundred regrets over mistakes she felt she made, things

she'd do differently if she had another chance. ~~But~~ It's hard

to ~~discover~~ find yourself living under the same roof with a

person you'd never have ~~had~~ anything to do with (I've heard her

say,) if you hadn't happened to give birth to him.

5   Usually my children are ~~all~~ around us--all over us--as we've

talked. ~~It-was-hard-for-me--as-my-18-month-old-son-danced-to-~~

~~the-Big-Chill-Soundtrack~~ We'd be in my living room, surrounded
tangible
by the ~~physical~~ chaos an 18 month old and a 5 year old make of

their parents' lives. Cars and blocks and Fisher Price people

flung in all directions, Audrey begging ~~for-another-cookie-or-~~

~~piece-of-cake~~ to stay up another half hour and Charlie ~~having-~~

~~had-one-set-of-diapers-removed~~ with one diaper just removed,

having successfully eluded getting taped into its replacement--
would
~~will-be~~ doing his wild, dervish dance to the Big Chill

Soundtrack, with a plastic fire chief's hat on his head and an

uncapped magic marker in his fist. They are children of an age,

still, to be picked up and put in another place, when they're

heading in the wrong direction. Children to whom one can still

hold out the threat of no dessert, and for whom that lyric about

"You better watch out, better not pout, cause Santa Claus is

coming to town" still carries a lot of power. My daughter

(though of course she can also get very mad at me) will still say ~~to me~~ sometimes, "You're the best mommy in the world." My son wakes in the night with my name on his lips.

6   ~~Fearing Janet is in no rush to go home, because her son wouldn't be there anyway--a child who won't speak, a child who goes to his room and shuts the door.~~ I try to imagine my two round-faced offspring ~~someday~~ being teenagers who will stop speaking to me someday. Going up to their rooms and closing the door, blasting me out of the house with their music. ~~What~~ I don't feel, certainly, immune to Janet's kind of disaster, and the invisible chaos an unhappy teenager can bring onto a household. When parents of older children, nodding in the direction of my ~~children~~ small ones, shake their heads and tell me "wait until they're teenagers"--I do not feel ~~fear~~ a cold hand grip my heart. I have to believe a person has some control over the way things turn out; ~~am not prepared to write off as a loss--years in advance--a whole set of~~ But neither do I believe that I control my children's universe and that I have the power ~~to make their survival.~~ to ensure ~~my children~~ Janet was, I know, a loving mother who did everything she could to save her son (very nearly destroying herself in the process) and still, ~~that boy~~ he just didn't make it. If he had been at the wheel of the car he died in, ~~no one would~~ his death would have been no less of a shock. ~~have made more sense of it.~~ He seemed as bent on destruction as the kids in our town who have lain down in the middle of the road, late at night, just waiting for someone to come and run over them. ~~The wonder is that--headed as he seemed to be, at full speed towards des~~

7   Where we live, the air is clean. More than one fundamentalist, survivalist religious group has settled in this particular valley in N.H., out of a conviction that we're situated in such a way as to avoid the worst of an atomic blast. There are--I ~~tell~~ reassure my daughter, tucking her in after a scary episode of ~~The Fall~~ T.J. Hooker, no bad guys around here.

8

So yesterday I let her, for the first time, walk off alone
down our ^dirt^ road, for a half mile journey through mostly woods, to
visit neighbors, just moved in, ~~who have a daughter just aged 5~~ ^who have a 5 year old^
daughter. I bundled her up warmly for the trip. Hat, mittens,
snowpants, and gave her a plastic bag filled with popcorn to eat
along the way. I stood at the window, watching ~~her go~~ the pom
pom on her hat bob off down the driveway. Then she dropped the
popcorn, and kernals were scattered in all directions, ~~and then~~
~~a strong gust of wind came~~ and she bent to pick them up, but with
her mittens still on, which made the job difficult. Then a
strong gust of wind came. She gathered up what ~~she could~~ hadn't
blown away and set out again and dropped the bag again. She bent
down a second time, picking up the kernals one by one. I thought
of how ~~(with my son asleep and wanting to savor some time alone)~~
impatient I'd been with her, just before she left: how I'd
complained that she was ~~dawdling, buttoning her sweater~~ ^taking too long putting on her boots,^, and the
way I'd brushed her hair--not unintentionally--just ^completely^ rough enough
that she cried out once. ~~Suddenly~~ I wanted, then, to run
outside and take her hand, walk her to her friend's house. ~~The~~ ^It seemed^
as if the sky had darkened, and there was a wolf behind every tree.
~~woods seemed suddenly filled with wolves.~~ Of course, what I
really did was just stand there; wondering how I'll ever manage,
when the trips she makes without me are taken in a car--with
friends I don't trust. It's a perilous journey through the
woods. For the child. For the mother.

Comparing Draft and Essay

Draft Paragraphs 1 through 3
Even a quick glance at the opening paragraphs of the draft and published versions
of "A Perilous Journey" shows major changes in the work. Maynard seems to
discover what she wants to emphasize while writing her draft. Rearrangement, her
main revision strategy, allows her to avoid the impression that her friend's tragedy
was less important and to end with the common peril shared by all children and
parents. Briefly, she has switched the end with the beginning.

1. Compare these paragraphs with the opening paragraphs of the published essay.
   Which opening gives you a better sense of the overall meaning?

2. Read paragraph 2 of the published essay. How does the depicted event lead into the main point of the essay?

Draft Paragraph 4

3. Maynard here applies addition as a revising strategy: note how details that make her friend more real have been added to published paragraph 8.

Draft Paragraph 6

4. Again, note the inclusion of additional detail about Janet's life and her fears for her son in published paragraph 11. Is published paragraph 11 more successful than the corresponding part in the draft? Why or why not?

Draft Paragraphs 7 and 8

5. How does Maynard's rearrangement of these paragraphs (see also published paragraphs 1 and 2) capitalize on their strengths? What do they accomplish as an introduction that the original opening paragraphs do not? (See Chapter 6, Composing Introductions and Conclusions, pp. 170–204.)

6. Compare the final paragraph in the draft with the final paragraph in the published version. Which is a more effective conclusion? Why?

Patrick Fenton

Patrick Fenton (b. 1944) is a freelance writer and teacher. "Confessions of a Working Stiff," which appeared in *New York* magazine in April 1975, was his first professionally published essay. Here is his answer to our question: "How did you discover the process of writing and revising?"

When I first started writing I thought I was doing something wrong. I would look at the first drafts with all the cross-outs, write-ins, and notes to myself, and I would think that it should come more easily to me. I would worry that I was working too hard at it. Then one day I was up in the Great Books section of the New York Public Library on Fifth Avenue and I saw something that amazed me. I looked at the actual, rough drafts of the poet Walt Whitman's *Leaves of Grass,* and I saw that it was filled with the same false starts, the same cross-outs, and the same write-ins that covered my own writing.

Later on when I started to write for some local newspapers where I lived, I had the experience of being around some seasoned writers and I got a chance to look over their shoulders at their deletions. It was here that I learned that good writing came from doing the thing over and over again. Since then, I have had a lot of my stuff published in daily newspapers and I have had the opportunity to learn about revisions from watching some famous journalists at work. I got to know the writer Jimmy Breslin after helping him with some ideas on a script he was trying to sell as a television series.

I used to go up to the *Daily News* and watch him struggle with his newspaper column with the pressure of a deadline. His coat would be thrown over a chair in the small office cubicle he worked in and his tie would be loose around his neck, as if he was getting ready for a street fight rather than the act of writing. The sweat would roll down his head in beads and all along his desk there would be piles of crumpled paper with his discarded words. With the intensity of a bullfighter he would stare at the typewriter that held paper covered with his pen marks.

When he was finished, the story would appear in that night's edition of the Sunday *Daily News* with all the smoothness and spontaneity of a great barroom tale. I didn't know much about it when I first started writing, but revision is simply something that is a natural part of the act of writing.

Confessions of a Working Stiff

1   The Big Ben is hammering out its 5:45 alarm in the half-dark of another Tuesday morning. If I'm lucky, my car down in the street will kick over for me. I don't want to think about that now; all I want to do is roll over into the warm covers that hug my wife. I can hear the wind as it whistles up and down the sides of the building. Tuesday is always the worst day—it's the day the drudgery, boredom, and fatigue start all over again. I'm off from work on Sunday and Monday, so Tuesday is my blue Monday.

2   I make my living humping cargo for Seaboard World Airlines, one of the big international airlines at Kennedy Airport. They handle strictly all cargo. I was once told that one of the Rockefellers is the major stockholder for the airline, but I don't really think about that too much. I don't get paid to think. The big thing

is to beat that race with the time clock every morning of your life so the airline will be happy. The worst thing a man could ever do is to make suggestions about building a better airline. They pay people $40,000 a year to come up with better ideas. It doesn't matter that these ideas never work; it's just that they get nervous when a guy from South Brooklyn or Ozone Park acts like he actually has a brain.

3   I throw a Myadec high-potency vitamin into my mouth to ward off one of the ten colds I get every year from humping mailbags out in the cold rain at Kennedy. A huge DC-8 stretch jet waits impatiently for the 8,000 pounds of mail that I will soon feed its empty belly. I wash the Myadec down with some orange juice and grab a brown bag filled with bologna and cheese. Inside the lunch bag there is sometimes a silly note from my wife that says, "I Love You—Guess Who?" It is all that keeps me going to a job that I hate.

4   I've been going there for seven years now and my job is still the same. It's weary work that makes a man feel used up and worn out. You push and you pull all day long with your back. You tie down pallets loaded with thousands of pounds of freight. You fill igloo-shaped containers with hundreds of boxes that all look the same. If you're assigned to work the warehouse, it's really your hard luck. This is the job all the men hate most. You stack box upon box until the pallet resembles the exact shape of the inside of the plane. You get the same monotonous feeling an adult gets when he plays with a child's blocks. When you finish one pallet, you find another and start the whole dull process over again.

5   The airline pays me $192 a week for this. After they take out taxes and $5.81 for the pension, I go home with $142. Once a month they take out $10 for term life insurance, and $5.50 for union dues. The week they take out the life insurance is always the worst: I go home with $132. My job will never change. I will fill up the same igloos with the same boxes for the next 34 years of my life, I will hump the same mailbags into the belly of the plane, and push the same 8,000-pound pallets with my back. I will have to do this until I'm 65 years old. Then I'll be free, if I don't die of a heart attack before that, and the airline will let me retire.

6   In the winter the warehouse is cold and damp. There is no heat. The large steel doors that line the warehouse walls stay open most of the day. In the cold months, wind, rain and snow blow across the floor. In the summer the warehouse becomes an oven. Dust and sand from the runways mix with the toxic fumes of fork lifts, leaving a dry, stale taste in your mouth. The high windows above the doors are covered with a thick, black dirt that kills the sun. The men work in shadows with the constant roar of jet engines blowing dangerously in their ears.

7   Working the warehouse is a tedious job that leaves a man's mind empty. If he's smart he will spend his days wool-gathering. He will think about pretty girls that he once knew, or some other daydream of warm, dry places where you never had a chill. The worst thing he can do is think about his problems. If he starts to think about how he is going to pay the mortgage on the $30,000 home that he can't afford, it will bring him down. He will wonder why he comes to the

cargo airline every morning of his life, and even on Christmas Day. He will start to wonder why he has to listen to the deafening sound of the jets as they rev up their engines. He will wonder why he crawls on his hands and knees, breaking his back a little bit more every day.

8   To keep his kids in that great place in the country in the summer, that great place far away from Brooklyn and the South Bronx, he must work every hour of overtime that the airline offers him. If he never turns down an hour, if he works some 600 hours over, he can make about $15,000. To do this he must turn against himself, he must pray that the phone rings in the middle of the night, even though it's snowing out and he doesn't feel like working. He must hump cargo late into the night, eat meatball heroes for supper, drink coffee that starts to taste like oil, and then hope that his car starts when it's time to go home. If he gets sick—well, he better not think about that.

9   All over Long Island, Ozone Park, Brooklyn, and as far away as the Bronx, men stir in the early morning hours as a new day begins. Every morning is the same as the last. Some of the men drink beer for breakfast instead of coffee. Way out in Bay Shore a cargoman snaps open a can of Budweiser. It's 6 A.M., and he covers the top of the can with his thumb in order to keep down the loud hiss as the beer escapes. He doesn't want to awaken his children as they dream away the morning in the next room. Soon he will swing his Pinto wagon up onto the crowded Long Island Expressway and start the long ride to the job. As he slips the car out of the driveway he tucks another can of beer between his legs.

10   All the men have something in common: they hate the work they are doing and they drink a little too much. They come to work only to punch a timecard that has their last name on it. At the end of the week they will pick up a paycheck with their last name on it. They will never receive a bonus for a job well done, or even a party. At Christmastime a card from the president of the airline will arrive at each one of their houses. It will say Merry Christmas and have the president's name printed at the bottom of it. They know that the airline will be there long after they are dead. Nothing stops it. It runs non-stop, without sleep, through Christmas Day, New Year's Eve, Martin Luther King's birthday, even the deaths of Presidents.

11   It's seven in the morning and the day shift is starting to drift in. Huge tractors are backing up to the big-mouth doors of the warehouse. Cattle trucks bring tons of beef to feed its insatiable appetite for cargo. Smoke-covered trailers with refrigerated units packed deep with green peppers sit with their diesel engines idling. Names like White, Mack, and Kenworth are welded to the front of their radiators, which hiss and moan from the overload. The men walk through the factory-type gates of the parking lot with their heads bowed, oblivious of the shuddering diesels that await them.

12   Once inside the warehouse they gather in groups of threes and fours like prisoners in an exercise yard. They stand in front of the two time clocks that hang below a window in the manager's office. They smoke and cough in the early morning hour as they await their work assignments. The manager, a nervous-looking man with a stomach that is starting to push out of his belt, walks out with the pink work sheets in his hand.

13   Eddie, a young Irishman with a mustache, has just bolted in through the door. The manager has his timecard in his hand, holding it so no one else can hit Eddie in. Eddie is four minutes late by the time clock. His name will now go down in the timekeeper's ledger. The manager hands the card to him with a "you'll be up in the office if you don't straighten out" look. Eddie takes the card, hits it in, and slowly takes his place with the rest of the men. He has been out till four in the morning drinking beer in the bars of Ozone Park; the time clock and the manager could blow up, for all he cares. "Jesus," he says to no one in particular, "I hope to Christ they don't put me in the warehouse this morning."

14   Over in another group, Kelly, a tall man wearing a navy knit hat, talks to the men. "You know, I almost didn't make it in this morning. I passed this green VW on the Belt Parkway. The girl driving it was singing. Jesus, I thought to myself, it must be great going somewhere at 6:30 in the morning that makes you want to sing." Kelly is smiling as he talks. "I often think, why the hell don't you keep on going, Kelly? Don't get off at the cargo exit, stay on. Go anywhere, even if it's only Brooklyn. Christ, if I was a single man I think I would do just that. Some morning I'd pass this damn place by and drive as far away as Riverhead. I don't know what I'd do when I got there—maybe I'd pick up a pound of beefsteak tomatoes from one of those roadside stands or something."

15   The men laugh at Kelly but they know he is serious. "I feel the same way sometimes," the man next to him says. "I find myself daydreaming a lot lately; this place drives you to that. I get up in the morning and I just don't want to come to work. I get sick when I hit that parking lot. If it wasn't for the kids and the house I'd quit." The men then talk about how hard it is to get work on "the outside." They mention "outside" as if they were in a prison.

16   Each morning there is an Army-type roll call from the leads. The leads are foremen who must keep the men moving; if they don't, it could mean their jobs. At one time they had power over the men but as time went by the company took away their little bit of authority. They also lost the deep interest, even enjoyment, for the hard work they once did. As the cargo airline grew, it beat this out of them, leaving only apathy. The ramp area is located in the backyard of the warehouse. This is where the huge jets park to unload their 70,000-pound payloads. A crew of men fall in behind the ramp lead as he mopes out of the warehouse. His long face shows the hopelessness of another day.

17   A brutal rain has started to beat down on the oil-covered concrete of the ramp as the 306 screeches in off the runway. Its engines scream as they spit off sheets of rain and oil. Two of the men cover their ears as they run to put up a ladder to the front of the plane. The airline will give them ear covers only if they pay for half of them. A lot of men never buy them. If they want, the airline will give them two little plugs free. The plugs don't work and hurt the inside of the ears.

18   The men will spend the rest of the day in the rain. Some of them will set up conveyor belts and trucks to unload the thousands of pounds of cargo that sit in the deep belly of the plane. Then they will feed the awkward bird until it is full and ready to fly again. They will crawl on their hands and knees in its belly, counting and humping hundreds of mailbags. The rest of the men will work up

topside on the plane, pushing 8,000-pound pallets with their backs. Like Egyptians building a pyramid, they will pull and push until the pallet finally gives in and moves like a massive stone sliding through sand. They don't complain too much; they know that when the airline comes up with a better system some of them will go.

19   The old-timers at the airline can't understand why the younger men stay on. They know what the cargo airline can do to a man. It can work him hard but make him lazy at the same time. The work comes in spurts. Sometimes a man will be pushed for three hours of sweat, other times he will just stand around bored. It's not the hard work that breaks a man at the airline, it's the boredom of doing the same job over and over again.

20   At the end of the day the men start to move in off the ramp. The rain is still beating down at their backs but they move slowly. Their faces are red and raw from the rain-soaked wind that has been snapping at them for eight hours. The harsh wind moves in from the direction of the city. From the ramp you can see the Manhattan skyline, gray- and blue-looking, as it peeks up from the west wall of the warehouse. There is nothing to block the winter weather as it rolls in like a storm across a prairie. They head down to the locker room, heads bowed, like a football team that never wins.

21   With the workday almost over the men move between the narrow, gray rows of lockers. Up on the dirty walls that surround the lockers someone has written a couple of four-letter words. There is no wit to the words; they just say the usual. As they strip off their wet gear the men seem to come alive.

22   "Hey, Arnie! You want to stay four hours? They're asking for overtime down in Export," one of the men yells over the lockers.

23   Arnie is sitting about four rows over, taking off his heavy winter clothing. He thinks about this for a second and yells back, "What will we be doing?"

24   "Working the meat trailer." This means that Arnie will be humping huge sides of beef off rows of hooks for four hours. Blood will drip down onto his clothes as he struggles to the front of the trailer. Like most of the men, he needs the extra money, and knows that he should stay. He has Master Charge, Korvettes, Times Square Stores, and Abraham & Straus to pay.

25   "Nah, I'm not staying tonight. Not if it's working the meat trailer. Don wanted to stop for a few beers at The Owl; maybe I'll stay tomorrow night."

26   It's four o'clock in the afternoon now—the men have twelve minutes to go before they punch out. The airline has stopped for a few seconds as the men change shifts. Supervisors move frantically across the floor pushing the fresh lot of new men who have just started to come in. They hand out work sheets and yell orders: "Jack, get your men into their rain gear. Put three men in the bellies to finish off the 300 flight. Get someone on the pepper trailers, they've been here all morning."

27   The morning shift stands around the time clock with three minutes to go. Someone says that Kevin Delahunty has just been appointed to the Fire Department. Kevin, a young Irishman from Ozone Park, has been working the cargo airline for six years. Like most of the men, he has hated every minute of it.

The men are openly proud of him as they reach out to shake his hand. Kevin has found a job on "the outside." "Ah, you'll be leaving soon," he tells Pat. "I never thought I'd get out of here either, but you'll see, you're going to make it."

28   The manager moves through the crowd handing out timecards and stops when he comes to Kevin. Someone told him Kevin is leaving. "Is that right, Delahunty? Well I guess we won't expect you in tomorrow, will we? Going to become a fireman, eh? That means you'll be jumping out of windows like a crazy man. Don't act like you did around here," he adds as he walks back to his office.

29   The time clock hits 4:12 and the men pour out of the warehouse. Kevin will never be back, but the rest of them will return in the morning to grind out another eight hours. Some of them will head straight home to the bills, screaming children, and a wife who tries to understand them. They'll have a Schaefer or two, then they'll settle down to a night of television.

30   Some of them will start to fill up the cargo bars that surround Kennedy Airport. They will head to places like Gaylor's on Rockaway Boulevard or The Dew Drop Inn down near Farmers Boulevard. They will drink deep glasses of whiskey and cold mugs of Budweiser. The Dew Drop has a honky-tonk mood of the Old West to it. The barmaid moves around like a modern-day Katie Elder. Like Brandy, she's a fine girl, but she can out-curse any cargoman. She wears a low-cut blouse that reveals most of her breasts. The jukebox will beat out some Country & Western as she says, "Ah, hell, you played my song." The cargomen will hoot and hollar as she substitutes some of her own obscene lyrics.

31   They will drink late into the night, forgetting time clocks, Master Charge, First National City, Korvettes, mortgages, cars that don't start, and jet engines that hurt their ears. They will forget about damp, cold warehouses, winters that get longer and colder every year, minutes that drift by like hours, supervisors that harass, and the thought of growing old on a job they hate. At midnight they will fall dangerously into their cars and make their way up onto the Southern State Parkway. As they ride into the dark night of Long Island they will forget it all until 5:45 the next morning—when the Big Ben will start up the whole grind all over again.

Considering Content

1. In paragraph 2 Fenton says, "I don't get paid to think." What does he get paid to do? Why does he say in paragraph 7 that the worst thing a man with his job can do is "to think about his problems"?

2. What does Fenton mean when he says in paragraph 8 that to earn $15,000 a year on his job he must "turn against himself"? Is this the worst effect that his job has on him?

3. In paragraph 10 Fenton tells us that all the men hate their work and drink a little too much. What causes the men to keep going to a job they hate? To what extent does the drinking of someone like Eddie, for example, help make the work any easier to accept?

4. Why don't the men complain about the way the airline treats them? What is it, ultimately, that breaks a man at the airline?

5. Who ultimately is responsible for the poor working conditions from which the men described by Fenton suffer? Do you blame the airline? If so, what causes the airline to exploit the men the way it does? Do you blame the men for allowing themselves to be exploited? Why or why not?

Considering Craft

1. What is Fenton's purpose in "Confessions of a Working Stiff"?

2. In paragraph 4 Fenton says that this job gives him "the same monotonous feeling an adult gets when he plays with a child's blocks." What other comparisons does Fenton make to convey the feelings of monotony and hopelessness that his job causes him? Which parts of his description of the job itself and the way he is treated by his employer are most effective in helping us understand why he feels as he does?

3. Why throughout the essay does Fenton picture the planes and the warehouse as creatures with "insatiable" appetites that must be fed? What impact does this have on the essay's meaning?

4. What is the effect of concluding the essay by comparing Kevin, who will never go back, with the rest of the men, who either go home to a night of television or go to places like the Dew Drop Inn?

5. Characterize Fenton's attitude about his situation. Is he angry, resigned, frustrated? Explain your answer.

6. What effect does using slang expressions like "kick over" and "humping" have on the essay's meaning? Does Fenton maintain this style consistently?

Anna Quindlen

Anna Quindlen (b. 1952) lives in New York City and writes frequently for the Op-Ed page of *The New York Times,* where "I am a Catholic" originally appeared (1987). Her most recent novel, *Object Lessons* (1991), received wide critical acclaim. In 1992, she received the Pulitzer Prize for her personal and political reporting. This is her response to our question: "How do you usually get started on a piece?"

If I did not write under deadline, I would never write. The most liberating moment in the writing of my novel came when it was actually purchased and I was given a date by which I had to complete it. When I told my editor I would be delivering it on time, she was stunned. "Nobody ever delivers on time," she said. "How many former Catholic school girls write for you?" I replied. I have written under deadline my entire life and I think it's too late for me to change.

I Am a Catholic

1   *Dominus vobiscum. Et cum spiritu tuo.* These are my bona fides: a word, a phrase, a sentence in a language no one speaks anymore. *Kyrie eleison. Confiteor dei.* I am a Catholic. Once at a nursing home for retired clergy, I ate lunch with a ninety-year-old priest, a man who still muttered the Latin throughout the English Mass and ate fish on Fridays. When he learned how old I was, he said with some satisfaction, "You were a Catholic when being a Catholic still meant something."

2   What does it mean now? For myself, I cannot truly say. Since the issue became material to me, I have not followed the church's teaching on birth control. I disagree with its stand on abortion. I believe its resistance to the ordination of women as priests is a manifestation of a misogyny that has been with us much longer than the church has. Yet it would never have occurred to my husband and me not to be married in a Catholic church, not to have our children baptized. On hospital forms and in political polls, while others leave the space blank or say "none of your business," I have no hesitation about giving my religion.

3   We are cultural Catholics. I once sneered at that expression, used by Jewish friends at college, only because I was not introspective enough to understand how well it applied to me. Catholicism is to us now not so much a system of beliefs or a set of laws but a shared history. It is not so much our faith as our past. The tenets of the church which I learned as a child have ever since been at war with the facts of my adult life. The Virgin Birth. The Trinity. The Resurrection. Why did God make me? God made me to know Him, to love Him, and to serve Him in this world and to be happy with Him forever in the next. I could recite parts of the Baltimore Catechism in my sleep. Do I believe those words? I don't know. What I do believe are those guidelines that do not vary from faith to faith, that are as true of Judaism or Methodism as they are of Catholicism: that people should be kind to one another, that they should help those in need, that they should respect others as they wish to be respected.

4   And I believe in my own past. I was educated by nuns, given absolution by priests. My parents were married in a Catholic church, my grandparents and mother buried from one. Saturday afternoons kneeling on Leatherette pads in the dim light of the confessional, listening for the sound of the priest sliding back the grille on his side. Sunday mornings kneeling with my face in my hands, the Communion wafer stuck to the roof of my dry mouth. These are my history. I could no more say I am not Catholic than say I am not Irish, not Italian. Yet I have never been to Ireland or Italy.

5   Some of our Jewish friends have returned to the ways of their past, to Shabbat without automobiles and elevators, to dietary laws and the study of Hebrew. We cannot do the same. There is no longer a Latin Mass, no Communion fast from midnight on. Even the inn is gone from the Bible; now Mary and Joseph are turned away from "the place where travelers lodged."

6   The first time my husband and I went to midnight mass on Christmas Eve in our parish church, we arrived a half-hour early so we would get a seat. When the bells sounded twelve and the priest came down the center aisle, his small acolytes in their child-size cassocks walking before him, the pews were still half empty. We were thinking of a different time, when the churches were packed, when missing Mass was a sin, when we still believed that that sort of sin existed—sins against rules, victimless sins.

7   There are more families coming to that church now, families like us with very small children who often have to leave before the Gospel because of tears, fatigue, temper tantrums. (I remember that, when I was growing up, my family's parish church was shaped like a cross, and one of the short arms was for the women with babies. It had a sheet of glass walling it off and was soundproof. And through the glass you could see the babies, as though in a movie with no audio, their little mouths round, their faces red. Inside that room, the noise was dreadful. But missing Mass was a sin.)

8   I think perhaps those families are people like us, people who believe in something, although they are not sure what, people who feel that in a world of precious little history or tradition, this is theirs. We will pass down the story to our children: There was a woman named Mary who was visited by an angel. And the angel said, "Do not be afraid" and told her that though she was a virgin she would have a child. And He was named Jesus and was the Son of God and He rose from the dead. Everything else our children learn in America in the late twentieth century will make this sound like a fairy tale, like tales of the potato famines in Ireland and the little ramshackle houses with grape arbors on hillsides in Italy. But these are my fairy tales, and so, whether or not they are fact, they are true.

9   I was born a Catholic and I think I will die one. I will ask for a priest to give me Extreme Unction, as it was given to my mother, and to her mother before her. At the end, as in the beginning, I will ask for the assistance of the church, which is some fundamental part of my identity. I am a Catholic.

Considering Content

1. What meaning does Catholicism have for Quindlen? How have her concepts of Catholicism changed with the passage of time? How do her views about religion compare with yours?

2. How have marriage and raising children affected her religious observance? What role does family tradition play?

3. Explain the significance of her title. What examples does she cite in her essay to best support it?

Considering Craft

1. What is Quindlen's purpose in "I Am a Catholic"? Where does she state it?

2. How do the details she includes in paragraph 3 enhance her essay's meaning?

3. Read over the first and last paragraphs of the essay. How do they reinforce her purpose? What is their impact on the essay's meaning?

4. Effective writing should be simple, clear, and concise. Cite examples from Quindlen's essay that meet these criteria.

Anne Taylor Fleming

Anne Taylor Fleming is a freelance writer living in Los Angeles. She writes most regularly for *The New York Times,* does weekly radio commentary for CBS, and contributes essays to the "MacNeil/Lehrer News Hour." Her writing career began shortly after she graduated from the University of California in 1971. Returning to her native Los Angeles, she wrote a number of "My Turn" essays for *Newsweek.* As you read "Losing People," which first appeared in *The New York Times,* speculate as to her purpose in writing this essay.

Losing People

1   For Christmas, I was given a new telephone–address book of sleek caramel-colored leather, made in France, that smells like the inside of a fancy imported car. My name is embossed in gold in the lower right-hand corner. It is the first address book I have had with my name on it. The books I had before were like the ones from school days, small and plastic, and I usually bent them and tore them and finally lost them, feeling nothing when I did. This one, I think, will outlast me; its beauty seems so invincible. Having it, owning it, holding it in my hands makes me feel greedy and giddy and almost elegant. I cannot imagine harming it. I wipe my hands before touching it; then, as if it were a mirror, I wipe its surface clear of my handprints with a cuff or sleeve. I carry it as I move from room to room, imagining myself, brave and lovely, pulling it from my shoulder bag while leaning against a dusty window in some seedy telephone booth in some foreign city.

2   The problem with the book is that I have not been able to use it; as yet, I have not made a single entry in it. I had anticipated with such pleasure the process of transferring the names from my old book to my new. I bought new

pens, three of them, with the finest felt tips to write the names in my new book. I practiced my printing. I counted the lines on each page, the number of pages for each letter, discovering that I had room for 400 A's and 60 X's. Then, ready, I sat before the book as if I were sitting down to a meal.

3   I skimmed through the A's in my old book, deciding whom to transfer to the new book and whom not to transfer, a simple clerical chore, I thought. Not so. Each name caught me up. I could not get out of the A's. There was my friend from high school who sometimes uses her own name, sometimes that of her husband. Should I put her in my new book under the name I first knew and loved her by, the name I had heard her called a thousand times in a thousand study halls, or should I wait and list her later by her married name? After all, I mused, we were grown-ups now, over 30, married, men's names after our own. It had all gone too fast. I wanted her here under the A's, under her own name. But who was I to make that judgment?

4   Then there was my sister, listed by her first name. Brothers and sisters, however old, never seem to have more than first names. Yet again, I thought, my sister and I are grown, I will give her a last name finally. I turned to the M's to enter her — her married name is Moore — but I couldn't do it. To me she was only that one name, that two-syllable first name I could hear my pleading child's voice using when I had done something awful to her and she had locked me out of her room, and I pounded, saying her name over and over, to get through that door and back into her heart.

5   I turned back to the A's, my page still empty. I set the new book aside for a moment. I went on through the old book, bumping into the names of people I hardly knew anymore, old classmates who in that frantic hour before graduation insisted on leaving their names in my book, knowing I would never call — just as I knew and they knew they would never call me. If I left them there in the old book and didn't bring them into the new, they would be gone forever, lost from my memory. Should I take them with me into my new book, knowing that I would never see them again? That was silly. Yet I was reluctant to abandon them. I thumbed on, finding names of cousins I barely knew, telephone numbers of people I had met at parties and never seen again. Half the impulse was to retain everybody, simply copy the old book verbatim, no questions asked, no memories aborted. The other half of the impulse was to purge, to clean out, moving only the best of best of friends into my beautiful new book, leaving behind anyone who had ever hurt me, even slightly, as if not transferring their names would somehow keep them from ever hurting me again.

6   By the time I was midway through the old book, I had not crossed off a single name nor made a single entry in the new one. The new book was, I realized, intimidating in its loveliness, more intimidating in its implication of permanence. Leather, my name in gold, it would last a lifetime and outlast the lifetimes of at least half the people whose names I would write in it. So later, much later, carrying it still, I would see names and addresses of people I had loved, people who had been at the very center of my life when I was young.

Considering Content

1. Why, despite its beauty, does Fleming have difficulty writing in her new address book?

2. What does she discover about her relationships as she leaves through her old address book?

3. Throughout the essay, Fleming makes references to names and their significance. What point is she making about names and identity? Can you relate to her comments on family names? Why or why not?

4. "The new book was, I realized, intimidating in its loveliness, more intimidating in its implication of permanence." What point is Fleming making? What connection does it have to the essay's title? What meaning does it have for you?

Considering Craft

1. Fleming's primary purpose is to inform her readers about her experiences with her new address book. Do you also find evidence that she is trying to clarify this experience for herself? What is it?

2. How do the details she includes in paragraph 3 enhance her essay's meaning?

3. Read over the first and last paragraphs of the essay. How do they reinforce her purpose? What is their impact on the essay's meaning?

Guidelines for Establishing Meaning

1. Generate as many ideas as you can about your topic by using freewriting, brainstorming, or journal-writing.

2. Narrow your topic if it is too broad for the scope of the assignment.

3. Write a sentence that sums up the main point of your essay—your working version of a thesis statement.

4. If it helps you, create an informal or formal outline.

5. Write a first draft. Remember to be receptive to discovering new ideas about your topic as you go along.

6. Let your reader-self take over, and read your draft. Now ask yourself the following questions:

   - Is the thesis clear and appropriate?
   - Does the essay support and/or defend the thesis?

- Do all the points relate to the thesis?
- Have I successfully said what I meant to say?

7. Revise your draft to solve any problems raised by these questions. If you did not create an outline earlier, you might create one now that includes any new ideas that you have discovered in your first draft.

Warm-up Exercises

1. Which of the following statements are too general to serve as the thesis of a paper of 300 to 500 words? Narrow these broad topics so that you could use them. Are any too narrow?

    a. Americans value religion.

    b. Native Americans are adopting the techniques of the civil rights movement of the 1960s.

    c. TV has forever changed American politics.

    d. Americans do not value their writers as much as the French do.

    e. The sexual revolution really occurred.

    f. Shakespeare's comedies are as good as his tragedies.

    g. Friends are more important than family.

    h. Shakespeare was born and died on the same date (April 23) fifty-two years apart.

    i. Some old-fashioned home remedies really work.

2. Discuss in groups how you would support the following theses:

    a. The freshman year of college is a test of endurance, character, and nerve.

    b. America is not a classless society.

    c. Most of us have more freedom than we want.

    d. *Sophistication* means different things to different people.

    e. The punk look is more than a change in dress.

3. Write a statement for each of the following topics that could serve as the thesis for a 300- to 500-word essay:

    | forgiveness | dreams |
    | movies | physical fitness |
    | ambition | rock music |

failure   presidential elections
loneliness   working the night shift

4. Look through your journal for an entry on which you might expand for a possible essay. Why are you writing about this particular topic? What more can you think of to say about it? Can you form a concise thesis statement on the subject? If so, write a draft.

5. Brainstorm about your associations with one of the following:

childhood   friendship
boredom   going to church
address books   Sundays
New Year's Eve   religion
reading a novel   parental authority
getting up early   playing an instrument

Look over your list. Are there enough specifics to form the basis of an essay in which you can establish your thesis and purpose? If so, write a first draft.

6.   (a) Freewrite about your own writing process. Can you, like Julia Alvarez (page 40), think of an analogy to describe it?

      (b) As an alternative, freewrite about your associations with music. To what extent have your musical tastes changed with the passage of time?

Writing/Revising Topics

1. Select the subject you chose to brainstorm about in Warm-up Exercise 5 and write a first draft of your essay. Then review the Guidelines for Establishing Meaning. If your main idea is not supported throughout the essay, rewrite it using the Revising Strategies (pages 32–39), such as addition, deletion, and rearrangement, that will be most effective in making your thesis and purpose clear.

2. Use one of the following statements, or a similar one, as a thesis for a draft of an essay. Before you write, brainstorm or create an outline for your essay.

   a. There are times when your life depends on keeping your mouth shut.
   b. Participation in a sport teaches you a lot about yourself.
   c. Child abuse is not always physical.
   d. Mothers and daughters or fathers and sons can be rivals of the worst sort.

3. Write an essay on one of the following topics:

   risk-taking

   privacy

   growing up in the city (or country)

   raising children in the city (or country)

   mixing motherhood and a career

   working at a dead-end job

   First write down all your ideas on your topic as they occur: do not censor content as long as the thoughts even remotely relate to your topic. Now read over what you have written. Is a recurring idea present? Now write a first draft in which this recurrent idea appears as your thesis statement. If your main idea is not supported throughout the essay, rewrite it using revision strategies such as addition and rearrangement to make your thesis and purpose clear.

4. Using one of the thesis statements from Warm-up Exercise 2 or 3, write a draft. Review the Guidelines for Establishing Meaning, and revise any parts of your essay in which your thesis is not clear.

5. Write an essay about yourself. This essay may take many forms; for example, you might choose to write a partial autobiography or a description of one particular incident. You might choose to write about a brief episode in your life, either one that has occurred in the past or one that is now taking place. It is even possible to write about yourself in terms of the future.

   The following topics are examples of how you can narrow the overall assignment.

   • Write about an incident in the past that has affected you in some important way.

   • Write about an event that has inspired you to take action, preferably action that has directly affected your life.

   • Write about an important decision you have made and the implications of that decision.

   • Write about an incident that you found to be strange, threatening, or otherwise eventful.

   Use your peer group for guidance in selecting your topic and in preparing a draft.

6. Patrick Fenton associates writing and dreaming: "I suppose all good writing starts out from dreaming." Write a draft of an essay responding positively or negatively to this view using examples from your own experience to support your thesis statement. Before revising your essay, review the Guidelines for Establishing Meaning.

7. Fleming discusses human relationships and the many changes that occur as a result of factors such as moving away, changing jobs, or getting married. Write

an essay analyzing the changes that occurred in a significant personal relationship of yours. Your primary purpose is to explain.

8. Quindlen analyzes the extent to which Catholicism shaped her identity. Write an essay analyzing the role that religion played in your upbringing including its influence on your system of values.

Addressing Audience

When you speak or perform in public the concept of *audience* is clearly defined. You know exactly who the audience is and before the lecture, speech, or concert is over, you probably know how they react. In some cases, you may even alter your delivery in response to audience reaction. When you write, however, this issue is more complicated. Now when considering audience, you will find yourself addressing the question "Who will read what I write?" Your response will help you to resolve your understanding of your audience.

As a writer, you first need to be concerned with yourself as a reader; in effect, you are your own audience. Sometimes you may write something that you intend no one else to read (a journal entry, for example); sometimes your inner reactions to your writing determine whether or not the work will be shared. Thus before you consider pleasing an external audience, your work must first come under the scrutiny of your own audience-self. Most of the time, however, you are writing with someone else in mind. Review the Guidelines for Clarifying Purpose and for Establishing Meaning (pages 60 and 99). How many of them are geared to the benefit of your audience?

The relationship between purpose, meaning, and audience is a close one; only by knowing *why* you are writing and *what* you desire to write will you be able to determine *how* to write it, and all these considerations depend on *whom* you are writing for. Thus you need to think about the age of your readers, their educational background, their interest in what you are writing, and their reason for reading what you write. Each of these conditions will affect your evaluation of your audience. Your analysis, and any changes in it, will in turn influence what you say and how you say it. Clearly, a nuclear physicist would not write the same article for the *Journal of Applied Physics* that he would write for *Reader's Digest*. Similarly, a letter you write to a friend explaining why you wanted to attend college may differ substantially from what you wrote in your college application in response to the same question.

The following paragraphs were created by a student to accompany a photograph she had taken. The first was written for her curious young brother. The second was submitted to her advanced photography course.

(1) When I take a picture I try to keep still. If I jiggle the camera at all the picture will be blurred. I also pay attention to the light. When I took this picture I had to be extra careful because I was facing the sun. I looked through the lens to make sure that everything was the way I wanted. Finally, I pressed the button!

(2) The immediate problem I had to overcome when I made this photograph was the back lighting of the subject. To compensate for dark areas, I opened the lens aperture two stops to f 3.5. Since the subject was motionless, shutter speed was not a factor. The composition of the shot is traditional. By zooming in, the subject is accentuated by the out-of-focus background.

The differences in the information conveyed and the method of presentation should confirm that the above paragraphs have been written for different audiences. The first addresses an audience that is not so much concerned with the complicated nuts and bolts of photographic creation as with learning about basic picture taking. The second is directed toward an audience that is knowledgeable about photography and interested in the technical side of image making.

The unity of what you want to write, how you will write it, and for whom it will be written is necessarily dominated by the third consideration. Often, you cannot even begin to work on the first two until the last one is resolved. In order to write almost anything, you must make assumptions about your audience. Yet a danger that all writers face is that they will be misunderstood by their audience. Whether that audience consists of a friend, a classmate, a teacher, or even the writer himself or herself, a breakdown between what is intended by a writer and what is perceived by a reader will result in ineffective communication. Since the possibility of such a problem between writer and audience exists, what can you do to reduce this risk?

The best way for you, as a writer, to minimize the danger of alienating your audience is to carefully assess your readership. The better you know your readers, the more likely you will gear your writing toward them and get your point across. Another effective way to ensure that you will be understood is to try to make your meaning and appeal universal. Read carefully what Linda Bird Francke has to say about audience:

There is a great knack to writing personal stuff. Often, such material is just a boring recital of self-interest. The point is to make the description of an individual experience universal, to take the step back so that the reader, any reader, can apply one person's story to his or her own. Only if such personal forms of writing form a connection to human experience are they valid and successful.

Just as Francke in "The Ambivalence of Abortion" (Chapter 2) revised her essay with a general readership in mind whom she wanted to reach, so you should aim to do likewise. Add information and details where they are needed: if you know more about a topic than your readers, you want to fill this knowledge gap to keep from losing them.

Conversely, to resolve this same predicament, a writer may cut out potentially alienating information. Anything that is either above or below your audience's knowledge level should be deleted. The lesson to be learned here is that as a writer you need to assess and adjust what you write in terms of your audience's understanding. A choice phrase, no matter how proud you may be of it, must be cast aside if it endangers comprehension.

Addressing your readership, whether a general or specific one, is yet another aspect of the writing process that you will be able to control through the conscious application of prewriting and revising activities. As you become more familiar with the general concept of audience, your ability to assess your readers and their requirements will improve. This effectiveness in meeting the needs of your audience will be reflected by your success in conveying your purpose and meaning.

Marshall Glickman

Marshall Glickman (b. 1961) majored in philosophy at Northwestern University and after graduation worked for three years as a stockbroker for Shearson Lehman Brothers. Since then he has been traveling, reading, meditating, writing, and spending time with family and friends. The following are his reasons for keeping a journal:

> I keep a journal for recording thoughts and ideas that are appealing for either their content or phrasing—usually taken from something I've read. I also record ideas for our book and potential articles.

Money and Freedom

Introduction to the Essay and Draft

Every writer faces that same basic problem whenever setting words to paper: How can I convey my personal knowledge and feelings to someone I have never met? This presentation of a unique understanding to unseen readers is the great challenge of audience. In the following essay, "Money and Freedom," Marshall Glickman is faced with the primary problem of audience and revises his draft to convey his ideas clearly to his readers.

One aspect of addressing audience made evident by this particular case is the potential gap between a writer and his or her readers. Sometimes there is virtually no distance between a writer and an audience; at other times the distance is great. It is almost certain that Glickman is different from his readers: how many of us at the age of 24 make $200,000 a year? And, achieving that, how many of us would dare to retire? Glickman attempts in his essay to answer the throng of questions generated by these circumstances, and he does so in a way that tries to bridge the gap that exists between himself and his audience. While his personal story can only be told from his own perspective, Glickman strives to reach every reader.

The strategy that Glickman employs to overcome any gap is to generalize his essay so that every reader understands the questions he is attempting to answer for himself. In this way he prevents his essay from becoming solely a rationalization of his actions and changes the central question from "Why did you quit?" to "What is meaningful in life?" This redirection is what makes the essay universal, and this universality helps general readers identify with the author: they are no longer limited to a particular case but can extend their vision to vital issues that concern everyone.

Glickman resolves the differences between himself and his audience by writing for a general reader. However, selecting a general reader—a universal audience—is tricky because this reader is difficult to write for. Little is known about him or her, and specific data regarding education, likes, dislikes, and motives are unavailable. A general reader (whom you might encounter in a composition course) is a person somewhat interested in the topic written about but whose willingness to read to the end is not to be taken for granted. He or she, when confused or bored, would rather go and do something else than stay and struggle with an unclear or uninteresting essay. As a result, Glickman must approach this reader on a common ground and then provide clear, interesting explanations to convey his particular viewpoint. With a clear comprehension of the author's ideas, a general reader can then apply them to his or her own life and to life in general.

As mentioned, in writing his essay, Glickman runs the risk of alienating many readers; after all, there are many people who have never shared his experiences. Knowing the capacities of a universal audience, the author revises to reduce this risk. He takes care to avoid including too much specialized language, though enough is present to capture the flavor of the moment. If the essay becomes too impersonal, he immediately places himself back into it, thereby restoring the personal dimension of the work. In short, Glickman modifies his essay to make it general, interesting, and sympathetic. To suit the requirements of his audience, words, sentences, and paragraphs are added, deleted, substituted, or rearranged. In fact, the author makes many changes in his own perspective as a writer to appeal to the sensibilities of his projected audience. By skillfully revising his draft to respond to his reader's needs, Glickman is able to reach beyond the limitation of a purely personal essay.

Published Essay

1   Making money has always been a passion of mine. At the age of 12, I was a hustling newspaper boy and baby sitter, squirreling away dollar bills in a small red plastic safe that I hid behind my socks. While my brother was out playing basketball, I was devising plans to build my fortune. I cut lawns, delivered pizza, worked in a warehouse and as a security guard. I even had a scheme in college to capitalize on student birth control and sell condoms by mail order.

2   When I left the brokerage house of Shearson Lehman Brothers last June, I was 24 and earning over $200,000 a year. Today I have no job. I'm not unemployed. I'm retired.

3   "You'd be a good lawyer," my mother always used to say. My mother is a lawyer and college professor who routinely puts in a 60-hour week. She loves the law, loves working and loves the $350,000 suburban home she and my dad live in.

4   My first career plan *was* to become a lawyer, and I entered Northwestern University as the necessary first step. I hoped to impress Stanford Law by majoring in philosophy. Maybe it was the philosophy, maybe the break from home and the exposure to people of different backgrounds, but I began to question my motivations. I read. I spent my summers traveling—out West, through Europe and in Kenya. I met people who had little of the respect for the legal profession that had been bred in me. I began thinking of life as a writer, artist or adventurer.

5   In my senior year, partly to relieve the anxiety I felt over my future, I began meditating—first for a half-hour, then up to two hours a day. Zen meditation quieted my scheming mind and taught me to focus on the present. I took the

test to enter law school, and my scores were good, within 20 points of what I'd predicted. But I knew I was marching toward a life I wasn't interested in.

6   I fantasized about trekking in the Himalayas, bicycling cross-country, meditating in Kyoto and writing a novel. But while I spoke bravely about freedom and choice, my suburban upbringing rejected a hand-to-mouth existence on the road. I had the heart of a wanderer but the head of an accountant.

7   So I postponed my adventures until I could afford them. I wouldn't have a career, I said, I would simply make money—fast. Enough money to make me feel I was a success but not so much that I would get sidetracked. My goal was a nest egg of $100,000, but I promised myself I'd work for only three years, even if I fell short of that. Wall Street seemed the most direct route.

8   The first months at Shearson were a nightmare. "Hello, my name is Marshall Glickman from. . . ." Slam! Busy signal. Wrong number. To reach 60 people, I had to make 200 to 300 calls a day. I took 15-minute lunches, hired three college students to help me call, and purchased names and numbers of prospective clients. Each morning I rose at 5:30, meditated for an hour and ran around Prospect Park. As the sun broke through the darkness, I imagined myself in India, in Oregon.

9   All images of a better life had faded by the time I shuffled home from the office at 9:30 P. M., wolfed my dinner and collapsed on the couch with the same half-read book. My eyes burned from staring at the green glow of my Quotron machine. My neck had a permanent crick from cradling the phone. Three years, I told myself. You just have to hold out for three years.

10   "You're living for tomorrow," said my brother, who is a writer.

11   Then the market went crazy. Interest rates dropped, and suddenly my phone rang nonstop. The groundwork I had done paid off. I raked in $30,000 to $40,000 a month in gross commissions. By year two, I was the top producer in my office, managing a portfolio of $14 million. Names on my Rolodex included C.E.O.'s, television journalists, professional athletes, actors and a world-renowned architect. Not to mention my grandmother.

12   I was a 10-year-old again, successful beyond my wildest dreams, stuffing money into mutual funds and money markets instead of into my little red safe. My meditating dwindled to 20 minutes. I found myself eyeing the price of cars, homes and exotic vacations. One more good year, I calculated, and I'd double my savings. I'd be a millionaire at 30. Although by now I'd socked away my $100,000, could I walk away while the market was this hot?

13   I enjoyed the gambling, enjoyed calculating my commissions at the end of each day. I was riding the momentary high, the thrill of the hunt. At the same time, all this unnerved me. I kept reminding myself that Shearson was a means to an end, and I was still committed to that end. Trusting my earlier instincts, I gave notice to my incredulous branch manager two weeks before my third year was up—$135,000 richer.

14   "In another five years you could have been set for life," said my father, who is a businessman.

15   For weeks after I left Shearson, I didn't know what to say when someone asked me what I did. I weighed the value of each day that passed against what I could have earned if I'd still been working. It was a while before I could pick up a book on a Monday morning without feeling guilty—and poor. Even after I began to travel and those feelings passed, my interest in making money remained. It probably always will.

16   But with $135,000 in the bank and frugal habits, I figure I can continue without working for a long time. I'm going to renovate a house and use the profits to finance a trip to the Orient. I have plans to do some real estate deals, to do some writing, work on a fishing boat in Alaska. It seems possible to do what I want and make some money, too.

17   Last fall, I pedaled my bike through the Catskill Mountains on the last leg of a trip from Minnesota. At a one-pump station in a town called Big Indian, I called my broker in New York to check on a volatile stock I own. I used to share an office with him. "How's it going, Dave?" I asked. Dave sounded as if he were a soldier reporting bad news from the front. "The market's off 50 points," he moaned. "I'm getting killed." I hung up and chuckled. My worries revolved around saddle sores and flat tires. I climbed back on the bike and felt the sun on my shoulders as the road raced beneath my wheels.

Draft

Final Draft

1   Making money has always been a passion of mine. At the age of 12 I was a hustling newspaper boy and babysitter, squirrelling away dollar bills in a red plastic vault that I hid behind my socks. While my brother was out playing basketball, I was devising plans to build my fortune. I cut lawns, delivered pizza, worked in a warehouse and as a security guard. I even had a scheme in college to capitalize on the low prices of student birth control and sell condoms by mail order.

2   When I left Shearson/Lehman Brothers, I was the highest-paid stockbroker in my office. At the age of 24, I was earning ~~over~~ $200,000 a year. Today I have no job. I'm not unemployed. I'm retired.

3   ¶   "You'd be a good lawyer," my mother always said. My first career plan, dating back to my pizza-delivery days, was to become a lawyer. My mother is a lawyer and college professor who routinely puts in a 60-hour week. She loves the law, loves working, and loves the $350,000 suburban home

she and my dad live in--a far cry form the two-family house
she grew up in the Flatbush section of Brooklyn.

4

I entered Northwestern University as the necessary first
step in filling out my law school applications. Maybe it was
the break from home and the exposure to people of different
backgrounds, or maybe it was the philosophy major with which
I had hoped to impress Stanford Law, but, as will happen in
college, I began to question my motivations. Did I care
about the law? For that matter, did I care about any one

career? I didn't have my mother's motivations; I had a love
of money and a need for security, and I couldn't see building
my life around two traits that I didn't respect.

5

What, then, did I want to do? I fantasized about
trekking in the Himalayas, bicycling cross-country,
meditating in Kyoto and writing a novel. The list
represented an ideal of adventure, freedom and choice.
Obviously, I would need money. My compromise: make a lot of
money fast, retire, and live off the income. My career
planning became simply a search for the most efficient way to
make money. After accepting that it was too late to make my
fortune on the Alaskan pipeline, I settled on Wall Street.

6

The first months at Shearson were a nightmare. "Hello
my name is Marshall Glickman from..." Slam! Busy signal.
Wrong number. To reach 60 people, I had to made 200 to 300
calls a day. I took 15-minute lunches, hired three college
students to help me call and purchased names and numbers of
prospective clients. I shuffled home at 9:30, wolfed my
dinner and collapsed on the couch with the same half-read
book. My eyes burned from staring at the green glow of my
Quotron machine. My neck had a permanent crick from cradling
the phone. Three years, I told myself. You just have to
hold out for three years.

7   "You're living for tomorrow," my brother, a writer, said.
Then the market went crazy. Interest rates dropped and
suddenly my phone rang nonstop. The groundwork I had laid
paid off -- I wasn't working hard and still made $30,000 to
$40,000 a month in gross commissions. By year two, I was the
top producer in my office, managing a portfolio of 14 million
dollars. Names on my rolodex included CEO's, TV journalists,
professional athletes, actors, and a world-renowned
architect. Not to mention my grandmother.

8   I was the ten-year-old again, successful beyond my
wildest dreams, stuffing my money in mutual funds and pension
plans instead of my little red safe. I found myself eyeing
the price of cars, homes, and exotic vacations. One more
good year, I calculated, and I'd double my savings. By
thirty I'd be a millionaire. And even though I'd reached my
goal of $100,000 in the bank, the market was too hot to
quit. I told myself, just a little longer.

9   I watched my clients chasing money, rarely satisfied
with their earnings, seeking the momentary high, the thrill
of the hunt. I heard people with hundreds of thousands of
dollars in the bank complain that they had grown old before
they could enjoy their money. One day the wife of a wealthy
lawyer called to tell me her husband had been murdered in a
hold-up. He had over 3 million dollars. What should she do?
I watched them, and one day I saw me.

10   The Talmud says that a rich man is one who is happy with
his lot. Maybe meditating on a mountain top was not the
answer -- maybe it was a naive notion, an intellectual
exercise. But I would give myself the chance to find out.
"In another five years you could be set for life," my
businessman father said.

11   My last day at work, a balmy Friday in June, held none
of the emotion I'd imagined. When I left the office for the
last time, I waited for the elation to hit. I let out a
hoot, but I knew I sounded like a man walking into a surprise
party he already knows about.

12   Not working is not easy. The hardest thing, maybe, is giving up a tangible measure of your productivity. For weeks after I left Shearson, I weighed the value of each day that passed against what I could have earned if I'd still been working. And it's still hard not to sound defensive whenever *I'm still uncomfortable when* I encounter the innocent question "And what do you do?"

13   But things are changing. This summer, as I pedalled my bike through the Catskill Mountains on the last leg of a trip from Minnesota, my mind drifted to my windowless office on Kings Highway. At a one-pump station in a town named Big Indian, I called the office to check on a volatile stock I own. "How's it going, Dave?" I asked the broker I used to share my office with. His answer was as impassioned as that of a private reporting bad news from the front. "The market's off 50 points," he cried. "I'm getting killed." I hung up the phone and chuckled. My worries revolved around saddle sores and flat tires. I climbed back on the bike and felt the sun on my shoulders as the road raced beneath my tires.

14   I'm beginning to embrace the uncertainty of my life. But I still wish the market would improve.

Comparing Draft and Essay

Draft Paragraphs 1 and 2
1. This draft, designated by the author as his "Final Draft," has already incorporated earlier revisions. Perhaps this is why these opening paragraphs do not differ greatly from the published version. How does Glickman approach his audience in these paragraphs? What information does he provide to help you understand him? How does the shift from the first to the second paragraph influence your perception of his meaning?

Draft Paragraphs 3 and 4
Compare these paragraphs with published paragraphs 3 through 5.

2. In these paragraphs, Glickman uses addition, deletion, and rearrangement as his primary revising techniques. In draft paragraph 3 he moves any information that does not pertain to his mother and reserves judgment on her profession until the next paragraph. Why do you think that Glickman has chosen to make these

changes? How might they reflect his perception of the gap between himself and his audience?

3. Compare draft paragraph 4 with its published counterpart. What differences do you notice between them? How do these differences affect your response? How might these differences be attributed to Glickman's awareness of audience?

4. In the margin and at the bottom of the draft paragraph, Glickman writes: "More about changing role . . . want to deny $ . . . passions . . . commuting in 3 piece suit" and "As I bounce around, I cont[inue to] scheme about renovate[ing] old brownstones, etc. . . . " How has he incorporated these comments into his published essay? (Also take into consideration published paragraphs 5 through 7.) How do these changes reflect the author's attention to his readers?

Draft Paragraph 5
Glickman believes that receiving feedback from readers helps him to revise. As a result of suggestions made by peers, he makes the following notes to himself in the margin (after the third sentence):

> (1) Yet, I didn't have the courage to be a total free-spirit. Need to feel diff[erent] (superior). (2) Need to prove to myself can succeed . . . Still had influence which made me want to be a $ earner. I made a compromise. I had a plan: give myself 3 years to make $100M then live off income."

5. Compare this draft paragraph (including Glickman's notes) with published paragraphs 5 through 7. How has he used his margin comments to guide his revision so that he conveys his ideas more clearly to a general audience? Which comments are accepted and which rejected by the author as reviser?

Draft Paragraph 6
Glickman again asks other readers to monitor what he has written and again finds he needs to include more information to help a general reader understand his feelings. Note how the marginal comment "Put in meditating & running & fantasies of quitting, daydreams of farming in Australia, etc." has been incorporated into the body of the draft and ultimately into the last two sentences of the published paragraph.

Draft Paragraph 9
6. If you compare this draft paragraph with published paragraph 13, you will notice many changes. However, perhaps the most marked revision concerns the author's perspective. Up until the last sentence in the draft, Glickman separates himself from his clients and their motives; in the published version he is one of them. Why do you think that Glickman has made this revision? How does this change in perspective affect your perception of him?

Draft Paragraph 10

This paragraph is the author's initial explanation of why he left his job. After reading the draft, Glickman decides to rewrite it entirely and makes many notes in the margin that address the issue more directly. These notes include such comments as:

Include 'practical' reasons [I] finally quit. (1) Upset . . . (saw myself slipping) . . . (2) (seeing myself in clients) greed > want more (3) Hold myself to my word Ghad "purity of vision" We shed against $ calling (4) confronted myself: can always go back or into biz. My compromise plan decision was: ~~to give myself 6 months of pure fun~~ to set aside $7000 & have no responsibilities for 6 months. Thereafter I could work part time & devote most of my time to what I enjoyed or work some when travelling e.g. teaching english in Japan.

7. How have the *ideas* present in draft paragraph 10 (both in the original typescript and the marginal comments) been incorporated into published paragraphs 13, 15, and 16?

8. How has a consideration of audience affected Glickman's decision to delete his original paragraph?

Draft Paragraph 11

9. How does the change from "businessman father" to "my father, who is a businessman" reflect Glickman's awareness of a possible gap between himself and his readers?

Draft Paragraphs 12 and 13

10. These paragraphs have been almost completely rewritten in the published essay (see published paragraphs 15 and 16). How do Glickman's revisions affect you as a reader? Why do you think that he has deleted draft paragraph 12?

11. How has Glickman expanded the ideas in the draft so that his personal experiences appeal to a larger audience?

Draft Paragraph 15

12. Why do you think that Glickman has deleted this paragraph? How might his choice reflect his awareness of his audience?

Hana Wehle

Hana Wehle (b. 1917) was born in Czechoslovakia. She is a survivor of the Theresienstadt, Auschwitz, and Stutthof concentration camps. Her first husband was killed by an SS man in Theresienstadt. After the defeat of the Nazis in 1945, she returned to Czechoslovakia where she remarried. In 1951, she and her husband, also a survivor of Auschwitz, emigrated to the United States. She has published several essays about her concentration camp experiences. This is how she describes her purpose in writing "Janushinka":

> For Franz Kafka, "writing is a form of prayer." For me, writing is a form of conveying a message. I remember the time in Auschwitz, when every prisoner in our part of the camp was destined to die in the gas chambers. How much did I then want to live, so that I could bring the message to the world about the absurdity of our existence during that period of madness. I survived and I want to help young people understand this event through a form which is easier to grasp than a strictly historical account. I like to share my experiences with a college-aged audience on the threshold of adult life, since they are the makers of the future. I wish to give them certain awareness of things they would not encounter otherwise. Last, but not least, I want them to understand that what I write contains an important message for them.

As you read "Janushinka," determine what message it contains for you.

Janushinka

Introduction to the Essay and Draft

Like many authors, Wehle has a specific readership in mind as she sets out to write. Consequently, meaning and purpose are tailored to the needs and demands of this audience. Fitting one's ideas to an external audience does not occur all at once; rather, the meeting of writer and reader is the result of deliberate choices made throughout the writing process. Here is what Wehle says about writing and revising:

> *My first draft is unorganized thoughts about what I have to write. I write initially in paragraphs paying no attention to how I'm writing but what. How do I recreate in words the picture I have in my mind? In revising, I reorganize first by checking chronology. Then I rearrange material as I would in making a collage. . . . Later I look at specific points in the essay which need more elaboration.*

As you will see in the portions of the draft reproduced below, Wehle makes many changes based on her understanding of her audience. Perhaps because of the message she bears, she strives to address younger people, people she believes capable of making a difference in the future of their world. Yet because she is writing for this readership, she is faced with a complex set of problems. How can she convey the meaning of her experiences to people who have not lived through what she has and who were not even alive at the time these events occurred? This disparity between author and audience might seem irreconcilable but it is the same problem faced by Marshall Glickman in "Money and Freedom" and by all writers who set pens to paper. That is, how can anyone convey personal knowledge and experience to others?

Published Essay

1   With Janushinka's birth the passionate bond was sealed. She was swept into the happy orbit of her parents, Henry and Pepinka, and became the focal point of their life. Whenever they looked at her, they transformed all their soul into that look. They tasted with pleasure bordering on reverence every move, touch and exploration of the child, as well as, later, the cascade of words scrambled in nonsense combinations. Today, forty years later, I am still able to draw from my memory the sweet melody of Janushinka's laughs and cries coming from the nursery.

2   Henry was my father's cousin, a successful, hard working businessman, in his thirties. Pepinka, a few years younger, was a beautiful woman with velvety brown eyes radiating with love and happiness. I stayed with them for a short time, after arriving in Prague from the German-occupied Sudetenland in the northern region of Bohemia.

3   Before long, I too gravitated toward the sweet child. I remember how one or the other of us would tip-toe in and out of the nursery to make sure that the sleeping Janushinka was not too cold or too hot. When the weather became chilly and rainy, we would brace ourselves with a surgical cotton mask so that germs would not invade her delicate system. Unquestionably, Henry and Pepinka's happiness was also heavily tinted by shadows of fear and anxiety for the safety of their precious jewel.

4   At a time when love and affection still warmed every corner of their home, the German army already occupied Prague. My recollection of being frightened as the clatter of marching soldiers could be heard through the windows is still clear. The dissonance between the dim winter morning when the Germans marched into our city and the sanctity of that loving home was an unbearable experience.

5   Very soon the tide of the events turned against the Jews. The curtains of their homes were drawn, the lights went out. They were deported to an unknown destination . . . Also the lights in the nursery were turned out, the curtains drawn. The chuckle of Janushinka was silenced.

6   After I was deported to Auschwitz, I never thought that I would see Henry and his family again. However, it did happen in the "Familien-lager," one of the many sections of Auschwitz-Birkenau. I was on my way to the "latrine" (toilet), a large wooden barrack, used by prisoners under the watchful eyes of the SS guards. Inside the large area on one side were women, on the other side were men, exposed to one another in utter humiliation. The entrance was always crowded with prisoners waiting for their turn. For some of them it was too late: they collapsed into their own excrement, unable to lift themselves from the muddy ground. We had to bypass these human forms as we moved on in silence.

7   The air was damp and the rags of clouds hung over us. As we were slowly inching away, I heard somebody softly calling my name. Carefully, so as not to dispel the feeble voice behind me, I turned my head in the direction of a tiny cloud steaming from the frozen mouth of a man. I looked at the still face and

suddenly felt as if a sword were splitting the web of my brain. There stood Henry! His sunken eyes were fixed upon me and the narrow line of his mouth twisted into a strange, almost embarrassed smile. The unshaven face hung between his shoulders, and the once translucent, blue eyes signaled an unspeakable anguish. His rasping voice was cutting through the silence around us: "Janushinka is very sick. Pneumonia. Pepinka is desperately trying to save her life." In these words there was something that killed all hope. The memory of the gulf between Henry in the nursery and the man standing in front of me that day will never allow me to forget the perversity of fate. I remember the dreamer's dreams and how they were shattered under the wheels of the trains rushing through the German and Polish countrysides, carrying in their dark bellies thousands of little Janushinkas, Henrys, and Pepinkas . . .

8   I slipped back through time and recaptured the fragrance of the little child in the nursery and the sight of Pepinka pulling the soft pink blanket over the sleeping Janushinka. Henry is lovingly watching the young woman in the bright opening of the door, as she steps out of the nursery. She then sets a bowl of steaming soup on the table covered with a starched, hand-embroidered table cloth; the silver spoons touching the fine porcelain send pleasant tinkles through the cozy dining room.

9   The urgency in Henry's eyes jolted me back into the present. I looked past Henry and glanced at the watch towers above the barbed wire surrounding the camp. What consolation could I offer to this man? I felt so cold and hungry. A picture of Pepinka and Janushinka struggling in some dark corner of a barracks pushed its way upon me. Janushinka's body is so thin that it appears translucent. Pepinka bends over the little girl and with an almost childlike expression hopes for a miracle. Her hand caresses the sweet forehead, covered with beads of sweat and her gentle lips brush the feverish face as she intently follows the quickening breath of her child, fighting for life . . . I leaned toward Henry and whispered: "Meet me here tomorrow at this time, I will bring you some soup." The crowd behind pushed us into the latrine barrack. As we parted, it seemed to me that Henry's face somewhat brightened.

10   Once in a while the workers at the camp post office got an additional portion of soup. I was one of them and, therefore, was able to share that precious "premium" with my mother, who had been deported with me to Auschwitz. Suddenly I panicked. What if I did not get the special soup tomorrow? Henry would be waiting . . . and what about my mother? How could I deprive her? Would she be able to understand?

11   The night seemed long because I could not sleep. Will I get the additional soup, and if I do, how shall I divide it? We all are so hungry! The barrels of soup paraded endlessly in front of my tired mind. Will any of them stop in front of me? Will there be some soup for Henry? The last barrel is finally set in front of me. What a relief! Eagerly I bend over the slippery edge of the barrel and realize with horror—the vessel is empty!

12   Finally daylight crept into our barrack. The dead were carried behind the barrack, the half dead and the healthy filed out for the roll-call. That day the

counting and recounting of prisoners was endless. It was almost midday before we could return. I could not rest. My eyes were glued to the road stretching between the rows of the wooden barracks. At last two women surfaced in the fog. Between them, they carried the long awaited barrel of soup. I followed eagerly the wooden clogs marching in unison with the swinging barrel suspended from two heavy poles. They headed toward us, the poles in the grip of their bony hands. Around their necks, attached to the poles, was a strong strap, which pulled their heads forward. As they came closer I could see their distorted faces reflecting the enormous strain of their bodies as they struggled to distribute the weight of the barrel between their arms and necks.

13   Finally they arrived at our barrack. Amid the pushing of the hungry prisoners a line was formed. There stood the vessel with a grayish, slimy liquid dripping down its sides. We all followed eagerly every drop. One full ladle was dropped into each bowl. My turn came . . . in an almost hypnotic trance I traced the movement of the ladle. It emptied once and dipped in—and emptied into my bowl again!

14   Victoriously I carried the full bowl to my place, where my mother was waiting for her share of the soup. I reluctantly explained to her why we would from now on divide the soup into three parts. She understood the urgency and shared in the sacrifice. I hurried with the rest of the soup to the latrine barrack. As I pushed my way through the waiting crowd to meet Henry, icy rain dropped into the soup. The hand on my shoulder was Henry's. His face seemed thinner than the day before. As I was transferring the soup into his dish, Henry's eyes were transfixed on that thick, gray stream barely filling the bottom of his bowl. He just nodded and disappeared into the crowd.

15   I met Henry several times, sometimes with the soup, sometimes without it. Meanwhile, Janushinka, he told me, was still in the grip of death. The question as to whether I could actually prevent her imminent death never left me. What if the recovery never took place?

16   The subhuman conditions in the camp were sapping the strength of Henry's frail body. His walking had become visibly slower, his back stooped increasingly and he was more listless. One day, however, I noticed some change. He tried to straighten his haggard body and across his face the cruel play of fear and hope was gone. The words rolled from his mouth like pieces of gold: "Janushinka's fever has subsided—she ate the soup!" Henry's and my eyes connected in a new alliance with life. In his face lingered a flicker of hope. For myself, I freed my conscience from the burden of guilt about having deprived my mother of the additional soup.

17   As Janushinka's health slowly improved so Henry's strength quickly evaporated. One day Henry did not show up. As usual, I waited in front of the latrine barrack, the gelatinous soup cold in my bowl . . . That day I returned to my mother's place, overtaken by fatigue. We shared Janushinka's soup in silence.

18   The only place where men and women were able occasionally to share a fleeting moment was the latrine barrack. For a long time I looked into the faces around me in vain. I never saw Henry again. At the far end of our camp was the

so called children's block where some of the mothers and their young children were housed; they helped take care of the youngsters' needs. There Pepinka and Janushinka lived also. Any contact between the occupants of the children's block and the rest of the camp prisoners was forbidden. Apparently, Henry had found some clandestine way to get the soup to Janushinka during her sickness. After his disappearance I lost track of their whereabouts.

19   Not until the beginning of July 1944, when the prisoners of the "Familien-lager" were about to be gassed, did I learn about Pepinka's and Janushinka's fate. Daily selections, grouping and regrouping of the old and young, the sick and healthy, took place. The younger and more healthy men and women were transported to other camps for work; the old and sick were exterminated in the gas chambers and to the mothers of young children a choice was given: "Leave your child behind and save yourself by joining the group of working women, or—go to your death together with your children." Three hundred young mothers made their choice: Pepinka was one of them. She held the tiny hand of Janushinka as if she would lead the child to school, like other mothers, in another world. In her lonely hour of anguish once again Pepinka hoped for a miracle. This time, however, there was none . . . Janushinka had to die, before she even learned to live. By a twist of fate Janushinka's recovery had led to Pepinka's death. Such was the notorious "law" in the world of Auschwitz!

Partial Draft

9   The dense vapors pushed their way out of the latrine. I looked past Henry and glanced at the watch towers above the barbed wire surrounding the camp. I was trying to recapture the sweet fragrance of the little child in the nursery, Pepinka, is pulling the blanket, warm, soft pink blanket, over the sleeping Janushinka. Henry observes her as she tip-toes out of the nursery. They exchange a smile of never-ending happiness. The face of the young woman in the bright opening of the doors is mirrored in the transparency of Henry's blue, loving eyes. With a gentle smile, Pepinka puts a steaming soup on the table covered with a starched, hand embroidered table cloth. The silver spoons touched occasionally the fine porcelain and send a pleasant, cling sound through the peaceful atmosphere.

10   As I stared at Henry again, another picture pushed its way to me. Somewhere in the shadow of a barrack, people stumble in and from the wooden bunks filled with dirt and stench. Children are crying. Janushinka is prabably not crying any more. Her weakened body is prostrated on a dirty, wrinkled blanket on her pale cheeks, fever has painted two rosy spots. Her parched lips are crusted. Pepinka, bent over the little girl, hopes for a miracle. With an almost child-like expression of amazement, she follows intensely the quickening breath of the child, fighting for life. Her hand caresses the sweet forhead, covered with beats of sweat..

11 I stood there with a kind of bewilderment. My eyes burned. I could
hardly speak. <u>What was I supposed to do?</u> What kind of consolation could I
offer to this totally broken man? I felt cold and hungry. An image of a
steaming bowl of soup poured suddenly through all my senses. All of a
sudden, I leaned toward Henry's ear and whisper: "Meet me here tomorrow at
this time; I will bring you some soup." ...The crowd behind pushed us int
the latrine barack. As we parted, Henry's face, seemed to me, brightened
2 with glimmer of hope,

rearrangement

20 As Janushinka's health did slowly improve, so Henry's strength
did quickly evaporate. One day, Henry did not show up. As usual, I wait
in front of the latrine barrack, the gelatinous soup cold in my bowl...
That day, I returned to my mother's place, overtaken by fatigue. We shared
Janushinka's soup in silence. I never saw Henry again. For a long time, lik
a sprawling octopus, sadness poisoned the taste of every spoon of soup
I ate.

21 Pepinka's shaky motherhood in the camp did not last very long.
The "Family Camp" in Auschwitz was about to be liquidated. To the mothers
of young children, a choice was given: Leave your child behind and save
yourself by joining the working group of women who will be transported to
other camps, or — — stay and perish with your child....

22 Pepinka made her choice — she stayed with her child. At that time,
Janushinka was about six years old. Her mother anxiously held her tiny hand.
She did not lead the child to school as other mothers, in an other world
did! In the world of Auschwitz, a mother had to lead her child into the gas
chambers...! Pepinka caressed Janushinka's pale cheeks and once again
hoped for a miracle. — This time, however, there was no miracle...
Janushinka had to die, before she even learned to live. By the twist of
fate, the recovery of Janushinka led, in a sense, ultimately, to Pepinka's
death. Such was the notorious law of Auschwitz!

23 Sifting through the memories of my childhood, I was excavating
the broken pillars of values, once carefully erected in my soul by my
mother. Could she have been so wrong? What happened in Auschwitz?

Comparing Draft and Essay

Draft Paragraph 9

If you compare this paragraph with published paragraph 8, the depth of the changes
becomes evident. Although redistribution is present (the second sentence is moved
to a new paragraph), the primary revising technique is deletion.

1. What information has been omitted from the draft version? What common
sentiment characterizes the deleted phrases and sentences?

2. How might the deleted portion of this paragraph reflect the author's awareness of audience? How do you respond to such details as "a smile of never-ending happiness" or "the face of the young woman in the bright opening of the doors is mirrored in the transparency of Henry's blue, loving eyes"?

3. To what extent does the inclusion of romantic details counteract the purpose and meaning of the essay? What message might these details convey to a reader?

Draft Paragraphs 10 and 11

4. Compare these paragraphs to published paragraph 9. What revising techniques are operating? How do they combine to affect a reader more profoundly? Why, at this moment, would the author want her audience to *feel* rather than *think*?

5. How do you respond to the details presented here? How might they increase or decrease the author's credibility? Why, given the author's intended audience, would credibility be an issue?

6. Which version of this event is more interesting to read? Which one is more challenging? If the author's purpose is to inform and motivate her audience, which version is more effective in achieving these goals?

Draft Paragraphs 20 through 23

Compare these paragraphs to published paragraphs 17 through 19. Draft paragraph 20, which leads into the essay's conclusion, is revised moderately (redistribution, deletion). The remaining draft paragraphs, however, are changed radically. In fact, with the exception of some rearrangements, these paragraphs are rewritten.

7. Which version of these paragraphs offers more information to a reader? Is everything you learn in the draft present in the published essay? Do you find any new information in the final copy?

8. Why does Wehle delete draft paragraph 23 and conclude with draft paragraph 22? Which ending has greater impact? Which helps her audience to see clearly the dreadful irony?

9. In the introduction to the draft, Wehle states that she is addressing a "college-aged audience on the threshold of adult life." What specific information is presented to help you understand "the notorious 'law' of Auschwitz"? How does the presentation of such information represent the author's awareness of her audience? What assumptions have been made about the reader?

Adrienne Rich

Adrienne Rich (b. 1929) was born in Baltimore and educated at Radcliffe College. She has published many volumes of poetry including *Diving into the Wreck* (1973), *The Dream of a Common Language* (1978), and *An Atlas of the Difficult World* (1991). Both her poetry and prose reflect different stages in her awareness of herself as a woman and an artist. Her study of motherhood, *Of Women Born: Motherhood as Experience and Institution* (1976), has been compared in importance to Simone de Beauvoir's *The Second Sex*. In "Claiming an Education," a talk she delivered in 1977 at Douglass College for Women, Rich examines the purpose of college education from the perspective of gender. As you read her address, ask yourself if she raises any ideas about education that pertain to men as well as women.

Claiming an Education

1   For this convocation, I planned to separate my remarks into two parts: some thoughts about you, the women students here, and some thoughts about us who teach in a women's college. But ultimately, those two parts are indivisible. If university education means anything beyond the processing of human beings into expected roles, through credit hours, tests, and grades (and I believe that in a women's college especially it *might* mean much more), it implies an ethical and intellectual contract between teacher and student. This contract must remain intuitive, dynamic, unwritten; but we must turn to it again and again if learning is to be reclaimed from the depersonalizing and cheapening pressures of the present-day academic scene.

2   The first thing I want to say to you who are students, is that you cannot afford to think of being here to *receive* an education; you will do much better to think of yourselves as being here to *claim* one. One of the dictionary definitions of the verb "to claim" is: *to take as the rightful owner; to assert in the face of possible contradiction.* "To receive" is *to come into possession of; to act as receptacle or container for; to accept as authoritative or true.* The difference is that between acting and being acted-upon, and for women it can literally mean the difference between life and death.

3   One of the devastating weaknesses of university learning, of the store of knowledge and opinion that has been handed down through academic training, has been its almost total erasure of women's experience and thought from the curriculum, and its exclusion of women as members of the academic community. Today, with increasing numbers of women students in nearly every branch of higher learning, we still see very few women in the upper levels of faculty and administration in most institutions. Douglass College itself is a women's college in a university administered overwhelmingly by men, who in turn are answerable to the state legislature, again composed predominantly of men. But the most significant fact for you is that what you learn here, the very texts you read, the lectures you hear, the way your studies are divided into categories and fragmented one from the other—all this reflects, to a very large degree, neither

objective reality, nor an accurate picture of the past, nor a group of rigorously tested observations about human behavior. What you can learn here (and I mean not only at Douglass but any college in any university) is how *men* have perceived and organized their experience, their history, their ideas of social relationships, good and evil, sickness and health, etc. When you read or hear about "great issues," "major texts," "the mainstream of Western thought," you are hearing about what men, above all white men, in their male subjectivity, have decided is important.

4   Black and other minority peoples have for some time recognized that their racial and ethnic experience was not accounted for in the studies broadly labeled human; and that even the sciences can be racist. For many reasons, it has been more difficult for women to comprehend our exclusion, and to realize that even the sciences can be sexist. For one thing, it is only within the last hundred years that higher education has grudgingly been opened up to women at all, even to white, middle-class women. And many of us have found ourselves poring eagerly over books with titles like: *The Descent of Man; Man and His Symbols; Irrational Man; The Phenomenon of Man; The Future of Man; Man and the Machine; From Man to Man; May Man Prevail?; Man, Science, and Society;* or *One-Dimensional Man* — books pretending to describe a "human" reality that does not include over one-half the human species.

5   Less than a decade ago, with the rebirth of a feminist movement in this country, women students and teachers in a number of universities began to demand and set up women's studies courses—to *claim* a woman-directed education. And, despite the inevitable accusations of "unscholarly," "group therapy," "faddism," etc., despite backlash and budget cuts, women's studies are still growing, offering to more and more women a new intellectual grasp on their lives, new understanding of our history, a fresh vision of the human experience, and also a critical basis for evaluating what they hear and read in other courses, and in the society at large.

6   But my talk is not really about women's studies, much as I believe in their scholarly, scientific, and human necessity. While I think that any Douglass student has everything to gain by investigating and enrolling in women's studies courses, I want to suggest that there is a more essential experience that you *owe* yourselves, one which courses in women's studies can greatly enrich, but which finally depends on you, in all your interactions with yourself and your world. This is the experience of *taking responsibility toward yourselves.* Our upbringing as women has so often told us that this should come second to our relationships and responsibilities to other people. We have been offered ethical models of the self-denying wife and mother; intellectual models of the brilliant but slapdash dilettante who never commits herself to anything the whole way, or the intelligent woman who denies her intelligence in order to seem more "feminine," or who sits in passive silence even when she disagrees inwardly with everything that is being said around her.

7   Responsibility to yourself means refusing to let others do your thinking, talking, and naming for you; it means learning to respect and use your own

brains and instincts; hence, grappling with hard work. It means that you do not treat your body as a commodity with which to purchase superficial intimacy or economic security; for our bodies and minds are inseparable in this life, and when we allow our bodies to be treated as objects, our minds are in mortal danger. It means insisting that those to whom you give your friendship and love are able to respect your mind. It means being able to say, with Charlotte Brontë's *Jane Eyre:* "I have an inward treasure born with me, which can keep me alive if all the extraneous delights should be withheld or offered only at a price I cannot afford to give."

8   Responsibility to yourself means that you don't fall for shallow and easy solutions—predigested books and ideas, weekend encounters guaranteed to change your life, taking "gut" courses instead of ones you know will challenge you, bluffing at school and life instead of doing solid work, marrying early as an escape from real decisions, getting pregnant as an evasion of already existing problems. It means that you refuse to sell your talents and aspirations short, simply to avoid conflict and confrontation. And this, in turn, means resisting the forces in society which say that women should be nice, play safe, have low professional expectations, drown in love and forget about work, live through others, and stay in the places assigned to us. It means that we insist on a life of meaningful work, insist that work be as meaningful as love and friendship in our lives. It means, therefore, the courage to be "different"; not to be continuously available to others when we need time for ourselves and our work; to be able to demand of others—parents, friends, roommates, teachers, lovers, husbands, children—that they respect our sense of purpose and our integrity as persons. Women everywhere are finding the courage to do this, more and more, and we are finding that courage both in our study of women in the past who possessed it, and in each other as we look to other women for comradeship, community, and challenge. The difference between a life lived actively, and a life of passive drifting and dispersal of energies, is an immense difference. Once we begin to feel committed to our lives, responsible to ourselves, we can never again be satisfied with the old, passive way.

9   Now comes the second part of the contract. I believe that in a women's college you have the right to expect your faculty to take you seriously. The education of women has been a matter of debate for centuries, and old, negative attitudes about women's role, women's ability to think and take leadership, are still rife both in and outside the university. Many male professors (and I don't mean only at Douglass) still feel that teaching in a women's college is a second-rate career. Many tend to eroticize their women students—to treat them as sexual objects—instead of demanding the best of their minds. (At Yale a legal suit [*Alexander* v. *Yale*] has been brought against the university by a group of women students demanding a stated policy against sexual advances toward female students by male professors.) Many teachers, both men and women, trained in the male-centered tradition, are still handing the ideas and texts of that tradition on to students without teaching them to criticize its antiwoman attitudes, its omission of women as part of the species. Too often, all of us fail to

teach the most important thing, which is that clear thinking, active discussion, and excellent writing are all necessary for intellectual freedom, and that these require *hard work*. Sometimes, perhaps in discouragement with a culture which is both antiintellectual and antiwoman, we may resign ourselves to low expectations for our students before we have given them half a chance to become more thoughtful, expressive human beings. We need to take to heart the words of Elizabeth Barrett Browning, a poet, a thinking woman, and a feminist, who wrote in 1845 of her impatience with studies which cultivate a "passive recipiency" in the mind, and asserted that "women want to be made to *think actively*: their apprehension is quicker than that of men, but their defect lies for the most part in the logical faculty and in the higher mental activities." Note that she implies a defect which can be remedied by intellectual training; *not* an inborn lack of ability.

10   I have said that the contract on the student's part involves that you demand to be taken seriously so that you can also go on taking yourself seriously. This means seeking out criticism, recognizing that the most affirming thing anyone can do for you is demand that you push yourself further, show you the range of what you *can* do. It means rejecting attitudes of "take-it-easy," "why-be-so-serious," "why-worry-you'll-probably-get-married-anyway." It means assuming your share of responsibility for what happens in the classroom, because that affects the quality of your daily life here. It means that the student sees herself engaged *with* her teachers in an active, ongoing struggle for a real education. But for her to do this, her teachers must be committed to the belief that women's minds and experience are intrinsically valuable and indispensable to any civilization worthy the name; that there is no more exhilarating and intellectually fertile place in the academic world today than a women's college— *if* both students and teachers in large enough numbers are trying to fulfill this contract. The contract is really a pledge of mutual seriousness about women, about language, ideas, methods, and values. It is our shared commitment toward a world in which the inborn potentialities of so many women's minds will no longer be wasted, raveled-away, paralyzed, or denied.

Considering Content

1. Why does Rich believe that "claiming" an education is preferable to "receiving" one? Which reasons did you find most convincing? What is your attitude toward your education?

2. Rich claims that much "university learning," at least until the early 1970s, focused primarily on male contributions and experiences. How does she support her thesis? To what extent do you agree that women's and other minorities' experiences should be reflected in college curricula?

3. Rich considers personal autonomy for women a major part of their "claiming" an

education. What does she mean by "taking responsibility toward yourselves"? Should this also be part of a man's educational experience? Explain.

4. Rich believes that students have the right to expect faculty to take them seriously. What does that involve, according to Rich? Should teachers take students seriously? What can students do to influence teachers' attitudes?

5. What new aspects of "claiming" an education does Rich include in her last paragraph of the talk? What is involved in her "contract" between teachers and students? How does Rich's philosophy on education differ from yours?

Considering Craft

1. Define Rich's purpose in "Claiming an Education." Is there evidence that she wishes to persuade as well as inform her audience?

2. Rich uses the third person "they" in the first five paragraphs of her talk. Why does she change to the second person "you" for paragraph 6 on? How does this change her purpose and meaning?

3. Does the change in point of view also affect her relationship with her audience? How? Characterize that relationship. What effect might it have on audience response?

Daniel Meier

Daniel Meier (b. 1959) graduated from Wesleyan University in 1982 and the Harvard Graduate School of Education in 1984. He is currently an elementary school teacher in Boston and has published many essays on educational issues and on the art of teaching. As you read "One Man's Kids," written for the "About Men" series in *The New York Times Magazine,* speculate on possible audience responses to Meier's experiences as a first-grade teacher.

One Man's Kids

1   I teach first graders. I live in a world of skinned knees, double-knotted shoelaces, riddles that I've heard a dozen times, stale birthday cakes, hurt feelings, wandering stories, and one lost shoe ("and if you don't find it my mother'll kill me"). My work is dominated by 6-year-olds.

2   It's 10:45, the middle of snack, and I'm helping Emily open her milk carton. She has already tried the other end without success, and now there's so much paint and ink on the carton from her fingers that I'm not sure she should drink

it at all. But I open it. Then I turn to help Scott clean up some milk he has just spilled onto Rebecca's whale crossword puzzle.

3   While I wipe my milk- and paint-covered hands, Jenny wants to know if I've seen that funny book about penguins that I read in class. As I hunt for it in a messy pile of books, Jason wants to know if there is a new seating arrangement for lunch tables. I find the book, turn to answer Jason, then face Maya, who is fast approaching with a new knock-knock joke. After what seems like the 10th "Who's there?" I laugh and Maya is pleased.

4   Then Andrew wants to know how to spell "flukes" for his crossword. As I get to "u," I give a hand signal for Sarah to take away the snack. But just as Sarah is almost out the door, two children complain that "we haven't even had ours yet." I stop the snack mid-flight, complying with their request for graham crackers. I then return to Andrew, noticing that he has put "flu" for 9 Down, rather than 9 Across. It's now 10:50.

5   My work is not traditional male work. It's not a singular pursuit. There is not a large pile of paper to get through or one deal to transact. I don't have one area of expertise or knowledge. I don't have the singular power over language of a lawyer, the physical force of a construction worker, the command over fellow workers of a surgeon, the wheeling and dealing transactions of a businessman. My energy is not spent in pursuing, climbing, achieving, conquering, or cornering some goal or object.

6   My energy is spent in encouraging, supporting, consoling, and praising my children. In teaching, the inner rewards come from without. On any given day, quite apart from teaching reading and spelling, I bandage a cut, dry a tear, erase a frown, tape a torn doll, and locate a long-lost boot. The day is really won through matters of the heart. As my students groan, laugh, shudder, cry, exult, and wonder, I do too. I have to be soft around the edges.

7   A few years ago, when I was interviewing for an elementary-school teaching position, every principal told me with confidence that, as a male, I had an advantage over female applicants because of the lack of male teachers. But in the next breath, they asked with a hint of suspicion why I chose to work with young children. I told them that I wanted to observe and contribute to the intellectual growth of a maturing mind. What I really felt like saying, but didn't, was that I loved helping a child learn to write his name for the first time, finding someone a new friend, or sharing in the hilarity of reading about Winnie the Pooh getting so stuck in a hole that only his head and rear show.

8   I gave that answer to those principals, who were mostly male, because I thought they wanted a "male" response. This meant talking about intellectual matters. If I had taken a different course and talked about my interest in helping children in their emotional development, it would have been seen as closer to a "female" answer. I even altered my language, not once mentioning the word "love" to describe what I do indeed love about teaching. My answer worked; every principal nodded approvingly.

9   Some of the principals also asked what I saw myself doing later in my career. They wanted to know if I eventually wanted to go into educational

administration. Becoming a dean of students or a principal has never been one of my goals, but they seemed to expect me, as a male, to want to climb higher on the career stepladder. So I mentioned that, at some point, I would be interested in working with teachers as a curriculum coordinator. Again, they nodded approvingly.

10   If those principals had been female instead of male, I wonder whether their questions, and my answers, would have been different. My guess is that they would have been.

11   At other times, when I'm at a party or a dinner and tell someone that I teach young children, I've found that men and women respond differently. Most men ask about the subjects I teach and the courses I took in my training. Then, unless they bring up an issue such as merit pay, the conversation stops. Most women, on the other hand, begin the conversation on a more immediate and personal level. They say things like "those kids must love having a male teacher" or "that age is just wonderful, you must love it." Then, more often than not, they'll talk about their own kids or ask me specific questions about what I do. We're then off and talking shop.

12   Possibly, men would have more to say to me, and I to them, if my job had more of the trappings and benefits of more traditional male jobs. But my job has no bonuses or promotions. No complimentary box seats at the ball park. No cab fare home. No drinking buddies after work. No briefcase. No suit. (Ties get stuck in paint jars.) No power lunches. (I eat peanut butter and jelly, chips, milk, and cookies with the kids.) No taking clients out for cocktails. The only place I take my kids is to the playground.

13   Although I could have pursued a career in law or business, as several of my friends did, I chose teaching instead. My job has benefits all its own. I'm able to bake cookies without getting them stuck together as they cool, buy cheap sewing materials, take out splinters, and search just the right trash cans for useful odds and ends. I'm sometimes called "Daddy" and even "Mommy" by my students, and if there's ever a lull in the conversation at a dinner party, I can always ask those assembled if they've heard the latest riddle about why the turkey crossed the road. (He thought he was a chicken.)

Considering Content

1. Explain your response to the first five paragraphs of Meier's essay. Why did he introduce his pupils with incidents from his classroom experience?

2. "My work is not traditional male work." How does Meier define male work? How is it different from female work? What do these distinctions suggest about gender stereotypes in the workplace?

3. What does Meier's essay suggest about our attitudes toward teaching as a professional choice for a male? Review the descriptions of his encounters at

interviews and at parties. What is your response to his having chosen teaching as opposed to a career in law or business? Explain your answer.

4. Discuss the significance of the essay's title.

Considering Craft

1. Create a profile of the intended audience of this piece ("About Men," *The New York Times Magazine*). How might his intended audience respond to his essay? How did you respond?

2. What is Meier's purpose? Is he seeking only to inform or does he also wish to persuade his readers?

3. Read over his introduction and conclusion. How do they enhance meaning? How might they affect audience response?

Guidelines for Addressing Audience

1. Answer as many of the following questions as you can to establish a profile of the audience you will be addressing.

- What are their ages?
- What are their backgrounds? (familial, ethnic, religious, political)
- What is their education level?
- How much do they know about my topic?
- What pre-established opinions might they have?
- How much interest do they have in my topic?
- Why are they reading my essay?
- What information do they expect to get out of my essay?

2. Keep in mind the main point that you think your readers need or want to know. Clearly express your meaning, and emphasize it with adequate supporting ideas and details.

3. As you write, keep in mind who your audience is. Try to avoid going above or below their knowledge level.

4. Look over your draft carefully, as if you were a reader encountering it for the first time. Now let your reader-self answer the following:

- What is the purpose of this essay?
- What is the meaning of this essay?

If meaning or purpose is unclear for *this* audience, revise your essay.

5. Look over your first draft imagining that you are a typical member of your perceived audience. Are there places where the writing is above or below your knowledge level? Are there words or concepts that you do not fully understand? Do you stay interested? Do you learn what you wanted to learn from the essay? If at any point you feel discouraged with or uninterested in what has been written, a gap between writer and audience exists. Now it is up to you as a *reviser* to close this gap.

Warm-up Exercises

1. Read through your journal entries and select one in which you expressed strong feelings about something important to you. Can you elaborate on this entry for an essay for a specific audience of your choice? What would you need to add, change, or delete if you, like Francke, decided to "go public"?

2. Choose five different people who vary in sex and age and ask them questions about at least four of the following:

occupation	favorite music	favorite hobbies,
religion	educational background	leisure activities
last movie seen	last book read	favorite politician
favorite magazines	favorite TV programs	

Then ask their views on *one* of the following controversial topics:

abortion

low-income housing in middle-class neighborhoods

nuclear weapons

mandatory testing of people for AIDS

Now, if you should write on this topic, would you be able to assume that these five people are typical of the audience you are writing for? Would you alter your approach to this topic as a result of these interviews? If so, how? Do you have any other way of getting a profile of your audience? In the absence of such information, what is the best way to address your audience?

3. Clip two advertisements from different magazines and be prepared to cite evidence from the ads in answering the following:

What is the purpose of the advertisement?

Is there more than one purpose?

Who is the perceived audience?

Is there more than one potential audience?

How effective is the advertisement in relation to purpose and audience?

4. Freewrite for 15 minutes and read over what you have written. Have you hit on a subject you can expand into an essay? What person or group of persons that you know would be interested in this subject? To continue this assignment, proceed to Writing/Revising Topic 5.

5. Brainstorm about your associations with one of the following after reading the essays in this chapter:

money	freedom	success	professions
death	holocaust	possessions	sacrifice
teaching	education	gender	college

To continue this assignment, proceed to Writing/Revising Topic 6.

Writing/Revising Topics

1. Select a short article from a specialty magazine (*Astronomy, Business Week, Rolling Stone, Ms., Modern Photography, Esquire, Stereo Review*) that you think could be made to appeal to your class by revising it with this audience in mind. Revise the revision, and ask your classmates whether you succeeded in addressing them more effectively than the original does.

2. Hana Wehle wrote about an experience she had in a concentration camp, and although you may not have known much about her subject, you were able to understand her essay because she revised it to make her meaning clear to a general audience. Choose a subject you know well and write an essay about it. Look over the Guidelines for Addressing Audience. Which parts of your essay need to be revised to make your meaning clear to a reader who doesn't know much about your subject? Rewrite your essay for that particular audience.

3. Write a letter to a prospective immigrant that highlights what you feel he or she should know about America. Read your letter again. Is its purpose and meaning sufficiently clear to someone who has high expectations about the experience of emigrating to America? Revise any parts of it that need clarification for this particular audience.

4. Select two reviews of a controversial movie you have seen, one from a very liberal newspaper and one from a more conservative source. Then write an essay giving a profile of the audience each review was addressing.

5. Using your freewriting from Warm-up Exercise 4, write a draft for the audience you selected. Now read your draft and determine if you have used what you know about this audience to make your essay appealing to them. If so, write your final draft.

6. Using your brainstorming from Warm-up Exercise 5, write a draft of an essay for an audience of your own age. Read over your essay and the Guidelines for Addressing Audience. Have you written an essay that will appeal to your intended audience? If so, write your final draft. If you decide you have included elements that should be deleted, or omitted others that might be added, review the Revising Strategies in Chapter 2 (pages 32–39) and revise your essay accordingly.

7. Rich, in her convocation address, urges her audience to take themselves and their education seriously. Write an essay discussing your views on the implications of actively pursuing your educational goals. Cite examples from your own experiences.

8. Meier and Rich discuss education and gender from different perspectives. Reread both essays and write an analysis of the extent to which audience gender influenced their choices of situation, examples, and vocabulary.

*S*etting Tone

When you are addressing an audience in a speech or conversation, you choose words that communicate your purpose and meaning. But an additional factor, the tone of your voice, is simultaneously conveying your attitude toward your subject and audience. Anger, compassion, disbelief, love, enjoyment, or confusion are all carried in the simple, immediate alteration of a voice. In fact, the range of feelings and attitudes that may be expressed by a speaker's voice is extensive.

Writing too has something called *tone*. It originates in the writer's attitude toward his or her topic and audience and expresses itself primarily through *diction* and *sentence style*. Diction refers to a writer's choice of words—their level of formality (slang, colloquialisms, jargon) and their connotations. Some words, such as *communist, jazz, feminist,* or *blue collar,* imply attitudes not stated in a mere dictionary definition (see more on connotation in Chapter 10, page 341). Sentence style concerns among other things sentence lengths and structures: long, complex sentences can set a different tone from short, simple ones. The number and types of clauses (groups of words containing subject and predicate) and phrases contained within sentences can also affect tone.

Since tone grows out of a writer's feelings about his or her *purpose, subject,* and *audience,* it is thus a matter of people interacting, a highly "personal" matter. Within the spectrum running from intimacy to detachment, the tone may be serious, joking, angry, ironic, joyous, timid, forthright—practically any emotion or mixture of emotions you encounter in person-to-person contacts. In general, a writer who desires distance will set a detached, cool, unemotional tone.

Read the following paragraphs carefully, looking for differences in diction, sentence style, and tone:

The code of feminine politeness, instilled in girlhood, is no help in dealing with the unwanted approaches of strange men. Our mothers didn't teach us to tell a man to get lost; they told us to smile and hint that we'd be just delighted to spend time with the gentleman if we didn't have other commitments. The man in the Oak Room bar would not be put off by a demure lowering of eyelids; he had to be told, roughly and loudly, that his presence was a nuisance.

—Susan Jacoby, "Unfair Game"

The real objection to capital punishment doesn't lie against the actual extermination of the condemned, but against our brutal American habit of putting it off so long. After all, every one of us must die soon or late, and a murderer, it must be assumed, is one who makes that sad fact the cornerstone of his metaphysic. But it is one thing to die, and quite another thing to lie for long months and even years under the shadow of death. No sane man would choose such a finish.

—H. L. Mencken, "The Penalty of Death"

This is how I began to work out. I work out for a very simple reason, and it is not because it makes me feel invigorated and refreshed. The people who say that exercise is important because it makes you feel wonderful are the same people who say a mink coat is nice because it keeps you warm. Show me a woman who wears a mink coat to keep warm and who exercises because it feels good and I'll show you Jane Fonda. I wear a mink coat because it is a mink coat, and I work out so that my husband will not gasp when he runs into me in the bathroom and run off with an 18-year-old who looks as good out of her clothes as in them. It's as simple as that.

—Anna Quindlen, "Going to the Gym"

Jacoby's words and sentence structures set a direct and assertive tone. Such words as "get lost," "roughly," "loudly," "nuisance," and "commitments" help to establish the author's no-nonsense approach to her problem, while the succession of balanced sentences reinforces this tone. Note the contrast in the second sentence between what our mothers didn't teach us and what they did. Combining the two clauses into one sentence with a semicolon as the pivot strengthens the contrast—the irony—between "get lost" and "be just delighted." The next sentence reinforces this ironic dilemma in another pair of balanced independent clauses that contrast "demure lowering of the eyelids" and "roughly and loudly."

Mencken presents factual, informative arguments by using direct language; however, the inclusion of phrases like "brutal American habit," "to lie for long months and even years under the shadow of death" makes an emotional statement as well. His emphatic "no sane man would choose such a finish" complements the insistent tone. His diction and sentence style lend urgency to an emotional appeal for more prompt executions.

Quindlen's tone is informal, personal, and humorous. The diction she selects appeals to a general reader—it is neither elevated nor simplistic—and the use of the contractions "I'll" and "It's" echo the language of daily conversation. Sentence structures reflect this easygoing tone and range from more complex structures to direct ones; "It's as simple as that" again recalls everyday communication.

Underlying these structural techniques is Quindlen's content, for the meaning a writer wants to convey is inseparable from the tone selected. The writer's musings and illustrations put a reader at ease. In essence, the combination of diction, sentence structure, and content all contribute to a comfortable, lighthearted tone.

The relations between sentence structure and tone are too subtle to codify, but if you are alert to the possible variations on the basic sentence, you may be able to convey your attitude toward your subject more exactly. One way to set tone is to use questions, commands, and exclamations. Note the range of tones in the following groups of sentences:

> *I worried about that interview all night long. "Why shouldn't I get that job?" I thought to myself.*
>
> *The problem with today is the demands made on us. "Do this. Get this. Finish this." There's no time left for anything.*
>
> *I couldn't believe that this was actually going to happen! All those years of hard work were finally coming to an end. At last I was graduating!*

Even if you write only declaratory sentences, varying the length will control tone. Short, punchy sentences might set up a feeling of expectation as you wait for the next detail. Smooth, long sentences free you from anticipation as you allow yourself to be taken along by an easy, flowing tone. Sometimes you will want the impact of a very short sentence, while another passage may benefit from an unusually long one. As a rule, a mixture of long and short sentences is agreeable. Note how different Jacoby's paragraph would have been if she had used only short, simple sentences:

> *Politeness is useless in handling strange men. Our mothers didn't teach us to tell a man to get lost. They told us to be polite and agreeable. The man in the Oak Room bar would not be put off by a demure lowering of eyelids. He had to be insulted.*

Don't you find the tone here somehow less confident, less assertive, even plaintive?

Your *purpose* in writing necessarily influences your tone: why you are writing must affect the manner in which you express your ideas. If you are writing to amuse or entertain, you will try to set a lighthearted, humorous tone. Conversely, if you are trying to impress your audience with the urgency of an action or belief, you may feel that a light tone undermines your appeal. Compare the tone of the two passages below, both on the subject of running for public office. Which one strikes a note of urgency?

> *(1) We all like to complain about our politicians, but we know deep down in our hearts that we can't do without them. We know that there is a difference between an honest, efficient, caring officeholder and the other kind. We know that we are lucky when we get a competent person even if his or her motives are not 100 percent*

altruistic. Why don't we encourage good people to run for office? In fact, why don't we ourselves run? True, we have a dozen ready answers to that question: lack of time, interest, or ability; unpopularity; timidity. But, seriously, some of us are free of these faults and defects, and we ought to take a fresh look at the possibility of running for public office.

We should get acquainted with our local government and attend a few public meetings. We would find out how the party leadership functions. We would find out what officials are coming up for reelection. We could attend the social functions of our party, get to know the active people, and show that we are willing to work with the team. Perhaps at first we will do no more than help out some other candidates in their campaigns. But we will be learning for our own eventual candidacy.

(2) If you feel stirred to serve your community or to revamp the system, or perhaps—simply to "be in charge," you may someday decide to run for political office. If you do, and you live in a very small town (10,000 or less) here are some basic rules to follow.

Find out who is on your side. To enter a political race, you must present a petition signed by a designated number of registered voters composed of your family, friends, neighbors and people who owe you money. Your petition may or may not be greeted with hurrahs, depending upon whether the party leaders have you labeled as a winner or loser. Next, call on your supporters to serve as Campaign Manager, Activities Chairman, Publicity Chairman, Treasurer and Ego Chairman. Ego Chairman's job is to call you every morning during the campaign to tell you that you are a shoo-in and the whole town reveres you. . . .

Present a news release each week to your local newspaper. Each release must contain a different issue or a new version of an old one. Finding new issues is very difficult. The subject matter must be innocuous enough to offend no one and yet present you as a dedicated, innovative public servant and a wonderful human being. Accompany your article with a photograph of yourself staring with tight-lipped disapproval at some object of public concern, such as a pothole in the middle of Main Street.

—Shirley Weissenborn, "How to Run for Office in a Very Small Town"

Like purpose, *subject matter* also influences tone. If you are writing a research paper about a technical subject, the tone will most likely be detached and informative. On the other hand, the tone of a message on a birthday card will probably be personal, cheerful, and hopeful. In general, a serious subject will demand a serious tone, but there may be exceptions even to that!

The last important element in selecting tone is the *audience* a writer wants to reach. In one sense, the tone you choose reflects your understanding of your audience's expectations of you and how you wish to be perceived. The things you take for granted, or the liberties you take with language and information, might be permissible with one audience but unthinkable with another. Just as you vary your vocabulary when you address your parents, friends, teachers, or a three-year-old toddler, you may also modify your tone to suit different audiences.

In another sense, your knowledge of your audience enables you to "work the crowd." If you find yourself writing for an unsympathetic or even hostile audience, you can use tone to win them over. Being friendly, warm, and responsive and using words such as *us* and *we* will help to reduce the distance between yourself and your readers. On the other hand, if you find yourself on the right side of an "us versus them" situation, your tone can take ample advantage of this. The exuberant tone of political rallies is often attributable to the fact that the speechwriter is addressing an audience that shares his or her aims and needs.

The tone of your writing will depend on your reason for writing, the content of your work, and the reader for whom you are writing. Ultimately, the tone you select represents who you are, or who you choose to be, at a particular moment. Fortunately, how you present yourself to your reader is your choice and is one open to experimentation. Your decision to be friendly, distant, humorous, somber, scientific, dramatic, assertive, or ironic will depend on the writing project under consideration. Of course, should you write an essay with a tone that is inappropriate or unsatisfactory to you, you need to change it. Revision is the process that allows you to seek out the best way to express your attitudes toward your topic and reader.

Rachel L. Jones

Rachel L. Jones (b. 1961) was born in Cairo, Illinois. She attended Northwestern University and Southern Illinois University and held internships at *The New York Times* and the *Washington Post*. Her essays are widely anthologized and this particular piece was written especially for this edition of *The Writer's Craft*. After reading her essay, freewrite about the extent to which we tend to judge people on the basis of their appearance.

Judging a Book by Its Cover

Introduction to the Essay and Draft

As you read Rachel L. Jones' "Introduction" to her essay, you will learn how she has crafted "Judging a Book by Its Cover" from its beginning as an idea through its final revision. The writer's eye view provided by Jones should help to explain the choices she makes and that you and all writers must make. Some of these, such as purpose, meaning, and audience, have been examined in earlier chapters, and, as mentioned in the introduction to this chapter, your decisions regarding them will be related to the *tone* you choose. Indeed, Jones neatly explains how her purpose, meaning, and intended audience help her to establish her tone, and how her revision of her draft is primarily intended to make her tone—and the entire essay—more effective.

INTRODUCTION TO ESSAY, "JUDGING A BOOK BY ITS COVER," BY

Rachel L. Jones

1   Over the years, I've had many essays published in books and

newspapers, but I always point fondly to my very first published

piece--a MY TURN article in NEWSWEEK Magazine--as my crowning

glory.[1] I learned a valuable lesson from the overwhelming response

to that piece, which was that people respond more to essays

written conversationally and from a deeply held point of view.

2   With that knowledge, I've essentially tried to write about

what I've believed in, and that holds true with this essay. I had

read a quote from an editor at a major daily newspaper, in which

---

1. See Rachel Jones' "What's Wrong with Black English" on pages 316–318.

he lamented the lack of "qualified minorities" to staff newsrooms. I have long believed that this is an excuse used by many newspaper executives to avoid actively seeking minority candidates, and so I was compelled to go home that night and scratch off a tart response.

3   As you can see frm the draft, I started it off with a "memory"--relating the subject from something that had happened to me several years earlier. I've often found that to be a good way to pull people into your topic, by not just spouting facts and figures. Later, as I revised the draft, I decided that it was just a bit TOO informal, and without getting a good idea of what my topic was, readers might wonder what the heck I was writing about and then move on before the good stuff! I solved that problem by adding several introductory, "explanatory" paragraphs to prepare the reader.

4   Overall, the major changes from draft to final essay were to clean up some of the informal language. For example, in the fifth paragraph of the draft, I changed "I wish newspaper editors and publishers would find the guts to drop that term and say what they really mean" to "Newspaper editors and publishers should stop using that term and say what they really mean." I think the second version is much more authoritative, and though I think they need guts, it's a little too casual for a persuasive essay. Another good example is the sentence where I used the word "hellacious"--OUCH! Not only is that not a real word, but an essay writer should inform and provoke, not necessarily offend. Often, it's best to leave out such language until you've attained the status of a Mike Royko and can write whatever you want, with your editor's blessing!

5   Finally, towards the end, I decided that a two paragraph section where I described my travels and how my writing has

developed was too much off the subject, and it's an important thing to remember. Use your thoughts and experiences ONLY WHEN THEY HELP YOU MAKE A STRONG CASE. Otherwise, you risk prompting the reader to think, "I don't care what's she's been doing, I wish she'd stick to the point!" Near the end, I tried to broaden the scope by including all employers in my thesis and not just newspaper publishers and editors, because I think it's important that everyone understand and respect the differences of the people they work with.

Draft

 Rachel L. Jones

DON'T JUDGE A BOOK BY ITS COVER ?
~~JUDGING A BOOK BY ITS COVER~~
DESPERATELY NEEDS AN INTRODUCTORY PARAGRAPH OR TWO, TO SET UP THE ISSUE

1   In April of 1989, I interviewed at the Miami Herald's Fr. Lauderdale bureau wearing a button-down, yoked and pleated
not necessary ~~2-piece HATHAWAY~~ ensemble that would have done any east coast debutante proud. My hair was permed, neatly cut and Shaped, fanning back off my face in fluffy, short curls.

2   By by the time I started work, I'd pondered the cruel humidity of South Florida's and decided to have my hair braided. "Pinch braids," they're called, a head full of long, individual extensions, pulled back and neatly secured by A hair ties.

3   Yet there was no ~~escaping~~ mistaking the blanched expression on the face of the woman who'd hired me, nor the confused stares of ~~some of the~~ other editors. when I started work. "Oh, you got your hair braided," my benefactor gulped. "It's so...different."

4   That episode comes to mind because, once again, I've come across that journalistic catch phrase of the 90's, that red flag that invariably makes me furious. Yet another big newspaper recently was affirming its commitment to "cultural diversity" in the newsroom, but explained that they were stymied because of the ~~dearth~~ lack of "qualified minorities,"

5   ~~I wish Newspaper editors and publishers should find the guts to drop~~ stop using that term and say what they really mean. They are looking for ~~ACCEPTABLE~~ ACCEPTABLE MINORITIES, AND NOTHING ELSE. No dreadlocks, or braids, no social consciences, dashikis, political activism, cornrows, militant posturing, inner-city sensibilities, or any of that other messy stuff. They want

minorities so non-threatening you'd almost think they were
~~some of the~~ good old boys with a ~~M~~outh Florida suntan.

6   Personally, I'd be willing to bet that some of my own
success in this business could be attributed to a conservative
appearance and demeanor. Ove the years, my taste in clothes
has leaned toward the buttoned-down, almost preppy look,
permed hair and all. I'd like to say it was part of an ingenious
plan to secure a permanent place for myself in journalism,
but my small-town sensibilities precluded that kind of cunning.
~~M~~ strict religious background produced the prim and proper,
non-challenging "good girl" most editors have seen.~~   ~~*
I just wanted to work hard and give 150% to all the ~~good~~ nice
white males who had given me ~~all these~~ tremendous opportunities.

7   Couple that with my writing talent, and I've been the
"two-fer" most companies dream of. But I know many similarly
intelligent and articulate black reporters who left the business
because they were perceived as hostile, antagonistic or
non-conformist. I met a young man at the NABJ convention
last summer, who wore dreadlocks and sported ~~a hellacious~~   an impressive
clip portfolio. He didn't expect to be hired at a daily,
he explained, because of his hair. ~~And~~ But he wasn't going to
cut it, ~~he added.~~ either

"hellacious"
is not a real
word; plus, it's
too informal.

spell out

8   On the other hand, I've met a lot of white reporters
in the past eight years who were stunning in their averageness,
sometimes downright incompetence, as minorities often find
themselves portrayed. I often wondered ~~as~~ who had agonized
over their qualifications.

9   MEANWHIle, my travels led me to an alternative weekly
newspaper in St. Louis. After Eight years of mainstream journalism,
it was the first time I actively pursued my desire to write
about African Americans and our problems and successes.
I developed more of an edge, became more aggressive ~~and~~
in my reporting and more able to stand toe to toe with atuhority.
It led to my current position as a reporter for an investigative
monthly in Chicago that focuses on issues of race and poverty.

OPTIONAL
I can just
as easily
NOT mention
myself at
this point

10   Already I'm sporting a floppy black felt hat with a
pin that reads "Fight racism, Fight imperialism." When I
interviewed for this position, though, I still had braids.
Now, my hair is permed. ~~But Hey~~, I suppose diversity means never having
to ~~$$$$$$~~ explain your hairstyle.

Optional

11   But here's the moral to this tale: editors who constantly
harp on the lack of qualified minorities need to take a
long hard look at ~~what~~ their "qualifications" are. Did the
inner-city edge in one applicants voice make him ineligible?
Maybe the young female applicant was intelligent, appropiately
dressed and had great clips, but also had three holes in
her left ear and wore a "Free South Africa" button on her
lapel. "Oh my," thinks the editor who commutes from ~~Winnetka~~. the suburbs
"She's probably a radical who'll fight me every step of
the way. NEXT!"

readers may
not know that
Winnetka is an
affluent suburb

[handwritten margin note: Too informal, doesn't add anything]

12 ~~Just admit it,~~ you guys. Newspaper administrators want
mintorities who won't make them uncomfortable, personally
or jourñalistically. They want employees who won't call them
on editorial policy or push for stories they feĕl are important
to their particular ethnic groups, or castigate them for
a lack of empathy or insight. ~~But you see, I never learned~~
~~how to play the game, how to schmooze or hogwrto cozy up~~ *[handwritten: how]*
~~to the powers that be. I never learned the "good old boys"~~
~~game, so I just had to be me.~~

[handwritten margin note: Innappropriate here. take yourself out of the discussio]

13 →Those ~~who~~ decry quotas ~~$##-that~~ call for the dreaded
"d" word -- diversity -- need to realize that until white
~~males~~ actually spend morˢ time around minorities, of all different *[handwritten: employers]* *[handwritten: m e]*
types, attitudes and appearances, ~~this~~ this "color-blind,
even playing field" ideɛlogy that's cropping up is just as
appalling as the erstwhile abhorrent policy of filling spaces
with minorities simply because they're minorities. ~~I'm~~ *[handwritten: END IT HERE.]*
~~tired of you telling me what I need to be. Let me be myself,~~
~~and maybe~~

Final Essay

1   A great irony persists in mainstream America today, as attempts to deal with
a changing workforce and different ethnic perspectives are beginning. Though the
oft-heralded melting pot is becoming increasingly diverse and the numbers of
minorities are growing daily, Americans still cling to a notion of "sameness," a
uniformity in appearance and manner, as the key to making it in this society.

2   Whether in dress or speech, the "powers that be" still look for an ideal that's
based on just one model—and that model is largely a European-based one.
Granted, the use of standard English is vital for basic communication and should
be mastered by all who wish to succeed, but the need for conformity stretches
far beyond manner of speech.

3   For example, in April of 1989, I interviewed at the Miami Herald's Fort
Lauderdale Bureau wearing a buttoned-down, yoked and pleated ensemble that
would have done any East Coast debutante proud. My hair was permed, neatly
cut and shaped, fanning back off my face in short, fluffy curls.

4   But by the time I started work, I'd pondered South Florida's cruel humidity
and decided to have my hair braided. "Pinch braids" they're called, a head full of
long, individual hair extensions woven into my own hair, pulled back and neatly
secured by a hair tie.

5   There was no mistaking the blanched expression on the face of the woman
who'd hired me, or the confused stares of other editors when I started work.
"Oh, you got your hair braided," my benefactor gulped. "It's so . . . different."

6   That episode comes to mind because, once again, I've come across the
journalistic catch-phrase of the 90's, that red flag that invariably makes me
furious. Yet another big newspaper recently was affirming its commitment to

"cultural diversity" in the newsroom, but explained that they were stymied because of the lack of "qualified minorities."

7   Newspaper editors and publishers should stop using that term and say what they really mean. They are looking for ACCEPTABLE minorities, and nothing else. No dreadlocks or braids, no social consciousness, dashikis, political activism, cornrows, militant posturing, inner-city sensibilities, or any of that other messy stuff. They want minorities so non-threatening you'd almost think they were good old boys and gals with a South Florida suntan.

8   Personally, I'd be willing to bet that some of my own success in this business could be attributed to a conservative appearance and demeanor. Over the years my taste in clothes has leaned more toward that buttoned-down, almost preppy look, permed hair and all. I'd like to say it was part of an ingenious plan to secure a permanent place for myself in journalism, but my small-town sensibilities precluded that kind of cunning. A strict religious background produced the prim and proper, non-challenging "good girl" most editors have seen. I just wanted to work hard and give 150% to all the nice white males who had given me some tremendous opportunities.

9   Couple that with my writing talent, and I've been the "two-fer" most companies dream of. But I know many similarly intelligent and articulate black reporters who left the business because they were perceived as hostile, antagonistic or non-conformist. I met a young man at the National Association of Black Journalists convention last summer who wore dreadlocks and sported an impressive clip portfolio. He didn't expect to be hired at a daily newspaper, he explained, because of his hair, but he wasn't going to cut it, either.

10   On the other hand, I've met a lot of white reporters in the past eight years who were stunning in their averageness, and sometimes downright incompetence—two terms often used to portray minorities who've landed jobs formerly dominated by whites. I often wondered who had agonized over THEIR qualifications.

11   But here's the moral to this tale: editors who constantly harp on the lack of qualified minorities need to take a long hard look at what their "qualifications" are. Did the inner-city edge in one applicant's voice make him ineligible? Maybe the young female applicant was intelligent, appropriately dressed and had great clips, but also had three holes in her left ear and wore a "Free South Africa" button on her lapel. "Oh my," thinks the editor who commutes from the suburbs. "She's probably a radical who'll fight me every step of the way. NEXT!"

12   Newspaper administrators want minorities who won't make them uncomfortable, personally or journalistically. They want employees who won't call them on editorial policy or push for stories they feel are important to their particular ethnic groups, or castigate them for a lack of empathy or insight. And the same can be said of employers across the board; they hire people whom they feel will reflect their companies accurately and presentably. But unless it's in the food service or child care sectors, many employers still believe that a white candidate offers the best, most presentable image. Or, when a minority is chosen,

it's the one who most closely mirrors their view of what's presentable, and anything deviating from that narrow norm is instantly rejected.

13   As for me, I've solved that problem by landing a fellowship at an investigative monthly that focuses on issues of race and poverty. These days, I'm sporting a floppy black felt hat with a pin that reads "Fight racism, Fight poverty." When I interviewed for the position, I had braids; after I started, I took them down and got a perm. But Chicago's winter weather made me reconsider the braids.

14   I suppose diversity means never having to explain your hairstyle.

15   Those who decry quotas calling for the dreaded "d" word—diversity—need to realize that until white employers actually spend more time around minorities, of all different types, attitudes and appearances, this "color-blind, even playing field" ideology that's cropping up is just as appalling as the seemingly abhorrent policy of filling spaces with minorities simply because they're minorities. The playing field is not even when cobblestones of conformism and a disdain for difference dot the path for African Americans and other minorities.

Comparing Draft and Essay

Draft Paragraphs 1 and 2

1. From the very beginning, Jones' concern with tone is evident. Examine the two titles that are offered. What is the difference in tone between "Judging a Book by Its Cover" and "Don't Judge a Book by Its Cover"?

2. In paragraph 3 of her "Introduction," Jones explains that she feels that starting the essay with a memory is a good way to grab people's attention but that it creates a tone that is "just a bit TOO informal." Also note the handwritten comment on the draft saying that it "desperately needs an introductory paragraph or two, to set up the issue." Examine published paragraphs 1 and 2. How does the new introduction both establish a different tone from that of the draft and convey the writer's purpose more clearly? How would you characterize the tone of these paragraphs? How does the writer achieve this tone?

Draft Paragraphs 4 through 8

3. Compare draft paragraph 5 with published paragraph 7. What emotions do you think appear in these paragraphs, especially in the first sentence of the draft paragraph? How do you react to the tone of draft paragraph 5? How might other readers react to it? Note that in her "Introduction," Jones asserts that "an essay writer should inform and provoke, not necessarily offend." How has her revision of this paragraph acted on this idea?

4. Jones states that it is her intention to "clean up some of the informal language" in the draft (see statement paragraph 4). How does she accomplish this? What specific examples of revisions can you find?

Draft Paragraphs 9 and 10

5. Reread the first half of statement paragraph 5. From Jones' explanation of her intentions, what changes do you think she will make in these draft paragraphs? What revision strategies does she ultimately employ? (You might need to review published paragraphs 11 through 15.)

6. How is the overall tone of the essay affected by the rearrangement of these paragraphs? Why do you think Jones does not delete them but, instead, moves them to the end of the piece? Do you agree with the writer's decision? Why or why not?

7. Compare draft paragraphs 9 and 10 with published paragraphs 13 and 14. What tone is elicited by the draft paragraphs? How is this tone different from that found in the published paragraphs?

Draft Paragraphs 12 and 13
The arrow drawn in the draft indicates that Jones had originally intended to combine draft paragraphs 12 and 13. The published essay, however, does not follow this plan. Draft paragraphs 9 and 10 have now been rearranged to come between these paragraphs, and draft paragraph 13 has itself undergone revision. In essence, addition, deletion, and rearrangement have been used to revise draft paragraphs 12 and 13 so that their effect is quite different from what it was originally.

As you have learned, Jones has been concerned with finding and maintaining the tone that best suits her purpose, subject, and audience. While her immediate plan in writing this essay was to "scratch off a tart response" to a provocative statement she had read, you have seen how she uses the tools of revision to transform her initial draft into a unified whole that argues her opinion with a carefully constructed tone. In draft paragraphs 12 and 13 you can clearly see Jones' revision process as she works to bring her initial thoughts and emotions into line with the tone she has established.

8. Compare draft paragraph 12 with published paragraph 12. What tone do you think is evoked by the deleted sections of the paragraph? What specific words or phrases characterize this tone?

9. How does Jones' addition of the second half of published paragraph 12 affect her tone as well as her purpose, meaning, and audience?

10. Why do you think that the last sentence of draft paragraph 13 has been deleted? How does this deletion and the subsequent addition of the sentence that replaces it typify the revisions that Jones has made throughout the essay?

Margaret Cardello

Margaret Cardello (b. 1956) was born in Pennsylvania. As an infant her family moved to Queens, New York, where she was raised and currently resides. This is her first published piece. She has a full-time job, working with artists, writers, and mailshops in the production of getting what is commonly known as "junk mail" into mail boxes. This is her description of her writing process:

> For me the easiest part to write is the beginning and the end. I seem to be always sure of what I want to say (introduction) and my final feelings (finish). It is the middle of an essay that gives me the most difficulty. As such, I write the beginning and end first and work my way around them. For me writing gives me a chance to relive my life experiences and draw from what I learned.

I Wish

Introduction to the Essay and Draft

In a statement that describes both how she writes in general and how she produced "I Wish," Margaret Cardello says:

> *I look over my draft and think to myself, "How did the end project ever evolve from this?" Some of the main thoughts, however, have remained. For me, the only job the rough draft has is to offer me a guideline to what I want to write about (my inner feelings), serving as a checklist — giving me the insurance that all the important issues have been covered.*

As you look over the draft and compare it with the final version of the essay, you might keep the above statement in mind. Resembling Pete Hamill's brainstorming list (see pages 10–11), the "draft" is used by Cardello to fulfill several crucial functions. Most important is that by getting her ideas on paper, she is able to discover her "inner feelings," what she truly wants to say. Yet, in the complex set of interactions among purpose, meaning, audience, and tone, making a decision about one almost always requires rethinking the others. By discovering the true meaning of what she wants to say, the purpose of the essay is also clarified and Cardello commits herself to a particular audience. Perhaps the most perceptible and significant redirection of the draft is in the final selection of its *tone,* for the revised tone seems to unify the above considerations. That is, Cardello's discovery and reevaluation of meaning, purpose, and audience seem to make the selection of a particular tone inevitable.

As Cardello mentions, her draft offers her a "guideline" — for both content and form. Note how much of the draft has been revised and how different revision techniques contribute to the transformation of meaning, purpose, audience, and tone. Such substantial changes indicate how Cardello trusts addition, deletion, and rearrangement to help turn the draft into what she truly wants it to become.

The draft reproduced below is a typescript prepared from an original written in pencil on loose-leaf paper. That draft and this one both show how Cardello writes and revises at the same time. By examining the draft, you will notice how the author stops in the middle of a sentence, starts the sentence again, or abandons it in the middle. Similarly, changes are immediately inserted below or above a line as she tries out different ways of saying what she wants to say. What is seen, then, is not a first draft that is revised after it has been completed, but a work that changes as it emerges, a work that is taking shape as it is being created. As you read the draft, you might find yourself having to retrace your way through a sentence or paragraph as you, like Cardello, follow a sentence or thought to where it is going.

Draft

1　If I could give the most perfect
gift, it would be to myself.
　　,to someone
2　If I could give but one perfect
gift I would give myself the ability to
change into a man. Yes, a man. Not
necessarily a rich man. ~~But~~ I would
gladly start my life ~~at the economic~~
　　with the same family, same environment,
within the same　with the
　~~at the same~~ economic station I
~~had as a girl~~ but, I would be a man. boy.
was born into as a girl
3　Why you say, would I want to
be a man instead of a woman?　Well I'll tell you.

4　~~A man in the same position job~~
~~responsibility~~ ~~according to currently dated~~
Men currently earn $1.00 more to every .70¢
women earn. Unbelievable, a man could
　　　　　　have the
hold the same exact position ~~as~~ same
level of responsibility, do the exact same
job as I a woman does and ~~I do as a woman~~
~~and earn~~ for every 70¢ I am paid
he is paid $1.00! Why because he was
lucky enough to be born a man instead of
a woman.
5　What I like most is the way
men think. They have a knack of
turning a situation around

6

way men
~~Mostly~~, I like the ~~male~~ thinking
system. The majority of the men I've
have come in contact with and have

[margin: I have heard myself and plenty of other women folk]

7

think
~~My own I hear women~~ talking about
how wonderful it is to have husband who thinking is
way   Men who have
~~the are~~ "Old Fashioned." ~~They have~~ old fashioned
values, ~~they~~ believe in the home. They all

[margin: Believe in home cooked meals. ~~Feel that their clean bed was part~~]

want a nice home, good clean living. Three
kids a dog. Two cars. ~~Two homes~~
A year long home as well as a summer
retreat. They believe in vacations--it is
very important for the family to go out
and spend time together as a family. They
~~are just wonder - old fashioned we~~ Us
sure   such
women are so lucky to have some fine
old fashioned men ~~whose values are~~ with the
"right values." The perfect family man.

8

[margin: Mother or sons]

My question ~~or should I say questions~~
is who does all the work in this old

[margin: women cause]

fashioned life style? Women do--I can guess
because it just is the old fashioned thing
to do. Yes men think it is important

[margin: Divorce]

to maintain a clean home. ~~Their children~~
to be fed a home cooked   for
~~must have~~ a ~~fresh~~ meal served ~~at~~ dinner
~~time which is always an exact time~~ By the
way the exact dinner time varies from
man to man,--some feel 5 o'clock some
6 o'clock and some even feel 7 o'clock.
I tell you when the exact correct time
for dinner to be served is it is when
they ~~walk in the door~~ come home from work.
the proper
Men's thinking regarding ∧dinner time for
and day to day
dinner however, varies from man to man. ∧

9

Some men feel that 5-6-7 is the
proper time. Their choice is selfishly decided

```
                                 arriving
     by what time they will be home from
     office                     ^
     work or the gym
```

10
```
          Mother or son's work in

     about Rich's upbringing verses mine -

     woman cause - divorce - OH I DO WANT

     TO BE A MAN WORKED INTO COPY HERE AND THERE.
```

Final Essay

1   "Wish I may, wish I might, make my wish come true tonight."

2   I wish to be a man. Yes, I want to be a man. I do not have to necessarily be a rich man. I would gladly start my life over with the same family, same environment, and the same economic station. But instead of being a girl I would be a boy.

3   I close my eyes and my childhood as a girl as compared to my brother's childhood comes vividly to mind. HE was treated like a God. On weekends HE was permitted to sleep as late as HIS little heart desired. HE was allowed to stay out much later thán I. HE did not have to learn the fine art of housecleaning. I helped our mom clean our three story home. HE had no need to learn how to iron, as I ironed all his clothes. When HE completed taking a shower HE simply left the bathroom a mess. It was perfectly alright for HIM to let the wet towels fall where they would, as I would shortly be there to clean up after HIM. My family made sure to start a college fund for HIM, not so for me. I believe the only responsibility HE ever had was to wake up in the morning for school. From that point on everything else HE ever needed or desired, a woman member of the family would do for HIM. All this special treatment for HIM, and why? Simply because HE was a BOY child and would grow to be a fine MAN one day.

4   OH I DO WANT TO BE A MAN! As I grew, I found out that the outside world viewed MEN as my family did. It was amazing! MEN in general were believed to be God-like! In a way I was relieved to learn that my brother was not the only MALE God in the world. When we would have dinner in the home of relatives or friends the routine was the same as at home. The MEN would sit in the living room watching baseball or football or whatever sport was in season, while the women prepared the dinner. After the table was set and all the food placed on the table the MEN would honor us with their presence. We children had strict orders from our mothers not to disturb the MEN while they ate their dinner. After the MEN finished eating they would retire back to the living room. The clearing of the table and washing of the dishes would be done by the women. My brother was content and happy sitting there among HIS fellow Gods. It seemed to be where HE belonged.

5   OH I DO WANT TO BE A MAN! As a grown woman I have heard myself and other women folk remark on how lucky we are to have husbands with "Old

Fashioned Beliefs." You see, MEN who have old fashioned beliefs have old fashioned values. They believe in the home and the family. They believe and demand in their own fashion to have three home cooked meals a day. They see the importance of a clean home. They treasure clean clothes, neatly ironed. They love children and dogs. They are strong believers in family vacations.

6   And who does all the work in this old fashioned life style? Women do! I guess it simply is the old fashioned thing to do. Yes indeed, MEN think it is important to keep a clean home, have kids and pets, home cooked meals, but all this simply adds up to women's work. I am happy to say old fashioned MEN have changed one of their old fashioned beliefs. They no longer feel that a woman's only place is within the home. No, they have decided that it is OK for a woman to work a full time job. They have given us this new freedom, with some restrictions. One is that women are not to earn more than their husbands. Well in truth it is alright to earn more, as long as we never tell anyone. Women must maintain all their other household duties and work a full time job. You remember the household duties, don't you? The clean house, home cooked meals, clean clothing, rearing of the children, etc., etc., etc. . . .

7   OH I DO WANT TO BE A MAN! MEN currently earn $1.00 to every 70 cents we earn. A MAN and a woman have the same job, with the same level of responsibilities and for every 70 cents she earns HE earns $1.00. Why? Simply because HE is a MAN.

8   OH I DO WANT TO BE A MAN! My husband and I divorced when our son was five years of age. My son lives with me as does the dog. I have the full time job of being a mom and sometimes a dad to my son. When I want to go out I must arrange and pay for babysitting. I work a full time job during the day, which very rarely ends at five. I attend school one night a week. Therefore, I do not see my son all that much. This leaves me with guilt feelings. My ex-husband on the other hand is living a life of total freedom. The MAN does not have to worry about babysitters. I am HIS son's full-time free sitter. HE does not have the joy of doing homework with our son every night. HE does not have to discipline our son. HE is not worried about our son's social development. Nor does HE concern HIMSELF with tutors for our son, Cub Scouts, drum lessons, kids' birthday parties. No, this MAN is free to live HIS own life as HE likes. HE can go where HE wants. HE can stay out as late as HE wants. All this MAN needs to do is show up every Wednesday, take our son out to dinner and play video games. Give me child support, when HE can. And for this HE is a hero. My son's failures are all my fault and my son's successes are all due to HIS father.

9   OH I DO WANT TO BE A MAN! It seems to me that women are not judged by what they have accomplished but by the accomplishments of their husbands and sons.

10   What I find to be the saddest is that it is we women who create the world we live in. I see myself catering to my son as I saw my mom cater to my brother. I have already unknowingly created a very macho seven year old. The principal of my son's school is a woman and the vice principal is a man. My son believes

this can not be correct. He tells me, "Mommy, the Principal must be the man and the Vice Principal the woman, because the Principal is the boss and that must be the MAN, not the woman." God help the woman who falls in love with my son.

11   My writing gives evidence of my age. I've been told that the world is changing. Men are or will soon be more helpful around the house. Equality between the sexes is not far from being a reality. Perhaps, but from what I can see it is still a MAN's world. So please twinkling little star, make my wish to be a MAN come true, and please do not allow this equality thing to take place until I have lived my life to the fullest as a MAN!

Comparing Draft and Essay

Draft Paragraphs 1 through 3

1. As you look over these paragraphs, how would you characterize the tone that you think the writer is creating? What tone do you expect the rest of the essay to have?

2. Judging from these opening paragraphs, what do you think Cardello's purpose is? Who is her intended audience? How does your perception of tone help you to arrive at your answers to these questions?

3. Compare the draft paragraphs with published paragraphs 1 and 2. What is the tone of the published version? How has this tone met with your prediction of it in Question 1?

Published Paragraphs 3 and 4

4. These paragraphs are new and have no draft counterparts. How has Cardello created their tone? Find specific examples in the text to support your answer.

5. Review your answer to Question 2 above. How do you now assess Cardello's purpose and audience? What impact might the writer's tone have on them? What do you think the meaning is that Cardello has now discovered that had been absent from the draft essay?

Draft Paragraphs 4 through 6

Following draft paragraph 3 (which serves as the draft's thesis statement), these paragraphs are intended to begin the essay's body, where Cardello starts to explain why she would want to be born a man. Note that draft paragraph 4 has been rearranged in the final version of the essay (see published paragraph 7), while draft paragraphs 5 and 6 are abandoned.

6. What is the tone of draft paragraph 4? How does it compare with the tone established by earlier paragraphs? Do draft paragraphs 5 and 6 share this tone? Explain.

Draft Paragraphs 7 through 9

7. Examine draft paragraph 7. How does the tone of the first half of this paragraph compare with that of the second half? How would you characterize the tone of the sentence "Us women are so lucky to have such fine old fashioned men with the 'right values'"? How does the tone of draft paragraphs 8 and 9 help you to understand the tone of this paragraph?

8. Compare draft paragraphs 7 and 8 to published paragraphs 5 and 6. What revision strategies has Cardello applied to these paragraphs? What effect do these changes have on tone?

9. Cardello deletes draft paragraph 9 from the final version of her essay. She also moves draft paragraph 4 so that it now follows draft paragraph 8 (see published paragraph 7). Why do you think Cardello makes these revisions? How do they help her to maintain a consistent tone?

Draft Paragraph 10

This draft paragraph is critical in fulfilling the purpose Cardello assigns to first drafts, that is, "serving as a checklist—giving me the insurance that all the important issues have been covered." Several of these issues are mentioned in the brief brainstorming list that is draft paragraph 10: "work in Rich's upbringing verses mine," "woman cause," "divorce," and "OH I DO WANT TO BE A MAN WORKED INTO COPY HERE AND THERE." If you examine the draft and published versions of the essay, you can see how these ideas have become its backbone—"Rich's upbringing verses mine" appears in published paragraphs 3 and 4, and "woman cause" is the focus of published paragraphs 5 through 9. The final paragraphs of the published essay, particularly published paragraph 8, are Cardello's expanded treatment of the brief note "divorce." At this point, it has also become readily apparent how the author has "WORKED INTO COPY HERE AND THERE" the sentence "OH I DO WANT TO BE A MAN!"

10. Study the final paragraphs of the published essay and determine how they contribute to what already has been established regarding the essay's purpose, meaning, audience, and tone.

H.L. Mencken

H.L. Mencken (1880–1956) had only ten years of formal education, yet by age 23 he was city editor of the *Baltimore Herald*. Three years later he joined the staff of the *Baltimore Sun* and wrote for that paper for the next 40 years. He also wrote over two dozen books, including six volumes of *Prejudices* (1919–1927). In *A Mencken Chrestomathy* (1949) he collected his best essays on a variety of issues. As you read "The Death Penalty," written more than 50 years ago, note how Mencken uses humor to write effectively about a serious and controversial subject.

The Penalty of Death

1   Of the arguments against capital punishment that issue from uplifters, two are commonly heard most often, to wit:

> 1. That hanging a man (or frying him or gassing him) is a dreadful business, degrading to those who have to do it and revolting to those who have to witness it.
> 2. That it is useless, for it does not deter others from the same crime.

2   The first of these arguments, it seems to me, is plainly too weak to need serious refutation. All it says, in brief, is that the work of the hangman is unpleasant. Granted. But suppose it is? It may be quite necessary to society for all that. There are, indeed, many other jobs that are unpleasant, and yet no one thinks of abolishing them—that of the plumber, that of the soldier, that of the garbage-man, that of the priest hearing confessions, that of the sand-hog, and so on. Moreover, what evidence is there that any actual hangman complains of his work? I have heard none. On the contrary, I have known many who delighted in their ancient art, and practiced it proudly.

3   In the second argument of the abolitionists there is rather more force, but even here, I believe, the ground under them is shaky. Their fundamental error consists in assuming that the whole aim of punishing criminals is to deter other (potential) criminals—that we hang or electrocute A simply in order to so alarm B that he will not kill C. This, I believe, is an assumption which confuses a part with the whole. Deterrence, obviously, is *one* of the aims of punishment, but it is surely not the only one. On the contrary, there are at least a half dozen, and some are probably quite as important. At least one of them, practically considered, is *more* important. Commonly, it is described as revenge, but revenge is really not the word for it. I borrow a better term from the late Aristotle: *katharsis. Katharsis,* so used, means a salubrious discharge of emotions, a healthy letting off of steam. A school-boy, disliking his teacher, deposits a tack upon the pedagogical chair; the teacher jumps and the boy laughs. This is *katharsis.* What I contend is that one of the prime objects of all judicial punishments is to afford the same grateful relief (*a*) to the immediate victims of the criminal punished, and (*b*) to the general body of moral and timorous men.

4 These persons, and particularly the first group, are concerned only indirectly with deterring other criminals. The thing they crave primarily is the satisfaction of seeing the criminal actually before them suffer as he made them suffer. What they want is the peace of mind that goes with the feeling that accounts are squared. Until they get that satisfaction they are in a state of emotional tension, and hence unhappy. The instant they get it they are comfortable. I do not argue that this yearning is noble; I simply argue that it is almost universal among human beings. In the face of injuries that are unimportant and can be borne without damage it may yield to higher impulses; that is to say, it may yield to what is called Christian charity. But when the injury is serious Christianity is adjourned, and even saints reach for their sidearms. It is plainly asking too much of human nature to expect it to conquer so natural an impulse. A keeps a store and has a bookkeeper, B. B steals $700, employs it in playing at dice or bingo, and is cleaned out. What is A to do? Let B go? If he does so he will be unable to sleep at night. The sense of injury, of injustice, of frustration will haunt him like pruritus. So he turns B over to the police, and they hustle B to prison. Thereafter A can sleep. More, he has pleasant dreams. He pictures B chained to the wall of a dungeon a hundred feet underground, devoured by rats and scorpions. It is so agreeable that it makes him forget his $700. He has got his *katharsis*.

5 The same thing precisely takes place on a larger scale when there is a crime which destroys a whole community's sense of security. Every law-abiding citizen feels menaced and frustrated until the criminals have been struck down—until the communal capacity to get even with them, and more than even, has been dramatically demonstrated. Here, manifestly, the business of deterring others is no more than an afterthought. The main thing is to destroy the concrete scoundrels whose act has alarmed everyone, and thus made everyone unhappy. Until they are brought to book that unhappiness continues; when the law has been executed upon them there is a sigh of relief. In other words, there is *katharsis*.

6 I know of no public demand for the death penalty for ordinary crimes, even for ordinary homicides. Its infliction would shock all men of normal decency of feeling. But for crimes involving the deliberate and inexcusable taking of human life, by men openly defiant of all civilized order—for such crimes it seems, to nine men out of ten, a just and proper punishment. Any lesser penalty leaves them feeling that the criminal has got the better of society—that he is free to add insult to injury by laughing. That feeling can be dissipated only by a recourse to *katharsis,* the invention of the aforesaid Aristotle. It is more effectively and economically achieved, as human nature now is, by wafting the criminal to realms of bliss.

7 The real objection to capital punishment doesn't lie against the actual extermination of the condemned, but against our brutal American habit of putting it off so long. After all, every one of us must die soon or late, and a murderer, it must be assumed, is one who makes that sad fact the cornerstone of his metaphysic. But it is one thing to die, and quite another thing to lie for long months and even years under the shadow of death. No sane man would choose such a finish. All of us, despite the Prayer Book, long for a swift and unexpected

end. Unhappily, a murderer, under the irrational American system, is tortured for what, to him, must seem a whole series of eternities. For months on end he sits in prison while his lawyers carry on their idiotic buffoonery with writs, injunctions, mandamuses, and appeals. In order to get his money (or that of his friends) they have to feed him with hope. Now and then, by the imbecility of a judge or some trick of juridic science, they actually justify it. But let us say that, his money all gone, they finally throw up their hands. Their client is now ready for the rope or the chair. But he must still wait for months before it fetches him.

8   That wait, I believe, is horribly cruel. I have seen more than one man sitting in the death-house, and I don't want to see any more. Worse, it is wholly useless. Why should he wait at all? Why not hang him the day after the last court dissipates his last hope? Why torture him as not even cannibals would torture their victims? The common answer is that he must have time to make his peace with God. But how long does that take? It may be accomplished, I believe, in two hours quite as comfortably as in two years. There are, indeed, no temporal limitations upon God. He could forgive a whole herd of murderers in a millionth of a second. More, it has been done.

Considering Content

1. Do you agree that the two "most often" heard arguments against capital punishment are still the two that Mencken lists?

2. Executioners themselves, says Mencken, don't complain of unpleasantness and some actually enjoy the job. Does this point help to refute the first argument? If not, why not?

3. Mencken calls hanging an "ancient art." What unexpressed attitude does this phrase reveal in Mencken? How does it relate to the term "frying" used earlier?

4. What is Mencken's attitude toward deterrence as the (or an) aim of capital punishment? Does he simply dismiss it?

5. What neglected justification for capital punishment does Mencken advance?

6. Do you understand Mencken's distinction between revenge and *katharsis?* Do you agree that the story of the schoolboy and the tack is an example of katharsis, not revenge? Has Mencken gained support for his position by rejecting the term "revenge"? Would there be anything wrong (in any sense) in saying that "one of the prime objects of all judicial punishments is to afford" revenge? What is the difference between seeking justice and seeking revenge?

7. "The thing [the victims] crave primarily is the satisfaction of seeing the criminal actually before them suffer as he made them suffer." Is this true?

8. Reread the story of A, the storekeeper, and B, his bookkeeper. Does the story ring true? Is this a typical crime? Note that the punishment here is not death but

imprisonment with perhaps some additional dismemberment by rats and scorpions. Does this story belong in an essay on the penalty of death? Why?

9. Mencken obviously doesn't believe all punishment should be capital. For what crimes *should* the death penalty be used?

10. Mencken finds another (hidden) reason for "uplifters" to object to the death penalty: delay in carrying out the execution. Do you agree with him that fewer people would object to the death penalty if it were always carried out swiftly?

Considering Craft

1. Characterize the tone of Mencken's essay. Is it informative, serious, humorous? Is his tone consistent throughout the essay? Give examples to support your answer.

2. Mencken begins his essay by calling those who are not in favor of capital punishment "uplifters." What are the connotations of the word? For what purpose does he use it? How does it affect the essay's tone?

3. Where does Mencken state his main reason for his support of capital punishment? What is his thesis?

4. How effective is Mencken's comparison of making an analogy between the job of the executioner and other jobs that might be considered "unpleasant"?

5. What is the impact on the essay's meaning of Mencken's shifting his focus in paragraph 7 from the victims to the prisoners waiting in jail?

6. Does the shift from victim to criminal affect the purpose of the essay? What is Mencken's purpose: is he merely explaining a complex subject or does he want also to persuade? Explain.

7. Describe Mencken's intended audience in terms of sex, age, education, and social background. Would men and women respond differently to his essay? What is *your* response?

8. "Even saints reach for their sidearms." Comment on the choice of words here.

Susan Jacoby

Susan Jacoby (b. 1946) is a reporter and freelance writer who has written on a variety of women's issues for *The New York Times* and *McCall's. The Possible She,* a collection of her essays on women, was published in 1979. "Unfair Game" was originally published in 1978 in the "Hers" column of *The New York Times.* As you read the essay, speculate as to Jacoby's purpose in writing about these two personal experiences.

Unfair Game

1   My friend and I, two women obviously engrossed in conversation, are sitting at a corner table in the crowded Oak Room of the Plaza at ten o'clock on a Tuesday night. A man materializes and interrupts us with the snappy opening line, "A good woman is hard to find."

2   We say nothing, hoping he will disappear back into his bottle. But he fancies himself as our genie and asks, "Are you visiting?" Still we say nothing. Finally my friend looks up and says, "We live here." She and I look at each other, the thread of our conversation snapped, our thoughts focused on how to get rid of this intruder. In a minute, if something isn't done, he will scrunch down next to me on the banquette and start offering to buy us drinks.

3   "Would you leave us alone, please," I say in a loud but reasonably polite voice. He looks slightly offended but goes on with his bright social patter. I become more explicit. "We don't want to talk to you, we didn't ask you over here, and we want to be alone. Go away." This time he directs his full attention to me—and he is mad. "All right, all right, *excuse me.*" He pushes up the corners of his mouth in a Howdy Doody smile. "You ought to try smiling. You might even be pretty if you smiled once in a while."

4   At last the man leaves. He goes back to his buddy at the bar. I watch them out of the corner of my eye, and he gestures angrily at me for at least fifteen minutes. When he passes our table on the way out of the room, this well-dressed, obviously affluent man mutters, "Good-bye, bitch," under his breath.

5   Why is this man calling me names? Because I have asserted my right to sit at a table in a public place without being drawn into a sexual flirtation. Because he has been told, in no uncertain terms, that two attractive women prefer each other's company to his.

6   This sort of experience is an old story to any woman who travels, eats, or drinks—for business or pleasure—without a male escort. In Holiday Inns and at the Plaza, on buses and airplanes, in tourist and first class, a woman is always thought to be looking for a man in addition to whatever else she may be doing. The man who barged in on us at the bar would never have broken into the conversation of two men, and it goes without saying that he wouldn't have imposed himself on a man and a woman who were having a drink. But two women at a table are an entirely different matter. Fair game.

7   This might be viewed as a relatively small flaw in the order of the universe—something in a class with an airline losing luggage or a computer fouling up a bank statement. Except a computer doesn't foul up your bank account every month and an airline doesn't lose your suitcase every time you fly. But if you are an independent woman, you have to spend a certain amount of energy, day in and day out, in order to go about your business without being bothered by strange men.

8   On airplanes, I am a close-mouthed traveler. As soon as the "No Smoking" sign is turned off, I usually pull some papers out of my briefcase and start

working. Work helps me forget that I am scared of flying. When I am sitting next to a woman, she quickly realizes from my monosyllabic replies that I don't want to chat during the flight. Most men, though, are not content to be ignored.

9   Once I was flying from New York to San Antonio on a plane that was scheduled to stop in Dallas. My seatmate was an advertising executive who kept questioning me about what I was doing and who remained undiscouraged by my terse replies until I ostentatiously covered myself with a blanket and shut my eyes. When the plane started its descent into Dallas, he made his move.

10   "You don't really have to get to San Antonio today, do you?"

11   "Yes."

12   "Come on, change your ticket. Spend the evening with me here. I'm staying at a wonderful hotel, with a pool, we could go dancing . . ."

13   "No."

14   "Well, you can't blame a man for trying."

15   I do blame a man for trying in this situation—for suggesting that a woman change her work and travel plans to spend a night with a perfect stranger in whom she had displayed no personal interest. The "no personal interest" is crucial; I wouldn't have blamed the man for trying if I had been stroking his cheek and complaining about my dull social life.

16   There is a nice postscript to this story. Several months later, I was walking my dog in Carl Schurz Park when I ran into my erstwhile seatmate, who was taking a stroll with his wife and children. He recognized me, all right, and was trying to avoid me when I went over and courteously introduced myself. I reminded him that we had been on the same flight to Dallas. "Oh yes," he said. "As I recall you were going on to somewhere else." "San Antonio," I said. "I was in a hurry that day."

17   The code of feminine politeness, instilled in girlhood, is no help in dealing with the unwanted approaches of strange men. Our mothers didn't teach us to tell a man to get lost; they told us to smile and hint that we'd be just delighted to spend time with the gentleman if we didn't have other commitments. The man in the Oak Room bar would not be put off by a demure lowering of eyelids; he had to be told, roughly and loudly, that his presence was a nuisance.

18   Not that I am necessarily against men and women picking each other up in public places. In most instances, a modicum of sensitivity will tell a woman or a man whether someone is open to approaches.

19   Mistakes can easily be corrected by the kind of courtesy so many people have abandoned since the "sexual revolution." One summer evening, I was whiling away a half hour in the outdoor bar of the Stanhope Hotel. I was alone, dressed up, having a drink before going on to meet someone in a restaurant. A man at the next table asked, "If you're not busy, would you like to have a drink with me?" I told him I was sorry but I would be leaving shortly. "Excuse me for disturbing you," he said, turning back to his own drink. Simple courtesy. No insults and no hurt feelings.

20   One friend suggested that I might have avoided the incident in the Oak Room by going to the Palm Court instead. It's true that the Palm Court is a

traditional meeting place for unescorted ladies. But I don't like violins when I want to talk. And I wanted to sit in a large, comfortable leather chair. Why should I have to hide among the potted palms to avoid men who think I'm looking for something else?

Considering Content

1. To what extent do you empathize with Jacoby in the situations she describes?

2. Is it true that "a woman is always thought to be looking for a man in addition to whatever else she may be doing"? What kind of evidence do you need to prove or disprove this assertion?

3. Where does Jacoby make clear the distinction between fair and unfair game? Explain it.

4. What do you think Jacoby means by "sexual revolution." How does her attitude toward it compare with yours?

5. Jacoby proposes solutions in her last two paragraphs. Are they likely to work? Can you propose other solutions?

Considering Craft

1. Is Jacoby's tone objective or subjective? In other words, is she merely presenting her point of view or is she trying to influence yours? Cite examples to support your answer.

2. What tone is revealed by the title "Unfair Game"?

3. Describe the audience for which Jacoby is writing in terms of sex, age, education, and social background. Would men and women respond differently? What is your response to her essay?

4. Read the last paragraph of the essay. Does the tone change or remain the same? Explain.

Anna Quindlen

Anna Quindlen (b. 1952) lives in New York City and writes for *The New York Times*. Her response to our question: "How do you usually get started on a piece?" appears on page 94.

Going to the Gym

1   For most of my life I have pursued a policy toward my body that could best be characterized as benign neglect. From the time I could remember until the time I was 15 it looked one way, and from the time I was 15 until I was 30 it looked another way. Then in the space of two years, I had two children and more weight changes than Ted Kennedy, and my body headed south without me.

2   This is how I began to work out. I work out for a very simple reason, and it is not because it makes me feel invigorated and refreshed. The people who say that exercise is important because it makes you feel wonderful are the same people who say a mink coat is nice because it keeps you warm. Show me a woman who wears a mink coat to keep warm and who exercises because it feels good and I'll show you Jane Fonda. I wear a mink coat because it is a mink coat, and I work out so that my husband will not gasp when he runs into me in the bathroom and run off with an 18-year-old who looks as good out of her clothes as in them. It's as simple as that.

3   So I go to this gym three times a week, and here is how it works. First I go into the locker room. On the wall is an extremely large photograph of a person named Terri Jones wearing what I can only assume is meant to be a bathing suit. The caption above her body says Slim Strong and Sexy. It is accurate. I check to make sure no one else is in the locker room, then I take my clothes off. As soon as I've done this, one of two people will enter the locker room: either an 18-year-old who looks as good out of her clothes as in them who spontaneously confides in me that she is having an affair with a young lawyer whose wife has really gone to seed since she had her two kids, or a 50-year-old woman who has had nine children, weighs 105 and has abdominal muscles you could bounce a quarter off and who says she can't understand why, maybe it's her metabolism, but she can eat anything she wants, including a pint of Frusen Glädjé Swiss chocolate almond candy ice cream, and never gain a pound. So then I go out and exercise.

4   I do Nautilus. It is a series of fierce looking machines, each designed, according to this book I have, to exercise some distinct muscle group, which all happen in my case never to have been exercised before. Nautilus was allegedly invented by Arthur Jones, husband of the aforementioned slim and strong and sexy Terri, who is his 17th wife or something like that. But I think anyone who comes upon a Nautilus machine suddenly will agree with me that its prototype was clearly invented at some time in history when torture was considered a reasonable alternative to diplomacy. Over each machine is a little drawing of a human body—not mine, of course—with a certain muscle group inked in red. This is so you can recognize immediately the muscle group that is on fire during the time you are using the machine.

5   There is actually supposed to be a good reason to do Nautilus, and it is supposed to be that it results in toning without bulk: That is, you will look like a

dancer, not a defensive lineman. That may be compelling for Terri Jones, but I chose it because it takes me only a little more than a half hour—or what I like to think of as the time an average person burning calories at an average rate would need to read "Where the Wild Things Are," "Good Night Moon" and "The Cat in the Hat" twice—to finish all the machines. It is also not social, like aerobics classes, and will not hold you up to widespread public ridicule, like running. I feel about exercise the same way that I feel about a few other things: that there is nothing wrong with it if it is done in private by consenting adults.

6   Actually, there are some of the Nautilus machines I even like. Call it old-fashioned machisma, but I get a kick out of building biceps. This is a throwback to all those times when my brothers would flex their arms and a mound of muscle would appear, and I would flex mine and nothing would happen, and they'd laugh and go off somewhere to smoke cigarettes and look at dirty pictures. There's a machine to exercise the inner thigh muscles that bears such a remarkable resemblance to a delivery room apparatus that every time I get into it I think someone is going to yell push and I will have another baby. I feel comfortable with that one. On the other hand, there is another machine on which I am supposed to lift a weight straight up in the air and the most I ever manage is squinching my face up until I look like an infant with bad gas. My instructor explained to me that this is because women have no upper body strength, which probably explains why I've always found it somewhat difficult to carry a toddler and an infant up four flights of stairs with a diaper bag over one shoulder while holding a Big Wheel.

7   Anyhow, the great thing about working out is that I have met a lot of very nice men. This would be a lot more important if I weren't married and the mother of two. But of course if I was single and looking to meet someone, I would never meet anyone except married men and psychopaths. (This is Murphy's Other Law, named after a Doreen Murphy, who in 1981 had a record 11 bad relationships in one year.) The men I have met seem to really get a kick out of the fact that I work out, not unlike the kick that most of us get out of hearing very small children try to say words like hippopotamus or chauvinist. As one of the men at my gym said, "Most of the people here are guys or women who are uh well hmm umm. . . ."

8   "In good shape," I said.

9   "I wouldn't have put it like that," he answered.

10   Because I go to the gym at the same time on the same days, I actually see the same men over and over again. One or two of them are high school students, which I find truly remarkable. When I was in high school, it was a big deal if a guy had shoulders, never mind muscles. So when I'm finished I go back into the locker room and take a shower. The 18-year-old is usually in there, and sometimes she'll say something like, "Oh, that's what stretch marks look like." Then I put on my clothes and go home by the route that does not pass Dunkin' Donuts. The bottom line is that I really hate to exercise but I have found on balance that this working out is all worth it. One day we were walking down the street and one of the guys from my gym—it was actually one of the high school

guys, the one with the great pecs—walked by and said, "How ya doing?" My husband said, "Who the hell is that guy?" and I knew that Nautilus had already made a big difference in my life.

Considering Content

1. Why does Quindlen go to the gym?

2. Compare Quindlen and Jane Fonda.

3. What two types show up in the dressing room as soon as Quindlen takes her clothes off? What effect does their arrival have on her?

4. What, according to Quindlen, is wrong with running and aerobics classes?

5. Can you state Murphy's Other Law? What, by the way, is Murphy's Law? What is the relation between the two laws?

6. Finish this sentence the way the man at the gym would have if he weren't talking to Quindlen: "Most of the people here are guys or women who are uh well hmm umm. . . ."

7. Quindlen says she sees the same men over and over again, some of them high-school students. Would you say most men use gyms for plain exercising or for bodybuilding? Why do you think bodybuilding has become so popular? Is there any sign that Quindlen herself likes muscular men?

8. Do you find that most of the people you meet at a gym are already in good shape? Quindlen says in between the lines that she is not in good shape; are such people usually embarrassed to go to a gym? Women seem to be a minority at her gym; is that also true of your experience?

9. Quindlen says, "The bottom line is that I really hate to exercise. . . ." Do you believe her? Why or why not?

10. Quindlen has a lot of fun with this subject. Is there a serious issue behind the fun?

Considering Craft

1. What is Quindlen's purpose in working out? Where does she state it?

2. How do the details she includes in paragraph 3 enhance her essay's meaning?

3. Quindlen begins paragraph 4 with the short topic sentence "I do Nautilus." How does she support this statement in paragraphs 4, 5, and 6?

4. Create a profile of the intended audience for this piece ("Life in the Thirties," *The New York Times*).

5. Identify the tone of the essay. Is it objective, condescending, humorous, or informative? Is it appropriate for her subject? Explain.

Linda Weltner

Linda Weltner (b. 1938) was born in Worcester, Massachusetts, and educated at Wellesley College. She is a columnist at the *Boston Globe* and the author of two novels, *Beginning to Feel the Magic* (1981) and *The New Voice* (1983), as well as a collection of essays, *No Place Like Home* (1989). After reading "Every 23 Minutes," published originally in the *Boston Globe,* freewrite on your solutions to the problems of drinking and driving.

Every 23 Minutes . . .

1   My husband and I went to a funeral a few weeks ago. The man we honored had not been ill and will never grow old. He was killed in his car on a Sunday night, driving home along a divided highway.

2   It was an ordinary evening, no blacker than any other, when a car coming in the other direction jumped the median strip, broke through the guard rail, and hit two other cars before smashing head on into his. According to the newspaper, the driver, who was returning from a wedding, seemed puzzled. "I only had two bottles of beer and two glasses of champagne," she is reported to have said.

3   A wedding.

4   Followed by a funeral.

5   I wish she could have been there to see all the lives her act has changed forever, the wife, and four children, the extended family, the hundreds and hundreds of friends who sat in numbed silence, listening to words which barely touched the depths of their grief.

6   Strange to think that, according to the National Highway Traffic Safety Administration, this happens in America every 23 minutes.

7   Somebody drinks.

8   Somebody drives.

9   Somebody dies.

10   And other lives are altered forever, though sometimes the changes may be invisible to a casual observer. By chance, the day before the funeral I ran into a longtime acquaintance while shopping. He commented on my crutches. I asked if he had ever broken his leg.

11   "Uh, I have a long rod in this thigh," he said, "from an automobile accident two weeks after I came back from Vietnam."

12   "That's ironic. To leave a war zone and get injured," I teased him. "You're lucky it wasn't worse."

13   "Well, my wife was killed in the crash and so was the wife of the driver," he said uncomfortably. "We were hit by a drunk."

14   I've known this man for years, yet suddenly I realized there was a whole chapter of his life he never mentioned. I asked and discovered he'd remained in the hospital seven weeks, and that all that time he'd known his wife was dead. It was hard to know where to go from there, for there are questions you can't put to someone in a casual conversation, like "How could you bear it?" or "What did you do about wanting revenge?"

15   I wish I knew the answers to those questions. I wish I could offer those answers to the woman who, overwhelmed by grief, could barely walk as she followed her husband's coffin from the synagogue.

16   My friend Lynn saw a movie at the high school where she teaches in which the young male narrator recounted how he'd killed someone while driving drunk. "He said he didn't know how he'd stand it if he'd killed someone he loved," Lynn told me. "That really bothered me. Isn't everyone someone that somebody loves?"

17   Every 23 minutes, who dies?

18   A mother who will never comfort the child who needs her. A woman who will never know how very much her friends depended on her. A man whose contributions to his community would have made a difference. A wife whose husband cannot picture the future without her.

19   Every 23 minutes, who dies?

20   A son who involuntarily abandons his parents in their old age. A father who can never acknowledge his children's accomplishments. A daughter who can never take back her angry words in parting. A sister who will never be her sister's maid of honor.

21   Every 23 minutes, who dies?

22   A brother who will not be there to hold his newborn nephew. A friend whose encouragement is gone forever. A bride-to-be who will never say her vows. An aunt whose family will fragment and fall apart.

23   Every 23 minutes, who dies?

24   A child who will never fulfill his early promise. An uncle who leaves his children without guidance and support. A grandmother whose husband must now grow old alone. A lover who never had a chance to say how much he cared.

25   *Every 23 minutes.*

26   A void opens.

27   Someone looks across the table at a vacant chair, climbs into an empty bed, feels the pain of no voice, no touch, no love. Where there was once intimacy and contact, now there is only absence and despair.

28   *Every 23 minutes.*

29   A heart breaks.

30   Someone's pain shatters the confines of her body, leaking out in tears, exploding in cries, defying the healing power of tranquilizers and Seconal. Sleep offers no escape from the nightmare of awakening. And morning brings only the irreversibility of loss.

31   *Every 23 minutes.*

32   A dream ends.

33 Someone's future blurs and goes blank as anticipation fades into nothingness. The phone will not ring, the car will not pull into the driveway. The weight of tomorrow becomes unbearable in a world in which all promises have been forcibly broken.

34 *Every 23 minutes.*

35 Somebody wants to run. Somebody wants to hide.

36 Someone is left with hate. Somebody wants to die.

37 And we permit this to go on.

38 *Every 23 minutes.*

Considering Content

1. What are the effects of Weltner's using examples from the lives of ordinary people in the discussion of drunk driving accidents?

2. How does the title of the essay reinforce the magnitude of this problem?

3. Discuss substance abuse with your classmates. How do you account for its prevalence in our culture? What possible solutions can you suggest?

Considering Craft

1. Characterize Weltner's tone. Is it informative, serious, emotional? Is her tone consistent throughout the essay? Give examples to support your answer.

2. What is the impact on the essay's meaning of Weltner's shifting the focus from the victims of drunk driving accidents to their surviving family members?

3. Does this shift affect the essay's purpose? Explain.

4. Discuss the effects of repeating the phrase "every 23 minutes." What is the significance of Weltner's changing it from a question to a series of statements in the latter part of the essay?

Guidelines for Setting Tone

1. How do you feel about your subject and your audience? Try to characterize your attitude in a single word or phrase.

2. Can you point to specific words in each paragraph that set the tone? Why do these words have that effect? Is it because of their connotation? Check whether this is the connotation you want by substituting several synonyms, then choose the best.

3. Examine your sentence style. Can you control your tone by changing sentence types or lengths?

4. Does your tone suit your purpose? Your subject? Your audience? If your tone is unsuitable, look for ways—alternate diction or sentence style, for example—to set the tone you want.

5. Does your tone change from sentence to sentence or section to section? What is the change? Does it serve your purpose?

Warm-up Exercises

Connotation and Denotation

The following word groups have roughly the same denotation. Discuss the differences in connotation.

1. a. drunk
   b. intoxicated
   c. inebriated
   d. blasted

2. a. chubby
   b. fat
   c. plump
   d. obese

3. a. crazy
   b. insane
   c. psychotic
   d. nuts

4. a. stingy
   b. thrifty
   c. frugal

5. a. naive
   b. innocent
   c. ignorant

6. a. steed
   b. horse
   c. stallion

7. a. senior citizen
   b. old geezer
   c. old person

8. a. legs
   b. limbs
   c. pins

9. a. scribble
   b. write
   c. compose

Setting Tone

1. A job application usually requires that you write a paragraph explaining why you chose to major in a specific area such as computers, journalism, nursing, or data processing. Write such a paragraph using a tone suited to your purpose and audience. Now write a letter on the same subject to your best friend. How has your tone changed with this change of audience?

2. Write a paragraph describing one of the classes you are taking this term, keeping your tone as objective as possible. Then rewrite the paragraph, making your tone humorous, sarcastic, or angry. How has your tone affected your choice of words?

3. Freewrite on one of the following:

cultural diversity

manners

physical appearance

"The Death Penalty"

dating

stereotyping

wishing   conformity
"Judging a Book by Its Cover"   physical fitness
                                     hunting

Read over what you have written. Are there ideas on which you could expand for an essay? If so, decide what audience you wish to address, what your purpose in writing on this topic would be, and what tone you want to set.

4. Brainstorm on one of the following:

substance abuse   aerobics
drinking and driving   losing your job
Nautilus   affirmative action
stress   male children
gun control   ethnic identity

Read over what you have written and select the ideas on which you could expand for an essay. What audience will you address and how will this choice of audience affect your tone?

Writing/Revising Topics

1. Select an area in which you have some knowledge or experience, such as tennis, skiing, jogging, music, or cooking. Write an essay offering some basic instruction in the skill which might be suitable for publication in a magazine. Then rewrite the essay in a more personal tone for a friend who has asked for some information on the subject.

2. Write down an explanation of a difficult technical subject. (If you are studying for a biology test, you might try to explain the Krebs cycle; if you need to know about electromagnetic fields for an electrical engineering examination, you might write about that.) Rewrite your first version as a response to an examination question. Then write a third version for a general audience. What modifications did you have to make, particularly in choice of words?

3. Write a letter to your friend suggesting that he or she move in with you. Give reasons as to why you think it is a good idea. Then write a letter to your parents explaining the reasons for your decision to invite this person to share your lodgings. How has change of audience affected your purpose, tone, and style?

4. Using Warm-up Exercise 3 or 4, write an essay based on your freewriting or brainstorming topic. Before revising, review the Guidelines for Setting Tone. Then revise any parts of your essay in which your tone doesn't seem to support your purpose.

6

Composing Introductions and Conclusions

As you know from experience, first and last impressions are important. You probably want to project a positive image when you meet someone for the first time, and you want to reinforce this image when you leave. Similarly, an introduction and a conclusion are important parts of any essay. Together they provide the first and last contact you have with your readers. For these reasons, among others that will be explained, most writers spend much time and energy on opening and closing paragraphs.

It may be helpful to postpone writing your first and last paragraphs until you have written a draft of your essay. Often having a sense of the scope and direction of your essay will assist you in composing an effective introduction and conclusion.

The chief purpose of an introduction is to capture your reader's attention. For example, Brent Staples begins his essay in this chapter with a dramatic first sentence: "It has been more than two years since my telephone rang with the news that my younger brother Blake—just 22 years old—had been murdered." Likewise, Maya Angelou, in writing about her first summer job, starts her essay with the arresting statement: "My room had all the cheeriness of a dungeon and the appeal of a tomb." In "Noses, Naturally," Peter Steinhart chooses a striking statement, "There are times when only the smell of things will do," to arouse his readers' curiosity. Other effective ways of beginning an essay are to ask a question that will directly involve your reader or to evoke emotion with a passionate statement.

5. Write a draft of an essay about a frustrating experience you have l teacher in whose subject you were not particularly interested. In re particular attention to your tone. Is it consistent with your purpose?

6. During class discussion of Jacoby's "Unfair Game" note your classmate toward the essay and their answers to Considering Content questions 1 5. How well has Jacoby controlled her audience's response by controlli of her essay? Formulate a thesis that expresses your own attitude t relative freedom of men and women and write a draft that you th convince your classmates. In revising, focus on your tone. Does it : purpose?

7. Rachel L. Jones presents her personal and professional observatioi limitations of conformity in the American workplace. To what extei agree that there should be room for people with ethnic and gender pe that challenge the status quo? Should employers judge applicants base appearance? Write a letter to the editor of your college or local r responding to the issues that she raises.

8. Margaret Cardello is convinced by her personal, social, and pr experiences that it is better to be born male. Write an essay supp attacking her point of view using similar criteria. Before revisin(Guidelines for Setting Tone. Revise any part of your essay in which yo inconsistent.

9. Linda Weltner writes about the dangers of drinking and driving. What thoughts on this issue? Do you agree with Weltner that society as a who try to find solutions to this problem? Can society legislate people's l Write an essay expressing your views. Before writing, determine your and choose an appropriate tone.

Another function of the introduction is to present the purpose and main idea of the essay. Sometimes the thesis is the first sentence of the essay, as is the case in this student's introduction.

Meryl Streep is my favorite actress for many reasons. I think that she has much talent as an actress and that she also takes many risks when she selects her roles. In addition, I think that she has an on-screen presence that is superior to that of all other actresses working today. It is for these reasons that she is able to attract so many fans at movie theaters all over the country.

The rest of the essay, as stated in the thesis, will consist of an analysis of Meryl Streep's appeal to the writer. Already we know that one of the author's purposes is to convince a general audience by means of a straightforward, informative tone that he knows why he likes this actress. The organizational plan to be followed is briefly sketched in: body paragraphs will discuss Meryl Streep's talent, role choice, and screen presence.

The previous example is one way in which you may introduce your essay since it contains a thesis that establishes the essay's purpose and tone. Putting the thesis at the beginning, however, seems to lose some of the paragraph's impact. Consider the following introduction in which the last sentence is the thesis:

My interest in movies started when I was a young child. Something about theaters fascinated me. Entering a huge, dark auditorium in the middle of a hot summer's day was itself a mysterious adventure. Now some of that magic has disappeared, but I still can't find anything more enjoyable than watching a great actor or actress in an excellent film. Of all the actresses working today, there is one superior to all the rest. Because of her acting skill, the roles she selects, and her screen presence, Meryl Streep is the best actress around.

Concluding with the thesis has allowed the writer to invent a more creative, attention-getting introduction. Also, as she moves in her discussion from general ideas about the topic to her thesis, she helps the reader to participate in the narrowing process that a topic should undergo. One additional bonus is that this type of introduction smoothly leads a reader into the essay's body.

The placement of a thesis statement is dependent on the needs and goals of a specific writing project. Thus, while an introduction for an essay in your English class will probably conform to the considerations already discussed, other writing projects may demand different kinds of opening statements. The introductory paragraph of a business letter, for example, might not be a catchy general discussion, but a sober, pointed explanation of who you are, why you are writing, and what you want of the person to whom you are writing. The opening paragraph of a newspaper article is even more direct: in only one sentence it explains where something happened, what happened, when and why it happened, and who was involved.

Conclusions

Conclusions share some characteristics with introductions. However, whereas an introduction leads a reader into an essay, a conclusion leads a reader out of it. Whereas the primary functions of an introduction are to grab a reader's attention and establish a main point, those of a conclusion are to make a reader remember the essay and to restate the thesis for the last time.

How can you restate main points and the thesis without being repetitious? Avoid using exactly the same words and form you used in the introduction and topic sentences. Try to give them a fresh appearance. You might also try to put your summary in a new form: if you have used *narrative* in your introduction or body, switch now to literal, discursive language. If you have been using the language of logical *argument,* end with a *brief narrative.* If you have used *comparison and contrast* to make your point, turn now to personal opinion in your final restatement. (See the Glossary for an explanation of these terms.)

The other main objective of a conclusion is to make your reader remember your essay. How often have you read an essay and forgotten it an hour later? But last words can be as memorable as first impressions. A final handshake, a parting smile, a last bow—your conclusion is your farewell to your readers. It is your last chance to impress them, to win them over, to make them remember your ideas. When possible, directly involve your readers—conclude with a provocative question, an exclamatory statement, a passionate plea, or a call to action. Examine the two conclusions presented below:

(1) *For the reasons stated above in this paper, I think that drunk driving is bad. It is harmful to the driver, to his or her family, and to innocent people who are affected. I just don't believe that driving while drunk is an intelligent thing to do. Nobody should ever drive a car while intoxicated.*

(2) *The above arguments are true, but none of us in this school has to look far for examples of what it means to drink and drive. Maybe you yourself have received that midnight phone call from the state police, or you've been a mourner at a recent funeral, or you've seen yesterday's wreck on the highway. We have all been victims of this stupid, senseless act. Will an act of Congress tell us what we already know? What will it take to make us learn that driving while drunk kills?*

Both of these paragraphs are functional conclusions—they summarize the topic and restate the thesis. Yet what a difference in the tone! The second is an emotional appeal that uses charged language and images to engage a reader's interest. It is more likely to be remembered.

Remember also that a vivid picture or a spoken word often has great impact. Richard Selzer, in "Mercy," uses dialogue with a dying patient's family to leave his readers with a lasting impression.

"He didn't die," I say. "He won't . . . or can't." They are silent.
"He isn't ready yet," I say.
"He is ready," the old woman says. "You ain't."

Two words of caution and advice: avoid introducing an entirely new point or argument in your conclusion. To present a new line of reasoning here gives the impression that the new information is not important enough to receive its proper share of attention in the essay part reserved for it, and therefore ought to be deleted anyway. Such a late inclusion also calls in question your whole organization, thereby compromising the effect of your whole essay. Secondly, expect to write and rewrite your last paragraph until you get the right combination of familiar and new: present by-now-familiar ideas in new, memorable language.

Richard Selzer

Richard Selzer (b. 1928) was professor of surgery at the Yale School of Medicine who retired to pursue his writing career full-time. In recent years, he began writing about his experiences as a doctor for the general public. As you will see in the drafts of his introduction to "Mercy," he is a meticulous reviser. Unlike many of our authors who compose on the typewriter or word processor, Selzer writes in longhand. When we asked him to decipher his introductory paragraph to "Mercy" he graciously consented, adding, "only James Joyce's manuscripts, it seems, are messier and more illegible than mine." We think you will be interested in Selzer's explanation of how he came to write "Mercy."

> Revision is the act of pushing words around on a page until you like the way they look. This piece dawned with the incident of the dying flies. I was then put in mind of the patient with whom I shared the experience recounted. Obviously, the horror, guilt, *and* the dilemma had accompanied me to Italy. And beyond, into the imagination.

Mercy

Introduction to the Essay and Draft

The draft pages that are reproduced below are taken from four complete drafts of Richard Selzer's essay "Mercy." You might wonder why so many drafts have been created, but as some authors have already mentioned, revision is not primarily a correcting process but a means of discovery. Such discovery may result from cutting out digressions or adding ideas that help to focus a piece. Discovery may be achieved through the reorganization of a work or through the substitution of words, sentences, or ideas. Discovery may occur with rewriting an essay and finding an entirely new purpose or meaning. In Selzer's case, the sheer number of drafts indicates how revision is used to discover and then establish meaning. Nowhere is this better demonstrated than in the introduction.

The main purpose of any introduction is twofold: to establish an author's meaning and to grab a reader's attention. Selzer, like all other writers, is concerned with these requirements throughout his drafting process. Perhaps because of his subject he is able to catch his reader's interest easily. However, when he attempts to explain the meaning of his essay, his struggle for mastery over his writing begins.

In his search for an introduction, Selzer is seeking a way into the story he wants to tell. He tries many methods, ranging from a direct approach, which only presents the facts of the events, to an indirect, allegorical treatment, which deftly leads into the actual essay. In the allegorical treatment the respective paragraphs describing the fig tree and the cluster flies gradually introduce a reader to the main point of the essay. (An allegory is a kind of story where things stand for other things, and where meaning is hidden from immediate view; for further explanation, see the Glossary.) When taken together, these diverse opening paragraphs illustrate a transformation of meaning, and Selzer not only discovers a central image for his own understanding of the story he will tell, but he also allows a reader to discover the overall meaning of the essay.

Discovering meaning—for writer and reader alike—is the essence of revision. As a reader you can now concentrate on Selzer's introduction, but as a writer you should be on the lookout for discovered meanings throughout your essay.

Published Essay

1   It is October at the Villa Serbelloni, where I have come for a month to write. On the window ledges the cluster flies are dying. The climate is full of uncertainty. Should it cool down? Or warm up? Each day it overshoots the mark, veering from frost to steam. The flies have no uncertainty. They understand that their time has come.

2   What a lot of energy it takes to die! The frenzy of it. Long after they have collapsed and stayed motionless, the flies are capable of suddenly spinning so rapidly that they cannot be seen. Or seen only as a blurred glitter. They are like dervishes who whirl, then stop, and lie as quiet as before, only now and then waving a leg or two feebly, in a stuporous reenactment of locomotion. Until the very moment of death, the awful buzzing as though to swarm again.

3   Every morning I scoop up three dozen or so corpses with a dustpan and brush. Into the wastebasket they go, and I sit to begin the day's writing. All at once, from the wastebasket, the frantic knocking of resurrection. Here, death has not yet secured the premises. No matter the numbers slaughtered, no matter that the windows be kept shut all day, each evening the flies gather on the ledges to die, as they have lived, *ensemble*. It must be companionable to die so, matching spin for spin, knock for knock, and buzz for buzz with one's fellows. We humans have no such fraternity, but each of us must buzz and spin and knock alone.

4   I think of a man in New Haven! He has been my patient for seven years, ever since the day I explored his abdomen in the operating room and found the surprise lurking there—a cancer of the pancreas. He was forty-two years old then. For this man, these have been seven years of famine. For his wife and his mother as well. Until three days ago his suffering was marked by slowly increasing pain, vomiting and fatigue. Still, it was endurable. With morphine. Three days ago the pain rollicked out of control, and he entered that elect band whose suffering cannot be relieved by any means short of death. In his bed at home he seemed an eighty-pound concentrate of pain from which all other pain must be made by serial dilution. He twisted under the lash of it. An ambulance arrived. At the hospital nothing was to be done to prolong his life. Only the administration of large doses of narcotics.

5   "Please," he begs me. In his open mouth, upon his teeth, a brown paste of saliva. All night long he has thrashed, as though to hollow out a grave in the bed.

6   "I won't let you suffer," I tell him. In his struggle the sheet is thrust aside. I see the old abandoned incision, the belly stuffed with tumor. His penis, even, is

skinny. One foot with five blue toes is exposed. In my cupped hand, they are cold. I think of the twenty bones of that foot laced together with tendon, each ray accompanied by its own nerve and artery. Now, this foot seems a beautiful dead animal that had once been trained to transmit the command of a man's brain to the earth.

7   "I'll get rid of the pain," I tell his wife.

8   But there is no way to kill the pain without killing the man who owns it. Morphine to the lethal dose . . . and still he miaows and bays and makes other sounds like a boat breaking up in a heavy sea. I think his pain will live on long after he dies.

9   "Please," begs his wife, "we cannot go on like this."

10   "Do it," says the old woman, his mother. "Do it now."

11   "To give him any more would kill him," I tell her.

12   "Then do it," she says. The face of the old woman is hoof-beaten with intersecting curves of loose skin. Her hair is donkey brown, donkey gray.

13   They wait with him while I go to the nurses' station to prepare the syringes. It is a thing that I cannot ask anyone to do for me. When I return to the room, there are three loaded syringes in my hand, a rubber tourniquet and an alcohol sponge. Alcohol sponge! To prevent infection? The old woman is standing on a small stool and leaning over the side rail of the bed. Her bosom is just above his upturned face, as though she were weaning him with sorrow and gentleness from her still-full breasts. All at once she says severely, the way she must have said it to him years ago:

14   "Go home, son. Go home now."

15   I wait just inside the doorway. The only sound is flapping, a rustling, as in a room to which a small animal, a bat perhaps, has retreated to die. The women turn to leave. There is neither gratitude nor reproach in their gaze. I should be hooded.

16   At last we are alone. I stand at the bedside.

17   "Listen," I say, "I can get rid of the pain." The man's eyes regain their focus. His gaze is like a wound that radiates its pain outward so that all upon whom it fell would know the need of relief.

18   "With these." I hold up the syringes.

19   "Yes," he gasps. "Yes." And while the rest of his body stirs in answer to the pain, he holds his left, his acquiescent arm still for the tourniquet. An even dew of sweat covers his body. I wipe the skin with the alcohol sponge, and tap the arm smartly to bring out the veins. There is one that is still patent; the others have long since clotted and broken down. I go to insert the needle, but the tourniquet has come unknotted; the vein has collapsed. Damn! Again I tie the tourniquet. Slowly the vein fills with blood. This time it stays distended.

20   He reacts not at all to the puncture. In a wild sea what is one tiny wave? I press the barrel and deposit the load, detach the syringe from the needle and replace it with a second syringe. I send this home, and go on to the third. When they are all given, I pull out the needle. A drop of blood blooms on his forearm. I blot it with the alcohol sponge. It is done. In less than a minute, it is done.

21   "Go home," I say, repeating the words of the old woman. I turn off the light. In the darkness the contents of the bed are theoretical. No! I must watch. I turn the light back on. How reduced he is, a folded parcel, something chipped away until only its shape and a little breath are left. His impatient bones gleam as though to burst through the papery skin. I am impatient, too. I want to get it over with, then step out into the corridor where the women are waiting. His death is like a jewel to them.

22   My fingers at his pulse. The same rhythm as mine! As though there were one pulse that beat throughout all of nature, and every creature's heart throbbed precisely.

23   "You can go home now," I say. The familiar emaciated body untenses. The respirations slow down. Eight per minute . . . six . . . It won't be long. The pulse wavers in and out of touch. It won't be long.

24   "Is that better?" I ask him. His gaze is distant, opaque, preoccupied. Minutes go by. Outside, in the corridor, the murmuring of women's voices.

25   But this man will not die! The skeleton rouses from its stupor. The snout twitches as if to fend off a fly. What is it that shakes him like a gourd full of beans? The pulse returns, melts away, comes back again, and stays. The respirations are twelve, then fourteen. I have not done it. I did not murder him. I am innocent!

26   I shall walk out of the room into the corridor. They will look at me, holding their breath, expectant. I lift the sheet to cover him. All at once, there is a sharp sting in my thumb. The same needle with which I meant to kill him has pricked me. A drop of blood appears. I press it with the alcohol sponge. My fresh blood deepens the stain of his on the gauze. Never mind. The man in the bed swallows. His Adam's apple bobs slowly. It would be so easy to do it. Three minutes of pressure on the larynx. He is still not conscious, wouldn't feel it, wouldn't know. My thumb and fingertips hover, land on his windpipe. My pulse beating in his neck, his in mine. I look back over my shoulder. No one. Two bare IV poles in a corner, their looped metal eyes witnessing. Do it! Fingers press. Again he swallows. Look back again. How closed the door is. And . . . my hand wilts. I cannot. It is not in me to do it. Not that way. The man's head swivels like an upturned fish. The squadron of ribs battles on.

27   I back away from the bed, turn and flee toward the doorway. In the mirror, a glimpse of my face. It is the face of someone who has been resuscitated after a long period of cardiac arrest. There is no spot of color in the cheeks, as though this person were in shock at what he had just seen on the yonder side of the grave.

28   In the corridor the women lean against the wall, against each other. They are like a band of angels dispatched here to take possession of his body. It is the only thing that will satisfy them.

29   "He didn't die," I say. "He won't . . . or can't." They are silent.

30   "He isn't ready yet," I say.

31   "He *is* ready," the old woman says. "*You* ain't."

Draft A

1   Today I do not feel romantic about anything, especially
even
not about death. I admit to the Baroque habit of seeing death as
upon dying
a mysterious stranger both dreaded and at last welcomed or as the

passage from one material state to another. From such denials I

have drawn much comfort, domesticated my terrors, fended off my
I·
horror--but not today [You must be forgiven these little

whistlings in the dark.] Today Ron Martens taught me that a

death is not so easily had. He can be a petulant lover,

coquettish (un cocotte) who will tease and tease and then draw

back at the last moment.

2   Ron has been my patient for 7 years--ever since I explored

his abdomen and found the surprise lurking there--a cancer of the

pancreas. He was 42 then. The 7 years have been of famine for

Ron and his wife Lola and their 3 children. His suffering has

been squalid and steady--marked by pain, bloating, vomiting and

bowel obstruction. 3 days ago his pain abruptly lifted to

unimagined heights. He had entered an elect band of those whose

pain cannot be controlled by any amount of narcotic nor by any

means known to doctors. One watched him twisting in the bed and

felt awe at the magnitude of it as though Ron´s 80 lb. body had

been entered by a pure evil--a concentrate of pain, the core of

pain from which all the lesser pains--were made by serial

dilution.

1   *[handwritten draft]*

2 Ron has been my patient for 7 years — ever since I explored his abdomen & found the surprise lurking there — a cancer of the pancreas. He was 42 then. The 7 years have been of famine for Ron. And for his wife Lola & their 3 children. His suffering has been [illegible] squalid & steady — marked by pain, bloating, vomiting and bowel obstruction. 3 days ago his pain abruptly leapt to unimagined heights. He had entered an elect band of those whose pain cannot be controlled by any amount of narcotic, nor by any means known to doctors. One watched him twisting — [illegible] in the bed & [illegible] felt awe at the magnitude of it. As tho Ron's 80 lb body had been entered by a pure mind — a concentrate of pain, the core of [illegible] pain from which all the lesser pains were made by serial dilution. [illegible]

Draft B

1 There is a fig tree so rigorous and aggressive that it crushes a building to death. It is called fig of the ruins.

2 Ron Martens has been my patient for seven years, ever since the day I explored his abdomen in the operating room and found the surprise lurking there--a cancer of the pancreas. He was forty two then. These have been seven years of famine ~~for Ron~~. ~~And~~ for his wife, his mother, and his three children. Until three days ago his suffering was ~~steady and squalid~~, marked by slowly increasing pain, bloating, vomiting and fatigue. Three days ago the pain rollicked out of control, ~~Ron Martens~~ entered that elect band whose suffering cannot be relieved by any means short of death. ~~He twisted under the lash of it.~~ He was an eighty pound ~~remnant~~, who has been occupied by the concentrate of pain ~~itself~~, from which all other pains were made by serial dilution. An ambulance ~~and~~ brought him to the hospital. Nothing was to be done ~~there~~ to prolong his life. Only the administration of large doses of narcotics.

Draft C

What is this frenzy it takes to die!

Ron — present tense & write as a letter from Bellagio

1 The frenzy of the dying--it amazed him. He had watched, amazed, the interminable death of cluster flies in November. Even after they had collapsed on their backs on the window ledges, they were capable of

suddenly spinning so rapidly that they could not be seen. Only as a
blurred glitter. They were like dervishes who whirl to induce the
vertigo that is the only proper state for prayer. (In such an
ecstasy are these flies more receptive to their death?)
~~Xxixxxxxxxaftxxx~~ Whirl, then stop and lay as quiet as before,
only now and then waving a leg feebly, (then all four legs) in a
stuporous reenactment of locomotion. Until the moment of actual
death, this awful buzzing as though to swarm again.

2   What I most remember about Bellagio and the Villa Serbelloni
was the death of the cluster flies on ~~my~~ the window ledges of my
room. It was October, and the climate was full of uncertainty.
Should it cool down? Or warm up? As a result, it overshot the mark
veering from frost to steam. The flies had no such uncertainty. They
understood that the time had come.

Draft D

1   (Not long ago) I spent a month in Italy trying to write.
~~What I remember~~ Most about the Villa Serbelloni was the death of
the Cluster flies on the window ledges of my room. It was October,
and the climate was full of uncertainty. Should it cool down? Or warm up?
As a result, it overshot the mark, veering from frost to steam.
The flies had no such uncertainty. They understood that their time
had come.

2   What a lot of energy it takes to die! The frenzy of it.
Long after they had collapsed and stayed motionless, the flies ~~were~~ are
capable of suddenly spinning so rapidly that they ~~could not~~ cannot be seen. Or seen
only as a blurred glitter. They ~~were~~ are like dervishes who whirl to
induce the vertigo that is the only proper state for prayer. Just so
do these flies whirl, then stop, and lay as quiet as before, only now
and then waving a leg or two feebly, in a stuporous reenactment of
locomotion. Until the very moment of death, the awful buzzing
as though to swarm again.

Comparing Draft and Essay

Because an introduction is only part of a work, read Selzer's whole published essay before examining the draft openings. Then, in order to give you a clearer sense of the process the author undertook when writing and revising his essay, read all of the introductions before concentrating on each one.

Drafts A and B

1. A comparison between the one-sentence opening of draft B and the first paragraph of draft A will reveal no similarities! From where did this introduction come? Apparently, the writer's dissatisfaction with his original opening compels him to search for a new way into his topic. Try using the allegory of the fig tree to form your own understanding of the new introduction. What might the tree symbolize? How does it pertain to what comes later in the paragraph?

2. Examine the second paragraphs of both draft B and draft A. What kinds of revisions have been made? How do these changes affect meaning?

3. How is your reaction to the introduction to draft B similar to or different from your reaction to draft A? Which introduction is more effective in grabbing your interest? Explain your answer.

Drafts C and D

Suddenly it seems as if Selzer has abandoned all of his previous work: in these drafts there is no sign of the first two! As discussed earlier, sometimes a writer will evaluate a piece that he or she has written only to discover a new meaning, one that needs to be presented through a complete revision. On the other hand, this introduction may have been salvaged from another work. Perhaps it is part of a short story or reflection that the author has found to be suitable for the essay he is now writing. If so, this new introduction is an example of how writers mine other works for ideas and information. Perhaps you will find something in your journal that can be incorporated into a formal writing project. As you will discover, you can rarely know for certain how valuable something you write will prove to be later on.

1. The introduction to draft D picks up where the previous one has left off; the opening paragraph is a revision of the second paragraph of the previous draft. What has the author changed? What information has been included? What has been deleted? How do these revisions affect meaning?

2. How does the first sentence of the first paragraph of draft D affect meaning and tone? In particular, what do the words "trying to" indicate to you?

3. Where does Selzer hint at what will come in the pages to follow? What words or phrases indicate the purpose of the essay? What makes you suspect that the essay will not focus on cluster flies, the climate, or writing? How does the tone complement purpose and meaning?

Selzer's published essay begins with a four-paragraph introduction. The first two paragraphs will be familiar to you, and note the fourth one! Though it seemed that Selzer had abandoned his initial approach to his topic, it is now clear that he was searching for a proper lead-in to it. The first two paragraphs, the substance of drafts C and D, have served that purpose. (Paragraph 3, new to you here, helps to continue the purpose, meaning, and tone of the first two.)

Drafts A, B, C, and D

At last you can clearly see how both sets of introductions (drafts A and B and drafts C and D) work together. First, Selzer carefully controls his opening to gradually introduce his reader to his topic. Second, the complementary nature of the themes rivets his reader's attention and compels him or her to read on. As you study all of the draft versions, you will see how the author has arrived at his final introduction and how this last one represents the evolution of his ideas and technique. In particular, you can discover how changes in the first four drafts have been refined and incorporated into this one.

Myra Miller

Myra Miller (b. 1936) was born in New York to immigrant parents and is currently teaching composition at Queensborough Community College. These are her biographical comments.

> Their highest aspiration for me was that I attend college and become a teacher. Happily, my own inclinations were the same. After twenty-six years of teaching English I have no regrets about the challenging and satisfying career I've enjoyed. It even allowed me to enjoy time with my family as I juggled the responsibilities of being teacher and wife and mother.

Farewell to the Bird

Introduction to the Essay and Draft

The following statement by Myra Miller explains her purpose in writing "Farewell to the Bird" and the meaning she ultimately discovers:

> I wrote this piece the day after the accident. I was upset and anxious so I sat down and began to write. It seemed that putting the story down on paper helped me to gain some control over it. When I finished my first handwritten draft and looked back over it, I realized that I hadn't started with the accident, but with events that had occurred much earlier. I discovered that the essay was really about my relationship with my son and that the "Bird" had been more important to me than I had ever realized.

Miller's purpose for writing and her realizations after completing a first draft echo statements that you have already encountered. Indeed, it is common for writers to begin a piece because they want to release emotions or sort out their feelings. What frequently happens, as Miller acknowledges, is that what a writer intends as the meaning of a piece is not revealed to be so by the draft! The *process* of writing allows a writer to discover what he or she really wants to say: *your* first draft can lead you to discover your meaning in an essay.

Once Miller discovers her meaning, she revises to clarify it and to make it the focus of her essay. This process of clarification is best illustrated by the creation of the essay's conclusion. As the author works through successive drafts of her essay (there are five in all), the conclusion is shaped and refined so that it fulfills her purpose while providing the desired impact on a reader.

Reproduced below are the conclusions to three drafts as well as the published version. The first draft (draft A) is a typescript created from Miller's first handwritten version while the others are reproductions of the actual typed copies. When reading draft A, note that Miller revises as she composes: deletions are those portions of the draft that are crossed out, additions and substitutions are inserted between lines, and rearrangement is indicated by an arrow.

Perhaps the best strategy for studying how revision affects the essay's conclusion is to read the published version through before reading the drafts. Careful examination of drafts A, B, and C will help you to see and understand the evolution of Miller's ending to her essay.

Final Essay

1   My son bought his first car when he was seventeen. It was a four year old Firebird with a decal of a huge bird sprawled across the long, mustard-yellow hood. It was neither sparkling new nor elegantly old; it had incipient rust on its body and some signs of trouble to come in its innards. He loved it.

2   His inclination toward cars surfaced early. Before he was three he identified by manufacturer nearly every car we passed on our daily three block walk to and from the playground. "Ford, Chevy, Mercury," he would announce, running ahead of me and pointing at each one as he named it. Baffled, and feeling a bit foolishly proud of my little savant, I once asked him how he knew that a particular car was a Ford. His expression showed puzzled concentration for a brief moment, and he replied, "Because it looks like a Ford." I might as well have asked him how he recognized me as his mother!

3   The Firebird became a central element in his life. He prided himself on caring for it, saved his money in anticipation of maintenance costs, and drove it to and from the events and places that mark the life of a seventeen, eighteen, nineteen year old: the prom, the first three hour trip to college, the regular treks home and back during school breaks, the drive home after graduation. I know little about the friends and dates, conversations, laughter, and youthful angst that somehow became identified with that mass of mustard-yellow metal with the

bird on the hood. I do know that by the time my son returned home after four years of school, both he and his car had done their share of living.

4   He continued to nurture his car along during the years of transition from college life to the adult world of employment. I watched with practical, adult dismay as he spent his precious savings on parts, often tracked down diligently in distant locations when they were no longer available from any local source. One year the car emerged from a long stay at a body shop with brand new bumpers and fenders, and a sleek new hood. The bird was gone—my son's somewhat reluctant concession to adulthood.

5   Last week he called from a curbside telephone. He told me in gentle stages about having had some "car trouble," of a "fender-bender," and finally that his car had been "totalled." His voice was firm with only a hint of a tremor. The accident had occurred three hours earlier on a storm-washed highway; no other car was involved, he was not hurt, the police had come, and his car was on a flat bed truck. Towing was impossible because the front end had split away from the rest of the body, spilling its contents across two lanes of the highway.

6   I sat at the kitchen table, numbly absorbing the information. Inexpressibly grateful for his safety, terrified, though unable to fully conceive of what might have been, I waited to see him. I needed to reassure myself of his physical wholeness, but I worried too about his emotional state. He told me later that he had pounded the steering wheel in rage and frustration when the car hit a barrier after it had skidded on a sheet of water and veered out of control.

7   As I listened, I remembered once thinking that I never saw him more confident, more at ease, more graceful than he was while driving his car. Now he told me how he had at first gently guided the wheel one way and then the other, feeling for a split second that the tires were about to grip, then realizing that they weren't and that he was going to hit. He remembered the first instant of silence and then reaching down to shift into park—while the transmission and engine were scattered along the center lane and he and the rest of the car were in the right.

8   He set up a flashing yellow light which had survived the impact, waved traffic on with a flashlight, waited for the police, and walked off the highway to the nearest phone to call his office. Finally he watched his car collected into a mangled heap and driven to a collision shop. It was there that he got to work removing salvageable parts, feeling, as he said, as if he were cannibalizing a friend. A curious passerby stopped to look at the wreck and asked if that was his car. My son said it was and that it was for sale! No, he didn't get an offer.

9   He talked that day and the next, quietly, sporadically, to his father, sometimes to me, to a friend, to his sister, each time reliving the details, asking himself again and again if there was something he could have done and didn't. He always seemed to come up with the same stunned sense of triumph and pain: he was alive; he had lost his car.

10   Our driveway has a large oil stain, a reminder of one of the car's last ailments. I will not miss the Firebird very much, but I will never forget it. I look

at my son, admiring and proud of his quiet strength and resilience. He is hurt and chastened by his experience. He is glad to be alive and ready to move on.

11   The Bird is gone, and an era has ended, but there's a young man out there ready to start a new one.

Draft A

Our driveway has a large oil stain, a reminder of one of
                of the car's   Firebird
the last ailments. ~~He~~ I will not miss the car very much, but

I will never forget it. I look at my son, amazed one more

time at his ability to surprise me. He is hurt and chastened
                                   glad to be alive and
by his experience. He is ready to move on. ~~The seventeen~~

~~The car is gone, so is the seventeen year old who spent the~~

~~first thousand dollars along~~ An era has ended) ~~for him~~
                                                      young
Watch our driveway for newest developments. ↱there's a man

out there ready to start a new one.

Draft B

1   Our driveway has a large oil stain, a reminder of one of

the car's last ailments. I will not miss the Firebird very
                                                admiring
much, but I will never forget it. I look at my son, (amazed)
                                                      H
and proud of his quiet strength and resilience. He is hurt

and ⁄chastened by his experience. He is glad to be alive and

ready to move on.

2   Watch our driveway for newest developments. An era has

ended, and there's a young man out there ready to start a new

one.

Draft C

1   Our driveway has a large oil stain, a reminder of one of
the car's last ailments. I will not miss the Firebird very
much, but I will never forget it. I look at my son, admiring
and proud of his quiet strength and resilience. He is hurt
and chastened by his experience. He is glad to be alive and
ready to move on.

2   ⟨ ~~Watch our driveway for newest developments.~~ The Bird is gone, and an ~~An⟩~~ era has
ended, ~~and~~ but there's a young man out there ready to start a new
one.

Final Version

1   Our driveway has a large oil stain, a reminder of one of
the car's last ailments. I will not miss the Firebird very
much, but I will never forget it. I look at my son, admiring
and proud of his quiet strength and resilience. He is hurt
and chastened by his experience. He is glad to be alive and
ready to move on.

2   The Bird is gone, and an era has ended, but there's a
young man out there ready to start a new one.

Comparing Draft and Essay

As you read the drafts and the published version of the conclusion to "Farewell to the Bird," you might notice that draft B is primarily a clean copy of draft A and displays Miller's final decisions about the changes she made while composing. Draft C incorporates additional revisions and ultimately becomes the published version of the essay (see published paragraphs 10 and 11).

1. Why do you think that Miller chooses to rearrange draft A? What is gained by placing the last sentences of the draft into a new paragraph?

2. In her statement about why she wrote this piece, Miller asserts that the essay is really about her relationship with her son. How do these revisions of draft A help to convey her intended meaning? What do the revisions tell you about how she now perceives this relationship?

3. Draft C introduces important changes in its second paragraph. The addition of the clause "The Bird is gone" states the finality of the event. Why, however, do you think that Miller deletes the sentence "Watch our driveway for newest developments"? How does this revision affect the tone of the conclusion?

4. How do the paragraphs presented above help to conclude this essay? What impact do the revisions have on the essay's effectiveness?

Maya Angelou

Maya Angelou (b. 1928) was born in St. Louis. An actress and a poet, she has written several autobiographies, including *I Know Why the Caged Bird Sings* (1969) and *All God's Children Need Traveling Shoes* (1986), and is currently a professor at Wake Forest University. This is her description of *where* she writes and *what* she does.

> I keep in my writing room a Bible, a dictionary, *Roget's Thesaurus*, a bottle of sherry, cigarettes, an ashtray, and three or four decks of playing cards. During the five hours I spend there I use every object, but I play solitaire more than I actually write. It seems to me that when my hands and small mind (a Southern black phrase) are engaged in placing the reds on the blacks and the blacks on the reds, my working mind arranges and rearranges the characters and the plot. Finally, when they are in a plausible order, I simply have to write down where they are and what they say.

As you read her essay, from *Singin' and Swingin' and Getting Merry Like Christmas* (1976), prepare a mental profile of Angelou's intended audience.

Step Forward in the Car, Please

1   My room had all the cheeriness of a dungeon and the appeal of a tomb. It was going to be impossible to stay there, but leaving held no attraction for me, either. The answer came to me with the suddenness of a collision. I would go to work. Mother wouldn't be difficult to convince; after all, in school I was a year ahead of my grade and Mother was a firm believer in self-sufficiency. In fact, she'd be pleased to think that I had that much gumption, that much of her in my character. (She liked to speak of herself as the original "do-it-yourself girl.")

2   Once I had settled on getting a job, all that remained was to decide which kind of job I was most fitted for. My intellectual pride had kept me from selecting typing, shorthand, or filing as subjects in school, so office work was ruled out. War plants and shipyards demanded birth certificates, and mine would reveal me to be fifteen, and ineligible for work. So the well-paying defense jobs were also out. Women had replaced men on the streetcars as conductors and motormen, and the thought of sailing up and down the hills of San Francisco in a dark-blue uniform, with a money changer at my belt, caught my fancy.

3   Mother was as easy as I had anticipated. The world was moving so fast, so much money was being made, so many people were dying in Guam, and Germany, that hordes of strangers became good friends overnight. Life was cheap and death entirely free. How could she have the time to think about my academic career?

4   To her question of what I planned to do, I replied that I would get a job on the streetcars. She rejected the proposal with: "They don't accept colored people on the streetcars."

5   I would like to claim an immediate fury which was followed by the noble determination to break the restricting tradition. But the truth is, my first reaction was one of disappointment. I'd pictured myself, dressed in a neat blue serge suit, my money changer swinging jauntily at my waist, and a cheery smile for the passengers which would make their own work day brighter.

6   From disappointment, I gradually ascended the emotional ladder to haughty indignation, and finally to that state of stubbornness where the mind is locked like the jaws of an enraged bulldog.

7   I would go to work on the streetcars and wear a blue serge suit. Mother gave me her support with one of her usual terse asides, "That's what you want to do? Then nothing beats a trial but a failure. Give it everything you've got. I've told you many times, 'Can't Do is like Don't Care.' Neither of them has a home."

8   Translated, that meant there was nothing a person can't do, and there should be nothing a human being didn't care about. It was the most positive encouragement I could have hoped for.

9   In the offices of the Market Street Railway Company, the receptionist seemed as surprised to see me there as I was surprised to find the interior dingy and drab. Somehow I had expected waxed surfaces and carpeted floors. If I had met no resistance, I might have decided against working for such a poor-mouth-looking concern. As it was, I explained that I had come to see about a job. She asked, was I sent by an agency, and when I replied that I was not, she told me they were only accepting applicants from agencies.

10   The classified pages of the morning papers had listed advertisements for motorettes and conductorettes and I reminded her of that. She gave me a face full of astonishment that my suspicious nature would not accept.

11   "I am applying for the job listed in this morning's *Chronicle* and I'd like to be presented to your personnel manager." While I spoke in supercilious accents, and looked at the room as if I had an oil well in my own backyard, my armpits were being pricked by millions of hot pointed needles. She saw her escape and dived into it.

12   "He's out. He's out for the day. You might call him tomorrow and if he's in, I'm sure you can see him." Then she swiveled her chair around on its rusty screws and with that I was supposed to be dismissed.

13   "May I ask his name?"

14   She half turned, acting surprised to find me still there.

15   "His name? Whose name?"

16   "Your personnel manager."

17   We were firmly joined in the hypocrisy to play out the scene.

18   "The personnel manager? Oh, he's Mr. Cooper, but I'm not sure you'll find him here tomorrow. He's . . . Oh, but you can try."

19   "Thank you."

20   "You're welcome."

21   And I was out of the musty room and into the even mustier lobby. In the street I saw the receptionist and myself going faithfully through paces that were stale with familiarity, although I had never encountered that kind of situation

before and, probably, neither had she. We were like actors who, knowing the play by heart, were still able to cry afresh over the old tragedies and laugh spontaneously at the comic situations.

22   The miserable little encounter had nothing to do with me, the me of me, any more than it had to do with that silly clerk. The incident was a recurring dream concocted years before by whites, and it eternally came back to haunt us all. The secretary and I were like people in a scene where, because of harm done by one ancestor or another, we were bound to duel to the death. (Also because the play must end somewhere.)

23   I went further than forgiving the clerk; I accepted her as a fellow victim of the same puppeteer.

24   On the streetcar, I put my fare into the box and the conductorette looked at me with the usual hard eyes of white contempt. "Move into the car, please move on in the car." She patted her money changer.

25   Her Southern nasal accent sliced my meditation and I looked deep into my thoughts. All lies, all comfortable lies. The receptionist was not innocent and neither was I. The whole charade we had played out in that waiting room had to do with me, black, and her, white.

26   I wouldn't move into the streetcar but stood on the ledge over the conductor, glaring. My mind shouted so energetically that the announcement made my veins stand out, and my mouth tighten into a prune.

27   I WOULD HAVE THE JOB. I WOULD BE A CONDUCTORETTE AND SLING A FULL MONEY CHANGER FROM MY BELT. I WOULD.

28   The next three weeks were a honeycomb of determination with apertures for the days to go in and out. The Negro organizations to whom I appealed for support bounced me back and forth like a shuttlecock on a badminton court. Why did I insist on that particular job? Openings were going begging that paid nearly twice the money. The minor officials with whom I was able to win an audience thought me mad. Possibly I was.

29   Downtown San Francisco became alien and cold, and streets I had loved in a personal familiarity were unknown lanes that twisted with malicious intent. My trips to the streetcar office were of the frequency of a person on salary. The struggle expanded. I was no longer in conflict only with the Market Street Railway but with the marble lobby of the building which housed its offices, and elevators and their operators.

30   During this period of strain Mother and I began our first steps on the long path toward mutual adult admiration. She never asked for reports and I didn't offer any details. But every morning she made breakfast, gave me carfare and lunch money, as if I were going to work. She comprehended that in the struggle lies the joy. That I was no glory seeker was obvious to her, and that I had to exhaust every possibility before giving in was also clear.

31   On my way out of the house one morning she said, "Life is going to give you just what you put in it. Put your whole heart in everything you do, and pray, then you can wait." Another time she reminded me that "God helps those

who help themselves." She had a store of aphorisms which she dished out as the occasion demanded. Strangely, as bored as I was with clichés, her inflection gave them something new, and set me thinking for a little while at least. Later when asked how I got my job, I was never able to say exactly. I only knew that one day, which was tiresomely like all the others before it, I sat in the Railway office, waiting to be interviewed. The receptionist called me to her desk and shuffled a bundle of paper to me. They were job application forms. She said they had to be filled out in triplicate. I had little time to wonder if I had won or not, for the standard questions reminded me of the necessity for lying. How old was I? List my previous jobs, starting from the last held and go backward to the first. How much money did I earn, and why did I leave the position? Give two references (not relatives). I kept my face blank (an old art) and wrote quickly the fable of Marguerite Johnson, aged nineteen, former companion and driver for Mrs. Annie Henderson (a White Lady) in Stamps, Arkansas.

32   I was given blood tests, aptitude tests, and physical coordination tests, then on a blissful day I was hired as the first Negro on the San Francisco streetcars.

33   Mother gave me the money to have my blue serge suit tailored, and I learned to fill out work cards, operate the money changer and punch transfers. The time crowded together and at an End of Days I was swinging on the back of the rackety trolley, smiling sweetly and persuading my charges to "step forward in the car, please."

34   For one whole semester the streetcars and I shimmied up and scooted down the sheer hills of San Francisco. I lost some of my need for the black ghetto's shielding-sponge quality, as I changed and cleared my way down Market Street, with its honky-tonk homes for homeless sailors, past the quiet retreat of Golden Gate Park and along closed undwelled-in-looking dwellings of the Sunset District.

35   My work shifts were split so haphazardly that it was easy to believe that my superiors had chosen them maliciously. Upon mentioning my suspicions to Mother, she said, "Don't you worry about it. You ask for what you want, and you pay for what you get. And I'm going to show you that it ain't no trouble when you pack double."

36   She stayed awake to drive me out to the car barn at four-thirty in the mornings, or to pick me up when I was relieved just before dawn. Her awareness of life's perils convinced her that while I would be safe on the public conveyances, she "wasn't about to trust a taxi driver with her baby."

37   When the spring classes began, I resumed my commitment with formal education. I was so much wiser and older, so much more independent, with a bank account and clothes that I had bought for myself, that I was sure I had learned and earned the magic formula which would make me a part of the life my contemporaries led.

38   Not a bit of it. Within weeks, I realized that my schoolmates and I were on paths moving away from each other. They were concerned and excited over the approaching football games. They concentrated great interest on who was worthy

of being student body president, and when the metal bands would be removed from their teeth, while I remembered conducting a streetcar in the uneven hours of the morning.

Considering Content

1. Angelou's essay is from her autobiography published in 1969. What is the social or historical significance of the situation she describes?

2. What profile of Angelou emerges from the incidents she includes? Do you agree with her description of herself as possibly "mad." Explain.

3. Angelou frequently speaks of the mutual hypocrisy or "actions" of the participants in this account of racial antagonism. Were there also any moments of cooperation and mutual gain?

4. What values does Angelou share with her mother in addition to respect for privacy? To what extent did her mother influence her system of values? What values have you learned from your parents?

Considering Craft

1. Review the Guidelines for Introductions (page 201) and evaluate Angelou's opening paragraph.

2. What is Angelou's purpose in writing about her struggle to obtain this particular summer job? Is she simply recording an experience or is she also making a point? If so, state it.

3. Characterize Angelou's audience. Is she writing only for black people who have had similar experiences or is her intended audience more inclusive? Explain your answer.

4. Angelou makes references to her mother at various points in the essay. How does this affect its meaning? To what extent does including her mother broaden its appeal?

5. Characterize Angelou's tone. Is it objective, sarcastic, informative, angry? Is it consistent with her subject? Why or why not?

6. Read over the last two paragraphs of Angelou's essay. What technique does she use to link them together? Why is her conclusion effective? How has she avoided a boring summary statement?

Peter Steinhart

Peter Steinhart (b. 1943) is an editor at *Audubon* magazine. We think you will find his comments on his writing process informative:

> As to how I prepare for these essays, I take care to pick a subject that interests me and that fits the particular magazine audience I am writing for. I read extensively and talk to anybody who seems to have anything to say about the subject. I do not keep a journal, but I take a lot of notes when reading and interviewing. I don't begin writing until I have a first paragraph, usually an opening scene or an anecdote that suggests or encapsulates the central issue, clearly in mind. I revise heavily, and seldom send out a manuscript I haven't revised at least ten times.

As you read, "Noses, Naturally," first published in *Audubon,* pay particular attention to the first paragraph of the essay. To what extent does it conform to the comments in his statement?

Noses, Naturally

1   There are times when only the smell of things will do. The first whiff of pine when you go to the woods. The smell of new-mown hay. The aspirin tang of streamside willows. The scent of fresh beginnings on a summer morning when the rising sun reclaims the vapors of night and the earth breathes a warm must of grass and mold, sap and blossom. Such things delight the nose. They tell of the ease and promise of things left alone. And they reach into our souls, sneaking past the fortress gates of reason to speak directly to our feelings.

2   At such moments, we want to smell more. That sounds comical, because in the loftiness of our cultural elevation, noses are comical. We don't praise noses, except perhaps to admire the juvenile miniature of a movie starlet's. In the comics, we exaggerate noses to make it clear we may laugh at a character, or shrink noses to make a character seem tough, heroic, unlikely to trip over his own feelings.

3   We are slightly ashamed of what the nose does. In an age that makes perfection a civic duty, the nose still finds putrescence and decay. It taunts us with the news that bacteria are more potent than bank notes. It reminds us that we haven't yet figured out what to do with sewage, chemical waste, dead birds, windthrown trees, or misspent humanity. And the blessings of pleasing aromas seem trivial in an age of chemical mayhem and nuclear clouds. Spring weather and hot soup can't compete for headlines with airline crashes and summit talks. We no longer pretend, as men did in the Middle Ages, that nosegays can hide the smell of trouble.

4   Some of us nevertheless put great stock in the power of smell. There are scents we keep in memory, like favorite photographs or old songs, and they

trigger moments of intense feeling. Along a road I take into the mountains, there is a dry canyon where the scent of pine dives into my heart. I think of that place all winter when I am eager for days of sunlight and sparkling streams. My first memory of Africa is of standing at midnight on the runway of Entebbe Airport, breathing in rumors of grass and spice and mystery. A lion moved across the runway, a tawny shadow in the dim moonlight, and faded into the grass. I often think, too, of a June afternoon when the hills of Virginia were full of the perfume of honeysuckle and I rolled down the car windows and breathed deeply, the sugary air inflating my spirit until I felt I must sing. It is an odd memory, but it keeps returning, perhaps to tell me about the back roads to joy.

5   Some of us trust deeply in what we smell. Charles Dickens read character with his nose; he described E. W. B. Childers in *Hard Times* as "a smell of lamp oil, straw, orange peel, horses, provender, and sawdust." Dan McKenzie, a Scottish surgeon, noticed in some patients "a piney aromatic odor" which "becomes stronger on the approach of death." Rousseau had poor vision but could identify a hundred species of plants by smell. Helen Keller foretold the weather. Hours before a storm, she felt "a throb of expectancy, a slight quiver, a concentration in my nostrils. As the storm draws near, my nostrils dilate, the better to receive the flood of earth odors which seem to multiply and extend, until I feel the splash of rain against my cheek."

6   The sense of smell varies widely among men. Tests by osphresiologist John Amoore of Olfacto-Labs in California show that human sensitivity to odor generally fits a bell curve, but, says Amoore, "one person in a hundred will just go right through the whole kit and identify the smells. The sensitivity of such a person is at least five hundred times more than an average person's." A Japanese researcher reports that about one in five of his subjects has such super abilities. "It may be," says Amoore, "that there are still humans around who are just as sensitive as dogs."

7   The sense of smell is our oldest sense. It is an achievement made by aquatic ancestors, long before our mammalian forebears leapt into the trees, looked around, and found eyesight more dazzling. The olfactory lobe, deep in our brains, is called the paleocortex in men and rhinencephalon or nose brain in fish. Today, we still cannot smell anything unless it enters the watery medium of the mucous membrane in the nose.

8   Those mammals whose noses are close to the ground, where odors linger and eyesight isn't as dependable a means of judging what is going on, still exalt the sense of smell. Coyotes deposit scents as personal calling cards on rocks and bushes for other coyotes to read. Some deer have scent glands on their feet to mark their passage through fields. Dogs like to hang their heads out of car windows, not to cool off but to run the scenery through their noses, to drink in a delicious stew of people, dogs, skunks, dead cats, and decaying beetles. A dog can get as much mental exercise just sitting in a summer breeze as a man gets watching a Shakespearean play.

9   Men once had olfactory skills worth bragging about. Polynesian sailors followed the windblown scent of coco palms to colonize islands far beyond the

horizon. American Indians tracked game by smell. Columbus reported that New World natives could identify an individual's footprints by scent. Some African witch doctors claim to be able to smell witches. We don't see such abilities today. Most of us city slickers have trouble telling pomade from perfume.

10   Part of the reason is that in cities the human scents that ought to be of interest to us are masked in the whine of combustion and the stench of chemicals not of nature's making. We move about in a soup of automobile exhaust, industrial dust, paint fumes, the shriek of iron grating upon iron. The smell of oil and solvents loiters in our noses like street-corner toughs, scaring off more subtle and civil scents. The odor of combustion is a shackle on our souls. It tells us we are subject to purposes not of our own making, to wills as severe and unswerving as a four-lane highway.

11   But it's not just a matter of pickling our noses in oil. Olfactory ignorance is older than the automobile. The decline of the nose arises out of smell's special properties. The emotional centers of our brains developed out of the olfactory lobe, and because the two are intertwined, smell triggers strong feelings. Naturalist Roy Bedichek observed that "the words for smell mainly deal with the sensations they respectively arouse, as disgusting, pleasurable, suffocating, intoxicating." By smell we often pick our strong impulses. We can smell anger, fear, exhaustion. A friend of mine, walking up New York City's First Avenue to meet his domineering mother, said, "We must be close. I can smell guilt."

12   Scent tells us there is more going on than we can see on the evening news. And what we see may be at war with what we smell. Our cerebral hemispheres, which house our ability to see and to calculate, developed later and on top of the olfactory lobe. Reason and language are tied to sight, and we think of genius as the ability to think beyond the reach of the eye. Modern men trust vision over feeling. But our feelings are close to the sense of smell, and they live together in a different neighborhood in the brain. That can cause problems, for we cannot always retrieve what we smell or feel through language. A lady's perfume may thus become an argument that words cannot break. A foul smell, like an act of sorcery, attacks us where we breathe, not where we think. The sense of smell is speechless. And without words to govern it, rebellious. A perfume tester told Amoore that when he was fatigued, his nose failed him. "If he was stressed about something, he fell apart," says Amoore.

13   The conflict between smell and vision may have charted human history. Austin Meredith, a California science writer, thinks the loss of smell may have made it possible for men to live in cities. He theorized that the sense of smell once kept men dispersed in small groups. "It has been demonstrated," he says, "that mammals use the nose for population control." Female mice, for example, bred to one male may not reproduce if exposed to the odor of another male. Meredith thinks a similar mechanism may once have triggered aggression between men of different tribes, but that genetic change ended the use of smell as a dispersing agent perhaps five thousand years ago. He thinks we may find in the brains of some isolated tribal peoples a dully developed *pars intermedia*, an

area of the pituitary that is undeveloped in men and whales but elaborated in more olfactory mammals.

14   I see the decline of the nose as a consequence, rather than a cause, of city life. I believe our olfactory ignorance began when men sought to separate themselves from their biological roots, to make men a cultural wonder rather than a child of nature. The sense of human purpose, which in civic culture must ride above all others, requires that we free the air of subversive scents. Urban life bathes us in anguish, assaults us with the smells of anxiety and thwarted impulse. The cumulative odor of discomfort could drag us from our tasks. We must suppress the sense of smell lest strange odors lead us astray, like moths chasing pheromones in the wind of a summer night, or like idle youths chasing rebellion in the hopelessness of poverty.

15   So, we sanitize. We fight the smell of dumps and slaughterhouses. We spray our bedrooms and kitchens with lemon and rosewater, scents that will, in time, become so familiar that we no longer notice. Deodorizing is big business. We spend fortunes on underarm deodorants, poisoning sweat glands to hide the smell of anguish. At home, we deploy Airwick, which uses "proprietary chemical compound" to inhibit odors. A Monsanto chemist recently found a family of chemicals that prevent the nose from detecting the sulfurous smell of rotten eggs or the odors of fatty acids. There are perhaps one thousand flavor and fragrance companies in New York and New Jersey alone.

16   In Africa and Asia, where men do not wage this aerosal war, the villages smell no more of sweat and anger than, say, Atlanta or Duluth. There, however, men are less confined by space and use.

17   We shall not deodorize the world. The nose will never become merely an ornament on which to hang our eyes. It will go on being a part of the way we penetrate the mysteries that stir beyond our skins. There is yet a part of the brain that demands fresh air. We long to put our noses back into the wind. But to do so, we must clear our sinuses of smoke and haste. And clearing our heads is one of the great necessities of wild places. When we go to the woods, we wait expectantly for the first whiff of maple, the first scent of water. It comes furtively. It takes hours to get the city out of one's nose.

18   But then you suddenly notice that fir and pine and cedar each have their own distinctive smell. The air is full of rumors. The invisible currents that rise from the forest floor carry a banquet of scents: the vanilla of pine needles, the sweet smoke of forest molds, the familiar leather of your own boots. You want to breathe deeper, to expel the exhausts of the city and draw in the color and spice. And the more you smell, the more you trust your nose.

19   You change senses. While the eye keeps a distance between object and observer, the nose draws the world inside you. Barriers drop. There is none of the glare that gets in your eye, none of the noise that obscures birdsong. You are sharing the breath of bee and bear and birchwood, taking it deep into your heart.

20   I have at such moments become aware of things I could not see. The vinegary sadness of a tree, still green, dying beside the trail. The sour, wet

fustiness where a bear recently crossed the path. I have sensed not only other hikers but something of their moods. It seems possible, at times, to sort by smell those who have found what they are looking for in the woods from those who are still searching for it in the pages of their guidebooks. I believe I begin to smell joy, trust, betrayal, confusion.

21   At such moments, the engagement of the senses is full. I feel primitive and intensely alive. I am exploring an unseen world, head close to the ground, heart free in the forest. It is one of the reasons we need woods and meadows, tidal flats and desert washes, places where, like a snake, one can close one's eyes and know just what is going on. The smell of rain coming, the toasty aroma of the newly turned earth, the sweet hay smell of elephants passing, or the sharp mustiness of snakes in the grass are enlivening and real. And to know them is to reassert the man over the machine, our own nature over economic purpose. To know them is to be human again.

Considering Content

1. Is it true that "smell triggers strong feelings"? Are these stronger than those triggered by taste or touch? Is that why we cannot develop smells into a "fine art," as we can sounds or sights? Why do you suppose Steinhart never mentions either taste or touch?

2. What, according to Steinhart, is the physiological explanation for the close connection between smell and feeling?

3. How could a more powerful sense of smell have prevented the development of cities? Which came first, according to Steinhart, weakened smell or the development of cities? Why was weakened smell a necessary precondition for the development of cities?

4. Where does Steinhart think we learn to smell again? Do you agree? Can you suggest a better place?

5. To what extent do you share Steinhart's excitement about feeling "primitive"? Does this feeling have anything to do with being close to nature? Explain.

Considering Craft

1. "There are times when only the smell of things will do." Is this an appealing way to begin an essay? Does the last sentence of the first paragraph make you want to continue reading?

2. Are the specific examples in the first paragraph effective? Make a list of ten examples of pleasurable smells that Steinhart might have used to open the paragraph.

3. Make a list of other effective topic sentences in Steinhart's essay and explain what makes them effective.

4. Steinhart's purpose is to convince you of the importance of your sense of smell. What evidence does he provide to support his thesis that there is great diversity in ability to smell?

5. Read over Steinhart's conclusion. Does it mainly summarize his thesis, or does it introduce a new aspect of his subject? Explain your answer.

Brent Staples

Brent Staples (b. 1951) is from Chester, Pennsylvania. He has a Ph.D. in psychology from the University of Chicago. He is a frequent contributor to *Harper's, New York Woman,* and *The New York Times Magazine.* Since 1990 he has been on the editorial board of *The New York Times* and he is currently writing his first book, *Parallel Time.* After reading his essay, write a journal entry on what Staples reveals about himself in this piece about his brother.

A Brother's Murder

1   It has been more than two years since my telephone rang with the news that my younger brother Blake—just 22 years old—had been murdered. The young man who killed him was only 24. Wearing a ski mask, he emerged from a car, fired six times at close range with a massive .44 Magnum, then fled. The two had once been inseparable friends. A senseless rivalry—beginning, I think, with an argument over a girlfriend—escalated from posturing, to threats, to violence, to murder. The way the two were living, death could have come to either of them from anywhere. In fact, the assailant had already survived multiple gunshot wounds from an incident much like the one in which my brother lost his life.

2   As I wept for Blake I felt wrenched backward into events and circumstances that had seemed light-years gone. Though a decade apart, we both were raised in Chester, Pennsylvania, an angry, heavily black, heavily poor, industrial city southwest of Philadelphia. There, in the 1960's, I was introduced to mortality, not by the old and failing, but by beautiful young men who lay wrecked after sudden explosions of violence. The first, I remember from my 14th year—Johnny, brash lover of fast cars, stabbed to death two doors from my house in a fight over a pool game. The next year, my teenage cousin, Wesley, whom I loved very much, was shot dead. The summers blur. Milton, an angry young neighbor, shot a crosstown rival, wounding him badly. William, another teen-age neighbor, took a shotgun blast to the shoulder in some urban drama

and displayed his bandages proudly. His brother, Leonard, severely beaten, lost an eye and donned a black patch. It went on.

3   I recall not long before I left for college, two local Vietnam veterans—one from the Marines, one from the Army—arguing fiercely, nearly at blows about which outfit had done the most in the war. The most killing, they meant. Not much later, I read a magazine article that set that dispute in a context. In the story, a noncommissioned officer—a sergeant, I believe—said he would pass up any number of affluent, suburban-born recruits to get hard-core soldiers from the inner city. They jumped into the rice paddies with "their manhood on their sleeves," I believe he said. These two items—the veterans arguing and the sergeant's words—still characterize for me the circumstances under which black men in their teens and twenties kill one another with such frequency. With a touchy paranoia born of living battered lives, they are desperate to be *real* men. Killing is only *machismo* taken to the extreme. Incursions to be punished by death were many and minor, and they remain so: they include stepping on the wrong toe, literally; cheating in a drug deal; simply saying "I dare you" to someone holding a gun; crossing territorial lines in a gang dispute. My brother grew up to wear his manhood on his sleeve. And when he died, he was in that group—black, male and in its teens and early twenties—that is far and away the most likely to murder or be murdered.

4   I left the East Coast after college, spent the mid- and late-1970s in Chicago as a graduate student, taught for a time, then became a journalist. Within ten years of leaving my hometown, I was overeducated and "upwardly mobile," ensconced on a quiet, tree-lined street where voices raised in anger were scarcely ever heard. The telephone, like some grim umbilical, kept me connected to the old world with news of deaths, imprisonings and misfortune. I felt emotionally beaten up. Perhaps to protect myself, I added a psychological dimension to the physical distance I had already achieved. I rarely visited my hometown. I shut it out.

5   As I fled the past, so Blake embraced it. On Christmas of 1983, I traveled from Chicago to a black section of Roanoke, Virginia, where he then lived. The desolate public housing projects, the hopeless, idle young men crashing against one another—these reminded me of the embittered town we'd grown up in. It was a place where once I would have been comfortable, or at least sure of myself. Now, hearing of my brother's forays into crime, his scrapes with police and street thugs, I was scared, unsteady on foreign terrain.

6   I saw that Blake's romance with the street life and the hustler image had flowered dangerously. One evening that late December, standing in some Roanoke dive among drug dealers and grim, hair-trigger losers, I told him I feared for his life. He had affected the image of the tough he wanted to be. But behind the dark glasses and the swagger, I glimpsed the baby-faced toddler I'd once watched over. I nearly wept. I wanted desperately for him to live. The young think themselves immortal, and a dangerous light shone in his eyes as he spoke laughingly of making fools of the policemen who had raided his apartment

looking for drugs. He cried out as I took his right hand. A line of stitches lay between the thumb and index finger. Kickback from a shotgun, he explained, nothing serious. Gunplay had become part of his life.

7   I lacked the language simply to say: Thousands have lived this for you and died. I fought the urge to lift him bodily and shake him. This place and the way you are living smells of death to me, I said. Take some time away, I said. Let's go downtown tomorrow and buy a plane ticket anywhere, take a bus trip, anything to get away and cool things off. He took my alarm casually. We arranged to meet the following night—an appointment he would not keep. We embraced as though through glass. I drove away.

8   As I stood in my apartment in Chicago holding the receiver that evening in February 1984, I felt as though part of my soul had been cut away. I questioned myself then, and I still do. Did I not reach back soon enough or earnestly enough for him? For weeks I awoke crying from a recurrent dream in which I chased him, urgently trying to get him to read a document I had, as though reading it would protect him from what had happened in waking life. His eyes shining like black diamonds, he smiled and danced just beyond my grasp. When I reached for him, I caught only the space where he had been.

Considering Content

1. What do we learn about Blake's way of life from the first paragraph of the essay?

2. What examples does Staples cite to convey that he "was introduced to maturity not by the old and failing, but by beautiful young men who lay wrecked after sudden explosions of violence"?

3. Why does Staples include the argument between the Vietnam veterans? How does it add to your understanding of his thesis that "killing is only *machismo* taken to the extreme"? Do you agree? Why or why not?

4. How did the narrator escape the fate of the other young men in the ghetto? Does the fact that he made it alter your opinion of those who didn't? Explain.

5. "As I fled the past, so Blake embraced it." How does this choice affect the brothers' relationship?

6. In the concluding paragraph, Staples reveals that he is still haunted by his brother's death as well as guilty about what he had not done. Are his guilt feelings justified? Could he have altered his brother's destiny? Explain.

Considering Craft

1. Read over the first paragraph of the essay. What makes it an effective introduction? Describe your reaction to the first sentence.

2. Review the topic sentences (see Glossary) in each paragraph. How does the author support them? How do they contribute to the essay's meaning?

3. Staples uses flashback (see Chronology in Glossary) several times in the essay. Identify examples of this and discuss their impact on the essay's purpose.

4. Staples tries to maintain an objective tone. Are there points at which his tone becomes more personal? What examples can you cite? What is their effect?

5. Read over the conclusion and analyze the elements that make it effective. Why is the example of the recurring dream particularly compelling? What does it reveal about the author's attitude toward his subject?

Guidelines for Introductions and Conclusions

Introductions

1. Grab your audience's attention with a striking statement, anecdote, question, picture, quotation, definition, or description.

2. State the purpose and thesis of your essay.

3. Don't begin with a phrase such as "In this paper I am going to write about. . . ."

4. Avoid one-sentence introductions.

5. Omit sentences that are just fillers such as those beginning with "I hope to. . . ."

Conclusions

1. Make your ending memorable by presenting a vivid final image.

2. Try to involve your reader with a provocative question, a passionate plea, a call to action, or a prediction.

3. Avoid introducing a new point.

4. Avoid ending with a tacked-on moral lesson.

5. Avoid clichéd phrases such as "in conclusion," " I will now end my paper," or "to sum up" as ways of introducing the ending of an essay.

Warm-up Exercises

1. Make a journal entry on an idea that crystallized in your mind after a recent conversation. Read over what you have written. How could you most effectively introduce your journal entry? Review the guidelines for introductions and try

writing at least two possible introductory paragraphs reversing the position of the thesis statement just as the student did in writing about Meryl Streep.

2. Browse through your favorite magazine looking particularly at the introductory paragraphs of the articles. Clip three that you think effective and analyze them carefully. To what extent do they follow the guidelines for introductory paragraphs? How are they similar? Which introduction attracted you most? Why?

3. Write an introduction and a conclusion in support of one of the following thesis statements:

   a. Family members are not always predictable.
   b. Our society has taken the idea of "letting it all hang out" too far.
   c. Sex education in schools is harmful to children.
   d. Jazz is popular among college students.

4. Look through your journal for a controversial statement and write a concluding paragraph that supports it. Then assume an opposite point of view and write a concluding paragraph that refutes the statement.

5. Look through a magazine and select three articles that have convincing conclusions. Make notes on what makes them effective and then review the Guidelines for Introductions and Conclusions. What techniques have the authors used? Which conclusion is the most effective? Can you think of a way to use this method in your next essay?

6. Freewrite about your first summer job. Read over what you have written. Is there one idea on which you could elaborate? How might you effectively introduce it?

7. Brainstorm about one of the following:

ghetto	brothers
violence	families
drugs	memories
mortality	your first car
machismo	hustler
stereotypes	

Read over your list of associations and write two paragraphs. Then review the Guidelines for Introductions and Conclusions and write an introductory sentence and a concluding sentence for each of the paragraphs. Try to achieve an impact similar to that of the essayists in this chapter.

Writing/Revising Topics

1. Read through the "Help Wanted" section of your newspaper and clip an advertisement for a position you will be qualified for by graduation. Then write a letter of application, making sure you consult a handbook for the proper format of a business letter. When revising your letter, focus on the first and last paragraphs. Review the comments about business letters in this chapter's introduction and try to make your opening sentence interesting to a prospective employer. Remember that you want him or her to choose yours from among the many applications.

2. Brent Staples cites many examples of the violence and dangers inherent in ghetto life. Write an essay discussing the impressions that his brother's experiences you, including any ideas you had to modify as a result of reading about them. Clarify your purpose and meaning. Before revising, review Staples' introduction and conclusion. Think of a provocative statement to begin your essay and end with an effective comparison.

3. Peter Steinhart in "Noses, Naturally" wrote about the pleasures of smells. Write an essay on tastes using connotative language to appeal to your reader's sense of taste. Use your thesaurus to help you choose words associated with taste. In revising your essay, focus on the introduction and conclusion. Have you succeeded in introducing your subject in an appealing way? Is your reader likely to remember your conclusion?

4. Take notes during the class discussion of Richard Selzer's "Mercy," giving special attention to what your classmates say about Considering Content questions 5 and 7. Use these notes to generate a thesis on the topic of euthanasia. Write a draft reporting your and your classmates' positions and reasons. Then, following the Guidelines for Introductions and Conclusions, write these parts of the essay. Wait for a day or two, reread what you have written, make corrections and improvements, and write a final draft.

5. Using Warm-up Exercise 6 as the basis, write an essay for a specific audience discussing the finding of your first summer job and the impact of that experience. Before revising your essay, review Guidelines for Addressing Audience (page 130). Have you used examples that will appeal to your intended audience? Is your purpose clear? Now read over Angelou's introduction and conclusion and try to imitate her techniques in your first and last paragraphs.

6. Using Warm-up Exercise 7 as the basis, write an essay on the topic you selected, making sure that your tone is appropriate to your purpose, meaning, and intended audience. On revising, focus on your first and last paragraphs and experiment with different ways of beginning and ending your essay until you are satisfied with both paragraphs.

7. In relating her arduous efforts to obtain her first summer job, Maya Angelou writes, "In the struggle lies the joy." Have you also experienced a joyful struggle? If so, relate it in detail. Before revising, review the Guidelines for Introductions and Conclusions and pay particular attention to these two parts of your essay.

8. Have you recently acquired a possession that, like the "Bird," has affected your life or attitude in some way? If so, write an essay describing the changes that have occurred because of it. Consider your audience to be your English class. Have your group critique your first draft, then use their suggestions to revise the essay, paying particular attention to the introduction and conclusion.

Composing Narrative and Descriptive Essays

In Chapter 3 you were introduced to the three main parts of an essay, the introduction, body, and conclusion. The last chapter explained introductions and conclusions; this chapter and the next two will discuss the various kinds of body paragraphs.

The function of all body paragraphs is to support the thesis, but body paragraphs differ in the way they perform this function. Narrative and descriptive paragraphs are two of the most common, appearing, for example, in such diverse types of writing as personal letters, diaries, resumés, medical histories, laboratory reports, news stories, novels, and expository essays. A narrative essay is one in which narrative paragraphs predominate although the same essay may also contain paragraphs that support the thesis by other modes, such as those discussed in Chapters 8 and 9. Similarly, a descriptive essay would be one in which descriptive paragraphs predominate.

Narration

Narration is storytelling that makes a point. This definition implies that the purpose of a narrative is to share a main idea, and the meaning of a narrative is the main point to be shared.

Beyond these requirements, narration demands attention to *point of view, pacing, chronology,* and *transitions.* Whether you are writing fiction or nonfiction, you will have to choose a *point of view.* In everyday language the term *point of view* means opinion or attitude, as in the question, "What is your point of view on capital punishment?" In narration, however, point of view is a technical term meaning the consciousness through whom the story is conveyed or, simply, who is telling the story. There are four possible points of view, depending on the number of persons in the story whose thoughts and feelings are revealed—not by their speech or action but by "getting into their heads."

1. *First person*—narrator reveals *only his or her own* thoughts and feelings.
2. *Third person omniscient*—author reveals thoughts and feelings of *any number* of characters.
3. *Third person limited omniscient*—author reveals thoughts and feelings of *only one* character.
4. *Third person objective*—author reveals thoughts and feelings of *none* of the characters, as is usual in drama.

For a story in which you are a participant, first person with you as your own storyteller will probably seem the natural choice:

> *It was early morning when I went out to chop some wood for the kitchen. I had split hardly a dozen sticks when I turned toward the shed and saw a pair of green eyes staring from a hole in the wall. "Russell, bring me my shotgun," I yelled.*

But you could change the perspective by allowing Russell, another participant, to tell the story:

> *Al had just gone to the woodlot when all of a sudden I heard him yell to me to bring him his gun.*

Or you might want "green eyes" to be your narrator:

> *It's not easy finding shelter in these woods, so when I found an old woodshed I made it my home for the night. Whacks of an ax woke me the next morning, and I peered out a crack between the shingles to see, not five feet away. . . .*

Another way you can control how the story is told is to change the point of view to a third-person form.

> *Alan Smith paused after chopping half a dozen sticks of firewood to find a pair of green eyes peering out of a crack in the woodshed wall. Remembering the story he had heard last night, he yelled, "Russell, bring me my gun!"*

Deciding on a point of view is just as important as choosing the events (plot), the persons (characters), and the setting (place and time) of your story. Experiment with various points of view in your early drafts, and choose the one that best serves your purpose.

Pacing is the relative amount of detail apportioned to the various parts or scenes of your story. In some scenes every step of the action must be told; in others, the story must be sketched in only the boldest strokes. If you are writing about a race, for example, when is it important to detail every movement, when you are warming up or when you cross the finish line?

Chronology refers to the time sequence of the story. Many writers prefer to narrate a sequence chronologically, that is, as it actually occurred, starting at the beginning and stopping at the end. Others choose to reorganize time in flashbacks. Here the end of the story might be told first, with the beginning and middle added on to make the ending understandable. And there are other ways you can reorganize time. You can build to a climax by crowding more incidents into a shorter and shorter period of time. If you want a surprise ending, you simply withhold information. If you wish to create suspense you make your reader wait for the answer to the question "What happened next?" while at the same time giving just enough information to awaken curiosity.

Transition—words, phrases, or sentences—are important in all writing, but especially in narration. You are familiar with such ordering expressions as *first, second, finally, later, next, last.* Use them to direct the traffic in your stories. Put a clock or a calendar—figuratively speaking—in your story and use it to keep the reader alert and curious. Especially if you use flashbacks, you need words and phrases like *earlier, all at once,* and *at 3:41 sharp.*

The decisions you make regarding point of view, pacing, chronology, and transitions should aid you in establishing and reinforcing the purpose and meaning of your narrative, in addressing your audience, and in setting your tone. Using the *I* point of view (the first-person narrator) helps to bring an author closer to an audience; some narratives, however, benefit from a more distant point of view. Similarly, a fast-paced narrative will set an active, intense tone not usually found in a slow-paced one.

Description

A second fundamental method of paragraph development is *description*. Like narration, it is a kind of writing you encounter every day. Assessing your environment is primarily a function of description; you know your world through your sense of sight, hearing, smell, taste, and touch. When you attempt to communicate your knowledge of the environment, you rely on these senses.

Description, like narration and all the other methods of development, has its own specific requirements. You will need to *order* the details in some appropriate way, dramatic, spatial, or chronological. You can use dramatic order—building up to the most important details—with any kind of description, visual, olfactory, and so on. If your description is visual, you can use spatial order, beginning with the foreground and moving toward the farthest point, or vice versa. Some subjects, like a symphony, ballet, or battle, call for a primarily chronological order, that is, time order, but it may be necessary to combine spatial, chronological, and even dramatic order in one description, as you would, for example, in the description of a sunrise.

Most things lend themselves primarily to one kind of description: it is impossible to describe the view from a mountaintop without concentrating on vision, or to communicate the beauty of a symphony orchestra without mentioning sound, or to tell of an encounter with a skunk without invoking the sense of smell. Yet even though primarily one sense is operating, see if you can bring in other senses: what does the wind feel and sound like at the top of that mountain? What visual impression is made by the sight of twenty violinists playing a serenade for strings (for that matter, what does the serenade look like in your imagination?), and what does the deep thump of the timpani feel like? How did the skunk look before it sprayed you, and what did the spray feel like? Make the senses—as many as possible—work for you and the reader.

Another consideration you need to be aware of is the level of emotion that you will put into your description—its level of objectivity or subjectivity. Objective description is factual and exact. A laboratory technician, for example, must describe what he or she sees under the microscope in language stripped of personal and emotional overtones. Similarly, a witness in a courtroom must reproduce in words the defendant's or the victim's appearance detail by detail without embellishment. The purpose of subjective description, in contrast, is to give an emotional or personal interpretation or to create a mood; this type of description capitalizes on a *connotative* vocabulary that plays on the reader's values and attitudes.

If you are writing a subjective description, decide what *dominant impression* you require and choose vocabulary with the appropriate connotations. Puns and figures of speech such as *simile, metaphor, personification,* and *hyperbole* (see Figurative Language in the Glossary) can often convey more than a literal statement; for example, in the description of a sinister scene *creeper* can contribute more than the word *vine*. William Zinsser in his essay "Words" in Chapter 10 gives excellent advice on the search for the right word: "What is the difference," he asks, "between 'cajole,' 'wheedle,' 'blandish' and 'coax'?" He recommends *Webster's New Dictionary of Synonyms* and "that bulging grab-bag, *Roget's Thesaurus.*"

Since description is unified around a dominant impression, if you can decide what impression you want to create—sinister, lyrical, grotesque, innocent, calm, grand, or intimate, for example—you may be able to provide more unity through your choice of vocabulary. Note how D. H. Lawrence unifies his description of a ranch in the mountains of New Mexico:

> The black ants in her cupboard, the pack-rats bouncing on her ceiling like hippopotamuses in the night, the two sick goats: there was a peculiar undercurrent of squalor, flowing under the curious tussle of wild life. That was it. The wild life, even the life of the trees and flowers, seemed one bristling, hair-raising tussle. The very flowers came up bristly, and many of them were fang-mouthed, like the dead-nettle: and none had any real scent. But they were very fascinating, too, in their very fierceness. . . . So it was! the alfalfa field was one raging, seething conflict of plants trying to get hold. One dry year, and the bristly wild things had got hold: the spiky,

blue-leaved thistle-poppy with its moon-white flowers, the low clumps of blue nettle-flower, the later rush, after the sereness of June and July, the rush of red sparks and Michaelmas daisies, and the tough wild sunflowers, strangling and choking the dark, tender green of the clover-like alfalfa!

—from *St. Mawr*

This description may be more subjective and figurative than you need, but it certainly shows the effect of sticking to one dominant impression. What would you say that impression is? What are the words that most contribute to it? If you do decide to "grab" a synonym from Roget, beware of the exotic, splashy word where the simple, familiar one would do the job better.

As with all kinds of body paragraphs, you will need to keep in mind the purpose, meaning, and tone of your description. When you begin to develop your paragraph, ask yourself why you have chosen *this* object or group of objects. Why is it interesting or unique? The details you choose to emphasize, those you see as representing the essence of what you are describing, will ultimately convey your meaning. The tone you choose, your presence as an involved or a detached observer, the diction you choose, and the number of senses you bring to the description will influence its effect on your reader.

One last consideration is audience. How much information will your reader need? Is the described thing familiar? Try to give your reader new eyes, to make the familiar new and fresh. Or, if you are describing unusual objects, you may need to make the unusual familiar. In that case, use additional information, a simplified vocabulary, or a well-chosen comparison. Whichever problem you face, plan to get away from your description for a few hours or days, read it again, and revise.

Narration and description complement each other; after all, stories happen in specific places that may exert a powerful influence and so need to be made real to your reader. Because of the way these two techniques work together and in association with the other modes to be described in the next two chapters, you will probably want to include narration and description in most of your essays.

Julia Alvarez

Julia Alvarez (b. 1950) was born in New York City. Soon after her birth her family moved to the Dominican Republic, returning to the United States ten years later. She has published poetry, essays, and short fiction. Her most recent collection, *How the Garcia Girls Lost Their Accents,* was published in 1991. She is currently teaching creative writing at Middlebury College in Vermont. She wrote and revised "Daughter of Invention" over a period of seven years, giving credence to her conviction that "there is something purifying in the labor itself. Revision can be self-knowledge."

Daughter of Invention

Introduction to the Essay and Draft

Some essays are particularly difficult to write. Writer's block may prevent the onset of the writing process, a topic may not be to one's liking, or a writer may not know exactly what he or she wants to say or be unsure of the best way to get ideas down on paper. In the previous chapter you saw how Richard Selzer labored with the introduction to his essay "Mercy"; his satisfaction with the complete essay rested on finding the proper entrance to it. In the following pages you will again meet a writer who puts forth a maximum effort in order to tell a story.

Julia Alvarez, who in Chapter 2 describes her use of revision (see page 40), has worked on her essay for a long time. In the following excerpts from a letter, she explains in detail how she composed and revised what ultimately came to be "Daughter of Invention":

I wrote twenty or so pages, before abandoning the piece in a folder, tentatively labeled, "Mami." It was good writing, that's why I saved the pages, but something was wrong—I knew the form of the piece was too facile. . . .

From that first piece, two little details survived which seemed to be thread in the labyrinth of misconceptions, drafts, stories I wrote for the next seven years about my mother: one detail was my mother's habit of misnomers, misquoting passages, getting sayings and expressions wrong in English. . . . The other detail that stayed with me as a key one was how my mother started inventing gadgets the minute we arrived in this country. That was a gift experience had given me: that rich and ready gem of a detail, something that had "really happened" and was better than I could invent. They are all around, these freebies: I try to keep my eyes open, a pen and notebook handy. . . .

I'd try one thing or another, but the folders of "Mami" and "Mami?" and "Dona Julia" and "Household Earth" filled up my file box of pieces I had temporarily abandoned. . . .

"She wanted to invent something, my mother.": a first sentence came to me, a gift really, which carried inside it a rhythm and energy and attitude in its syntax which *led me forward through the first draft in a couple of sittings of six or so hours a piece, remarkably quickly, if you don't count, that is, the seven years I'd been writing this piece in my head and in other versions! I also wrote most of this piece out loud—I had to hear it, hear my mother's voice, so that from the beginning this has been a very readable piece I like to do at readings. The audience hears the mother, the drama between mother and daughter. And that's also how I did most of the revising of this piece: reading it at readings, I'd hear where the details weren't as sharp as they could be or where the voice went on too long, where I could cut. . . . I recommend that as a very helpful way to step back from a work you feel is finished—try it out on an audience. . . .*

In the above statements, the author traces the evolution of her piece, the germination of an idea, the twists and turns as the idea grew into a draft, and, later, the transformation of the drafts into a finished essay. Alvarez follows processes common to many writers you have already studied and adopts approaches to writing that you are already using: brainstorming about a topic, writing in a journal, creating a first draft, and revising thoroughly until your final version emerges. In addition, Alvarez stresses the importance of being receptive to one's ideas and experiences, and of using them as the basis of the narrative essay. She also notes the value of feedback from an audience—and this may be your instructor, a peer writing group, or any other group of readers—to help with revising.

This essay exists because of the author's determination to create an effective narrative, and the success of "Daughter of Invention," like that of most successful essays, is largely attributable to painstaking revision. In the attempt to get the telling of her story just right, Alvarez alters her narrative to capture the exact meaning and tone that she desires. In this way, the revision of narrative technique—controlling point of view, pacing, and chronology—helps the author to achieve the intimacy that her purpose requires.

The draft version of Alvarez's portrait of her mother will not be reproduced in its entirety, yet the four pages included should help you to understand how the author has sculpted her tribute into a finished work. Of course, you will probably not take seven years to create your essay, but you will have to make many of the same decisions that Alvarez had to make regarding *how* to tell a story. As Alvarez has implied, careful, sensitive revision of your drafts is the most powerful way to make your story truly your own.

Yet, as you read the following pages of Julia Alvarez's draft, you will not notice the signs of revision you now might be used to seeing. Alvarez, like many writers who use a word processor, probably finds it easier to revise text directly on her computer screen and to print out newly revised versions than to revise on the drafts themselves. This flexibility of the text simplifies revision because a writer does not have to retype sections that have not been altered significantly, but the newly printed product can be misleading in terms of demonstrating how much work has gone into the revision. That is, the additions, deletions, substitutions, and rearrangements that are hidden by a clean copy demand more attention from a reader who desires to learn what has been guiding a writer's revisions. As you read through the draft, pay close attention to the changes that Alvarez makes from her "early draft" to the final version.

Published Essay

1   She wanted to invent something, my mother. There was a period after we arrived in this country until five or so years later when my mother was inventing. They were never pressing, global needs she was addressing with her pencil and pad. She would have said that was for men to do, rockets and engines that ran on gasoline and turned the wheels of the world. She was just fussing with little house things, don't mind her.

2   She always invented at night, after settling her house down. On his side of the bed, my father would be konked out for an hour already, his Spanish newspaper draped over his chest, his glasses propped up on his bedside table, looking out eerily at the darkened room like a disembodied body guard. But in her lighted corner like some devoted scholar burning her midnight oil, my mother was inventing, sheets pulled to her lap, pillows propped up behind her, her reading glasses riding the bridge of her nose like a schoolmarm's. On her lap lay one of those innumerable pads of paper my father always brought home from his office, compliments of some pharmaceutical company, advertising tranquilizers or antibiotics or skin cream; in her other hand, my mother held a pencil that looked like a pen with a little cylinder of lead inside. She would be working on a sketch of something familiar, but drawn at such close range so she could attach a special nozzle or handier handle, the thing looked peculiar. Once, I mistook the spiral of a corkscrew for a nautilus shell, but it could just as well have been a galaxy forming.

3   It was the only time all day we'd catch her sitting down, for she herself was living proof of the *perpetuum mobile* machine so many inventors had sought over the ages. My sisters and I would seek her out now when she seemed to have a moment to talk to us: we were having trouble at school or we wanted her to persuade my father to give us permission to go into the city or to a shopping mall or a movie—in broad daylight! My mother would wave us out of her room. "The problem with you girls. . ." I can tell you right now what the problem always boiled down to: we wanted to become Americans and my father—and my mother, at first—would have none of it.

4   "You girls are going to drive me crazy!" She always threatened if we kept nagging. "When I end up in Bellevue, you'll be safely sorry!"

5   She spoke in English when she argued with us, even though, in a matter of months, her daughters were the fluent ones. Her English was much better than my father's, but it was still a mishmash of mixed-up idioms and sayings that showed she was "green behind the ears," as she called it.

6   If my sisters and I tried to get her to talk in Spanish, she'd snap, "When in Rome, do unto the Romans . . ."

7   I had become the spokesman for my sisters, and I would stand my ground in that bedroom. "We're not going to that school anymore, Mami!"

8   "You have to!" Her eyes would widen with worry. "In this country, it is against the law not to go to school. You want us to get thrown out?"

9   "You want us to get killed? Those kids were throwing stones today!"

10   "Sticks and stones don't break bones . . . ," she chanted. I could tell, though, by the look on her face, it was as if one of those stones the kids had aimed at us had hit her. But she always pretended we were at fault. "What did you do to provoke them? It takes two to tangle, you know."

11   "Thanks, thanks a lot, Mom!" I'd storm out of that room and into mine. I never called her *Mom* except when I wanted her to feel how much she had failed us in this country. She was a good enough Mami, fussing and scolding and giving advice, but a terrible girlfriend parent, a real failure of a Mom.

12   Back she'd go to her pencil and pad, scribbling and tsking and tearing off paper, finally giving up, and taking up her *New York Times*. Some nights, though, she'd get a good idea, and she'd rush into my room, a flushed look on her face, her tablet of paper in her hand, a cursory knock on the door she'd just thrown open: "Do I have something to show you, Cukita!"

13   This was my time to myself, after I'd finished my homework, while my sisters were still downstairs watching TV in the basement. Hunched over my small desk, the overhead light turned off, my lamp shining poignantly on my paper, the rest of the room in warm, soft, uncreated darkness, I wrote my secret poems in my new language.

14   "You're going to ruin your eyes!" My mother would storm into my room, turning on the overly bright overhead light, scaring off whatever shy passion I had just begun coaxing out of a labyrinth of feelings with the blue thread of my writing.

15   "Oh Mami!" I'd cry out, my eyes blinking up at her. "I'm writing."

16   "Ay, Cukita." That was her communal pet name for whoever was in her favor. "Cukita, when I make a million, I'll buy you your very own typewriter." (I'd been nagging my mother for one just like the one father had bought her to do his order forms at home.) "Gravy on the turkey" was what she called it when someone was buttering her up. She'd butter and pour. "I'll hire you your very own typist."

17   Down she'd plop on my bed and hold out her pad to me. "Take a guess, Cukita?" I'd study her rough sketch a moment: soap sprayed from the nozzle head of a shower when you turned the knob a certain way? Coffee with creamer already mixed in? Time-released water capsules for your potted plants when you are away? A key chain with a timer that would go off when your parking meter was about to expire? (The ticking would help you find your keys easily if you mislaid them.) The famous one, famous only in hindsight, was the stick person dragging a square by a rope—a suitcase with wheels? "Oh, of course," we'd humor her. "What every household needs: a shower like a car wash, keys ticking like a bomb, luggage on a leash!" By now, as you can see, it'd become something of a family joke, our Thomas Edison Mami, our Benjamin Franklin Mom.

18   Her face would fall. "Come on now! Use your head." One more wrong guess, and she'd tell me, pressing with her pencil point the different highlights of

this incredible new wonder. "Remember that time we took the car to Bear Mountain, and we re-ah-lized that we had forgotten to pack an opener with our pick-a-nick?" (We kept correcting her, but she insisted this is how it should be said.) "When we were ready to eat we didn't have any way to open the refreshments cans?" (This before flip-top lids, which she claimed had crossed her mind.) "You know what this is now?" A shake of my head. "Is a car bumper, but see this part is a removable can opener. So simple and yet so necessary, no?"

19   "Yeah, Mami. You should patent it," I'd shrug. She'd tear off the scratch paper and fold it, carefully, corner to corner, as if she were going to save it. But then, she'd toss it in the waste basket on her way out of the room and give a little laugh like a disclaimer. "It's half of one or two dozen of another. . . ."

20   I suppose none of her daughters was very encouraging. We resented her spending time on those dumb inventions. Here, we were trying to fit in America among Americans; we needed help figuring out who we were, why these Irish kids whose grandparents were micks two generations ago, why they were calling us spics. Why had we come to this country in the first place? Important, crucial, final things, you see, and here was our own mother, who didn't have a second to help us puzzle any of this out, inventing gadgets to make life easier for the American moms. Why it seemed as if she were arming our own enemy against us!

21   One time, she did have a moment of triumph. Every night, she liked to read *The New York Times* in bed before turning off her light, to see what the Americans were up to. One night, she let out a yelp to wake up my father beside her, bolt upright, reaching for his glasses, which in his haste he knocked across the room. *"Que pasa? Que pasa?"* What is wrong? There was terror in his voice, fear she'd seen in his eyes in the Dominican Republic before we left. We were being watched there; he was being followed; he and Mother had often exchanged those looks. They could not talk, of course, though they must have whispered to each other in fear at night in the dark bed. Now in America, he was safe, a success even; his Centro Medico in Brooklyn was thronged with the sick and the homesick yearning to go home again. But in dreams, he went back to those awful days and long nights, and my mother's screams confirmed his secret fear: we had not gotten away after all; they had come for us at last.

22   "Ay, Papi, I'm sorry. Go back to sleep, Cukito. It's nothing, nothing really." My mother held up the *Times* for him to squint at the small print, back page headline, one hand tapping all over the top of the bedside table for his glasses, the other rubbing his eyes to wakefulness.

23   "Remember, remember, how I showed you that suitcase with little wheels so we should not have to carry those heavy bags when we traveled? Someone stole my idea and made a million!" She shook the paper in his face. She shook the paper in all our faces that night. "See, see! This man was no bobo! He didn't put all his pokers on a back burner. I kept telling you, one of these days my ship would pass me by in the night!" She wagged her finger at my sisters and my father and me, laughing all the while, one of those eerie laughs crazy people in movies laugh. We had congregated in her room to hear the good news she'd

been yelling down the stairs about, and now we eyed her and each other. I suppose we were all thinking the same thing, wouldn't it be weird and sad if Mami did end up in Bellevue as she'd always threatened she might?

24   "*Ya, ya!* Enough!" She waved us out of her room at last. "There is no use trying to drink spilt milk, that's for sure."

25   It was the suitcase rollers that stopped my mother's hand; she had weather-vaned a minor brainstorm. She would have to start taking herself seriously. That blocked the free play of her ingenuity. Besides, she had also begun working at my father's office, and at night, she was too tired and busy filling in columns with how much money they had made that day to be fooling with gadgets!

26   She did take up her pencil and pad one last time to help me out. In ninth grade, I was chosen by my English teacher, Sister Mary Zoe, to deliver the teacher's day address at the school assembly. After our arrival in America, I had become something of a writer. Back in the Dominican Republic growing up, I was a terrible student. No one could ever get me to sit down to a book. But in New York, I needed to settle somewhere, and the natives were unfriendly, the country inhospitable, so I took root in the language. By high school, the nuns were reading my stories and compositions out loud to my classes as examples of imagination at work.

27   This time my imagination jammed. At first I didn't want and then I couldn't seem to write that speech. I suppose I should have thought of it as "a great honor," as my father called it. But I was mortified. I still had a pronounced lilt to my accent, and I did not like to speak in public, subjecting myself to my classmates' ridicule. Recently, they had begun to warm towards my sisters and me, and it took no great figuring to see that to deliver a eulogy for a convent full of crazy, old nuns was no way to endear myself to the members of my class.

28   But I didn't know how to get out of it. Week after week, I'd sit down, hoping to polish off some quick, noncommittal little speech. I couldn't get anything down.

29   The weekend before our assembly Monday morning I went into a panic. My mother would just have to call in tomorrow and say I was in the hospital, in a coma. I was in the Dominican Republic, Yeah, that was it! Recently, my father had been talking about going back home to live.

30   My mother tried to calm me down. "Just remember how Mister Lincoln couldn't think of anything to say at the Gettysburg, but then, Bang! 'Four score and once upon a time ago,'" she began reciting. Her version of history was half invention and half truths and whatever else she needed to prove a point. "Something is going to come if you just relax. You'll see, like the Americans say, 'Necessity is the daughter of invention.' I'll help you."

31   All weekend, she kept coming into my room with help. "Please, Mami, just leave me alone, please," I pleaded with her. But I'd get rid of the goose only to have to contend with the gander. My father kept poking his head in the door just to see if I had "fulfilled my obligations," a phrase he used when we were a little younger, and he'd check to see whether we had gone to the bathroom before a car trip. Several times that weekend around the supper table, he'd recite

his valedictorian speech from when he graduated from high school. He'd give me pointers on delivery, on the great orators and their tricks. (Humbleness and praise and falling silent with great emotion were his favorites.)

32   My mother sat across the table, the only one who seemed to be listening to him. My sisters and I were forgetting a lot of our Spanish, and my father's formal, florid diction was even harder to understand. But my mother smiled softly to herself, and turned the Lazy Susan at the center of the table around and around as if it were the prime mover, the first gear of her attention.

33   That Sunday evening, I was reading some poetry to get myself inspired: Whitman in an old book with an engraved cover my father had picked up in a thrift shop next to his office a few weeks back. "I celebrate myself and sing myself . . ." "He most honors my style who learns under it to destroy the teacher." The poet's words shocked and thrilled me. I had gotten used to the nuns, a literature of appropriate sentiments, poems with a message, expurgated texts. But here was a flesh and blood man, belching and laughing and sweating in poems. "Who touches this book touches a man."

34   That night, at last, I started to write, recklessly, three, five pages, looking up once only to see my father passing by the hall on tiptoe. When I was done, I read over my words to myself, and my eyes filled. I finally sounded like myself in English!

35   As soon as I had finished that first draft, I called my mother to my room. She listened attentively while I read it out loud, as she had to my father's speech, and in the end, her eyes were glistening too. Her face was soft and warm and proud. "That is a beautiful, beautiful speech, Cukita. I want for your father to hear it before he goes to sleep. Then I will type it for you, all right?"

36   Down the hall we went, the two of us, faces flushed with accomplishment. Into the master bedroom where my father was propped up on his pillows, still awake, reading the Dominican papers, already days old. He had become interested in his country's fate, again. The dictatorship had been toppled. The interim government was going to hold the first free elections in thirty years. There was still some question in his mind whether or not we might move back. History was in the making, freedom and hope were in the air again! But my mother had gotten used to the life here. She did not want to go back to the old country where she was only a wife and a mother (and a failed one, at that, since she had never had the required son). She did not come straight out and disagree with my father's plans. Instead, she fussed with him about reading the papers in bed, soiling their sheets with those poorly printed, foreign tabloids. "The *Times* is not that bad!" she'd claim if my father tried to humor her by saying they shared the same dirty habit.

37   The minute my father saw my mother and me, filing in, he put his paper down, and his face brightened as if at long last his wife had delivered a boy, and that was the news we were bringing him. His teeth were already grinning from the glass of water next to his bedside lamp, so he lisped when he said, "Eh-speech, eh-speech!"

38   "It is so beautiful, Papi," my mother previewed him, turning the sound off

on his TV. She sat down at the foot of the bed. I stood before both of them, blocking their view of the soldiers in helicopters landing amid silenced gun reports and explosions. A few weeks ago it had been the shores of the Dominican Republic. Now it was the jungles of Southeast Asia they were saving. My mother gave me the nod to begin reading.

39   I didn't need much encouragement. I put my nose to the fire, as my mother would have said, and read from start to finish without looking up. When I was done, I was a little embarrassed at my pride in my own words. I pretended to quibble with a phrase or two I was sure I'd be talked out of changing. I looked questioningly to my mother. Her face was radiant. She turned to share her pride with my father.

40   But the expression on his face shocked us both. His toothless mouth had collapsed into a dark zero. His eyes glared at me, then shifted to my mother, accusingly. In barely audible Spanish as if secret microphones or informers were all about, he whispered, "You will permit her to read *that*?"

41   My mother's eyebrows shot up, her mouth fell open. In the old country, any whisper of a challenge to authority could bring the secret police in their black VWs. But this was America. People could say what they thought. "What is wrong with her speech?" My mother questioned him.

42   "What ees wrrrong with her eh-speech?" My father wagged his head at her. His anger was always more frightening in his broken English. As if he had mutilated the language in his fury—and now there was nothing to stand between us and his raw, dumb anger. "What is wrong? I will tell you what is wrong. It show no gratitude. It is boastful. 'I celebrate myself'? 'The best student learn to destroy the teacher'?" He mocked my plagiarized words. "That is insubordinate. It is improper. It is disrespecting to her teachers." In his anger he had forgotten his fear of lurking spies: each wrong he voiced was a decibel higher than the last outrage. Finally, he was yelling at me, "As your father, I forbid you to say that eh-speech!"

43   My mother leapt to her feet, a sign always that she was about to make a speech or deliver an ultimatum. She was a small woman, and she spoke all her pronouncements standing up, either for more projection or a carryover from her girlhood in convent schools where one asked for, and literally, took the floor in order to speak. She stood by my side, shoulder to shoulder; we looked down at my father. "That is no tone of voice, Eduardo—" she began.

44   By now, my father was truly furious. I suppose it was bad enough I was rebelling, but here was my mother joining forces with me. Soon he would be surrounded by a house full of independent American women. He too leapt from his bed, throwing off his covers. The Spanish newspapers flew across the room. He snatched my speech out of my hands, held it before my panicked eyes, a vengeful, mad look in his own, and then once, twice, three, four, countless times, he tore my prize into shreds.

45   "Are you crazy?" My mother lunged at him. "Have you gone mad? That is her speech for tomorrow you have torn up!"

46   "Have *you* gone mad?" he shook her away. "You were going to let her read that . . . that insult to her teachers?"

47   "Insult to her teachers!" My mother's face had crumpled up like a piece of paper. On it was written a love note to my father. Ever since they had come to this country, their life together was a constant war. "This is America, Papi, America!" she reminded him now. "You are not in a savage country anymore!"

48   I was on my knees, weeping wildly, collecting all the little pieces of my speech, hoping that I could put it back together before the assembly tomorrow morning. But not even a sibyl could have made sense of all those scattered pieces of paper. All hope was lost. "He broke it, he broke it," I moaned as I picked up a handful of pieces.

49   Probably, if I had thought a moment about it, I would not have done what I did next. I would have realized my father had lost brothers and comrades to the dictator Trujillo. For the rest of his life, he would be haunted by blood in the streets and late night disappearances. Even after he had been in the States for years, he jumped if a black Volkswagen passed him on the street. He feared anyone in uniform: the meter maid giving out parking tickets, a museum guard approaching to tell him not to touch his favorite Goya at the Metropolitan.

50   I took a handful of the scraps I had gathered, stood up, and hurled them in his face. "Chapita!" I said in a low, ugly whisper. "You're just another Chapita!"

51   It took my father only a moment to register the hated nickname of our dictator, and he was after me. Down the halls we raced, but I was quicker than he and made it into my room just in time to lock the door as my father threw his weight against it. He called down curses on my head, ordered me on his authority as my father to open that door this very instant! He throttled that doorknob, but all to no avail. My mother's love of gadgets saved my hide that night. She had hired a locksmith to install good locks on all the bedroom doors after our house had been broken into while we were away last summer. In case burglars broke in again, and we were in the house, they'd have a second round of locks to contend with before they got to us.

52   "Eduardo," she tried to calm him down. "Don't you ruin my new locks."

53   He finally did calm down, his anger spent. I heard their footsteps retreating down the hall. I heard their door close, the clicking of their lock. Then, muffled voices, my mother's peaking in anger, in persuasion, my father's deeper murmurs of explanation and self defense. At last, the house fell silent, before I heard, far off, the gun blasts and explosions, the serious, self-important voices of newscasters reporting their TV war.

54   A little while later, there was a quiet knock at my door, followed by a tentative attempt at the door knob. "Cukita?" My mother whispered. "Open up, Cukita."

55   "Go away," I wailed, but we both knew I was glad she was there, and I needed only a moment's protest to save face before opening that door.

56   What we ended up doing that night was putting together a speech at the last moment. Two brief pages of stale compliments and the polite commonplaces on teachers, wrought by necessity without much invention by mother for daughter late into the night in the basement on the pad of paper and with the same pencil she had once used for her own inventions, for I was too upset to compose the

speech myself. After it was drafted, she typed it up while I stood by, correcting her misnomers and mis-sayings.

57   She was so very proud of herself when I came home the next day with the success story of the assembly. The nuns had been flattered, the audience had stood up and given "our devoted teachers a standing ovation," what my mother had suggested they do at the end of my speech.

58   She clapped her hands together as I recreated the moment for her. "I stole that from your father's speech, remember? Remember how he put that in at the end?" She quoted him in Spanish, then translated for me into English.

59   That night, I watched him from the upstairs hall window where I'd retreated the minute I heard his car pull up in front of our house. Slowly, my father came up the driveway, a grim expression on his face as he grappled with a large, heavy cardboard box. At the front door, he set the package down carefully and patted all his pockets for his house keys—precisely why my mother had invented her ticking keychain. I heard the snapping open of locks downstairs. Heard as he struggled to maneuver the box through the narrow doorway. Then, he called my name several times. But I would not answer him.

60   "My daughter, your father, he love you very much," he explained from the bottom of the stairs. "He just want to protect you." Finally, my mother came up and pleaded with me to go down and reconcile with him. "Your father did not mean to harm. You must pardon him. Always it is better to let bygones be forgotten, no?"

61   I guess she was right. Downstairs, I found him setting up a brand new electric typewriter on the kitchen table. It was even better than the one I'd been begging to get like my mother's. My father had outdone himself with all the extra features: a plastic carrying case with my initials decaled below the handle, a brace to lift the paper upright while I typed, an erase cartridge, an automatic margin tab, a plastic hood like a toaster cover to keep the dust away. Not even my mother, I think, could have invented such a machine!

62   But her inventing days were over just as mine were starting up with my school-wide success. That's why I've always thought of that speech my mother wrote for me as her last invention rather than the suitcase rollers everyone else in the family remembers. It was as if she had passed on to me her pencil and pad and said, "Okay, Cukita, here's the buck. You give it a shot."

Draft

1   She wanted to invent something, my mother. There was a period after

we arrived in this country until five or so years later when my mother was

inventing. They were never pressing, global needs she was addressing with

her pencil and pad. She would have said that was for men to do, rockets

and engines that ran on gasoline and turned the wheels of the world. She

was just fussing with little house things you'd kind of overlooked because

they weren't anything important. But then, something came up, and you'd
wish someone had taken the time to solve the problem. That someone was my
mother after our emigration and before we sunk roots in this country.

2   She always worked at night, after settling her house down. From room
to room, she went, turning on lights, scanning the furniture, unplugging
lamps, taking stock. The things that are in the world. Up the stairs she
came at a clip--she went from on to off, no winding down, picking up
invisible motes of dust as she rose. At the upstairs hall window, she
checked on our front yard, the hedge of azaleas was still there; the little
dogwood that surprised us with blooms every spring stood guard, my father's
car. Then, a tug of the cord, the blinds lidded shut, and we were safe and
settled, a little outpost of civilized foreign people, surrounded by the
wild, dangerous, exciting country of the Americans.

3   On his side of the bed, my father would be konked out for an hour
already, his Spanish newspapers or a book of history draped over his
chest like a tent, his glasses propped up on his bedside table, looking out
eerily at the darkened room like a disembodied body guard. But in her
lighted corner like a devoted scholar burning her midnight oil, my mother
was inventing, sheets pulled to her lap, pillows propped up behind her, her
reading glasses riding the bridge of her nose like a schoolmarm's. On her
lap lay one of those innumerable pads of paper always found in our house,
given to my father by pharmaceutical companies advertising their
tranquilizers, their antibiotics, their skin cream; in her other hand, my
mother held a drafting pencil that looked like a pen with a little cylinder
of lead inside. She would be working on a sketch of something familiar but
drawn at such close range so my mother could insert a nozzle or attach a
handle or affix a knob, the thing looked peculiar. Once I mistook the
spiral of a screw for a nautilus shell, but it could just as well have been
a galaxy forming.

4   It was the only time all day we'd catch her sitting down, for she
herself was living proof of the perpetuum mobile machine so many inventors
had sought over the ages. My sisters and I would seek her out now when she
seemed to have a moment to talk to us: we were having trouble at school or

we wanted her to persuade my father to give us permission to go into the city alone or to the movies or overnight to a neighbor's house. My mother would wave us out of her room, "This is not Grand Central Station!" Then before we could leave the room, she would start in on one of her lectures. "The problem with you girls..." I can tell you right now what the problem always boiled down to: we wanted to become Americans and my father, and my mother at first, would have none of it.

5   "You girls are going to drive me crazy!" She always threatened if we kept nagging. "When I end up in Bellevue, you'll be safe and sorry!"

6   She always spoke in English when she argued with us, even though, in a matter of months, her daughters were the fluent ones. Her English was much better than my father's; she was a good mimic, easily picking up the accent, the body language. Her talk was full of cliches. For us, immigrants, to sound like everyone else was a great plus. We were as original as we hoped to be with our dark hair and eyes, our food that that made our house smell like a restaurant, as one repairman noted. But her idioms and sayings were so jumbled up and misquoted that it showed she was "green behind the ears," as she called it. "You know what I mean," she'd snap if my sisters and I tried to get her to talk in Spanish. "When in Rome..." That might very well be true, the courtesy of the native tongue, but I don't put it beyond her ingenuity to have used language barriers to keep us cooped up in her way of seeing the world.

7   I was the daughter who persisted, blurting out what we all needed desperately to talk to her about. "I'm not going to school anymore!"

8   "You have to. In this country, it is against the law not to go to school." Her eyes widened with worry. "You want us to get thrown out?"

9   "You want us to get killed? The kids were throwing stones today!"

10   "Sticks and stones don't break bones..." She chanted. I could tell, though, by the look on her face, it was as if one of those stones the kids had aimed at us had hit her. But she always pretended we were at fault. "What did you do to provoke them, it takes two to tangle, you know."

11   I'd storm out of that room and into mine. "Thanks, thanks a lot, Mom!" I'd toss over my shoulder as casual as an American. I never called her <u>Mom</u>

```
except when I was angry and wanted her to feel how much she had failed us
in this country.  She was a good enough Mami, fussing and scolding and
giving advice, but a terrible girl-friend parent, we thought, a real
failure of a Mom.
```

Comparing Draft and Essay

Draft Paragraph 1

1. What is the point of view of this paragraph? How does it compare to that of the final version? What specific words indicate Alvarez's perspective?

2. Why do you think that the author has deleted the last two sentences? How does her revision affect you as a reader?

3. Applying what you have learned from the previous chapter, how would you evaluate the draft's introductory paragraph and the final version's? Which do you prefer? Why?

Draft Paragraphs 2 and 3

4. What major revision strategies is Alvarez employing in these paragraphs? Why do you think that she has chosen to make these changes?

5. How do Alvarez's revisions affect the pacing of her narrative? How are meaning and purpose affected?

6. Small details can sometimes be of great importance in an essay. In a narrative, where a writer is presenting a meaningful experience, each word contributes to the overall impact. What seemingly minor revisions do you find in these paragraphs? How do they shape your response to the story?

Draft Paragraphs 4 and 5

7. You may notice that these paragraphs differ little from the corresponding ones of the final version (paragraphs 3 and 4). Indeed, aside from the deletion of sentences 3 and 4, both versions are virtually the same. How does Alvarez use these paragraphs to further her narrative? What meaning does she develop?

Draft Paragraph 6

8. Compare this paragraph with paragraph 5 in the final version. Which one seems more effective to you? How can you explain your opinion?

9. What revisions does Alvarez make to this paragraph? How do these changes affect point of view and pacing?

Draft Paragraphs 7 through 11

10. As you read these paragraphs, you will notice that Alvarez includes much dialogue. How do you react to the verbal exchanges between mother and daughter? Why would the author choose to use this stylistic device?

11. These draft paragraphs, like preceding ones, illustrate Alvarez's concern with strengthening the perspective offered by her first-person narrator. What advantage is to be gained by the author in clarifying this narrator?

12. In earlier draft paragraphs, Alvarez has tended to delete information that was general and that did not directly develop her portrayal of her mother. Much of this deleted information concerned the family's feelings about being immigrants and their response to their new country. How has this topic been incorporated into *these* paragraphs? How have revisions affected your perception of this information?

13. If one defines a narrative essay as a story that makes a point, then what do you think the point of "Daughter of Invention" is? How can you use your observation of Alvarez's revisions to back up your prediction?

Christine Donaghy

Christine Donaghy (b. 1950) is a nursing student at Queensborough Community College in Bayside, New York. She plans to work in pediatrics when she graduates.

A Second Chance

Introduction to the Essay and Draft

A primary aim and responsibility of a writer are to convey meaning as accurately and interestingly as possible. Yet, as we have observed, the meaning that often emerges from a first draft is not the meaning originally intended by a writer. This search for meaning becomes even more complicated when one writes a first-person narrative. Precisely because we are participants in our lives we frequently confuse what is and what is not essential to the event being narrated. Also, because we have experienced and know about the event, we might take for granted how episodes relate to each other and how background information relates to the story being told. Most important, we sometimes do not see clearly a particular event for what it is. In short, when writing about oneself, a writer might lack sufficient perspective on an event to understand and convey its full meaning.

Yet, a first-person narrator, being a participant in the event being written about, also has several advantages. He or she knows the details and has experienced and felt directly the sensations and emotions associated with the event. Writing down your thoughts and feelings, and including concrete descriptions, will almost always capture a reader's attention. Here is what Christine Donaghy writes about what she wants to say, her predictions of her audience's expectations, and her reconsideration of audience and meaning.

> In my first draft of this story, I was trying to write what I thought the reader would be interested in. In my revision, I wrote as if I was talking to someone and just relating what was in my head. I think the more natural approach to writing ends up being the more interesting version to the reader.

Donaghy's search for the story she wants to narrate leads her to reevaluate her first draft of "A Second Chance." Her revision is indeed a "seeing again" of her essay; the changes she makes are substantial and affect directly a reader's response to it. Once again, a narrative is a story that has a point. The primary search for and clear expression of meaning are what motivate Donaghy to revise.

Final Essay

1   Starting school and beginning a new career in mid-life always seemed to me to be something that "other" people did. I had read and heard many success stories about Super-Moms who were able to do it all without ever having a hair out of place or breaking a nail. I never believed them. I had raised 3 boys, and I knew that there had never been any time left over for me. I didn't think it was possible.

2   In the summer of 1989, as I was approaching the age of 39, I ran into an old friend of mine. We were both visiting our mothers in our old neighborhood and had brought our kids to the local playground where we had played as children. We started talking, and she told me that she had one more year of school left and she would be a registered nurse. I couldn't believe it. A real live Super-Mom—and she was someone I knew! She had 2 daughters in elementary school and had been going to school part-time for 5 years. She told me about how she managed it—by taking her classes during the hours that her children were in school, and by arranging for her mother to baby-sit on days off or when she had schedule problems. It sounded complicated and very hectic, but as I was listening to her, it became very clear that she was enjoying it and felt very good about herself. We had both always wanted to be nurses when we were young, and she was almost there.

3   As I listened to her and then as I walked back to my mother's house with my children, my mind was racing. With my youngest child about to start nursery school, I was approaching the first time in my life that I could be considered a "Lady of Leisure"—even if it was only going to be for 3 hours a day. I had started working right after high school for the telephone company and I stayed there until I had my second child which was 13 years later. It was never my dream career, but it paid well and helped me prove to myself how much I was

capable of. I didn't have a lot of self-confidence as a teenager, and that's what kept me from going to nursing school when I was 18. It seemed to me that it was fate that I ran into my friend when I did. The timing was perfect for me to start school. I just needed someone to show me the way. I couldn't wait to tell my mother about my new plan.

4   My mother's reaction was even better than I expected. She had wanted me to go to college 20 years before and was very disappointed when I didn't. Her face lit up like a Christmas tree. She was totally positive about it and told me she would help me in any way that she could. Her supportive attitude made me feel even more determined. Now it was becoming a reality in my mind, and the whole idea was only about 3 hours old!

5   That evening at the dinner table, I presented my plans to my husband. Being a college graduate himself, he never looked at the idea of me going to school with any apprehension in the first place. He had more confidence in me than I had in myself. He had been a stock broker for 16 years but had just gone into a new career after the market had fallen apart. The prospect of me going into a promising field when we weren't too sure about his new business seemed very practical. Besides, he had been after me for years after I left my job to do something stimulating for myself. I don't think he expected me to do this, but he thought it was a great idea. Now I had everyone behind me; there was no turning back.

6   During my first term I took two classes, English Composition I and a fundamental biology course. It wasn't easy, but I loved it. On some days, I would have just 10 minutes to get from my school to my sons' school to pick them up. I even bought running shoes so I could get to my car faster and wouldn't be late. All my studying and writing had to be done after the boys were in bed, which was the only time the house was quiet. Many nights I just wanted to go to bed myself, but I was driven. I wanted to do this, and I wanted to be good at it.

7   The generation gap between students my age and the younger students soon became obvious. We wanted the A's— they were very often satisfied with just passing. We found the English class stimulating—they were bored and complained a lot about the material we were reading. There are many factors that I feel contribute to these differences in attitude. The most obvious one is what one's priorities are at different ages. College-age teenagers are often preoccupied with their social lives and regard school as a secondary activity. They may also be in college only to please their parents and may not have any real goals of their own yet. Finally, they have not yet experienced the responsibility of having to be financially independent and don't fully associate their schooling with their future careers. For the older students, the opposite of these factors is true. How perfect it would be if we could only combine experience with youth!

8   I'm half-way through my schooling now. It's been difficult for me and for my family, but there are other benefits that have come from this besides my eventual nursing career. My children, as young as they are, are learning to pitch in and help at home because I need them to. They've been given responsibilities that I used to take care of myself. My older sons, ages 10 and 8, have learned

how to fold and separate laundry. They may whine that they would rather be playing Nintendo as they're putting the clothes away, but they're beginning to realize how much work goes into running a household and that everyone has to do his part. You would be amazed at how well a 4-year-old can clean up his toys. I know I was. I have also been able to use myself as an example for being responsible for one's own schoolwork. When they know that I've studied hard for a big test, they're always anxious to know what my mark is, and they are just as happy for me when I do well as I am for them with their tests. I also feel that I'm much more in tune with today's teenagers than I had been, which I hope will help me when my boys reach those volatile years.

9   Being home with your children while they are babies is a wonderful experience and I am grateful that I was able to do it. I do feel, however, that when children reach school age, it is beneficial for the entire family for mothers to have another interest—a job, school or even volunteer work. You become more well-rounded when you have more to think about than housework or your child's science project that's due. The housework and the science projects will still have to get done, and you may have less time to devote to these things, but you will be amazed how you will still find the time to do them anyway.

10   In the past two years, I have met many other women in school who also are raising children, both with husbands and without. There's a comraderie among us because we understand both the difficulties of "doing it all" and the rewarding feeling of doing something for ourselves. There is never any mention of quitting, only of how long it will take to finish. We all seem to fiercely guard our school time because it is "our own" time and we move mountains if necessary rather than miss a class. We get excited over new registration schedules and look forward to new Septembers and summer's end. Going to school for us is a wonderful experience, even for those who didn't feel that way about it as teenagers. We've been part of the "real world" since we left high school and now we appreciate the "luxury" of being students. I'm grateful that my friend ignited that spark in me two years ago, and I hope that my story will convince someone who is undecided about school to make the move and better herself. She will never regret it.

Draft

1   In the spring of 1989, as I was approaching the age of 39, I decided to do something that I believe had been in the back of my mind since I was a teenager. I decided to go to school to become a nurse. I can remember exactly when I made this decision, and once it was made I knew there was no turning back.

2   I really shouldn't say that the idea was in the back of my mind, because when I was in high school, a nurse is all I ever wanted to be. I had been a candystriper in a local hospital when I was 13 and 14

(I lied about my age) and I loved it. I applied for a Regents Nursing Scholarship — and I got it, but something as foolish as hearsay from my peers kept me from pursuing my goal. I kept hearing about how important chemistry was in a nurse's training and I hated chemistry. I had had a terrible chemistry teacher in high school and I never quite caught on to it. So based on this 'expert' advice, I dropped the whole idea and took a job with the telephone company after I graduated.

3   My career with Ma Bell lasted for 13 years. During that time I got promoted to supervisor, got married and had two children. I held a lucrative position with many possibilities for advancement, but I couldn't wait to leave. For me, it was not fulfilling.

4   When my third child was almost 3, I ran into an old friend of mine who told me she had one more year of school and she would become a registered nurse. She also had children and told me how she juggled her hours with their school hours and managed to get through it. She gave me an incentive for something I never would have thought manageable. She never made it sound easy, but somehow the challenge of it all made it seem so exciting. After raising babies for 8 years, I couldn't wait to get my hands on the very thing I had turned my back on when I was younger and without responsibilities. My attitude was so positive toward my new plan that no one could have talked me out of it. My husband ~~said: 'Go for it!'~~ thought it was a great idea; my mother was thrilled and offered whatever babysitting help I needed — how could I lose? I took a ride over to Queensborough and got the paperwork starrted.

5   My first indication that being older than the majority of students would make me different was apparent on the day of the placement test. I had studied the sample test I had been sent for a few weeks in advance — after all, I hadn't had algebra for 20 years! About half-way through the allotted time for the math segment, I picked my head up and looked around the auditorium. It was half-empty! I was finding the problems difficult and the steady clearing of the room was beginning to make me feel very unsure of myself. I remember thinking that maybe ~~this was~~ I was making a mistake, that too much time had passed and I wouldn't be able to keep up with the teenagers. I finished the test, using almost all the time allowed, and feeling a little more nervous than when I started.

6   *my self-confidence was refortified when I received my test*
     ~~Well, I passed the placement tests, which meant I didn't have to~~
     results — I passed!
     ~~take any remedial classes. That bolstered my self-confidence somewhat.~~
     And after talking to other students, I found out that most of them
     give up on the math section - they just walk out! They resolve them-
     selves to taking a remedial math course (for no credit) rather than
     try to pass the test. I was shocked. I was also enlightened as to how
     the average modern college student approaches school.

7   During my first term I took two classes, English Composition I and
     a fundamental biology course. It wasn't easy, but I loved it. On
     some days, I would have just 10 minutes to get from my school to my
     I even bought running shoes so I could get to my car
     sons' school to pick them up. *faster and wouldn't be late.* All my studying and writing had to be done
     after the boys were ~~all~~ in bed, which was the only time the house
     was quiet. Many nights I just wanted to go to bed myself, but I was

     driven. I wanted to do this, and I wanted to be good at it.

8   The generation gap between students my age and the younger students
     was becoming more obvious. We wanted the A's - they were very often
     satisfied with just passing. We found the English class stimulating -
     they were bored and complained a lot about the material we were read-
     ing. [I would often hear them asking each other before class, "Did you
     read the story?" or "Did you study for the test?" and the answers
     would very often be "No" with no explanation. It didn't make
     sense. They didn't have to be there, and they were paying for these
     classes. My only guess was that they were in school for their parents'
     sake, not their own. So many times when I'd hear someone complaining
     or talking about how he's failing and he "really doesn't care", I
     wanted to shake him and tell him to do it now when it's easy instead
     of waiting until he has a family and responsibilities. I know, though,
     when I was 18, I probably wouldn't have listened to a 40 year old
     woman telling me what I should do with my life. So I kept my mouth
     shut, and I only gave advice if someone asked for it.]

9   I'm ~~almost~~ half-way through my schooling now. It's been difficult
     for me and for my family, but there are other benefits that have come
     from this besides my eventual nursing career. My children, as young as

they are, are learning to pitch in and help at home because I need
them to. I have ~~used~~ myself as an example for being responsible
for ~~their~~ own schoolwork. ~~It's~~ a lot more effective than saying,
'When I was a child in school....' ~~That~~ falls on deaf ears. I also feel
that I'm much more in tune with today's teenagers than I had been,
which I hope will help me when my boys reach those volatile years.

(handwritten annotations: "been able to since", "K?", "one's", "This is", "which often")

10   Being home with your children while they are babies is a wonderful
experience and I am grateful that I was able to do it. I do feel,
however, that when children reach school age it is beneficial for the
entire family for mothers to have another interest – a job, school or
even volunteer work. You become more well-rounded when you have more
to think about than housework or your child's science project that's due.
The housework and the science projects will still have to get done,
and you may have less time to devote to these things, but you will be
amazed at how they do get done anyway. ~~Responsibilities can be
delegated to children or husbands that you used to take care of
yourself — and yes, they can do it. Folding laundry may take away
some Nintendo playing time, but it teaches a child to be a little more
self-reliant. This can only be regarded as an asset.~~

11   Going back to school has done more for me than I expected it to.
So many times I've heard from other women like myself, 'I'd love to go
to school, but I don't think I could ever do it.' I want to jump up
and down, yelling 'Go for it!'. There's so much to be gained, and the
only way to find out is by trying it. I know that I'm glad I ran into
my friend that day who started the wheels turning for me. My life,
and my family's, took a whole new direction from that point on –
a better one.

Comparing Draft and Essay

1. Read the complete draft of "A Second Chance." What do you think is the writer's
   main point in telling her story? (Perhaps a paragraph-by-paragraph inspection of
   the essay will help you to grasp the author's meaning more easily.)

2. Now examine the published version of the essay. What is the main point of this
   narrative?

Draft Paragraphs 1 through 3

3. Compare draft paragraphs 1 through 3 with published paragraphs 1 through 3. How has Donaghy revised her draft in terms of *chronology* and *pacing*? How do these changes affect your perception of the main point of the narrative?

4. How would you characterize the tone of the draft and published versions of these paragraphs? Which do you find more interesting? Why?

Draft Paragraph 4

If you compare draft paragraph 4 with published paragraphs 3 through 5 you will see many important revisions. Donaghy is using addition, deletion, and rearrangement to bring out the ideas she wants to emphasize. In short, the changes made to this draft paragraph are critical to establishing the main point of the story. That is, if the story Donaghy wants to tell is her decision to start school, now is the time for her to slow down the action to *show* a reader what is happening. In the draft, meeting her friend, thinking that the time is right, and telling her mother and husband of her decision are all quickly reported and dispensed with. Yet such an important decision must have had more *action* to it! In the published version of the essay, note how the decision-making story is introduced at the beginning (the pivotal friend is now presented much earlier). Also observe how the actual decision is explained in greater detail: you are with Donaghy as her mind is "racing" with the possibility of being a "Lady of Leisure" (published paragraph 3). You are placed in the room to see her mother's face light up like "a Christmas tree" (published paragraph 4). And you are also present at the dinner table with the writer and her husband as he offers his support (published paragraph 5). In addition, note how background information, which had dominated draft paragraphs 2 and 3, is selectively woven into published paragraph 3 (past working experience with the phone company, self-confidence, and nursing). Such substantial changes in pacing and chronology help to keep the writer focused on and the reader interested in what is being discussed.

Draft Paragraphs 5 and 6

5. Why do you think Donaghy has deleted draft paragraphs 5 and 6 from the final version of the essay?

Draft Paragraphs 7 through 10

6. Compare draft paragraphs 7 through 10 with published paragraphs 6 through 9. What similarities exist among these versions of the essay? What differences can you find? What reasons can you provide for why Donaghy makes the changes she does? What specific revising strategies does she employ?

Draft Paragraph 11

7. Compare draft paragraph 11 with published paragraph 10. Which of these two conclusions do you think is more effective? (You might want to review the functions of conclusions on page 172.) Which conclusion most accurately represents the main point of Donaghy's narrative?

Louis J. Russo III

Louis J. Russo III is a student at Queensborough Community College. We think you will enjoy his autobiographical comments.

> Louis J. Russo III is a man who no matter what he puts his hands on will always put his full effort into it. Although I would like writing to be my life, I feel that effort shown is the whole ballgame. Being 20 and a sophomore in college, I feel that my life is flying by but I know the best is yet to come. My goals are kind of simple, pick a profession, try my best, and make sure that I always remain happy.

A Shot at Dreams

Introduction to the Essay and Draft

In past chapters, we have examined how purpose, meaning, audience, and tone affect a writer's approach to a work. Assignments that are part of a writing class introduce additional concerns to a writer. In effect, students completing course assignments need to juggle many considerations. In "A Shot at Dreams," Louis J. Russo III is responding to an assignment that requires him to write a story about something important that happened to him. In addition, the essay must be a *narrative* with a clear main point, it must be short—the length recommendation is two typed pages—and, last, it has to be completed within three weeks.

Russo acknowledges the above constraints and explains how he came to terms with them:

> *Short essays are the hardest to write because you really don't know which ideas you want to leave out. They are all important, just that some are more important than others. I've learned that if you just stick to the point that people will always understand what you're getting at.*

In the draft and published versions of "A Shot at Dreams" that follow, you will be able to examine how Russo ultimately complies with the demands placed on him as a writer. In particular, you will see how he negotiates meaning, pacing, and chronology to guide his revision and make his narrative more effective.

Final Essay

1   Did you ever have a dream, a dream you wanted so bad that you would have done anything to have it? And then when you could almost taste it, it got crushed before you even knew what happened. Well, I got to experience both, the dream and the disaster.

2   It all began when I was ten. I decided to take up a sport called hockey. When I turned fourteen I was asked to play for a team called the Flames. I was

invited on a one year tryout basis. The coach told me that at times professional scouts come and view his team.

3   The next year came up quickly and before I knew it I was back on the ice again. This was a great year for me; I was tearing up the league and making a name for myself. I was approached by three professional farm team scouts; they all told me the same thing, if I keep playing like this I will go pro in five years. I knew this could be my chance, so I worked harder and harder trying not to blow it.

4   At the end of the season I developed some pain in my left knee. I was told by my doctor not to play. He said that there was some ligament damage and if I played it could worsen. This hit home because I knew that one missed season could cost me my career. I made my decision and prepared for next season.

5   The year was going great and I once again was tearing up the league. Midway through the season I began to feel noticeable pain in my left knee. With five games left in the season we played the toughest team in the league. This was the roughest game that I ever played.

6   Midway through the third period we were up 3 to 2. The face-off was deep in our end. We were one man down because of a penalty. When the shot was taken, our goalie deflected it right to me. I saw an opening down the right side of the ice. I had everyone beat, or at least I thought I did. I didn't think he was that close and I was about to take a shot. That's when he hit me. The pain that I felt was like someone had just rammed a three foot needle through the side of my left knee. At first all I could think about was that it was over, but the pain was so intense I didn't think long.

7   When I awoke the next day, I was in a hospital listening to a doctor tell me that I should never play hockey again. I was so upset that I cried for days. To this day all I keep thinking about is that game and how I should have listened to my doctor and not played. The only good that came out of this is the way I run my life now.

8   Nowadays, I still keep my dreams in sight, and still hope that someday they will come true. I also put everything into perspective and make sure that I look at it from all angles. I usually try not to think about what happened. Now that I write about it, I realize that it is better to have almost had something than to never have had anything at all.

Draft

A Shot At Dreams

1   Did you ever ~~have~~ have a dream, a dream that you wanted so bad that you would have done anything to have it. ~~XXXXXXXX~~. And then when you could almost taste it, it got crushed before you even new what happened. Well, I got to experience both, the dream, and the disaster.

2   It all began when I was ten.
I decided to take up a sport called Hockey.
I began to purchase the equipment for
the sport hoping that I will ~~thoroughly~~ thoroughly
enjoy the game. Well, I did. I enjoyed
the game so much, I began to play it
everyday untill I got good at it.
Then, when I felt I was good enough
I joined a team. ~~the most fun I ever
had was when I started playing for
this team. We were named the Bruins.
We weren't such a good team, but I
was having fun and I guess thats
all that counts.~~

3   When I turned fourteen I was
asked to play for a team on the
Island called the Flames. They
were a really good team, and I was
excited to play for them. I was invited
on a one year tryout basis, ~~so this
made me work harder than ever
before.~~ The coach told me that at times
proffesional scouts come and ~~see~~ scout his
team. I was virtually a nobody, bieng a rookie
and all. At the end of the season

4   I was third on the team in goals
and second in assists. I new for sure
that I would be asked to come back
and play again next year, well I was.

New
Paragraph ⟩ The next year came up quickly and
before I new it I was back on the
Ice again. This was a great year for
me. I was tearing up the league and
making a name for myself. I was
approached by three proffesional farm
team scouts, they all told me the
same thing, If I keep playing like
this I will go pro in five years. ~~When
my friends and family had heard this
they all went~~ went crazy with enthusiasm.
I new this could be my chance so
I worked harder and harder trying
not to blow it.

5

At the end of the season I developed some pain in my left knee. ~~When I had a specialist look at it he told me that I strained the ligaments in the knee.~~ He told me that I shouldn't play Hockey next year. ~~I said "no way, you only get one shot with those scouts" he said that if I tear the ~~~~ligaments the consequences my be that I will be unable to play at all.~~ I totaly ignored his orders and prepared for next season. The year was going great and I was once again tearing up the league. I once again meet with

Being sent to a specialist made me feel Inferior because of the Consequences I new might arise.

Because of the severity of Damages to the ligaments in my left knee

Reel

New Paragraph

~~Scouts~~ scouts, they told me that I am ~~on~~ my way. ~~I never even felt a twinge in my knee until about ten games before the season ended, but I was have to good of a season to sit down now, so I continued to play.~~ With five games left in the season we played the toughest team in the league. They were the hardest hitters around. I new going into this game that they would go ~~after~~ me because I was my teams ~~leading~~ leading scorer. This was the roughest game that I ever played, and then it happened, midway through the third we were up. ~~3~~ 3-2. I was skating down Ice, with the puck, when the guy hit me, he hit me square in my left knee. I then fell to the ground and was unable to get up. The pain was just to great to remember, and the only other thing I remember was the doctor telling me I would never play the game again.

Midway through the season I Began to feel Noticable pain In my left knee

6   *I was so upset about this,*
         that I cryed for days. To this
         day all I keep thinking about
         is that game and how I should
         have Listened to my doctor, and not
         played. The only good that could
         have came out of this is the fact
    New *of the way I run my life now.*

Paragraph → *Nowadays I still keep my dreams*
         in sight, and still hope that
         someday they will come true, but
         I also put every thing into
         perspective and make sure I look
         at it from all angles. I usually
         try not to think about what happened
         but now that I write about it, I realize
         that is better to have almost had
         something then to never have had anything
         at all.

Comparing Draft and Essay

In a narrative essay, a useful organizing strategy is *time*. That is, an effective way to organize body paragraphs is to arrange them along the sequence of individual events that actually occur in time. Organizing along the beginning, middle, and end of an event will provide a writer with a rough outline; refining this sketch to accommodate contributing minor episodes will help to coordinate the complete organization of the narrative. This control over *chronology* is an important concern that Russo brings to the revision of his essay and is reflected by his use of *rearrangement* to reorganize the draft.

Another primary concern for Russo is *meaning*, the *main point* that he wants to get across to his readers. Because he covers much time in his narrative, he revises carefully to help a reader zero in on the part of the story that contains the main idea he wants to convey. The targeting of the main point is largely accomplished by *pacing*; background information is quickly provided while the central action is slowed down to show it more clearly and in greater detail.

Draft Paragraphs 2 and 3

1. Compare these draft paragraphs with published paragraphs 2 and 3. How do Russo's revisions affect pacing and chronology? What specific revising strategies does he use?

Draft Paragraphs 4 and 5

2. Note that draft paragraph 4 has been divided among published paragraphs 4, 5, 6, and part of 7. Why do you think Russo has made these changes? How does his use of *addition* and *deletion*—as well as rearrangement—help you to understand his meaning?

3. How is revision used to create published paragraph 6? What is this paragraph's role in the essay?

Draft Paragraph 5

Once again, Russo uses the sequence of events in time to reorganize his draft. He moves the first half of this paragraph to published paragraph 7, as it is the chronological continuation of the hospital episode. The second half of the draft paragraph is then used to form a chronologically distinct conclusion that explicitly states his meaning.

Eudora Welty

Eudora Welty (b. 1909) was born in Jackson, Mississippi. Her publications include novels, short stories, and essays. *One Writer's Beginnings* (1984), from which the following excerpt is taken, is her account of how she became a writer. Her most recent publication is *The Norton Book of Friendship* (1991). In an interview about her writing process, Welty talked about how she uses "scissors and pins" to revise her work:

> My ideal way to write . . . is to write the whole first draft through in one setting, then work as long as it takes on revisions, and then write the final version, all in one, so that in the end the whole thing amounts to one long sustained effort. . . . I can correct better if I see it in typescript. After that I revise with scissors and pins. Pasting is too slow, and you can't undo it but with pins you can move things from anywhere to anywhere, and that's what I really love doing—putting things in their best and proper place, revealing things at the time when they matter most.

Miss Duling

1   From the first I was clamorous to learn—I wanted to know and begged to be told not so much what, or how, or why, or where, as when. How soon?

Pear tree by the garden gate,
How much longer must I wait?

This rhyme from one of my nursery books was the one that spoke for me. But I lived not at all unhappily in this craving, for my wild curiosity was in large part suspense, which carries its own secret pleasure. And so one of the godmothers of fiction was already bending over me.

2   When I was five years old, I knew the alphabet, I'd been vaccinated (for smallpox), and I could read. So my mother walked across the street to Jefferson Davis Grammar School and asked the principal if she would allow me to enter the first grade after Christmas.

3   "Oh, all right," said Miss Duling. "Probably the best thing you could do with her."

4   Miss Duling, a lifelong subscriber to perfection, was a figure of authority, the most whole-souled I have ever come to know. She was a dedicated schoolteacher who denied herself all she might have done or whatever other way she might have lived (this possibility was the last that could have occurred to us, her subjects in school). I believe she came of well-off people, well-educated, in Kentucky, and certainly old photographs show she was a beautiful, high-spirited-looking young lady—and came down to Jackson to its new grammar school that was going begging for a principal. She must have earned next to nothing; Mississippi then as now was the nation's lowest-ranking state economically, and

our legislature has always shown a painfully loud reluctance to give money to public education. That challenge *brought* her.

5   In the long run she came into touch, as teacher or principal, with three generations of Jacksonians. My parents had not, but everybody else's parents had gone to school to her. She'd taught most of our leaders somewhere along the line. When she wanted something done—some civic oversight corrected, some injustice made right overnight, or even a tree spared that the fool telephone people were about to cut down—she telephoned the mayor, or the chief of police, or the president of the power company, or the head doctor at the hospital, or the judge in charge of a case, or whoever, and calling them by their first names, *told* them. It is impossible to imagine her meeting with anything less than compliance. The ringing of her brass bell from their days at Davis School would still be in their ears. She also proposed a spelling match between the fourth grade at Davis School and the Mississippi Legislature, who went through with it; and that told the Legislature.

6   Her standards were very high and of course inflexible, her authority was total; why *wouldn't* this carry with it a brass bell that could be heard ringing for a block in all directions? That bell belonged to the figure of Miss Duling as though it grew directly out of her right arm, as wings grew out of an angel or a tail out of the devil. When we entered, marching, into her school, by strictest teaching, surveillance, and order we learned grammar, arithmetic, spelling, reading, writing, and geography; and she, not the teachers, I believe, wrote out the examinations: need I tell you, they were "hard."

7   She's not the only teacher who has influenced me, but Miss Duling in some fictional shape or form, has stridden into a larger part of my work than I'd realized until now. She emerges in my perhaps inordinate number of schoolteacher characters. I loved those characters in the writing. But I did not, in life, love Miss Duling. I was afraid of her high-arched bony nose, her eyebrows lifted in half-circles above her hooded, brilliant eyes, and of the Kentucky R's in her speech, and the long steps she took in her hightop shoes. I did nothing but fear her bearing-down authority, and did not connect this (as of course we were meant to) with our own need or desire to learn, perhaps because I already had this wish, and did not need to be driven.

8   She was impervious to lies or foolish excuses or the insufferable plea of not knowing any better. She wasn't going to have any frills, either, at Davis School. When a new governor moved into the mansion, he sent his daughter to Davis School; her name was Lady Rachel Conner. Miss Duling at once called the governor to the telephone and told him, "She'll be plain Rachel here."

9   Miss Duling dressed as plainly as a Pilgrim on a Thanksgiving poster we made in the schoolroom, in a longish black-and-white checked gingham dress, a bright thick wool sweater the red of a railroad lantern—she'd knitted it herself—black stockings and her narrow elegant feet in black hightop shoes with heels you could hear coming, rhythmical as a parade drum down the hall. Her silky black curly hair was drawn back out of curl, fastened by high combs, and

knotted behind. She carried her spectacles on a gold chain hung around her neck. Her gaze was in general sweeping, then suddenly at the point of concentration upon you. With a swing of her bell that took her whole right arm and shoulder, she rang it, militant and impartial, from the head of the front steps of Davis School when it was time for us all to line up, girls on one side, boys on the other. We were to march past her into the school building, while the fourth-grader she nabbed played time on the piano, mostly to a tune we could have skipped to, but we didn't skip into Davis School.

10   Little recess (open-air exercises) and big recess (lunch-boxes from home opened and eaten on the grass, on the girls' side and the boys' side of the yard) and dismissal were also regulated by Miss Duling's bell. The bell was also used to catch us off guard with fire drill.

11   It was examinations that drove my wits away, as all emergencies do. Being expected to measure up was paralysing. I failed to make 100 on my spelling exam because I missed one word and that word was "uncle." Mother, as I knew she would, took it personally. "You couldn't spell *uncle?* When you've got those five perfectly splendid uncles in West Virginia? What would *they* say to that?"

12   It was never that Mother wanted me to beat my classmates in grades; what she wanted was for me to have my answers right. It was unclouded perfection I was up against.

13   My father was much more tolerant of possible error. He only said, as he steeply and impeccably sharpened my pencils on examination morning, "Now just keep remembering: the examinations were made out for the *average* student to pass. That's the majority. And if the majority can pass, think how much better *you* can do."

14   I looked to my mother, who had her own opinions about the majority. My father wished to treat it with respect, she didn't. I'd been born left-handed, but the habit was broken when I entered the first grade in Davis School. My father had insisted. He pointed out that everything in life had been made for the convenience of right-handed people, because they were the majority, and he often used "what the majority wants" as a criterion for what was for the best. My mother said she could not promise him, could not promise him at all, that I wouldn't stutter as a consequence. Mother had been born left-handed too; her family consisted of five left-handed brothers, a left-handed mother, and a father who could write with both hands at the same time, also backwards and forwards and upside down, different words with each hand. She had been broken of it when she was young, and she said she used to stutter.

15   "But you still stutter," I'd remind her, only to hear her say loftily, "You should have heard me when I was your age."

16   In my childhood days, a great deal of stock was put, in general, in the value of doing well in school. Both daily newspapers in Jackson saw the honor roll as news and published the lists, and the grades, of all the honor students. The city fathers gave the children who made the honor roll free season tickets to the baseball games down at the grandstand. We all attended and all worshiped some

player on the Jackson Senators: I offered up my 100's in arithmetic and spelling, reading and writing, attendance and, yes, deportment—I must have been a prig!—to Red McDermott, the third baseman. And our happiness matched that of knowing Miss Duling was on her summer vacation, far, far away in Kentucky.

Considering Content

1. Create a profile of Miss Duling that includes both favorable and unfavorable characteristics. How might you respond to her as a teacher?

2. How does Miss Duling acquire so much power in the community? To what extent does her appearance contribute to her authority?

3. Characterize Welty's attitudes toward Miss Duling. How are they similar to or different from those of her parents?

4. Welty's parents had different viewpoints on the subject of "majority." What were they? How did they affect Welty? Which of their attitudes best reflect yours?

Considering Craft

1. Welty's description of Miss Duling is both objective and subjective. Is there a pattern to the details she has selected? How do you react to Miss Duling?

2. Welty also includes details about her parents and herself. How effectively does she connect all of these? Consider, for example, whether the story of Welty's left-handedness detracts from or contributes to the essay's unity.

3. Discuss Welty's use of dialogue. How does that affect the tone of her essay? Characterize her tone. Is it appropriate for her subject?

4. Read over Welty's introduction. Why is it effective? How does her concluding sentence contribute to the unity of her essay?

Loren Eiseley

Loren Eiseley (1907–1977) was a prolific essayist and poet who also taught anthropology at the University of Pennsylvania for several years. A philosopher by nature, he was intrigued by the role of fate and its interrelationship with nature and the individual. In "How Flowers Changed the World" from *The Immense Journey* (1957), Eiseley presents a scientific subject in a poetic way, seeking to reach a more general audience. As you read his essay, evaluate the extent to which he fulfills this purpose.

How Flowers Changed the World

1   When the first simple flower bloomed on some raw upland late in the Dinosaur Age, it was wind pollinated, just like its early pine-cone relatives. It was a very inconspicuous flower because it had not yet evolved the idea of using the surer attraction of birds and insects to achieve the transportation of pollen. It sowed its own pollen and received the pollen of other flowers by the simple vagaries of the wind. Many plants in regions where insect life is scant still follow this principle today. Nevertheless, the true flower—and the seed that it produced—was a profound innovation in the world of life.

2   In a way, this event parallels, in the plant world, what happened among animals. Consider the relative chance for survival of the exteriorly deposited egg of a fish in contrast with the fertilized egg of a mammal, carefully retained for months in the mother's body until the young animal (or human being) is developed to a point where it may survive. The biological wastage is less—and so it is with the flowering plants. The primitive spore, a single cell fertilized in the beginning by a swimming sperm, did not promote rapid distribution, and the young plant, moreover, had to struggle up from nothing. No one had left it any food except what it could get by its own unaided efforts.

3   By contrast, the true flowering plants (angiosperm itself means "encased seed") grew a seed in the heart of a flower, a seed whose development was initiated by a fertilizing pollen grain independent of outside moisture. But the seed, unlike the developing spore, is already a fully equipped *embryonic plant* packed in a little enclosed box stuffed full of nutritious food. Moreover, by featherdown attachments, as in dandelion or milkweed seed, it can be wafted upward on gusts and ride the wind for miles; or with hooks it can cling to a bear's or a rabbit's hide; or like some of the berries, it can be covered with a juicy, attractive fruit to lure birds, pass undigested through their intestinal tracts and be voided miles away.

4   The ramifications of this biological invention were endless. Plants traveled as they had never traveled before. They got into strange environments heretofore never entered by the old spore plants or stiff pine-cone-seed plants. The well-fed, carefully cherished little embryos raised their heads everywhere. Many of the older plants with more primitive reproductive mechanisms began to fade away under this unequal contest. They contracted their range into secluded environments. Some, like the giant redwoods, lingered on as relics; many vanished entirely.

5   The world of the giants was a dying world. These fantastic little seeds skipping and hopping and flying about the woods and valleys brought with them an amazing adaptability. If our whole lives had not been spent in the midst of it, it would astound us. The old, stiff, sky-reaching wooden world had changed into something that glowed here and there with strange colors, put out queer, unheard-of fruits and little intricately carved seed cases, and, most important of all, produced concentrated foods in a way that the land had never seen before or dreamed of back in the fish-eating, leaf-crunching days of the dinosaurs.

6   That food came from three sources, all produced by the reproductive system of the flowering plants. There were the tantalizing nectars and pollens intended to draw insects for pollenizing purposes, and which are responsible also for that wonderful jeweled creation, the hummingbird. There were the juicy and enticing fruits to attract larger animals, and in which tough-coated seeds were concealed, as in the tomato, for example. Then, as if this were not enough, there was the food in the actual seed itself, the food intended to nourish the embryo. All over the world, like hot corn in a popper, these incredible elaborations of the flowering plants kept exploding. In a movement that was almost instantaneous, geologically speaking, the angiosperms had taken over the world. Grass was beginning to cover the bare earth until, today, there are over six thousand species. All kinds of vines and bushes squirmed and writhed under new trees with flying seeds.

7   The explosion was having its effect on animal life also. Specialized groups of insects were arising to feed on the new sources of food and, incidentally and unknowingly, to pollinate the plant. The flowers bloomed and bloomed in ever larger and more spectacular varieties. Some were pale unearthly night flowers intended to lure moths in the evening twilight, some among the orchids even took the shape of female spiders in order to attract wandering males, some flamed redly in the light of noon or twinkled modestly in the meadow grasses. Intricate mechanisms splashed pollen on the breasts of hummingbirds, or stamped it on the bellies of black, grumbling bees droning assiduously from blossom to blossom. Honey ran, insects multiplied, and even the descendants of that toothed and ancient lizard-bird had become strangely altered. Equipped with prodding beaks instead of biting teeth they pecked the seeds and gobbled the insects that were really converted nectar.

8   Across the planet grasslands were now spreading. A slow continental upthrust which had been a part of the early Age of Flowers had cooled the world's climates. The stalking reptiles and the leather-winged black imps of the seashore cliffs had vanished. Only birds roamed the air now, hot-blooded and high-speed metabolic machines.

9   The mammals, too, had survived and were venturing into new domains, staring about perhaps a bit bewildered at their sudden eminence now that the thunder lizards were gone. Many of them, beginning as small browsers upon leaves in the forest, began to venture out upon this new sunlit world of the grass. Grass has a high silica content and demands a new type of very tough and resistant tooth enamel, but the seeds taken incidentally in the cropping of the grass are highly nutritious. A new world had opened out for the warm-blooded mammals. Great herbivores like the mammoths, horses and bisons appeared. Skulking about them had arisen savage flesh-feeding carnivores like the now extinct dire wolves and the sabertoothed tiger.

10   Flesh eaters though these creatures were, they were being sustained on nutritious grasses one step removed. Their fierce energy was being maintained on a high, effective level, through hot days and frosty nights by the concentrated

energy of the angiosperms. That energy, thirty per cent or more of the weight of the entire plant among some of the cereal grasses, was being accumulated and concentrated in the rich proteins and fats of the enormous game herds of the grasslands.

11   On the edge of the forest, a strange, old-fashioned animal still hesitated. His body was the body of a tree dweller, and though tough and knotty by human standards, he was, in terms of that world into which he gazed, a weakling. His teeth, though strong for chewing on the rough fruits of the forest, or for crunching an occasional unwary bird caught with his prehensile hands, were not the tearing sabers of the great cats. He had a passion for lifting himself up to see about, in his restless, roving curiosity. He would run a little stiffly and uncertainly, perhaps, on his hind legs, but only in those rare moments when he ventured out upon the ground. All this was the legacy of his climbing days; he had a hand with flexible fingers and no fine specialized hoofs upon which to gallop like the wind.

12   If he had any idea of competing in that new world, he had better forget it; teeth or hooves, he was much too late for either. He was a ne'er-do-well, an inbetweener. Nature had not done well by him. It was as if she had hesitated and never quite made up her mind. Perhaps as a consequence he had a malicious gleam in his eye, the gleam of an outcast who has been left nothing and knows he is going to have to take what he gets. One day a little band of these odd apes—for apes they were—shambled out upon the grass; the human story had begun.

13   Apes were to become men, in the inscrutable wisdom of nature, because flowers had produced seeds and fruits in such tremendous quantities that a new and totally different store of energy had become available in concentrated form. Impressive as the slow-moving, dim-brained dinosaurs had been, it is doubtful if their age had supported anything like the diversity of life that now rioted across the planet or flashed in and out among the trees. Down on the grass by a streamside, one of those apes with inquisitive fingers turned over a stone and hefted it vaguely. The group clucked together in a throaty tongue and moved off through the tall grass foraging for seeds and insects. The one still held, sniffed, and hefted the stone he had found. He liked the feel of it in his fingers. The attack on the animal world was about to begin.

14   If one could run the story of that first human group like a speeded-up motion picture through a million years of time, one might see the stone in the hand change to the flint ax and the torch. All that swarming grassland world with its giant bison and trumpeting mammoths would go down in ruin to feed the insatiable and growing numbers of a carnivore who, like the great cats before him, was taking his energy indirectly from the grass. Later he found fire and it altered the tough meats and drained their energy even faster into a stomach ill adapted for the ferocious turn man's habits had taken.

15   His limbs grew longer, he strode more purposefully over the grass. The stolen energy that would take man across the continents would fail him at last.

The great Ice Age herds were destined to vanish. When they did so, another hand like the hand that grasped the stone by the river long ago would pluck a handful of grass seed and hold it contemplatively.

16   In that moment, the golden towers of man, his swarming millions, his turning wheels, the vast learning of his packed libraries, would glimmer dimly there in the ancestor of wheat, a few seeds held in a muddy hand. Without the gift of flowers and the infinite diversity of their fruits, man and bird, if they had continued to exist at all, would be today unrecognizable. Archaeopteryx, the lizard-bird, might still be snapping at beetles on a sequoia limb; man might still be a nocturnal insectivore gnawing a roach in the dark. The weight of a petal has changed the face of the world and made it ours.

Considering Content

1. What stages does Eiseley delineate in the process by which "flowers" changed plant life? How did angiosperms change animal life?

2. Why did the human being, "a strange old-fashioned animal," hesitate to become involved in the changing world? How did flowers eventually change even this creature?

3. Exaggeration is often used to describe the process of evolution, be it a statement that "flowers changed the world," that man descended from monkeys, or that heaven and earth were created in six days. Why does this subject lend itself to exaggeration, or hyperbole? What other subjects are likewise subject to hyperbole?

4. Our earliest ancestors are a fascinating topic for research and speculation. How do *you* imagine them? How *many* of them do you include in your earliest scene? How do they act? Speak? Are they vicious or gentle? Are their feelings like yours?

Considering Craft

1. Eiseley uses description in this narrative of evolution. At what points in the essay does he describe the visual appearance of evolving life? What spatial arrangements does he use?

2. How does Eiseley's choice of a third-person narration affect the tone of his essay? Is his tone objective? Scientific? Informative? Explain.

3. Eiseley uses many figures of speech to dramatize the story of evolution. He uses simile, as in "All over the world, like hot corn in a popper, these incredible

elaborations of the flowering plants kept exploding" (paragraph 6), and he also uses personification, as in "These fantastic little seeds skipping and hopping and flying about" (paragraph 5). Find other examples of personification in his essay. How are they effective?

4. Eiseley was both a poet and an anthropologist. Make one list of the scientific words he uses and a second list of the poetic words. Define unfamiliar words on both lists such as "vagaries" (1), "metabolic" (8), and "prehensible" (11). Is the combination of scientific and poetic language effective? Discuss.

Christopher Hallowell

Christopher Hallowell (b. 1945) has been a freelance writer since 1978, contributing to several environmental and ecological journals including *Audubon* and *National Geographic*. "Man Talk" appeared originally in the "About Men" column of *The New York Times*. As you read his essay, speculate as to why he selected this particular audience. Write a journal entry about someone you know who has the AIDS virus.

Man Talk

1   A priest rang my door bell not long ago. I do not know any priests, but I always notice them. I have always assumed that priests know great secrets bestowed from Above. I sensed that this one was about to deliver a portentous message and, as I opened the door, I shooed my curious 5-year-old son back into the depths of our home.

2   I was right. The priest told me that one of my tenants, Sam, who was also a member of his church, had been admitted to the hospital a few days earlier with a severe case of pneumonia. He was in intensive care. No visitors were permitted except family.

3   I was as shocked by the message as by the way the priest delivered it. He was a sensitive-looking man with fragile eyes, one who I expected would impart unhappy news with softness. But his manner to me was clipped, almost brusque. I asked him if Sam would recover. It flashed through my mind that this was the kind of secret a priest would know. The man probed my eyes with his, and an expression crossed his face that communicated more than words ever could. It told me why Sam was in the hospital and confirmed all the statistics I had read about survival rates these days of young men with pneumonia.

4   My comprehension, evident, I imagine by the expression on my face, embarrassed the priest. I understood why he had been so brusque; he had not

wanted our exchange to go this far. He lowered his eyes, and we both reddened in recognition that we shared the kind of private information that men who are strangers find hard to acknowledge.

5   Poor sweet Sam, a gentle man, the only person who could ascend or descend the four creaking flights of our old brownstone to and from his little apartment on the top floor without making a sound. A buyer for a clothing store, he would noiselessly leave for work at 8 A.M. dressed in fine suits and natty ties. He rarely returned before midnight. On weekends, he sometimes met my children on the stairs and engaged them in conversation. He asked them serious questions about their toys.

6   Once, Sam found me a writing assignment. He gave my wife, a fashion photographer, the names of possible clients. Something of a history buff, he always steered our conversations to what he knew of the past. Sam did not wish to reveal much about his present and I, perhaps fearful that revelations would change our pleasant relationship, did not want him to.

7   Sam's condition did not worsen immediately. But after a few weeks had passed, my doorbell rang again. It was his mother. She was a small, spirited woman who had come from New England to be near her son until, as she said, "We lick this thing." She was going to stay in his apartment. I wondered where her husband, Sam's father, was.

8   More weeks passed, and an uneasy waiting settled over our house, broken only by the return of Sam's mother each afternoon from her daily visit to her son's bedside. My son kept asking her when Sam was going to come home. She always said, "He'll be home soon."

9   One day, Sam's mother looked deeply changed, and the next day the halls of our house were filled with the acrid smell of strong tobacco. I heard a man's voice upstairs. A while later, Sam's mother introduced me to Sam's father. He looked like an older and tired version of Sam. I greeted him emphatically and with concern, but he would not look at me. He kept staring at the walls. As we struggled for a language in common, jumbled words fell from his mouth.

10   His facial muscles began twitching, and he mumbled something about "high fever" and "doctors don't know." Then he turned away. He could not acknowledge that I knew something about his son's life that he could not, or would not, publicly recognize. I wondered if he ever thought about that part of Sam's life or if he just refused to let it enter his consciousness, whether he blamed himself, or blamed Sam. I wondered if Sam's father saw it coming in Sam, whether fathers were helpless, what I would think or do if my son ever disappeared into that world.

11   My son asked why Sam's father acted "so funny." I told him it was because his son was sick. "Daddy, is Sam going to die?" I told him the truth, that Sam was very sick and might die soon. "Well, Daddy, if Sam dies, he'll go to Heaven, won't he?" I answered that maybe he would. "And when Sam's daddy dies," my son continued, "he'll go to Heaven, too. And then Sam and his daddy will be happy together, right?" I said yes. If Heaven exists, I thought, my son is right.

12   Sam died a week later, three months after he went into the hospital. At a gathering following the funeral his mother wept. His father stood off by himself, an impenetrable wall around him.

13   Soon after, the couple began clearing out their son's apartment. I thought about them up there, going through Sam's things, saving this, throwing out that. One night, they put out a full plastic trash bag for the next morning's garbage pickup. In the darkness somebody or some animal broke into it, spewing its contents about—black motorcycle boots, leather, black underwear. I quickly returned the contents to the bag and hoped that Sam's parents were not looking down at me.

14   Sam's father changed. Bumbling confusion no longer controlled him. He took control of the job. He called moving services and storage companies, thrift shops and used furniture stores. He came to me to complain about the malfunctioning doorbell in Sam's apartment. He suggested that I examine the transformer in the basement. When I told him that I had, he wondered if I had checked the contacts. We talked. We had a conversation about wiring and moisture in the circuits, kinds of intercoms and installation costs. It was traditional man-to-man talk, familiar across generations and empty of emotion. As we went on, Sam's father's face took on an animation I had not thought possible two weeks before. Its lines seemed to settle into the skin more naturally. He looked me in the eye. Now Sam's father could face the world.

Considering Content

1. When Hallowell asked the priest if Sam, a "young" man, would survive pneumonia, we know that Hallowell suspected what disease? Is the disease ever named in the essay? Is this a good idea? Why had the priest hoped that Hallowell's "comprehension" would not "go this far"?

2. How well did Hallowell know Sam? How does Hallowell describe their relationship?

3. Why wouldn't Sam's father look at Hallowell at their first meeting?

4. Compare Sam's father and his mother. Does the father change? How? Why?

5. Hallowell's son asks about Sam and his father being reunited in Heaven. Can you tell what Hallowell feels when his son asks this question? What do you think of Hallowell's answer?

6. "It was traditional man-to-man talk. . . ." What, in general, is man-to-man talk? What point is Hallowell making about that talk or about men? Do you agree with that point?

7. Hallowell wonders what he would do if *his* son "ever disappeared into that world." Judging from this essay, what do you think Hallowell would do?

Considering Craft

1. What details most effectively convey the cause of Sam's pneumonia during the encounter between the priest and the narrator?

2. What portrait of Sam emerges from the essay? How is it enhanced by the details of Sam's relationship with Hallowell's wife and children?

3. How does the title "Man Talk" relate to Hallowell's including so many details of Sam's father's reaction to his illness and death? Characterize your response to the father.

4. Define the tone of the essay and evaluate its appropriateness in terms of the author's audience.

5. Is Hallowell's essay limited to a male audience or does it also have something to say to females? Why or why not?

Joan Ackermann

Joan Ackermann is a freelance journalist who has been published in *Time, Sports Illustrated, The Atlantic, Esquire,* and numerous other publications. She is also a playwright whose plays include "Zara Spook and Other Lures," "Rescuing Greeland," and "Don't Ride the Clutch." She lives in Berkshire County in western Massachusetts with her rooster, rabbit, and dog.

In New Mexico: A Family Lives in Its Own World

1   "Chicken power," says Ron Oest, exulting in his chicken house in northern New Mexico. "That's what keeps our winter water supply from freezing. See, they roost right under the tank." Up on the roost, two dozen hens ride out the winter, unwittingly warming a thousand gallons of mountain stream water stored in the black tank that bellies down from the ceiling. It is an efficient use of passive poultry energy, harnessed by a resourceful man who supports his family handsomely on $5,000 a year.

2   "We don't have any money in the bank," explains his wife Nora, who is part Spanish, part Chiricahua Apache. She can butcher a bear and cook up a steak in the Franklin stove so tender it softens a person's attitude toward grizzlies. "We don't have any credit. No life insurance," she says with a smile, the earthy enduring smile that heroines in South American novels bequeath to their daughters.

3   "People don't realize how much earning money costs," says Oest, 55. "Having a job is expensive. The clothes, the car, the house with the mortgage

payments. If you spend all your time working for someone else, you don't have time to learn to do things yourself."

4   Unemployed for nearly 20 years since he was a high school speech coach and creative-writing teacher, he has had time to learn, among other things, how to build his own house, overhaul VW engines in his living room, keep bees for honey and make his own bullets out of wheel weights. He grew up in Rutherford, N.J., disliking cities and laying a 75-trap line for muskrats down through what is now the Meadowlands. A wounded Korean War vet, he collects $333 a month veteran's compensation, and that, along with $1,200 he and Nora make each year selling their crafts, is enough to buy the various items—gas, Postum, margarine—that they can't grow in their garden, hunt, sew, fish for, trade for or find in the Taos County dump.

5   Married for 18 years, the Oests met when he was teaching in a high school in Albuquerque and she was a sophomore. "She walked by and I handed her a book, and I felt myself falling in love," says Ron. After she graduated, he wrote her a poem, they dated, went to Mexico, got married and lived for three years in a 1948 yellow school bus parked in a coconut grove.

6   For the past 15 years, the Oests have lived in the Valdez Valley on three acres of land that Nora inherited from her father, land he acquired by trading a La Salle automobile to his Uncle Pedro, who needed it to get to Wyoming.

7   "The way we live now isn't that different from how I lived here as a child," says Nora, 36, whose great-great-great-grandfather on her father's side settled in the valley in the early 1800s to work the local gold mine, and whose great-great-grandfather on her mother's side was shot in the back delivering mail for the Pony Express.

8   Nora's childhood house was made of adobe, but she and Ron built their two-story, five-room house for $6,000 out of logs and cement. It is a handsome, organically grown house with unpredictable flourishes: the door handle made out of a part from a lawn mower, the recesses in the stone walls for candles, the richly ornate wood carvings throughout. Although the Oests don't have plumbing, a telephone or a well, they do have electricity and a refrigerator they bought for $10 from a neighbor who later shot himself because his condominiums failed.

9   In their front yard, snow melts off six other refrigerators, piles of tires, three Maytag washing machines, a dozen bicycles, several bed frames and various orderly piles of useful treasures, all harvested from the dump. Their toaster, broiler, blender, coffeepot, clock, heaters and just about every other electrical item in the house are also from the dump, repaired by Ron, along with down jackets, chairs, front ends for cars, wood, French windows and jars for canning.

10   "We've given away lots of bicycles and wagons to people less fortunate than us," says Nora. She has joined Ron on the porch and sips a cup of Yerba Buena herb tea. Today even the witches, famous in this valley, must be yielding to the sun, loosening their joints in this welcome reprieve from the chill.

11   "Once I found a typewriter in the dump that had five rusty keys and didn't work," says Ron. "I fixed it and traded it with a guy for a pig. Well, the pig had

eight piglets, and I traded five of them for three VW bugs, none of which ran. I overhauled one of them to get it going; cost me $40. The next litter I traded five more piglets for another VW. We named the pig Tubby Typewriter after the typewriter."

12   "She was a very mellow pig," says Nora, who makes wild-chokecherry wine and bakes all her breads and biscuits with homegrown wheat and rye. "When she had her first litter, we took a bottle of wine and some glasses into the pig house to help her through."

13   Indoors in the kitchen, the Oests' pretty daughter Laura, 8, entertains a school chum. "This is my survival knife," she says, deftly slipping a 14-in. knife from its canvas sheath.

14   "You aren't afraid to touch it?" asks her playmate, aghast and giggling, her hands stuffed into her open mouth.

15   "No," says Laura, who also has a pellet gun, two .22s, a .45-cal. muzzle-loading rifle and muzzle-loading pistol, a bow and arrows, a wild pony named Wild Rose and her own row of flowers and vegetables in the garden. "I use it to skin squirrels." She puts the knife back into its sheath as if she were tucking one of her Barbie dolls into bed. "Squirrels are good," she adds, reaching for one of her mother's hot homemade donuts, "but there's not much meat on them."

16   "Laura got her hunting license when she was seven," says Ron. "She was the youngest female in New Mexico ever to earn a hunting license."

17   The family often goes camping together, hunting and fishing, and Ron takes Laura to the Taos County dump to shoot bottles.

18   "When I was a kid in New Jersey," says Ron, "I used to go to the dump to hunt rats. There was this guy named Mike who lived there in a big refrigerator crate. I remember one day he was cooking up some potatoes he'd found, and he suddenly looked around and said to me, arms outstretched, 'This place is rich. *Rich.*' It really made an impression on me.

19   "I grew up in two devastating times: I was old enough as a kid to see people in the Depression, and then later I saw items rationed during the Second World War. There are times when there's nothing, and you can't get it anywhere. Why not have your own little world where you have everything you need so no one can ever say no to you?"

20   Although some aspects of their world seem idyllic, there are difficulties— constant battles to protect the environment, to keep the water in the nearby Rio Hondo clean, jaunts down to Mexico for cheaper dental work, the three-hour drive to the veteran's hospital in Albuquerque, the hopes that Laura's teeth don't grow in crooked and that her A grades will earn her a scholarship later on.

21   "Some people think it's scary to live the way we do," says Ron. "No life insurance. No savings. But if I die, the house is all paid for. We have four years' worth of food—canned, frozen and dried. We have three years' worth of firewood. No bills. We have stockpiles of clothes. Living like this you just don't ever suddenly need a lot of money."

Considering Content

1. Characterize the Oests' attitudes toward money and material possessions. On what do they base their system of values? How does it differ from yours?

2. Although materially poor, is there any sense in which the family is rich? Explain.

3. How has Laura's life been affected by her parents' values? How might you respond in her situation?

4. Would you describe this family as un-American? Why or why not?

Considering Craft

1. The essay begins and ends with a quotation from Ron Oest. How effective is this technique?

2. Create a profile of the author's intended audience (*Time* magazine). How might this readership respond? Does it surprise you that many letters to the editor accused the family of *not* contributing to society and expecting assistance for their daughter's college and dental work?

3. Characterize the tone of the essay. Is it objective, persuasive, neutral? Does the author reveal her attitude toward the family's way of life? If so, where?

Guidelines for Narrative and Descriptive Essays

Narration

1. For your own clarification, state in one sentence the main point of your essay. Then decide whether this point is clearly embodied or dramatized by the story.

2. What details or incidents are essential to the story? Decide where you need to slow your pacing with ample detail and where a quick summary will allow you to pick up your pace.

3. Decide on a point of view and stick to it. How close do you want to be to the action? Do you want to tell the story in your own voice or allow another character to tell it for you?

4. Which time sequence will work best, chronological or flashback?

5. Where will you need to indicate a transition from one section or phase of the story to the next? What transitional words, phrases, or even sentences will you use?

Description

1. Determine your purpose. Do you want to provide a factual, scientific, objective description? Or do you intend a sensuous, interpretive, subjective description?

2. What distinguishes the object(s) you are describing? List the essential details.

3. Try to appeal to more than one or two senses. What about the neglected senses of smell and touch, not to mention taste?

4. Arrange the essential details on your list in an effective order (dramatic, spatial, chronological). Will you begin with the nearest details, or the most obvious? Decide on a path for your camera.

5. What dominant impression do you want to create? How can attention to connotation help you choose your vocabulary?

Warm-up Exercises

1. Describe, using spatial order, a stationary object, such as a car or a stereo, from as many different angles as you can. How does your perspective affect your description?

2. Freewrite for ten minutes about AIDS including as many impressions as you can think of. Read over what you have written. What dominant impression do you want to create?

3. Write a journal entry about a pleasant or unpleasant event that took place in your childhood. First, use chronological order in recalling the event. Then rewrite it using flashback. How has the change in sequence affected your narrative?

4. Brainstorm about your association with one of the following: bakery, swimming pool, beach, health club, coffee shop, pizza parlor. Have you chosen adjectives that evoke sight, sound, taste, smell, and touch?

5. Write a paragraph to be placed on your college bulletin board, advertising a room for rent. Describe the room for a prospective renter using spatial order. Have you included as many visual details as you can?

6. Describe a scene, a person, or an object using figures of speech—simile, personification, or hyperbole—to enhance your description wherever possible.

Writing/Revising Topics

1. Write a three-paragraph *objective* description of someone you know well. You might include in your description physical details, personality traits, emotional

characteristics, or even a brief narrative describing your subject's behavior. After you have finished, write a three-paragraph *subjective* description about the same person. Compare both descriptions with regard to purpose, meaning, and tone. What general statements can you now make about the nature of objective and subjective description?

2. Try to describe a midsummer thunderstorm as objectively (scientifically) as possible. Next rewrite your description from a subjective (emotional) viewpoint. Consider which description will mention such details as the following: your fear of thunder and lightning, raindrops one centimeter in diameter, rain accumulating at the rate of two inches per hour, Mother Nature's light show, zero visibility, the romantic feeling rainstorms give you, a one-half-mile cloud ceiling, cumulonimbus clouds, or sudden coolness after the storm.

3. Welty and Alvarez write about people who influenced them while growing up. Write about a person whom you knew well. Choose, as did these writers, two or three specific experiences that best reveal the person. In revising your essay, look for parts that could be improved using the revision strategies of substitution and redistribution, as Alvarez did in "Daughter of Invention."

4. Write an essay on one of the following topics using flashbacks. Begin with a scene in the present—one that holds conflict for you—then recall earlier events. Create suspense by concealing until the end how your conflict is resolved.

   a. An educational experience outside school, such as something learned on the streets, in the family, or on a trip.
   b. An experience in strange and frightening surroundings.
   c. An experience with a bully.

5. Describe a place as you perceived it when you were feeling particularly romantic, either because you were in love with another person or because you were feeling in love simply with life itself. Re-describe the same place as you perceived it another time, when you were feeling less romantic. Which description is more realistic? How much is a person's perception of nature colored by his or her feelings at a particular moment? Organize your subjective and objective descriptions so that they illustrate a discussion of this question.

6. Make an outline for an essay on a sports or other action event that you witnessed. Write the essay using action verbs and dialogue. Pace the action in such a way as to capture the highlights while keeping the less significant aspects of the activity in the background through summary. In revising your essay, focus on tone, the introductory paragraph, and the main points of your narrative.

7. Using your freewriting from Warm-up Exercise 2 as the basis, write an essay about AIDS. Before beginning, review the Guidelines for Narrative Essays and determine your main point and your point of view. In revising your essay, make sure that both your thesis and your point of view will be clear to the reader.

8. Write a narration that teaches a lesson or moral. As much as possible avoid explaining the lesson or moral; instead, let your narration communicate the meaning through your selection of events and details. In revising your essay, make sure that your point of view is consistent and that the specific details you have presented will make your meaning clear to your reader.

9. Describe the street on which you are living today. Which details are most important to focus on to give the reader the general impression of what life is like in your neighborhood? In revising, review the Guidelines for Narrative and Descriptive Essays, focusing specifically on 2 and 4 under Description.

10. Write an essay about a family you know who, like the Oests, have a different concept of the American dream. Focus on specific details that will highlight for your reader the differences in their system of values.

*C*omposing Expository Essays

You are familiar with the word *exposition*. It used to mean World's Fair, as in EXPO '81, when nations of the world got together in Los Angeles to show off their products and skills. Expository essays are also in "show" business: they show the meaning of things, they explain, they "expose" to the understanding. In this chapter we examine another type of body paragraph with several subtypes, the expository paragraph. Essays whose body paragraphs are predominantly of this type are expository essays. The opening paragraph of Edward Hoagland's essay prepares the reader for the main point to follow by explaining that strange bird the anhinga:

> *The anhinga is a big snake-necked dagger-billed darkish bird with silver on its wings. It's all but peerless at catching fish in Southern swamps, and doesn't wait like a statuesque heron for food to swim to it, but tucking its wings against its sides, kicks fast underwater, ruddering with its tail.*

The subtypes of exposition to be examined here are comparison and contrast, definition, and division/classification. A fourth subtype, cause and effect, will be examined in the next chapter, along with persuasive writing.

Comparison and Contrast

Comparison is the examination of two or more subjects for the purpose of noting similarities and differences. In expository comparison, you examine specific likenesses and differences in detail, and by making both subjects better known, aid your general purpose for writing. One basic requirement is that the subjects you are comparing are comparable; you cannot authentically compare a baseball player and a spoon, or a musician and a soft drink, but you can compare or contrast two athletes, two utensils, two countries, or two ideas. Another requirement is that the same basis of comparison is applied to both items: if you intend to compare two politicians, you should not examine the first one's intelligence, morality, and experience and then analyze the second one's physical appearance, taste in clothing, and musical preferences. Quite simply, there is no basis for comparison or contrast here because no common ground is explored.

When you are organizing contrast, you have two options: (a) group the material *subject by subject,* finishing with subject *x* before you move on to subject *y,* or (b) organize *point by point,* switching back and forth between subjects *x* and *y* even within the same paragraph. In "Youth and Old Age," Aristotle uses the first method, fully explaining the attributes of youth before moving on to those of old age. In this way a reader forms a complete mental picture of the first subject before going on to the next one. Marcus Mabry applies the second organizational pattern to his essay "Living in Two Worlds." Mabry shuttles a reader between New Jersey and California as he describes and explains the significance of these two places.

Most important of all, comparison and contrast can be useful only if you know and tell why you are using it. Why compare? Why contrast? *Listing* similarities and differences is not sufficient to command someone's interest; make it clear to your reader *why* you are comparing *x* with *y.* Aristotle presents his contrast as a lesson about oration; by understanding youth and old age, "we can now see how to compose our speeches so as to adapt both them and ourselves to our audiences." For Mabry, comparison and contrast provides a framework for him to understand and explain his feelings about his firsthand experiences of affluence and poverty.

Definition

Definition may be thought of as description of words, or as setting limits to the meaning of words: the second syllable, *fin,* means end or limit, as in finish or final. Most people are familiar with only one kind of definition, that found in a dictionary and called the *dictionary* or *lexical definition.* You might begin a defining essay with a quotation of a definition from a dictionary, but it would probably be more interesting to try writing your *own* lexical definition. How do you write such a definition? Here is a dictionary definition of jujitsu:

> *A Japanese art of self-defense or hand-to-hand combat based on set maneuvers that force an opponent to use his weight and strength against himself.*

As usual, this dictionary definition falls into two parts: placement in a class and differentiation from other members of the same class. Here the class is "art of self-defense"; the differentiation is the rest of the definition. Try writing a dictionary definition of the following words:

	Word		Class		Differentiation
Ex:	A pancake	is	a hot breakfast food	that	is made from wheat
	Karate	is	_____	that	_____
	A mutual fund	is	_____	that	_____
	A haiku	is	_____	that	_____
	A bachelor	is	_____	that	_____

A more important kind of definition for the writer of exposition is *extended definition*. This type is most often used with words that have uncommon significance for you or provoke debate, because they are new, misused, technical, or abstract, or for some other reason. Such words as poverty, freedom, happiness, and love may have as many definitions as there are people to define them. Definition of such words can form the basis of a whole essay. Indeed entire libraries may be dedicated to the definition of a single word: a law library is established in the hope of defining but one word—justice. Hoagland's short essay "Hail the Anhinga" makes the definition of an unfamiliar word the starting point of an essay that moves from consideration of a water bird to consideration of one of the truths of life. Wendy Modeste, in her essay "Are You Really a Failure?" chooses to define the word "failure" before answering her topic question.

You might begin with a dictionary definition that you write yourself and then explore the feelings and ideas you attach to the word. In the extended part you can use any and all of the other modes—narration, description—and any of the other subtypes of exposition—comparison and contrast, classification, cause and effect, and so on—to clarify and enliven your thesis.

Division/Classification

Division/classification is a process by which something is divided into its constituent parts. Classification, like sorting clothes or silverware, is an act of dividing and organizing. The yellow pages, classified ads, catalogs, and indexes of all kinds use classification to bring order to a subject or a set of things by showing the relationship of parts to the whole and to one another. Classification is one of the best ways to understand and explain a subject.

Its purpose, like that of all exposition, is to explain and clarify. Classification, indeed, can be viewed as a special application of comparison and contrast because you place the items in their classes on the basis of their similarities: items in the same class are similar and the name or label of the class identifies the similarity. When making a classification, you are asking "What kinds of x are there?" and grouping these kinds on the basis of resemblances and differences.

Suppose your purpose is to convince the local school board to spend more money on certain sports. You might begin by classifying them, using as your basis of classification one of the following:

popularity with townspeople and alumni	local traditions
age at which the sport can be played	cost
number of players required	

You can see what a different classification each basis would produce. Your selection of the basis for your classification would finally have to depend on which one would most effectively get your point across. When applying division/classification, be careful to devise a logical basis for your final categories. Also remember that an effective classification will provide enough, but not too many, classes. Finally, classes must not overlap and items should appear in only one class.

Having devised a system, use other expository modes to develop it, such as explaining your purpose and the basis of classification, defining the names of classes, and perhaps comparing your classification to a less adequate one. Narration and description may also come to your aid.

Edward Hoagland

Edward Hoagland (b. 1932) writes short stories, novels, essays, and editorials. He lives part of the year with his family in New York City. But he also spends many months alone on a remote farm in Barton, Vermont. Hoagland's composing process usually begins with rough notes, which he then uses to write subsequent drafts. In one of his letters to us concerning his drafts of "Hail the Anhinga" he added a fascinating postscript: "I have not only no phone, but no electricity. I'm probably your only contributor who writes by kerosene lamp!"

Hail the Anhinga

Introduction to the Essay and Draft

Writers can sometimes make it look so easy! This brief essay by Edward Hoagland appears so simple, so effortlessly put together. It is as if every paragraph, sentence, and word has mysteriously fallen onto the page in perfect order. Even the author's statement regarding his method of organization and purpose contributes to the overall impression of ease.

> *In the first paragraph I was trying to establish the complexity of the personality possessed by this unusual species of bird. I wasn't yet going into the "flaws" that make it doubly interesting . . . Then the next couple of paragraphs elaborate on the anhinga's incongruities and difficulties, trying to make them poignant enough to lead into the last paragraph, which compares this bird . . . with Franklin Roosevelt directing the course of the Second World War from a wheelchair and Beethoven composing symphonies even as he went deaf—as well as all the rest of us as we become enfeebled and handicapped and old.*

Yet, do not let the *seeming* simplicity of "Hail the Anhinga" fool you. Hoagland has taken great care to convey his exact meaning in a form and style that are under his control at all times. Examine the draft page with the three introductions. These three versions of Hoagland's introductory paragraph visually demonstrate the revising process that he applies to his work—note the cross-outs, additions, and rearrangements that occur as he searches for the structure that will make his introduction an effective one. Such comprehensive writing and rewriting are responsible for the lucidity of Hoagland's prose; hard work, and not a mysterious, secret way of writing, is the process by which the author produces his completed essays. The introduction has been revised seven times, and each body paragraph has undergone at least three revisions.

Published Essay

1   The anhinga is a big snake-necked dagger-billed darkish bird with silver on its wings. It's all but peerless at catching fish in Southern swamps, and doesn't

wait like a statuesque heron for food to swim to it, but tucking its wings against its sides, kicks fast underwater, ruddering with its tail. Then it emerges to flourish, flip and gulp headfirst its piscatorial prey (or a crayfish, baby turtle, baby alligator). Afterward, as if to complement such mastery underwater, it may soar slowly aloft in towering circles on the thermals, like a hawk or buzzard, to entertain itself; and lays blue eggs and talks in grunts.

2   Darter, snakebird, water turkey—some local names give an idea of the anhinga's personality. It speeds sinuously through the water, and if it tasted better, might well resemble a slender turkey, if turkeys could both swim and soar. Indeed, being superbly at home in the water and the sky should make the anhinga a superbird—except for one poignant evolutionary flaw. It lacks the adequate preening glands with which, for instance, ducks and geese waterproof their feathers; so it would actually drown if it stayed in the water too long and its plumage got waterlogged. Nor can it fly until its wings are dry.

3   A flightless bird is terribly at risk, and even on bright days the anhinga stands spread-eagled facing the sun for lengthy periods between deep chases after fish. On cloudy days it has to skimp severely on its meals. Rainy days, it nearly fasts, posturing itself as straight as possible so gravity will make the wet run off. And when the weather clears, if you approach the anhinga with its wings spread to the sun before its feathers are dry enough for it to fly, it will plunge back underwater and get soaked all over again.

4   Flawed brilliance, or any marvelous facility greatly handicapped, is fascinating. Deaf Beethoven, Franklin Roosevelt waging war: or any one of us approaching Homer's "doorsill into old age." Think of the anhinga—nonpareil underwater but dragged down if it stays too long—triumphant when soaring high but looking for a sanctuary from which to warm its plumage enough to fly.

Draft

1   The anhinga is a snake-necked, spear-billed bird, or Florida's Everglades. but nonpareil/swamps like Georgia's Okefinokee. It doesn't which is all tops at catching fish in It tucks its wings wait like an egret or heron, but for an unaware fish to come to it. against its sides and swims fast underwater with its feet, ruddering then emerging to flourish and swallow whole itself with its tail, a piscatorial prize or crayfish, leeches, baby turtles, baby alligators.

1   The anhinga is a snake-necked, spear-billed,/bird blackish on its wings, Florida's Everglades or with silver//all but nonpareil at catching fish in swamps like/Georgia's for action/ a picturesque Okefinokee. It doesn't wait/like an egret or statuesque heron, swims about, tucking but its wings against its sides and swims fast underwater

                    its ~~the~~ tail a rudder. Then it
          with its feet, ~~ruddering/then~~ emerges to flourish and swallow

          whole a piscatorial prize, or crayfish, baby turtle, baby alligator.
                                                      may
          Yet to complement such mastery underwater, you ~~will~~ see it soaring
          in towering
slowly   ~~in/hawklike~~ circles on the southern thermals like a hawk to

          entertain itself

                                        big
1   The anhinga is a snake-necked, spear-billed, blackish bird
                                  nonpareil
          with silver on its wings, all but tops at catching fish in swamps
                                and
          like Georgia's Okefinokee ~~or~~ Florida's Everglades. It doesn't
                food to swim ~~xxxxx~~ to it, like a
          wait for ~~action/to/develop//like/a/picturesque/egret/or~~ statuesque
                          tucking its wings against its sides, kicks fast
          heron, but ~~swims/about//kicking/fast~~/underwater, ruddering ~~with~~
superbly/ Then it emerges to flourish, flip and gulp down whole/~~its piscatorial~~
~~itself~~ with its tail.//~~and~~ to complement such mastery underwater, ~~xxx~~ may ~~xxx~~ it
prize (or ~~a~~ crayfish, baby turtle, baby alligator). And yet
                          aloft afterwards
~~xxxxxxxx~~   ~~xxxxxx~~ soaring slowly/in towering circles on the Southern thermals
                  or buzzard
          like a hawk/to entertain itself. It lays blue eggs in a stick
                  communicates in
          nest and/grunts.

1   The anhinga is a big snake-necked, dagger-billed, blackish

          bird with silver on its wings, all but peerless at catching fish

          in swamps like Georgia's Okefinokee and Florida's Everglades. It

          doesn't wait for food to swim to it, like a statuesque heron, but,

          tucking its wings against its sides, kicks fast underwater,

          ruddering with its tail. Then it emerges to flourish, flip and

          gulp head-first its piscatorial prey (or a crayfish, baby alligator,

          baby turtle). Yet to complement such mastery underwater, it may

          soar slowly aloft afterwards in towering circles on the Southern

          thermals like a hawk or buzzard to entertain itself. It lays

          blue eggs in a stick nest and talks in grunts.

2   Several local names give an idea of the anhinga's variousness--

          darter, snakebird, water turkey. It speeds sinuously through

          the water, and if it tasted any good (which hunters say it

          doesn't) might resemble a turkey, if turkeys were much slenderer

          and could swim and soar. You would think that being so superbly at home both in the water and the sky would make the anhinga

(the word is Brazilian-Indian) a super-bird--as indeed it should,

except for one poignant evolutionary flaw. It lacks the oil

glands with which ducks and geese, for instance, waterproof and

preen their feathers, so it will drown if it stays in the water

too long and its plumage gets soaked and waterlogged. Nor can it

fly until its wings are dry. A flightless bird is terribly

at risk, and even on bright days it stands spread-eagled

facing the sun between fish-hunts. On cloudy days it skimps

         on
severely/ food. In rain it postures itself as straight as

possible on a branch, so gravity will make the wet run off;
               with its wings spread to the sun
    any d̶r̶y̶i̶n̶g̶ anhinga that you approach   feathers
and F̶l̶a̶w̶e̶d̶/̶b̶r̶i̶l̶l̶i̶a̶n̶c̶e̶/̶c̶o̶u̶l̶d̶ in a canoe before its w̶i̶n̶g̶s̶ are dry

enough to fly will plunge back underwater and get wet all over

again.   *physical or creature*

3   Flawed brilliance, g̶r̶e̶a̶t̶l̶y̶ a marvelous facility
        B̶r̶i̶l̶l̶i̶a̶n̶c̶e̶/greatly handicapped, is fascinating---that must

rest and plot how not to be caught---

the anhinga
i̶t̶ stands spread-eagled facing the sun for lengthy periods

between deep chases after fish. On cloudy days it has to skimp
                       virtually
         sevrely on its meals. Rainy days, it/fasts posturing itself as
An anhinga with wings spread/̶t̶h̶a̶t̶/you approach before its feathers have dried
        straight as possible so gravity will make the wet run off./enough to
fly will plunge back underwater and get wet all over again.

4   Flawed brilliance,̶/̶/or any marvelous physical or creative
                         "sill of age"
facility g̶r̶e̶a̶t̶l̶y̶ handicapped,̶/̶/is fascinating. Deaf Beethoven,
      D.   in   Homer's "doorsill into X̶X̶X̶ old age.
Franklin̷/̷Roosevelt i̶n̶ war. Or any one of us at O̶d̶y̶s̶s̶e̶u̶s̶/̶s̶/̶s̶i̶l̶l̶
               ---but dragged down if it stays too long,̶--
o̶f̶/̶a̶g̶e̶s̶s̶ Think of the anhinga, nonpareil underwater̶/̶/triumphant when
    high   ---   ---   to find a sanctuary
soaring/in the air, but/with wet wings,̶/̶plotting h̶o̶w̶/̶t̶o̶/̶g̶e̶t̶/̶t̶h̶e̶t̶e̶/
            heat its wings to
from which to/get therem

Comparing Draft and Essay

Draft Paragraph 1

As you study this paragraph—all four versions—watch how different expository
techniques are used in conjunction with each other. Definition present in the first
sentence is supplemented with description, and comparison and contrast is also in

evidence. The fact that these modes are combined and do not act independently contributes to the full development of this introduction.

1. Note the author's dependence on addition, deletion, and rearrangement in revising this introductory paragraph. What specific revisions can you locate? How do these changes affect meaning?

2. How does Hoagland use definition? Which characteristics place the anhinga within a class? Which differentiate it?

3. Yet another technique included in this paragraph is comparison and contrast. What is the anhinga compared to or contrasted with? How does the presentation of similarities and differences help to establish a *definition*?

Draft Paragraph 2

4. Why has this paragraph been split up in the published essay? How does this redistribution affect *pacing*?

5. Which expository techniques does Hoagland employ in this paragraph? For each technique you locate, provide an example of its use.

6. Compare the first three sentences to those of the published version. Which seem smoother to you? Which revising technique is primarily responsible for this difference? In general, how do the revisions affect tone?

7. What parts of this paragraph have been deleted in the final version? What kind of phrases are these? (How may punctuation be used to indicate the importance or unimportance of details?)

Draft Paragraph 3

The change from the beginning of Hoagland's complete draft to the end of it is visually striking. Whereas the beginning is free of revisions, the end is busy with changes. Cross-outs, strikeovers, and insertions give the impression of a draft in flux, of a working copy not yet resolved or permanent. The author appears to have been writing and revising section by section, completing each unit for the time being before going on to the next. In this case, draft paragraphs 1 and 2 may have been considered complete at the time this draft was created, whereas draft paragraphs 3 and 4 were still clearly in process.

Note that draft paragraph 3 begins with a new discussion, but then abruptly shifts direction to become a revision of the end of draft paragraph 2. It is as if the author has begun a new idea, but feeling dissatisfied with what he has just written, he immediately attempts to create another version.

8. Compare the revised section of draft paragraph 3 to draft paragraph 2. What changes has Hoagland made in his sentences? Which version do you think is

more effective? Now compare both draft versions to published paragraph 3. Which version has been retained? Why?

Draft Paragraph 4

9. As noted in the introduction, exposition can extend the meaning of a word beyond its dictionary definition. How has Hoagland extended his definition of the word *anhinga?* Provide specific examples.

10. Note how comparison and contrast are used again to bring out the paragraph's meaning. Which similarities or differences help you to understand the author's main idea?

Wendy C. Modeste

Wendy C. Modeste (b. 1960) was born in Trinidad, West Indies. She emigrated to the United States in 1976 and is currently a student at Queensborough Community College. She's a born-again Christian, which means that her relationship with God is her number-one priority.

Are You Really a Failure?

Introduction to the Essay and Draft

In her essay, Wendy Modeste comes to understand that the key to answering the question "Are You Really a Failure?" is defining the word "failure." Yet this shift in inquiry is not immediately apparent, and she joins the growing list of writers you have studied who use a first draft to discover what they want to say. A writer's primary goal is to convey his or her meaning to an audience as effectively as possible; Modeste learns that her meaning hinges on her ability to define a single word.

After reading the draft and final versions of the essay, you might wonder how the draft version became the published one. How Modeste was able to transform her essay is no secret; indeed, she has done what each writer in this text has and what you currently do with your drafts—revise, revise, and revise! Yet Modeste's method of revising is suited to her and might be different from yours and other writers'. This essay has at least five drafts, and Modeste prefers to work section by section as she moves through each version. Note how Modeste starts, stops, and restarts an idea, and how even when it seems that a paragraph has been completed, she often returns to it in another series of revisions. Thus a paragraph or group of paragraphs become the focus of a draft and are worked on until the author is satisfied with them. Once revised in this manner, they may change little in subsequent drafts; however, even as the drafts approach the final version, major changes in content still appear. In the early versions of the essay, all the changes on the same piece of paper produce a draft that is difficult to read; therefore all the material from the first draft has been typed from the author's original handwritten manuscript. As you read the first and published versions of the essay, be aware of how Modeste's first draft has helped her come to a deeper understanding of the topic, discover what she wants to say about it, and select the expository techniques that best convey her meaning.

Final Essay

1   How do you feel when you have failed, over and over and over again? Well, it's difficult to describe the inner pain, the discouragement, and the self-defeat. It hurts—it hurts because you know that you are not really a failure. It's also embarrassing because you are sitting in front of this professor for the fourth time repeating the same course. And it's devastating because your records show that you are a failure. How can you feel good about yourself again, how can you keep on smiling and holding your head high knowing that you have been labeled as a failure?

2   These are the questions I asked myself after failing over and over and over again. It was not until I came to the realization that failing at a task does not make you a failure. Failing occurs in the event of trying to do or accomplish something.

3   According to the *Random House College Dictionary,* a failure is a non-performer.[1] A non-performer is someone who does not do or accomplish anything. Therefore, if you are a performer you cannot be a failure. You may fail in your performance, but you are not a failure in yourself.

4   Then why do we fail if we are performers? Well, we fail as performers because our performance is insufficient to succeed at our task. Insufficient performance is the cause of our failings. Performance is the key to conquering our failings. How much? As much as necessary to succeed at our task. Remember, without performance you are a failure, and without sufficient performance you will fail.

5   Then how do we perform sufficiently to succeed at our task? We perform sufficiently when we are consistent performers. Consistency is the art of performing even when all the odds are against you.

6   I recall a children's video I have seen: *The Tortoise and the Hare* by Don Cooper. The hare, the fastest animal in the forest, challenged the tortoise, the slowest animal in the forest, to a race. Even though all the odds were against the tortoise, he accepted the challenge. The hare was so confident that he would win the race that during the race he stopped and took a nap. While he was napping, the turtle, who knows the art of consistency, kept on walking. When the hare awoke, the tortoise had reached the finish line and had won the race.[2] The race

1. Jess Stein, *Random House College Dictionary,* rev. ed. New York: Random House Inc., 1984.
2. Don Cooper, *The Video Music Box Story Songs.* New York: Random House Home Video, 1987.

was not won because the tortoise was the faster of the two, but the race was won because the tortoise was consistent in his performance.

7   Consistency doesn't require you to be the fastest, or the smartest, but it requires that you perform and keep on performing. If we ever learn the art of consistent performance we will overcome all of our failings and we will be conquerors at all of our tasks.

8   Here are some guidelines on overcoming failings:

9   1. Realize that you are not alone. As quiet as it's kept, failing is a part of all our lives. We act so negatively when we see it in someone else's life and we get devastated when we see it in our own lives, because we have not been taught that failing is a path to success. We all have tried and craved for success, only to find out that the way up is filled with bumps and bruises, mistakes, and yes, failings. I saw the title of a book recently which explains it fully: *The Bumps Are What You Climb On.*[3]

10   2. Get help. Why is it so difficult for us to ask for help when it's so readily available? Why? Is it because of that inner voice that constantly whispers to us, "prove it to them, you can do it without anyone's help." Well, you can't do it alone, that's why there are so many resource labs available to help. There are books written, seminars being given, videos being made on literally any subject matter today. Counselors, professors, tutors are willing and available to give help. Don't do it alone. Get help.

11   3. Share your failure with a genuine friend. A genuine friend will give genuine encouragement. We all need to be encouraged, especially at a time when we are experiencing failings. Our dreams seem to have been shattered. We are in a state of depression and self-pity tries to consume us. Genuine encouragement is very powerful. It has the capability to help us regain our self-confidence. It helps to ease the pain. It also helps us to lift our heads again and puts a smile back on our faces.

12   4. Perform again. This time perform at your maximum potential. Yes, go ahead and take that course for the fourth time. This time you will succeed because you have learned the art of consistent performance. I'm confident that you will succeed because I have. Perform! Perform! Perform!

Draft A

```
You will be a
failure if you don't try

            ARE You Really a failure


                      genuinely tried and
1     How does it feel when you have failed over & over & over

again.  Well, it's very painful    There are no words to
```

3. Warren W. Wiersbe, *The Bumps Are What You Climb On.* Grand Rapids, MI: Baker Book House, 1990.

describe the inner ~~feelings...   it's very painful~~   pain,

that you feel. ~~In a few words it hurts, and hurts and~~

~~hurts...~~!

In a few words it hurts! it's embarrassing! ~~It's~~   and

at times it's devastating, but life goes on. Failure is not

~~a thing~~ an experience that we seek.

2   Looking at the _____ and knowing that it's not difficult

but in a few words, It hurts, because deep down on the inside

you know "I am not a failure." It's embarrassing because you

are sitting in front of this professor for the fourth time

taking this class_∧ over again ~~(forever)~~. It's also devastating
to your ego

_∧because your records show that you are a failure. How can

you feel good about yourself ~~when~~ how can you keep on

smiling, ~~how can~~   and ~~you~~ walk with your head ~~up~~ knowing

that you are labeled as a failure.

3 Failure is not an experience we seek but if you have ever

tried at anything in life you know that there is a chance of

failing. Someone once said, not trying is worse than

failing.

4   Points on dealing with failure:

First,

5   ∧ Realize that you are not alone. As quiet as it's

kept, failure is a part of all our lives. We act so surprise

when we see it in someone else's life and we ~~are~~ get

devastated when we see it in our own lives, only because

success is so overrated. We all try and ~~It happens to all~~

~~of us. Noone is exempt~~.   crave for success but only to find

~~that~~

out ∧ ~~on the way up is not all smooth sailing. It's~~ that the

way up is filled with bumps and bruises, ~~and~~ mistakes, and

yes, failures.

6   Secondly, admit to the fact that you have failed. This
is very hard for us to do, because ~~we hate to see ourselves~~
~~as failures.~~ admitting that we have failed makes us feel
that we are failures. Failing doesn't necessarily mean that
you are a failure. There are genuine reasons why we have
failed at something. ~~find a~~ ~~Remember, failure is one of~~
~~the paths to success~~. We also hate to admit that we have
failed, because society have classified someone who has
failed as a failure. They look down on you and make you feel
belittled. Although you

7   Seek to find the reason/s why you have failed. There's
always a reason why. Why are you taking the class over ~~for~~ a
fourth time? Is it because you have not studied, ~~It is Is~~
~~it because you just have not given it your all~~ of personal
~~problems you are faced with.~~ ~~You will never overcome the~~
~~failure or~~ Is it because you don't know how to study. Is
it because you are experiencing personal problems at that
time. Whatever your reasons are, ~~try to~~ before repeating the
class a fourth time try to find out why. Remember, you are a
failure if you don't try.

8 failing is a part of society, noone wants to admit to it and
pretends that it's all been perfect. We are so good at
covering up. Remember, failure is one of the paths to
success, admit the fact that you have failed.

9   ~~Get help! If you find out that you need hel~~
                              realize that your
        Get help! If you ̸ ⋀problem is that you just don't know
how to study. Get help. There are many articles, books
videos, cassettes, seminars on ~~studying~~ the subject of
studying.

10   If you realize that your problem is not knowing how to
study, get help. There are many articles, ^books^ videos, cassettes,
~~seminars on books~~, seminars on the subject of studying. You
can also ~~get with a study group,~~ talk with the professor
about your problem. ~~In most cases~~ The professor always is
willing and able to give help or give advice on getting help.
You can also get with a study group.

11   Last, but ~~not~~ most important is to share your failure
with a ~~friend or someone~~ genuine friend ~~or even a counselor.~~
~~We all need to be encouraged and a genuine friend will do~~
~~just that, encourage you.~~

      We all need to be encouraged and especially at a time
when we have failed. Depression wants to step in, self-pity
wants to take over but a genuine friend will give genuine
encouragement ~~that will cause us to~~
Genuine encouragement helps ~~to~~ us to regain our self-
confidence helps us to smile again. Helps ~~us to walk with~~
~~our heads high knowing that we are not failures but on our~~
~~own~~

Helps us to lift our shoulders and walk with our heads high.
It
                    is powerful. It
12 Genuine encouragement ^eases the hurts. It helps us to regain
our self-confidence. It lifts our shoulders and puts a smile
back on our faces. It helps us to walk with our heads high
and helps ~~to~~ us to regain our shattered dreams.
  Remember,
^It's easy to isolate ourselves and hide behind our masks of
pretense Share your failure ~~w~~

13 Start over--

    4. Perform Again. This time perform ~~to succeed~~ at your
                                              that
maximum potential and I guarantee ~~you~~ you will ~~have nothing~~

~~but success.~~ reach success. Success is failure overcome.

Comparing Draft and Essay: Part I

Perhaps the most significant difference between the first draft and final version of "Are You Really a Failure?" is the emphasis and arrangement of major essay parts. The draft version contains two major sections, draft paragraphs 1 through 3, the introduction and transition into the essay's body, and draft paragraphs 4 through 13, which explain the "points on dealing with failure." In contrast, the final version of the essay contains three main sections. The first of these, final paragraphs 1 and 2, are the essay's introduction and transition into the essay's body. The second section, consisting of published paragraphs 3 through 7, presents the writer's definition of "failure." The third and final section, containing final paragraphs 8 through 12, explains the "guidelines on overcoming failings." The subtle change in the body section titles from "failure" in draft paragraph 4 to "failings" in final paragraph 8 is revealing, for Modeste uses her definition and redefinition of the word "failure" to shift the overall meaning of her essay.

Draft Paragraphs 1 through 3
Compare these draft paragraphs to published paragraphs 1 and 2. Although three complete drafts separate these versions, it is still evident how the first draft has influenced the final set of revisions. Published paragraph 1 is a cleaner version of draft paragraphs 1 and 2. Published paragraph 2 is similar in *function* to draft paragraph 3 (each ends its essay's introduction and begins the body) but is completely different in *content*.

1. If you examine both parts of draft paragraph 1, you will see how they immediately are revised to become draft paragraphs 2 and 3. Modeste employs addition, deletion, and rearrangement to convey her meaning more effectively. What specific examples of revision can you locate in draft paragraphs 2 and 3? Explain the changes the writer makes.

2. What tone is present in draft paragraph 3 and published paragraph 2? How does each paragraph help to prepare a reader for the paragraphs that follow?

Published Paragraphs 3 through 7
These paragraphs, which have no counterparts in the draft version and which were added after the writer received feedback about her work, indicate and confirm a

change in the essay's direction. The central focus is no longer on giving advice about "dealing with failure" but is on establishing a definition that places the advice part of the essay in a context. Published paragraphs 3 through 5 provide a lexical definition of "failure" while indirectly establishing a definition of success ("consistent" performance). Published paragraphs 6 and 7 extend the definition by adding "consistency" as a qualification and as a goal.

3. How do the author's revisions of her purpose and meaning affect her tone and appeal to an audience?

Draft Paragraph 5

Once again, you can see how Modeste revises as she composes. Sentences build on each other and are revised or discarded until the paragraph conveys what the writer intends. To examine this paragraph in its final form, see published paragraph 9.

4. Which paragraph gives you more information? How have revisions helped the author to express her meaning?

Draft Paragraphs 6 through 10

Sometimes one or two thoughts contain the essence of the meaning a writer wants to convey. In draft paragraph 6, Modeste begins to discover her meaning and purpose; this draft paragraph contains the writer's first recognition that the essay might require a definition—and a redefinition—of the word failure. Indeed, in some of these sentences are the seeds of the idea that Modeste discovers and then actively presents in published paragraphs 3 through 7.

5. How do you feel after reading draft paragraphs 6 through 10? Compare these paragraphs to published paragraph 10. How has Modeste revised them? Why do you think she made these changes?

Draft Paragraphs 11 and 12

6. Compare draft paragraphs 11 and 12 with published paragraph 11. What do the changes Modeste makes tell you about her revising process?

Draft Paragraph 13

7. Compare this paragraph with published paragraph 12. What revisions has Modeste made? How are you affected by these changes?

8. Modeste partially builds her essay on lexical and extended definitions of the word failure. What other writing modes and expository techniques (narration, description, comparison and contrast, division/classification) does she use to develop her ideas? Provide specific examples.

Comparing Draft and Essay: Part II

As mentioned earlier, Modeste seeks to define "failure" in her essay. However, only reproducing the first and fifth (published) drafts of the essay would be misleading, for it might seem that using definition as an exposition technique for developing ideas (published paragraphs 3 through 7) occurs suddenly and completely after its rudimentary expression in draft paragraph 6. On the contrary, Modeste's implementation of definition continues through a series of drafts. Below are excerpts from Modeste's second, third, and fourth drafts of her essay. You will be able to examine how she revises each draft and comes closer and closer to defining her terms and conveying what she wants to say.

Draft B

ARE YOU REALLY A FAILURE

1   > A failure is someone who does not perform.
     How do you feel when you have failed, over and over and over
                    it's difficult to
again. Well, ~~there are no words~~ to describe the inner pain,
                                   you feel.
the discouragement, the self-defeat, ~~In a few words,~~ It

hurts. It hurts because deep down on the inside you know
                                   also
that you are not a failure. ►It's ᴧembarrassing because you

are sitting in front of this professor for a fourth time
                          and
repeating the same course; ᴧ It's ~~also~~ devastating because

your records show that you are a failure. How can you feel

good about yourself again, how can you keep on smiling and
     holding
keepᴧyour head high knowing that you have been labeled as a

failure. These are the questions I asked myself after

failing over, and over, and over again.

2   ► ~~Failure, someone said, is just a path to success.~~

3   It was not until I came to the realization that failing ~~is~~

~~no does not nece~~ at something does not make you a failure.

Failing happens when you try to do or accomplish a task ~~or~~

(something).

4   According to the RHCD of EL a failure is ~~someone who does~~

~~not perform~~ a non performer. We know, that to perform means to do, to accomplish something (task). Therefore, if you are a performer, you cannot be a failure. You may fail in your performance

Failing is defined by the (Insert)

You are a failure if you let the situation defeat you.

5   Failure is not an experience that we seek, but if you have ever tried at anything in life you know that there is a chance of failing. The RH College Dictionary of EL ~~defined failure~~ as a nonperformance of something due, required or expected.
To perform, we know, means to do or ~~to acc~~ to accomplish something; therefore if you perform you are not a failure you may fail in your performance but you are not a failure. A failure according to the definition is a nonperformer.

6   Failure is not an experience that we seek but it's a situation that we all encounter at one time or another.

7   Failure as defined by the RHCD of EL is a nonperformance of something

Final

8   Here are some steps that have helped me to overcome my failings

9   The RH Dictionary also describes failing as

10   The dictionary went on to describe failure as a ~~as a nonperformer~~ insufficient

11   The dictionary also went on to describe a failure as an insufficient performance. We also know that insufficient means not enough. Therefore, you are still not a failure in

```
your self but the reason why you failed is because you did

not perform enough.
```

If you compare draft paragraph 1 of Modeste's draft B with the corresponding sections of the first and published versions of the essay, you will discover that it is an intermediate stage between them. Although not as polished as the final copy, the writer has made much progress in this version. A study of how this draft paragraph has been revised from the first draft will show you how Modeste patiently crafts her revisions. You might also notice how the transitional paragraph of this draft (draft paragraph 3) has been changed; as Modeste begins to use definition to establish her ideas, she realizes that she needs a new way of getting into the essay's body. This paragraph (in its second draft version), like previous ones, now shows a clear relationship to what ultimately becomes the published version.

Modeste introduces definition in draft paragraph 4 and there establishes the lexical definition of "failure." Draft paragraph 5 shows a revision of draft paragraphs 3 and 4, but note how the idea "Failure is not an experience that we seek . . ." is brought back from the first draft. Unsatisfied with these changes, Modeste makes two false starts toward revision in draft paragraphs 6 and 7. In draft paragraph 8, the author seems to move into the essay's body by introducing the "steps" section; however, draft paragraphs 9 through 11 show that she has returned to the lexical definition of failure. In essence, what this second draft reveals most clearly is the writer's relentless search for the exact meaning she wants to convey to her audience.

Draft C

ARE YOU REALLY A FAILURE

```
1     How do you feel when you have failed, over and over and over

again?  Well, it's difficult to describe the inner pain, the

discouragement, and the self-defeat.  It hurts--it hurts because

you know that you are not really a failure.  It's also

embarassing, because you are sitting in front of this professor

for the fourth time repeating the same course.  And it's

devastating because your records show that you are a failure.

How can you feel good about yourself again, how can you keep on

smiling and holding your head high knowing that you have been

labeled as a failure?

2     These are the questions I asked myself after failing over
```

and over and over again. It was not until I came to the
realization that failing at a task does not make you a failure.
Failing happens when you try to do or accomplish something.
According to the <u>Random House Dictionary of the English Language</u>,
a failure is a nonperformer. We know that to perform means to
do, or to accomplish a task. Therefore if you are a performer
you cannot be a failure. You may fail in your performance, but
that does not make you a failure in yourself.

3   The dictionary also describes a failure as an insufficient
performer. We also know that insufficient means not enough.
Therefore, you have not failed because you are a failure, but you
have failed because you have not performed enough.

4   Performance is the key to conquering your failings. How
much?--as much necessary to succeed at your task. Remember,
without performance you are a failure.

5   Here are some of my personal guidelines to help overcome
failures:

Draft D

ARE YOU REALLY A FAILURE

1   How do you feel when you have failed, over and over and over
again? Well, it's difficult to describe the inner pain, the
discouragement, and the self-defeat. It hurts--it hurts because
you know that you are not really a failure. It's also
embarassing, because you are sitting in front of this professor
for the fourth time repeating the same course. And it's
devastating because your records show that you are a failure.
How can you feel good about yourself again, how can you keep on
smiling and holding your head high knowing that you have been
labeled as a failure?

2   These are the questions I asked myself after failing over and over and over again. It was not until I came to the realization that failing at a task does not make you a failure. Failing occurs in the event of trying to do or accomplish something.

3   According to the <u>Random House Dictionary of the English Language</u>, a failure is a nonperformer. A nonperformer is someone who does not do or accomplish anything. Therefore, if you are a performer you cannot be a failure. You may fail in your performance, but not a failure in yourself.

4   Then why do we fail if we are performers? Well, we fail as performers because our performance is insufficient to succeed at our task. Insufficient performance is what causes failure. Performance is the key to conquering our failings. How much?--as much necessary to succeed at your task. Remember, without performance you are a failure, and without sufficient performance you will fail.

5   Here are some guidelines to help overcome failures:

Reproduced above are the first five paragraphs of Modeste's drafts C and D of "Are You Really a Failure?" These drafts show the continued shaping of the essay, particularly of those paragraphs that help to establish the definition that lies at the center of the piece.

You will notice that the first paragraph of draft C is different from that of draft B, yet it is unchanged in draft D and is the opening paragraph of the published version. This series of revisions illustrates the evolution of the introduction as Modeste moves from her first to fifth draft. As mentioned earlier, the author revises revises each section of her essay, but when a paragraph or group of paragraphs rey the meaning she wants, she preserves them while continuing to revise other sections. One section that is still being revised, though the changes are less substantial than those revisions you have seen in the first two draft versions, is that presented in paragraphs 2 through 4 of drafts C and D. Before answering the following questions, you might look over the corresponding sections of these paragraphs in the drafts discussed earlier.

Draft C, Paragraph 2

9. Compare this draft paragraph with draft paragraphs 2 and 3 of Draft D. Why do you think that she has chosen to split this paragraph into two?

Draft C, Paragraphs 3 and 4

10. Compare these draft paragraphs with draft paragraph 4 of draft D. What revising strategies has Modeste applied? How do some of the revisions reveal the writer's shift from a lexical to an extended definition? What effect do these changes have on you?

Marcus Mabry

Marcus Mabry (b. 1970) was born in New Jersey and educated at Stanford University. He wrote "Living in Two Worlds" for the 1988 issue of *Newsweek on Campus*. As you read his essay, speculate as to his purpose in writing this piece. To what extent do you as a college student also live in two worlds?

Living in Two Worlds

1   A round, green cardboard sign hangs from a string proclaiming, "We built a proud new feeling," the slogan of a local supermarket. It is a souvenir from one of my brother's last jobs. In addition to being a bagger, he's worked at a fast-food restaurant, a gas station, a garage and a textile factory. Now, in the icy clutches of the Northeastern winter, he is unemployed. He will soon be a father. He is 19 years old.

2   In mid-December I was at Stanford, among the palm trees and weighty chores of academe. And all I wanted to do was get out. I joined the rest of the undergrads in a chorus of excitement, singing the praises of Christmas break. No classes, no midterms, no finals . . . and no freshmen! (I'm a resident assistant.) Awesome! I was looking forward to escaping. I never gave a thought to what I was escaping to.

3   Once I got home to New Jersey, reality returned. My dreaded freshmen had been replaced by unemployed relatives; badgering professors had been replaced by hard-working single mothers, and cold classrooms by dilapidated bedrooms and kitchens. The room in which the "proud new feeling" sign hung contained the belongings of myself, my mom and my brother. But for these two weeks it was mine. They slept downstairs on couches.

4   Most students who travel between the universes of poverty and affluence during breaks experience similar conditions, as well as the guilt, the helplessness and, sometimes, the embarrassment associated with them. Our friends are willing to listen, but most of them are unable to imagine the pain of the impoverished lives that we see every six months. Each time I return home I feel further away from the realities of poverty in America and more ashamed that they are allowed to persist. What frightens me most is not that the American socioeconomic system permits poverty to continue, but that by participating in that system I share some of the blame.

5   Last year I lived in an on-campus apartment, with a (relatively) modern bathroom, kitchen and two bedrooms. Using summer earnings, I added some expensive prints, a potted palm and some other plants, making the place look like the more-than-humble abode of a New York City Yuppie. I gave dinner parties, even a *soirée française*.

6   For my roommate, a doctor's son, this kind of life was nothing extraordinary. But my mom was struggling to provide a life for herself and my

brother. In addition to working 24-hour-a-day cases as a practical nurse, she was trying to ensure that my brother would graduate from high school and have a decent life. She knew that she had to compete for his attention with drugs and other potentially dangerous things that can look attractive to a young man when he sees no better future.

7   Living in my grandmother's house this Christmas break restored all the forgotten, and the never acknowledged, guilt. I had gone to boarding school on a full scholarship since the ninth grade, so being away from poverty was not new. But my own growing affluence has increased my distance. My friends say that I should not feel guilty: what could I do substantially for my family at this age, they ask. Even though I know that education is the right thing to do, I can't help but feel, sometimes, that I have it too good. There is no reason that I deserve security and warmth, while my brother has to cope with potential unemployment and prejudice. I, too, encounter prejudice, but it is softened by my status as a student in an affluent and intellectual community.

8   More than my sense of guilt, my sense of helplessness increases each time I return home. As my success leads me further away for longer periods of time, poverty becomes harder to conceptualize and feels that much more oppressive when I visit with it. The first night of break, I lay in our bedroom, on a couch that let out into a bed that took up the whole room, except for a space heater. It was a little hard to sleep because the springs from the couch stuck through at inconvenient spots. But it would have been impossible to sleep anyway because of the groans coming from my grandmother's room next door. Only in her early 60s, she suffers from many chronic diseases and couldn't help but moan, then pray aloud, then moan, then pray aloud.

9   This wrenching of my heart was interrupted by the 3 A.M. entry of a relative who had been allowed to stay at the house despite rowdy behavior and threats toward the family in the past. As he came into the house, he slammed the door, and his heavy steps shook the second floor as he stomped into my grandmother's room to take his place, at the foot of her bed. There he slept, without blankets on a bare mattress. This was the first night. Later in the vacation, a Christmas turkey and a Christmas ham were stolen from my aunt's refrigerator on Christmas Eve. We think the thief was a relative. My mom and I decided not to exchange gifts that year because it just didn't seem festive.

10   A few days after New Year's I returned to California. The Northeast was soon hit by a blizzard. They were there, and I was here. That was the way it had to be, for now. I haven't forgotten; the ache of knowing their suffering is always there. It has to be kept deep down, or I can't find the logic in studying and partying while people, my people, are being killed by poverty. Ironically, success drives me away from those I most want to help by getting an education.

11   Somewhere in the midst of all that misery, my family has built, within me, "a proud feeling." As I travel between the two worlds it becomes harder to remember just how proud I should be—not just because of where I have come from and where I am going, but because of where they are. The fact that they survive in the world in which they live is something to be very proud of, indeed.

It inspires within me a sense of tenacity and accomplishment that I hope every college graduate will someday possess.

Considering Content

1. What are some of the differences between Mabry's two worlds? In which does he feel more at ease?

2. "Once I got home to New Jersey, reality returned" (paragraph 3). What "realities" does he encounter? How does he respond?

3. Review the last paragraph of the essay. What is his family's legacy? How has it contributed to his survival?

4. What new insights about social class and upward mobility did you gain from reading this essay?

5. How do Mabry's views on poverty compare to those of Orwell (page 283)? With whom do you agree?

Considering Craft

1. Mabry uses contrast and comparison to discuss the dilemmas of his double identities in American society. Why is this an effective technique for highlighting the differences between his present life at Stanford and his past life in New Jersey?

2. In paragraph 9 Mabry states: "more than my sense of guilt, my sense of helplessness increases each time I return home." What evidence does he supply to support this thesis? Is it convincing? Why or why not?

3. Identify the tone of the essay. Is it objective, conversational, condescending, humorous, or informative? Is it appropriate for his subject? Explain.

4. An effective conclusion summarizes the author's points without being repetitive. To what extent does Mabry's conclusion fulfill this criterion?

Aristotle

Aristotle (384–322 B.C.) was a Greek philosopher who defined much of the content of Western thought. He spent twenty years at Plato's Athenian academy and in later life established his own institution, the Lyceum, which became a center for research into every field of inquiry. Of his numerous works, forty-seven remain, primarily in the form of notes used in his Lyceum lectures. In the following essay, he draws many contrasts between youth and age that are still pertinent today.

Youth and Old Age

1   Young men have strong passions, and tend to gratify them indiscriminately. Of the bodily desires, it is the sexual by which they are most swayed and in which they show absence of self-control. They are changeable and fickle in their desires, which are violent while they last, but quickly over: their impulses are keen but not deep-rooted, and are like sick people's attacks of hunger and thirst. They are hot-tempered and quick-tempered, and apt to give way to their anger; bad temper often gets the better of them, for owing to their love of honor they cannot bear being slighted, and are indignant if they imagine themselves unfairly treated. While they love honor, they love victory still more; for youth is eager for superiority over others, and victory is one form of this. They love both more than they love money, which indeed they love very little, not having yet learnt what it means to be without it—this is the point of Pittacus' remark about Amphiaraus.[1] They look at the good side rather than the bad, not having yet witnessed many instances of wickedness. They trust others readily, because they have not often been cheated. They are sanguine; nature warms their blood as though with excess of wine; and besides that, they have as yet met with few disappointments. Their lives are mainly spent not in memory but in expectation; for expectation refers to the future, memory to the past, and youth has a long future before it and a short past behind it: on the first day of one's life one has nothing at all to remember, and can only look forward. They are easily cheated, owing to the sanguine disposition just mentioned. Their hot tempers and hopeful dispositions make them more courageous than older men are; the hot temper prevents fear, and the hopeful disposition creates confidence; we cannot feel fear so long as we are feeling angry, and any expectation of good makes us confident. They are shy, accepting the rules of society in which they have been trained, and not yet believing in any other standard of honour. They have exalted notions, because they have not yet been humbled by life or learnt its necessary limitations; moreover, their hopeful disposition makes them think themselves equal to great things—and that means having exalted notions. They would always rather do noble deeds than useful ones: their lives are regulated more by moral feeling than by reasoning: and whereas reasoning leads us to choose what is useful, moral goodness leads us to choose what is noble. They are fonder of their friends, intimates, and companions than older men are, because they like spending their days in the company of others, and have not yet come to value either their friends or anything else by their usefulness to themselves. All their mistakes are in the direction of doing things excessively and vehemently. They disobey Chilon's precept[2] by overdoing everything; they love too much and hate too much, and the same with everything else. They think they know everything, and are always quite sure about it; this, in fact, is why they overdo everything. If they do wrong to others, it is because they mean to insult them, not to do them

1. Reference unknown.
2. "(Do) nothing in excess."

actual harm. They are ready to pity others, because they think every one an honest man, or anyhow better than he is: they judge their neighbour by their own harmless natures, and so cannot think he deserves to be treated in that way. They are fond of fun and therefore witty, wit being well-bred insolence.

2   Such, then, is the character of the Young. The character of Elderly Men— men who are past their prime—may be said to be formed for the most part of elements that are the contrary of all these. They have lived many years; they have often been taken in, and often made mistakes; and life on the whole is a bad business. The result is that they are sure about nothing and *under-do* everything. They "think," but they never "know"; and because of their hesitation they always add a "possibly" or a "perhaps," putting everything this way and nothing positively. They are cynical; that is, they tend to put the worse construction on everything. Further, their experience makes them distrustful and therefore suspicious of evil. Consequently they neither love warmly nor hate bitterly, but following the hint of Bias they love as though they will some day hate and hate as though they will some day love.[3] They are small-minded, because they have been humbled by life: their desires are set upon nothing more exalted or unusual than what will help them to keep alive. They are not generous, because money is one of the things they must have, and at the same time their experience has taught them how hard it is to get and how easy to lose. They are cowardly, and are always anticipating danger; unlike that of the young, who are warm-blooded, their temperament is chilly; old age has paved the way for cowardice; fear is, in fact, a form of chill. They love life; and all the more when their last day has come, because the object of all desire is something we have not got, and also because we desire most strongly that which we need most urgently. They are too fond of themselves; this is one form that small-mindedness takes. Because of this, they guide their lives too much by considerations of what is useful and too little by what is noble—for the useful is what is good for oneself, and the noble what is good absolutely. They are not shy, but shameless rather; caring less for what is noble than for what is useful, they feel contempt for what people may think of them. They lack confidence in the future; partly through experience—for most things go wrong, or anyhow turn out worse than one expects; and partly because of their cowardice. They live by memory rather than by hope; for what is left to them of life is but little as compared with the long past; and hope is of the future, memory of the past. This, again, is the cause of their loquacity; they are continually talking of the past, because they enjoy remembering it. Their fits of anger are sudden but feeble. Their sensual passions have either altogether gone or have lost their vigour: consequently they do not feel their passions much, and their actions are inspired less by what they do feel than by the love of gain. Hence men at this time of life are often supposed to have a self-controlled character; the fact is that their passions have slackened, and they are slaves to the love of gain. They guide their lives by reasoning more than by moral feeling; reasoning being directed to utility and

3. Bias of Priene; "they treat their friends as probable future enemies and their enemies as probable future friends."

moral feeling to moral goodness. If they wrong others, they mean to injure them, not to insult them. Old men may feel pity, as well as young men, but not for the same reason. Young men feel it out of kindness; old men out of weakness, imagining that anything that befalls any one else might easily happen to them, which, as we saw, is a thought that excites pity. Hence they are querulous, and not disposed to jesting or laughter—the love of laughter being the very opposite of querulousness.

3   Such are the characters of Young Men and Elderly Men. People always think well of speeches adapted to, and reflecting, their own character; and we can now see how to compose our speeches so as to adapt both them and ourselves to our audiences.

Considering Content

1. According to Aristotle, what are the basic character traits of youth? Why do young men overdo everything?

2. What are the basic character traits of old age as Aristotle defined them? Why do elderly men underdo everything?

3. What does Aristotle mean when he says that elderly men "love as though they will some day hate and hate as though they will some day love"?

4. In what ways are elderly men more selfish than young men? Why is the pity that old men feel less kind than that of young men?

5. How fair do you think Aristotle's characterization of youth and old age is? How would you characterize them?

6. Do you agree with Aristotle when he says that "we cannot feel fear so long as we are feeling angry"? Explain your answer.

Considering Craft

1. Aristotle offers one long paragraph that describes numerous characteristics of young men, then a second long paragraph that describes the contrasting characteristics of old men. What effect might he have gained had he instead organized a series of short paragraphs in each of which he contrasted one character trait of youth with one corresponding trait of old age?

2. How effectively does Aristotle use cause-and-effect analysis to explain the differences between youth and old age?

3. Characterize the tone of the essay. Is it appropriate for its subject? Explain.

4. Prepare a profile of the audience to whom Aristotle's essay would most appeal and include your rationale.

George Orwell

George Orwell (1903–1950) was born in India and educated in England. He served for many years as a member of the Indian Imperial Police in Burma but became discouraged by the injustices of colonialism and returned to England to try to establish himself as a writer. He published many books, the most famous of which is *1984*. "Poverty" is taken from *Down and Out in Paris and London* (1933). As you read his essay, list the techniques he uses to communicate his particular experiences with poverty to a universal audience. To what extent are his responses to poverty similar to or different from yours?

Poverty

1   It is altogether curious, your first contact with poverty. You have thought so much about poverty—it is the thing you have feared all your life, the thing you knew would happen to you sooner or later; and it is all so utterly and prosaically different. You thought it would be quite simple; it is extraordinarily complicated. You thought it would be terrible; it is merely squalid and boring. It is the peculiar *lowness* of poverty that you discover first; the shifts that it puts you to, the complicated meanness, the crust-wiping.

2   You discover, for instance, the secrecy attaching to poverty. At a sudden stroke you have been reduced to an income of six francs a day. But of course you dare not admit it—you have got to pretend that you are living quite as usual. From the start it tangles you in a net of lies, and even with the lies you can hardly manage it. You stop sending clothes to the laundry, and the laundress catches you in the street and asks you why; you mumble something, and she, thinking you are sending the clothes elsewhere, is your enemy for life. The tobacconist keeps asking why you have cut down your smoking. There are letters you want to answer, and cannot, because stamps are too expensive. And then there are your meals—meals are the worst difficulty of all. Every day at mealtimes you go out, ostensibly to a restaurant, and loaf an hour in the Luxembourg Gardens, watching the pigeons. Afterwards you smuggle your food home in your pockets. Your food is bread and margarine, or bread and wine, and even the nature of the food is governed by lies. You have to buy rye bread instead of household bread, because the rye loaves, though dearer, are round and can be smuggled in your pockets. This wastes you a franc a day. Sometimes, to keep up appearances, you have to spend sixty centimes on a drink, and go correspondingly short of food. Your linen gets filthy, and you run out of soap and razor-blades. Your hair wants cutting and you try to cut it yourself, with such fearful results that you have to go to the barber after all, and spend the equivalent of a day's food. All day you are telling lies, and expensive lies.

3   You discover the extreme precariousness of your six francs a day. Mean disasters happen and rob you of food. You have spent your last eighty centimes

on half a litre of milk, and are boiling it over the spirit lamp. While it boils a bug runs down your forearm; you give the bug a flick with your nail, and it falls, plop! straight into the milk. There is nothing for it but to throw the milk away and go foodless.

4   You go to the baker's to buy a pound of bread, and you wait while the girl cuts a pound for another customer. She is clumsy, and cuts more than a pound. *"Pardon, monsieur,"* she says, "I suppose you don't mind paying two sous extra?" Bread is a franc a pound, and you have exactly a franc. When you think that you too might be asked to pay two sous extra, and would have to confess that you could not, you bolt in panic. It is hours before you dare venture into a baker's shop again.

5   You go to the greengrocer's to spend a franc on a kilogram of potatoes. But one of the pieces that make up the franc is a Belgium piece, and the shopman refuses it. You slink out of the shop, and can never go there again.

6   You have strayed into a respectable quarter, and you see a prosperous friend coming. To avoid him you dodge into the nearest café. Once in the café you must buy something so you spend your last fifty centimes on a glass of black coffee with a dead fly in it. One could multiply these disasters by the hundred. They are part of the process of being hard up.

7   You discover what it is like to be hungry. With bread and margarine in your belly, you go out and look into the shop windows. Everywhere there is food insulting you in huge, wasteful piles; whole dead pigs, baskets of hot loaves, great yellow blocks of butter, strings of sausages, mountains of potatoes, vast Gruyère cheeses like grindstones. A snivelling self-pity comes over you at the sight of so much food. You plan to grab a loaf and run, swallowing it before they catch you; and you refrain, from pure funk.

8   You discover the *boredom* which is inseparable from poverty; the times when you have nothing to do and, being underfed, can interest yourself in nothing. For half a day at a time you lie on your bed, feeling like the *jeune squelette* in Baudelaire's poem.[1] Only food could rouse you. You discover that a man who has gone even a week on bread and margarine is not a man any longer, only a belly with a few accessory organs.

9   This—one could describe it further, but it is all in the same style—is life on six francs a day. Thousands of people in Paris live it—struggling artists and students, prostitutes when their luck is out, out-of-work people of all kinds. It is the suburbs, as it were, of poverty.

Considering Content

1. Is the poverty Orwell here describes a new experience or a lifetime condition? How does that affect his description?

---

1. *Jeune squelette* means young skeleton. Charles Baudelaire was a French poet (1821–1867).

2. Why, according to Orwell, does poverty require lying?

3. Why is the life of poverty precarious? (Is that the same as dangerous?) Why is it boring?

4. Poverty is "the thing you have feared all your life." Do you think the fear of poverty is common? What's the evidence? Have you ever been afraid of being poor or has poverty ever been a part of your life?

5. Orwell lived in Paris in the 1930s on six francs a day. How many dollars a day (or week) could you live on? How many dollars a day or week would you consider poverty? (The U.S. government defines poverty as about $10,000 for a family of *four*.)

6. Describe the life of the poorest person you know personally.

Considering Craft

1. Orwell uses classification to present his views on poverty. What is the basis of the subdivisions of his organization?

2. In addition to classifying types of poverty, Orwell uses comparison and contrast to discuss its effects. Cite two examples from the essay that illustrate comparison and contrast.

3. Select the example of poverty you found most effective and analyze why you reacted as you did to this particular illustration.

4. Although Orwell's "Poverty" is based on personal experience, he chooses the pronoun *you* rather than *I*. What is the effect of using this point of view? Does it make what he has to say about poverty more convincing? Why or why not?

5. How effectively does Orwell's introductory paragraph describe one's first contact with poverty? Explain.

6. Read over his concluding paragraph. What makes his last sentence particularly effective?

Guidelines for Expository Essays

Comparison and Contrast

1. Choose comparable subjects for comparison, that is, from the same general class. Stick to the same basis of comparison.

2. Choose the pattern that most clearly brings out the comparison—subject by subject, point by point, or a combination of the two.

3. Explain the purpose of your comparison. Why is it significant?

Extended Definition

1. Use this method as an organizing basis mainly when your subject involves a new, technical, or abstract word, or a word that has unusual interest for you.

2. Begin with a quoted dictionary definition or write your own dictionary definition.

3. Extend the dictionary definition by using other expository modes such as comparison and contrast or exemplification, or by using narration or description.

Division/Classification

1. Use this method when your subject can be divided into physical or logical classes.

2. Choose a basis of classification that serves your purposes; explain how this basis works.

3. Group items within their class by similarities; provide enough, but not too many, classes. Avoid overlapping classes: items may appear in only one class.

4. Use other expository modes and narration and description to explain and enliven your classification.

Warm-up Exercises

1. Hoagland uses a bird to symbolize genius or brilliance. Work out your own definition of genius by freewriting about it, using a different symbol that serves a similar purpose.

2. Brainstorm about your associations with personal space. How do they affect your way of relating to people? How conscious are you of a need for psychic space? Analyze your responses. Do you have enough material on which to write an essay?

3. Interview on a controversial topic four people who represent different sexes and ages and who differ in ethnic and educational backgrounds. Analyze their responses for points of comparison and contrast and formulate a thesis about the topic or the people interviewed.

4. Visit a disco, gym, or club and interview three people as to their reasons for being there. Then classify their responses. Do they have any points in common? Can you reach any generalizations as a result of your interviews?

5. Read over your journal for an opinion or impression that you had previously recorded and write another journal entry on the same subject recording your feelings about it now. Write a paragraph using comparison or contrast and examine the similarities or differences of the entries.

6. Write an extended definition of one of the following:

cool	star	upward mobility
jazz	myth	poverty
nationalism	patriotism	drugs

7. For a day or two keep a record of all the bumper stickers you see. Then classify them into several categories—comic, serious, erotic, political, or religious, for example. Review the guidelines for writing a division/classification essay. How can you best arrange your information?

Writing/Revising Topics

1. Write an essay comparing two important stages of your life: childhood and adolescence or adolescence and adulthood. When revising, highlight a specific experience through which you explain the similarities and differences.

2. Select a word with which you have strong associations, such as anxiety, stress, charm, success, or jealousy, and write an essay in which you classify its various types. Use a dictionary and a thesaurus to find words with similar meanings. In revising your essay, you may find rearrangement a useful revision strategy to make your classification as specific and complete as possible.

3. Write an essay comparing someone you know who has self-esteem primarily because of his or her character and feelings with someone you know who has self-esteem primarily because of his or her accomplishments. When revising, try, as did Hoagland, to use specific examples to heighten your comparisons.

4. What is the difference between being educated and being intelligent? Write an essay comparing these two concepts. In revising your essay, make sure that you have clearly defined what you mean by both terms.

5. Write a classification essay about television commercials, citing examples sufficient to form a conclusion about the American advertiser's perception of the marketplace. In revising, focus on the development of your paragraphs. Have you given specific examples to support each topic sentence?

6. Based on Warm-up Exercise 6, write an essay on the word you selected. Before revising, review the Guidelines for Extended Definitions. Consider using an object to unify your essay.

7. Using Warm-up Exercise 7 as the basis, write an essay classifying your information about bumper stickers. In revising your essay, focus on the first paragraph and introduce your essay with your favorite, the most unusual, or the most outrageous sticker.

8. Staples (Chapter 6) and Mabry contrast their past experiences in the ghetto with their present situations resulting from their college educations and middle class status. Compare their attitudes toward family, ethnicity, and class. To what extent do you empathize with their ambivalence about their success?

9. Using Warm-up Exercise 2 as the basis, write an essay comparing your attitude toward personal space with those of your best friend. When revising, focus on specific examples that heighten your comparisons.

10. Select a contemporary social problem that interests you, such as substance abuse, poverty, AIDS, or pollution, and speculate about its effects. List as many effects as you can think of. Do you need additional research to better document the effects? Before revising your essay, make sure that your purpose is clear and your tone is consistent.

11. Aristotle tells us experience teaches old men that "most things go wrong, or anyhow turn out worse than one expects." Write an essay in which you compare the validity of such a suspicious or "cynical" view of life to the validity of what Aristotle calls youth's "sanguine" or optimistic view.

Composing Persuasive Essays

We have seen that the purpose of exposition is to explain. Persuasive essays use all the techniques of exposition, narration, and description, but for their own purpose, which is to create in an audience the desire to do or believe something. They create this desire by appealing to the reader's emotions (*emotional appeal*), by establishing the writer's credibility (*ethical appeal*), and by showing how logical thinking and sound evidence lead to certain conclusions (*logical* or *argumentative appeal*). Since all three of these appeals are ways of answering the question "Why should one act or think as I propose?" they are most closely associated with one of the methods of exposition, *cause and effect*.

Persuasion aims to convince in compelling fashion. It appeals to the heart as well as the head. It aims to sell. It uses lively vocabulary and vivid examples tailored to its particular audience. No type of writing depends so heavily on the perception of what your audience knows and wants. More than narration, description, or exposition, persuasion is writing whose effectiveness can be tested because it calls for a more or less definite and immediate reaction from the audience. If it succeeds, your rewards can be immediate and substantial. In order to succeed, you must persuade your readers that what you advocate is for *their* benefit.

Emotional Appeal

Martin Luther King's "I Have a Dream," written as a speech to a huge outdoor audience at the Lincoln Memorial in Washington, DC, appeals largely to the emotions of his audience. The logic of the speech is too evident to need elaboration:

one hundred years after Emancipation is too long to wait for full citizenship. The speech is a challenge to Americans to live up to their ideals. It spends little time winning acceptance for the truth or validity of these ideals; its purpose is to inspire courage and hope. For its emotional appeal it relies on rhythm, repetition, Biblical quotations and vocabulary, historical parallels, and its author's personal identification with his audience and their problems.

Ethical Appeal

If you were participating in a live debate, you would have to convince the judges that your evidence is sound and your conclusions correct. Your opponents in the debate would be trying to do the same thing, and you can't pretend that they don't exist; you must acknowledge and refute their arguments if you are to win the judges' vote. The writer of an argumentative or persuasive essay is also facing an unseen opponent, and one of the most effective ways you can establish your right to debate, your credentials, is to show that you know the arguments for both sides. Louise Montague, for example, in her "Straight Talk About the Living-Together Arrangement" devotes the first four paragraphs to an acknowledgment of what her opponents are saying. This shows that she has considered both sides and still believes she is right. Your audience will accept your conclusions to the extent that they accept your claims to knowledge, honesty, and trustworthiness. They will be on the alert for your sense of ethics, your fairness, and consistency between what you say and how you say it—in a word, your tone. Montague further establishes her credentials by telling, in a straightforward, serious tone, about her long interest in the subject and experience with its problems.

Logical or Argumentative Appeal

Argumentation is a type of persuasion that appeals to your reader's sense of logic. Without going into the fine points of logic we can say that logical thought moves in one of two directions, either from the general to the particular (*deduction*), or from the particular to the general (*induction*). In deduction, *logic* means reaching valid conclusions from valid premises. The model in deductive thinking is the *syllogism,* consisting of two premises and a conclusion:

> All men are mortal.
> Socrates is a man.
> Therefore Socrates is mortal.

A syllogism assumes the truth of both premises and focuses on arriving at a *valid* conclusion within the system; the conclusion is valid if it correctly draws out the implications of the two interacting premises on the same principle as that used in geometry, that things equal to the same thing are equal to each other. The conclusion will be valid and *true* if both premises are true, but the closed system of a syllogism has no way of ascertaining the truth of its premises: that proof is left for *induction*.

How do we know that "All men are mortal" is true? By observation. Induction does not assume, but arrives at its concluding generalization by the observation of particular facts or events, which it accepts as *evidence*. It is the method of science, and its generalizations are called *hypotheses* because they are always subject to review, to later observation. But don't scientists apply hypotheses to particular cases? They do indeed, and at that point they are using deduction. When scientists reach a conclusion that explains the observed facts, they apply that conclusion, however hypothetical. For example, the discovery of DNA, the mechanism of genetics, led them to seek ways to produce in large quantities substances such as interferon and insulin through genetic recombination.

So the two, deduction and induction, are continually coexisting, alternating, in the thought of scientists and nonscientists too. Consider the following mixture of induction and deduction.

Over a period of time you observe ten girls working on their cars.

All are poor mechanics.

You generalize that girls make poor mechanics.

You meet an eleventh girl.

You conclude—without observation—that No. 11 will be a poor mechanic.

The syllogism is as follows:

Girls make poor mechanics.

No. 11 is a girl.

Therefore No. 11 will make a poor mechanic.

The deductive conclusion here is valid—logically correct—but is it true? Obviously the truth of statement 3 above depends on the quantity and quality of your inductive observation. Ten girls is not a large enough sample to establish the truth of 3; if you accept it, you commit the common fallacy of *hasty generalization*. If you use 3 as your first premise, your deductive conclusion (statement 5) cannot be true. You have committed the fallacy of *causal oversimplification* by attributing an effect (poor mechanical ability) to the wrong cause (sex), a fallacy to be further discussed below.

Cause and Effect

Cause-and-effect exposition is often used in argumentation and persuasion because it can support a logical appeal. The structure of cause and effect, like that of narration, is a series of events or conditions, the last of which, the effect, could not occur without the preceding one(s). The immediately preceding events or conditions are the "immediate" causes; if *one* immediate cause can alone produce the effect, it is called the "sufficient" cause. When scientists discovered that tuberculosis was caused by the tubercle bacillus and nothing else, they had found the sufficient cause of tuberculosis; they could stop prescribing mountain air, close the sanatoriums, and practically eliminate occurrence of the disease.

How do we know the constituents of this series of events? It's not always easy to identify them; in fact, causes are harder to identify than effects. One of the fallacies of causal thinking is the *non sequitur* (Latin for "it doesn't follow"), which is ascribing an effect to the wrong cause. For example, a character in Frank O'Connor's story "Guests of the Nation" says:

> *Mr. Hawkins, you can say what you like about the war* [World War I], *and think you'll deceive me because I'm only a simple poor countrywoman, but I know what started the war. It was the Italian Count that stole the heathen divinity out of the temple in Japan.*

We have all seen the damage done by this kind of "simple" fallacy; we should watch for it in our own and our opponents' arguments.

Another fallacy of causal thinking is to *assume* that an event is in the series of events. Just because event A happened before event B is no guarantee that A and B are in series, with A causing B. To make this assumption without evidence is to commit the fallacy called *post hoc, ergo propter hoc* in the Latin phrase meaning "after this, therefore, on account of this." For example, Mary Smith wins the lottery. John Russell then proposes marriage to her. To say the former caused the latter is an example of the *post hoc, ergo propter hoc* fallacy and an injustice to a couple who may be in love.

In answering the question "What caused the burglary?" you would look for a series of earlier events or conditions among which might be poorly lighted streets and yards, unlocked doors or windows, accessible fire escapes, an ineffective police and court system, high unemployment, drug use, and so on, some of which may have been recently aggravated or exacerbated, and you would certainly hope to find an immediate cause called "the perpetrator." But where you begin in this series will surely depend on your purpose in asking the question. You might also ask yourself the practical question "What had to happen before this particular burglary could occur?" For example, it is probably starting too far back in the series to say the burglary was caused by World War II, which deprived the burglar of a father, who might have made an honest man of his son. Conversely, to avoid beginning too *late* in your series (oversimplification again), remember that the causes may be numerous and various. Again, depending on your purpose, it is probably an oversimplification to say the burglary was caused by the burglar.

Cause-and-effect exposition can answer the corollary question "What is the effect of X?" You can ask, "What is the *effect* of the burglary?" (or, what amounts to the same thing, "What did the burglary cause?") Now the series begins with burglary and ends with later events or conditions: fear, anger, increased insurance costs, purchase of a burglar alarm, deterioration of a neighborhood, and so on. To keep the series from growing unmanageably long, keep in mind the practical question "What would not have happened if the robbery had not happened?"

Cause-and-effect exposition requires rigorous thinking and an awareness of the pitfalls and possibilities of diction. The words your questions are phrased in will determine to a large extent how they are answered. For example, Rachel L. Jones asks "What's wrong with black English?" in her essay of that name, intentionally tilting her discussion against a kind of "bi-dialectism" because she is "troubled by that colorful, grammar-to-the-winds patois that is black English."

Cause-and-effect exposition is often useful in argumentation or persuasion, whether that goal of changing behavior or belief is acknowledged or not. Rachel L. Jones, again, attempts to influence her reader's behavior for the alleged reason that black English hurts blacks. Louise Montague's "Straight Talk About the Living-Together Arrangement" is avowedly based almost entirely on the ill effects of living together in lieu of getting married. She says in many different ways, "Don't live together, because the consequences are bad." To meet Montague on her own ground, a reader must know and use the tools of cause-and-effect exposition, especially if the reader wants to compose a rebuttal.

In presenting your case for cause and effect, support your conclusions with proof or evidence. Use statistics, reports, your own experience and that of others. Don't expect readers to believe you merely because you say something is the cause: proof is the *writer's* job. Use any of the other expository modes, and narration and description, to help you present your case.

After writing your essay, vigorously reexamine the methods you have used to arrive at your conclusions. Make sure that generalizations are true, that conclusions are valid, that effects are in fact derived from their proper causes. Any deviation from your intended position or breakdown in logic will require you to make major revisions of your draft. If so, use addition, deletion, substitution, and/or rearrangement to make your essay serve your purpose well.

Jim Fusilli

Jim Fusilli (b. 1954) is a graduate of St. Peters College in Jersey City. For several years he worked at Dow Jones and has published essays in the *Wall Street Journal* and *The New York Times Magazine* as well as in other periodicals. His first novel will soon be published. When asked how he gets started, he responded:

> When I have an idea for a piece, I spend an inordinate amount of time thinking about it, refining it, studying its angles, before I commit an outline to paper. This process I think is my journal. In my essays, I begin by establishing tone. In fiction and in my critical reportage, I begin by establishing character.

As you read Fusilli's essay, pay particular attention to his tone and its influence on your response to his subject.

Criticizing Rock Music Critics

Introduction to the Essay and Draft

In his essay, "Criticizing Rock Music Critics," Jim Fusilli wants to convince his readers that artistic standards can and should be applied to a popular music form—rock and roll. To achieve this purpose, he turns to *persuasion*. As you read through the essay, try to keep track of *how* the author uses persuasion as he writes. Where does he try to convince you by using emotional appeal? How much of his argument depends on ethical and logical appeals? In addition, also note where and how he incorporates other writing strategies to make his point. How does Fusilli use narration, description, exposition, and cause and effect to strengthen his argument?

   Concerning his method of composing and revising, Fusilli states: "I usually write on a word processor and tend to edit as I go along. But I do find it helpful to, at some point, print out a draft and pencil edit it." Though previous drafts of "Criticizing Rock Music Critics" have been created, most have survived only momentarily in the memory of a computer. Reproduced below, however, are the last three pages of a late, "pencil-edited" draft. Also included is an introductory paragraph, taken from "a handwritten draft, material that, with the exception of the first sentence, never got into the story."

   After studying the drafts appearing in earlier chapters, you are now aware of the wide range of composing and revising styles available to writers, and to each writer as he or she approaches a specific writing task. In a writer's world, penciled drafts mingle easily with computer technology, but what remains the same are the procedures available to writers attempting to get their meaning across to readers. You will see again how one particular writer, Jim Fusilli, sharpens what he wants to present to his audience by using the same revising strategies that you have been applying to your own work.

Essay

1   I've worked for parts of the past 15 years as a rock critic. And in those years, I have seen the standards for rock critics and rock criticism dwindle to the point where I now rarely accept what I read. This gnaws at me; I believe rock is an art form subject to the same stringent critical standards as any other. If what I read is any indication, I may very well be close to alone in this belief.

2   Today there are fewer rock critics and more rock writers, journalists who view rock as entertainment which, of course, much of it is. But all of it isn't. There's an artful side that often is ignored. Accordingly, what's supposed to be ancillary—sales, popularity, image—has become primary. Thoughtful articles on a rock musician's mastery of craft, creativity and emotion appear with greater infrequency. You're more likely to see a piece on Michael Jackson's facial surgery than on his trembling falsetto. Cyndi Lauper has created a wonderful on-stage personality but it is such an easy handle for critics it has overshadowed her evocative voice.

3   To distinguish between entertainment and art isn't difficult. The entertainer's primary barometer is sales and popularity. For the rock's pure artist it may be depth of expression or ability to reveal the sublime. When the reporter plays critic and mistakes what's selling for what's good, a knack for tapping the mainstream with what's vital, he disserves his readers and contributes to the decline of artistic standards.

4   Most rock writers I come across aren't qualified to tackle artistic criticism. A puff profile of rock's newest Big Thing is the easiest piece to write, especially when a major record label's publicity machine lies ready to fill the writer's notebook with great color and quotes.

5   But to examine the Big Thing's music and determine whether it has any genuine artistic merit is something more. It requires a knowledge of music and the means to articulate what's been heard. It requires an application of standards to the music. And it may require the arrogance to tell people what they like may very well stink.

6   Lacking those qualifications, the writer is left with his own unsubstantiated opinion rather than a considered conclusion. What often follows is a review without critical substance, without *music,* and the reader is delivered 16 inches of unbridled and often unintelligible hyperbole. The *New York Daily News* reported a band's set "had all the awesome velocity of a Mac (sic) truck roaring down a mountain pass." Is that a pan or praise? From *Rolling Stone:* "Madonna prompted us to search for an answer that's expansive enough to fit this brilliant, chameleonlike performance." Imagine that guy describing a sunset. Or Ella Fitzgerald.

7   Hyperbole is the rock writer's crutch. I have a friend at a newspaper who, after reading a review, crosses out all the fatuous adjectives and rereads the piece. If it makes sense, he accepts the reviewer's point. But it rarely does.

8   This isn't to say every article should be a scholarly thesis dripping with musical terminology. English is a wonderful language for describing music. A

breezy profile can include some adroit critical observations. Further, the rock critic needn't know how to orchestrate for a symphony; he may not even have to know how to read a lead sheet. Half of his subjects don't. But he ought to know a 12-bar blues from a country waltz and he ought to be familiar with rock's history and its forerunners.

9   I can almost defend the unqualified critic. Editors, it seems to me, aren't looking for tough criticism when it comes to rock. They want a story they can run with a color photo to fill page one of the entertainment section or a concert review that can run alongside the TV listings. Perhaps conditioned by their own reporters, many editors think of today's rock as a vessel of meandering noise, satanic lyrics or formulaic pap and miss its masterful songwriters, instrumental virtuosos and heartfelt vocalists. I've more than once had to pitch a piece to an editor by giving him a cassette tape of the artist.

10   Add to that the writer's frustration of bucking record companies and what singer–songwriter Joni Mitchell called rock's "star-making machinery." Remember, most major record companies aren't altruistically developing artists. They want to make a lot of money; breaking commercially viable acts to their business. They'd rather work with friendly journalists, preferably from the market's major publication. Critics at small papers struggle for recognition. A snipe at a record company's latest Big Thing may guarantee months of unreturned phone calls.

11   Even critics at major dailies can suffer. I was free-lancing a piece on Bruce Springsteen for the *Wall Street Journal* around the time of "Born in the USA." I casually mentioned to a Columbia Records representative that I didn't particularly think the album was up to Mr. Springsteen's standards. Within hours, one of Mr. Springsteen's managers called and rejected my request for an interview with the artist. Days later, a puff piece appeared in *USA Today*, apparently arranged at the same time I was getting the brush.

12   But swimming upstream is a problem every journalist faces. And a critic with conviction easily reminds the publicist that it is he who must be served. By writing puff pieces, the writer is part of the "star-making machinery." By filing tough, objective criticism, he's not.

13   A handful of pop and rock journalists—I'm particularly thinking of the group at *The New York Times*—do a wonderful job of consistently reporting and reviewing the rock world. The *Times* group maintains what I perceive to be pretty high standards for their subjects. Interestingly, they move easily into other musical fields by applying similarly stringent standards. I also admire several jazz critics, particularly Leonard Feather, Nat Hentoff and Whitney Balliett, who manage to meld their love of the music with informed interpretation, exactly the way rock critics should.

14   The rock critic has to contend with two other obstacles. There's the view that rock can't be critically analyzed, that the difference between the blatantly commercial and the artistic is indistinguishable in a musical form that, by its nature, is simple. I disagree; in fact, it's rock's simplicity that makes it easy to find its best work. Passion often is the key. Rock's art strikes at the listener's

heart. If the critic takes that wonderful feeling and examines what caused it in a critical context, the music's truth will out.

15   There's also the argument that rock shouldn't be treated the same as other musical forms, that its main purpose is societal rather than artistic, that it exists for fun, not academic examination. Nowhere is it written that art and fun are mutually exclusive. One listen to Elvis Presley's husky vocal on "Teddy Bear," a whimsical lyric by Elvis Costello or the interplay between drummer John Bonham and guitarist Jimmy Page on any of several Led Zeppelin songs and you'll know art and fun coincide quite well.

16   In the foreward to his 1969 book *Outlaw Blues,* rock critic Paul Williams writes, "Most people see rock as a phenomenon . . . I see rock as a means of expression, an opportunity for beauty, an art." If a rock writer doesn't feel—or can't feel—that way and is unwilling to use that feeling as a springboard to undertaking serious criticism, he has no business critiquing rock.

Draft

I've worked for parts of the past 15 years as a rock critic.
And in those years, I have seen the standards for rock critics
and rock criticism dwindle to the point where I now rarely
accept what I read. This gnaws at me; I believe rock is an art
form subject to the same stringent critical standards as any
other. If what I read is any indication, I may very well be
close to alone in this belief.

2   Today there are fewer rock critics and more rock reporters,
journalists who view rock as entertainment which, of course,
much of it is. But all of it isn't. There's an artful side
that often is ignored. Accordingly, what's supposed to be
ancillary -- sales, popularity, image -- has become primary.
Thoughtful articles on a rock musician's mastery of craft,
creativity and emotion appear with greater infrequency. You're
more likely to see a piece on Michael Jackson's facial surgery
than on his trembling falsetto. Cyndi Lauper has created a
wonderful on-stage personality but it is such an easy handle for
critics it has overshadowed her evocative voice.

3   The entertainer's barometer is ~~sales and popularity~~ _financial_. For
rock's ~~the~~ pure artist it may be depth of expression or reve~~lation of~~ _ability to_
the sublime. When the reporter plays critic and mistakes

_It may be revealed in a single instrumental
phrase or an album's worth of songs. It
may be flat, monotonous, bordering on cacophony
or as sweet and smooth as silk and honey._

expression or ability to reveal the sublime. _Certainly_ ~~You may quibble
with this simple definition, sure, artists aren't opposed to
making money, and occasionally there comes along an entertainer
who may marry substance and form. But, for me, the distinction
is clear, if not in the performer then in the product.~~

~~But~~ when the reporter plays critic, and mistakes what's
selling for what's good, a knack for tapping the mainstream with
what's vital, he _misserves his readers and_ contributes to the decline of artistic
standards.

4   Most rock writers I come across aren't qualified to tackle
artistic criticism. A puff profile of rock's newest Big Thing
is the easiest piece to write, especially when the a major

record label's publicity machine behind him lies ready to fill the writer's notebook with great color and quotes.

5   But to examine the Big Thing's music and determine whether it has any genuine artistic merit is something more. It requires a knowledge of music and ~~how to articulate~~ the ~~many~~ means what's been heard. It requires an application of standards to the music. And it requires may the arrogance to tell people what they like may very well stink. There's a clear difference between what's popular and what's good and the critic must always be able then willing to determine that distinction with conviction.

6   Lacking that, *all qualifications* the reporter is left with his own, unsubstantiated opinion rather than a considered conclusion. What follows often is a review without critical substance, without music, and the reader is delivered 16 inches of unbridled and often unintelligible hyperbole. ~~Some examples~~: The New York Daily News reported a band's set "had all the awesome velocity of a Mac (sic) truck roaring down a mountain pass." Is that a pan or praise? From Rolling Stone: "Madonna prompted us to search for an answer that's expansive enough to fit this brilliant, chameleonlike performance." Imagine that guy describing a sunset. Or Ella Fitzgerald.

7   Hyperbole is the rock reporter's crutch. I have a friend at a newspaper who, after reading a review, crosses out all the *fatuos* adjectives and rereads it. If it makes sense, he accepts the reviewer's point. But it rarely does.

8   This isn't to say every article should be a scholarly thesis dripping with musical terminology. English is a wonderful *no critical* language for describing music. *A breezy profile can include some adroit observations* Further, the rock critic needn't know how to orchestrate for a symphony; he may not even have to know how to read a lead sheet. Half of his subjects don't. But he ought to know a 12-bar blues from a country waltz and he ought to be familiar with rock's history, *and its predecessors*.

9   I can almost defend the unqualified critic. Editors, it seems to me, aren't looking for tough criticism when it comes to rock. They want a story they can run with a color photo to fill page one of the entertainment section or a concert review that can run alongside the TV listings. Many editors, perhaps conditioned by their own reporters, think of today's rock as a vessel of meandering noise, satanic lyrics or formulaic pop and

miss its masterful songwriters, instrumental virtuosos and
heartfelt vocalists. I've more than once, pitched a piece to an _Had to_ ~
editor by giving him a cassette tape of the artist.
~~Add to that the~~ frustration of

10   ~~For a newspaperman,~~ bucking record companies and what
singer-singwriter Joni Mitchell called rock's "star-making
machinery" ~~is no feat~~. Remember, most major record companies
aren't altruistically developing artists. They want to make a
lot of money~~, and~~ breaking commercially viable acts is their   _a major's_
They'd rather work with friendly ~~reporters~~ journalists, P _referable from the major publication_
stock in trade. Critics ~~with~~ small papers ~~have to~~ struggle for
recognition~~, and~~ a snipe at a record company's latest Big Thing
may
~~can guarantee~~ months of unreturned phone calls. Even critics at
major dailies can suffer. I was free-lancing a piece on Bruce
Springsteen for The Wall Street Journal around the time of "Born
in the USA." I~~casually~~ mentioned to a Columbia Records representative
that I didn't particularly think the album ~~was~~ up to Mr.
Springsteen's standards. Within hours, one of Mr. Springsteen's
managers called and ~~told me "Bruce wouldn't be available for an~~ _rejected my request for an interview w/ the artist._
~~interview"~~ Days later, a puff piece appeared in USA Today,
apparently arranged at the same time I was getting the brush.

11   But ~~swimming upstream~~ is a problem ~~any~~ _every_ journalist ~~faces~~.
And a critic with conviction easily reminds the publicist that
it is he who must be served. Write puff pieces and the writer
is part of the "star-making machinery." File tough, objective
criticism and he's not.

12   Incidentally, a critic needn't have impeccable taste. In
~~my case, what~~ I like and what is good are often two different

the critic has to contend w/ the
things. In my record collection lies many well-worn albums that
don't hold up to critical standards. Just because their not up
to those standards, which, by the way, are established by the
artists and not the critics, that doesn't mean I can't like
them. I do but if I'm honest I make the distinction.

13   ~~There's a~~ view ~~among some folks~~ that rock can't be
critically analyzed, that the difference between the blatantly
commercial and the artistic is ~~virtually~~ indistinguishable in a
musical form that, by its ~~inherent~~ nature, is simple. I
disagree; in fact, it's rock's simplicity that makes it easy to

find its best work. Passion is the key; the difference between
something calculated for its sales potential and the heartfelt.
Record company executives are beating the bushes looking for a
group that can emulate the fervor delivered by Ireland's U2 but
the depth of passion in Bono's gritty tenor can't be faked.
Another example: Compare singer Rod Stewart's 1971 release
"Every Picture Tells a Story" and the junk he dashes off today.
The voice may sound the same but the difference is apparent.
Rock's art strikes at the heart. Examine it in a critical
context and the truth will out.

Jazz, it was said, couldn't be properly chronicled but
critics like Leonard Feather, Nat Hentoff and Whitney Balliett
proved that false. A handful of pop and rock journalists -- I'm
particularly thinking of the group at the New York Times -- do a
wonderful job of consistently reporting and reviewing the rock
world. The Times group maintains what I perceive to be pretty
high standards for their subjects. Interestingly, they move
easily into other musical fields by applying similiarly
stringent standards.

14   There's also the argument that rock shouldn't be treated
the same as other musical forms, that its main purpose is
societal rather than artistic, that it exists for fun, not
academic examination. The argument quotes the Rolling Stones'
lyric "It's only rock 'n' roll but I like it." But nowhere is
it written than art and fun are mutually exclusive. One listen
to Willie Mae Thornton's gruff, bluesy vocal on "Hound Dog," a
whimsical lyric by Elvis Costello or the interplay between
drummer John Bonham and guitarist Jimmy Page on any of several
Led Zeppelin songs and you'll know art and fun coincide quite
well.

15   In the foreward to his 1969 book "Outlaw Blues," rock critic
Paul Williams writes, "Most people see rock as a phenomenon...I
see rock as a means of expression, an opportunity for beauty, an
art." If a rock writer doesn't feel -- or can't feel -- that
way and is unwilling to use that feeling as a springboard to
undertaking serious criticism, he has no business critiquing
rock.

Comparing Draft and Essay

Draft Paragraph A

1. This handwritten draft paragraph is an early introduction to the essay. Compare it with paragraph 1 of the final version. What similarities or differences do you notice in the author's purpose and meaning?

2. What is your reaction to these paragraphs? In what way is your reaction related to the author's shift in *tone*? How does this change reflect Fusilli's reconsideration of the type of persuasive appeal he will use?

3. What do you think is the main idea (thesis) of each introduction? In which paragraph is the main idea stated more clearly?

Draft Paragraph 3

4. Compare this paragraph to paragraph 3 of the final version. Identify the kinds of revision strategies that Fusilli uses. How do these changes affect meaning, purpose, and tone?

5. What additional expository techniques is Fusilli using in the service of persuasion? How do they help develop the argument being presented?

Draft Paragraphs 5 and 6

Fusilli uses these paragraphs to develop his distinction between art and entertainment. Note how revision is used to sharpen his views. The changes made to the final sentences of draft paragraph 6 give the new version additional power: the writer is asserting his authority (ethical appeal). Here Fusilli reinforces his division classification by asserting that a rock *writer* only discusses *entertainment,* while a rock *critic* discusses *art*. This clarification is another example of the author's use of logical appeal.

Draft Paragraphs 7 through 10

6. These paragraphs have not been revised extensively; indeed, the changes mainly clarify or confirm the author's purpose and meaning. What types of appeals (emotional, ethical, or logical) is Fusilli using to back up his views? How does he use cause and effect to generate support?

Draft Paragraph 11

7. Fusilli again employs multiple revising strategies to convey his meaning to his readers. Examine the changes he makes and explain how you think they affect the paragraph as well as the overall essay.

Draft Paragraphs 13 through 15

8. Why do you think that draft paragraph 13 has been deleted?

9. Draft paragraphs 14 and 15 have been radically changed. In particular, Fusilli has rearranged their sequence (compare them with paragraphs 13 and 14 of the

final version) and deleted much information from draft paragraph 14. Why do you think that he has made these major changes?

Draft Paragraphs 16 and 17

10. These concluding paragraphs show only minor revisions, the most noticeable one being the deletion of the *Rolling Stones'* quotation from draft paragraph 16. Here, Fusilli tightens up his argument in an attempt to make a final pitch for his readers' support. How do you react to these paragraphs and, in particular, to the author's final sentence? Have you been convinced that rock and roll can and should be subjected to scrupulous criticism?

Tekla Devai

Tekla Devai (b. 1964) is a student from Hungary. After flunking out of the prestigious Technical University of Budapest, where she studied natural sciences, she decided to work on her English. Her curiosity has led her on an adventure to find out more about the American people living across the Atlantic and speaking a very different language.

Why I Don't Read the News Anymore

Introduction to the Essay and Draft

Rape is the subject of Tekla Devai's essay "Why I Don't Read the News Anymore." Rather than create an essay that clinically examines the topic or one that narrates a specific event, the writer engages the issue in several ways. By reading the draft and published versions of the essay, you will learn that the message Devai wants to convey defies easy classification; her thoughts about rape include a consideration of why it happens, strategies for avoiding or preventing it, and outrage about the way society has come to accept it.

The power of her topic is just one consideration Devai grapples with in her essay. As she mentions below, other concerns command her attention as she writes, yet putting her thoughts on paper is a challenge that is worth accepting.

Mastering English is quite a challenge and great fun at the same time. Using a language other than my native Hungarian forces me to think in a dramatically different way from the one I was used to when growing up. Suddenly, expressing simple thoughts can become a major problem when I try to do it in English. On the other hand, because of this difference, I look at life with different eyes, and this new take on things is very stimulating and refreshing.

Despite all the thrills, writing is quite a struggle. I am never done with a paper; I run out of time. I am never satisfied with my work because I always feel the need to change something to clarify my thoughts which are so clear in my head but are so hard to put on a piece of paper.

How Devai has chosen to convey her meaning reflects the depth and complexity of her thoughts and feelings, and her manipulation of argumentation and persuasion in turn mirrors this complexity. However, as you will see, the writer's selection of persuasive appeals (emotional, ethical, logical) is inextricably bound to her choice of audience and tone. By carefully examining how Devai balances her consideration of purpose, meaning, audience, and tone, and how she revises to maximize her effectiveness, you will gain insight into how she is able to control her appeal to a reader's heart and mind.

Final Essay

1   "BRONX MOM GANG-RAPED." I should stop peeking into people's newspapers on the subway, for I am always sorry afterwards. The headlines scare the hell out of me. They are even worse than the posters about AIDS or drugs. Taking the subway is an ordeal in itself because of my strong dislike of filth, ill odors, and crowdedness. On top of these come the pictures of alcoholics, drug addicts, and premature babies on the walls. What a treat! To find refuge and to pass the time I look at the newspaper headlines, and I am sorry I did.

2   A mother was gang-raped, says the *Newsday*. Please, do not let it happen to me! Please, please, please! I have already figured out that it is not supposed to be easy to be a woman, but rape is more than I have bargained for. I do not want it in the deal; nor does anyone else. So why does it happen to so many of us?

3   TIMES SQUARE—I get off here. My thoughts go back to that horrifying line about that gang-rape. Here I am all by myself in the middle of a strange crowd, and the butterflies start to beat their wings against my stomach. Am I frightened? Maybe I need a bodyguard, big, strong, somebody like Mike Tyson, to scare away rapists. Wait a minute! He was allegedly beating his wife between tournaments. Hiring him does not seem to be such a good idea; I do not think I would feel safe with him. Then who else? How about RoboCop? I have not heard anything bad about him. After all, he is a machine.

4   At home, in relative safety, and against my better judgement, I look up the article in the paper. "A 10-year-old Bronx boy and his stroller-bound baby sister were held at gun point . . . and forced to watch three men gang-rape their mother." OK, am I supposed to get used to this? To this constant threat to the female body and mind, including mine. There are reports about rape almost every day. It feels like playing Russian roulette on the streets: Am I going to be a victim or not? Am I safe at this part of the town at this time of the day? I have to face the fact that just because I am civilized does not mean that everybody will behave the same way and respect me as a human being. It is true, I do not go up to lonely men at secluded areas, demand their money, and rape them— obviously, I do not have either the interest or the strength—but this in itself

does not mean that I am saved from being harassed. Even if I expect everybody to stay away from antisocial behavior, the papers disillusion me day after day, and I do not know what to do to save myself.

5   If women would not care so much about being violated and abused, would it hurt less? One could tell this unfortunate mother of two not to take her rape to heart so much; she just happened to be a participant—the involuntary one—of a popular game in New York City. Did you get raped? Welcome to the club!

6   No, I do not think I could get used to it. Then what about a gun for self-defense? If rapists carry guns, logically, I should do the same in order to defend myself. I have to be realistic though and admit that most likely a shoot-out would be fatal for me. I have more important things to do than target practice, and so far I did not think that it should become part of my life. Or should it? Maybe my priorities need to change. On the other hand, the more guns are out out on the streets, the more often they will be used. That is not what I want either.

7   Back to square one: what can I do to avoid rape? There seems to be no satisfying answer. The problem is that rape happens practically anytime and anywhere, so it is very hard if not impossible to judge where and when I am safe, unless I expect to find monsters in every corner. In other words, I should trust nobody. But what kind of a life is it when a woman cannot have one male friend whom she is not afraid to be left alone with? I am cautious and play it safe but wonder from time to time whether it is going to be enough. It has been so far. But who can tell me how long?

Draft

1   "Bronx Mom Gang-Raped".
I should stop reading people's newspapers on the subway, for I am always sorry afterwards. The headlines scare the hell out of me. They are even worse than the posters about AIDS or drugs. Taking the subway is an ordeal in itself because of my strong dislike of filth, ill odors, and crowd. On top of these come the pictures of alcoholics, drug addicts, and premature babies on the walls. What

a treat! To find refuge and to pass the time I look at the newspapers head- lines and I am sorry I do. A mother was gang-raped, says the Newsday. Please, do not let that happen to me! Please, please, please! I have already figured out that it is not supposed to be easy to be a woman, but rape is more than I have bargained for. I did not want it in the deal, nor does anyone else. So why does it happen to so many of us women?

2   Times Square — I get off here. Maybe I should hire a bodyguard. Big, strong, somebody like Mike Tyson to scare away rapists. Wait a minute! He was allegedly beating his wife between tournaments. On second thought, having him does not seem to be a good idea. Then who else? How about RoboCop? I did not hear anything bad about him. After all, he is a robot.

3   At home, against my better judge- ment, I look up the article in the paper. " A 10-year-old Bronx boy and his stroller- bound baby sister were held at gun point ... and forced to watch three men gang-

rape their mother". OK, am I supposed
to get used to this? There are reports like
this in the news almost every day. Just
because I am civilized does not mean that
everybody else behaves the same way. I am
not refering to my table manners exclusively.
I do not go up to lonely men ∄ at secluded
areas, demand their money, and rape them
by using force. I would expect others to
stay away from this kind of beter behavior
also, but the papers disillusion me day
after day.

4   If women did not care so much
about being violated and abused, would it
hurt less? One could tell this unfortunate
mother of two not to take her rep rape to
heart so much; she just happened to be
a participant — an involuntary, though — of
a popu popular game in New York City.
Did you get raped? Welcome to the club!

5   No, I do not think I could get
used to it. What about a gun for self-
defense? If the rapist carry guns, I should
carry one also, in order to defend myself.
I have to be realistic and admit that most
likely I would loose in a shoot-out.

I have more important things to do than target practice, and I do not believe that it should become part of my life. Or should it? That is the question. On the other hand, the more guns are out on the streets, the more often they will be used. That is not what I want either.

6   Back to square one. What can I do to avoid rape? I do not seem to find a ~~dis satisfactory~~ <ins>satisfying</ins> answer. The problem is that rape happens practically anytime and anywhere. It's hard to judge where and when I am safe. I try to be ~~cook~~ cautious, not to take unnecessary risk, but still be able to enjoy life. I wonder from time to time whether this is enough. It has been so far. But who can ~~tt tell me~~ how long?

Comparing Draft and Essay

Draft Paragraph 1

The main revision undertaken by the writer in this draft paragraph is its rearrangement into two paragraphs (see published paragraphs 1 and 2). Making this change helps Devai to slow the pace of her essay by gradually introducing a reader to her topic.

1. What is the tone of this draft paragraph? What specific examples can you find to support your answer? On the basis of your decision about tone, what kind of appeal (emotional, ethical, or logical) do you think Devai will make in the rest of the essay?

2. What main idea is presented in this paragraph's last sentence? What do you think Devai will discuss next?

Draft Paragraph 2

3. Given the final sentence of draft paragraph 1, how does this paragraph fulfill your expectations?

4. Compare this draft paragraph to published paragraph 3. What revisions has Devai made? How do these changes help to establish emotional and ethical appeal?

Draft Paragraph 3

5. Once again, the primary revision strategy employed by Devai is addition. What specific ideas have been added to the published version of this paragraph (published paragraph 4)? What impact might they have on the writer's audience?

Draft Paragraphs 4 through 6

These draft paragraphs have been revised lightly. Draft paragraph 4 is nearly unchanged as Devai continues her strategy of mixing emotional with logical and ethical appeals (again reflected by corresponding shifts in tone). Also, the writer's control of pacing helps this paragraph build into a searing attack on the status quo. Draft paragraph 5 contains small but important changes. Devai's inclusion of the word "logically" calls attention to her use of argumentation in this paragraph; indeed, the analysis provided here is the least emotional of any in the essay. The sentence added in revision to published paragraph 6, "Maybe my priorities need to change," suggests the seriousness of the attraction of armed self-defense. Similarly, Devai adds one sentence to draft paragraph 6 in her published version ("But what kind of life is it when a woman cannot have one male friend whom she is not afraid to be left alone with?"), and it captures the depth of the meaning of this topic to the writer. In revising these draft paragraphs then, Devai once again adds details and analysis to enhance her initial opinions and convince a reader of the validity of her views.

6. What main point is being argued by the writer in the essay's conclusion? What tone does she leave the essay with and what is its impact on you as a reader?

7. How does Devai use narrative as a supporting technique in her essay? How does narrative contribute to the author's purpose and meaning?

8. How has Devai used emotional, ethical, and logical appeals in her essay? How has she used revision to moderate her tone and the appeals she employs?

George Kormos

George Kormos (b. 1969) was born in Brooklyn, New York. He is currently working toward his marketing degree at Queensborough Community College. He plans to use his writing and artistic skills in his future advertising career. But those plans are not set in stone!

Giving the Death Penalty to Drug Dealers

Introduction to the Essay and Draft

In his essay "Giving the Death Penalty to Drug Dealers," George Kormos is responding to an assignment that requires him to argue one side of a controversial issue. Having a time restriction of two class sessions to complete the assignment is another limitation; however, Kormos applies the following strategies to settle on a topic quickly:

> When I write on a certain subject it is usually something I feel strongly about. . . . I always like to feel comfortable with the topic I am working on. If I feel the piece is not workable, then I might try it from another perspective. However, if this just does not work, then I will select another topic. . . . I like to choose a topic that I can have fun with, a topic that I am fairly knowledgeable about. This gives me a chance to voice my opinions on certain issues and feelings I have.

Back in Chapter 1, William Stafford defined a "writer" as someone "who has become accustomed to trusting . . . grace, luck, or—skill" in getting across what he or she wants to say (see page 7). As evident from the above statement, Kormos' knowledge of himself as a writer helps him to do what needs to be done to complete his assignment. Although he is writing in a high-pressure situation with an imminent deadline, he makes several decisions that demonstrate his trust in himself and his abilities. First, he selects a topic that he feels strongly about, that he is comfortable with, and that he knows about. This understanding is critical, for any writer's strength is in what he or she knows about and is interested in. Second, if the writing is not coming as easily as he feels it should, Kormos does not give up on the topic but examines it from another perspective. Indeed, a writer at a dead end with a topic might discover that he or she has much to say about it if the topic is approached in a new way. Third, if the topic still does not work, Kormos will not allow himself to be trapped by it or the effort he has already expended but will trust himself to find something else to write about. Not looking on a piece that does not go where the writer wants it to as wasted effort is crucial to discovering ultimately what one wants to discuss. Indeed, an aborted effort sometimes yields a great amount of knowledge about oneself as a writer. As Stafford promises, "For the person who follows with trust and forgiveness what occurs to him, the world remains always ready and deep, an inexhaustible environment, with the combined vividness of an actuality and flexibility of a dream" (page 7).

Reproduced below is a typescript prepared from a portion of Kormos' handwritten first draft of "Giving the Death Penalty to Drug Dealers." Perhaps because the writer has connected with his topic (it is one that he feels strongly about, has knowledge of, and feels comfortable with), the first draft comes easily to him and you will notice that the published version is largely unchanged. Surface changes, those revisions of sentence constructions, diction, and grammar, are few, and little information has been added or deleted. What most concerns Kormos in his revision is reorganizing the essay to strengthen the argument he is presenting as well as tightening up specific ideas, changes that affect the larger context of the work.

Final Essay

1   There are many problems that the children in our society face today. Racial violence, sexual epidemics, teen-age pregnancy, and war. But the war that I am talking about has nothing to do with Saddam Hussein. It is a war whose victims get younger and younger every day. It is a war that is being waged against our children. The war is drugs.

2   Many people are asking, "What can be done to the drug dealers that plague our children's schoolyards and playgrounds? What can be done to the scum that when caught and convicted only return to claim more victims?" The answer is simple. Put into effect a mandatory death penalty for individuals caught and prosecuted for the selling of illegal drugs.

3   Let's face it, our justice system does not work. What kind of society do we live in if the drug dealers that are caught get sent to jail for six months only to watch cable television? That's punishment? Isn't jail supposed to be an unpleasant experience? What is to stop this kind of scum from continuing their distribution of death once they are released? The answer, nothing. Why should they? They make $15,000 a week, and when they get caught, they get three meals a day and a roof over their heads. And you know what's ironic? We the taxpayers are footing the bill for their holiday stay. No wonder there is overcrowding in our jails. It's a damn country club!

4   A mandatory death penalty would cut the drug dealing down considerably. At the very least the dealers would not be so arrogant as to deal openly in public places where our children fall prey. We owe our kids the guarantee of growing up in a drug free environment. With a death penalty for drug dealers in place, our children would be a lot safer.

5   I believe the death penalty should be taken one step further. People do not grasp or comprehend what they cannot see. So, I suggest that when a dealer is sent to his death, it should be televised. The scene of that person's life being taken away would be an excellent deterrent in the war on drugs. For example, the graphic scene of an electrocution would make many dealers and would-be drug dealers think twice about what they are doing.

6   People and politicians argue that two wrongs don't make a right. This response is not going to satisfy the thousands of grieving families that have lost their loved ones due to overdoses. The politicians say they want a clear conscience. Their argument is always over the slim chance that they might execute an innocent individual. This does not come before our kids who are getting slaughtered in the streets over crack. If the politicians want a clear conscience then they should stay home. Let a person with some backbone do the job they are unwilling to do. We as voters should send a clear message to these politicians. Stop making excuses and start working on a solution. A mandatory death penalty for drug dealers is the only way.

7   Who knows how many kids have died at the hands of drug dealers each day. What a waste of life. The only solution is to put a swift end to the problem. Catch the dealer, end his life, and he will never deal drugs again. End of problem. A death penalty for drug dealers is the only logical way to bring a quick end to a problem that will only get much worse.

Draft (Excerpt)

3   A mandatory death penalty would cut the drug dealing down considerably. At the very least the dealers would not be so arrogant as to deal openly in public places where our children fall prey. With a death penalty in place, our youth would be alot safer. We owe them the privilege of growing up in a drug free environment.

4   I believe the death penalty should be taken one step further. People do not grasp or comprehend what they cannot see. So, I suggest that when a dealer is sent to his death, it should be televised. The scene of that persons life being taken away would be an excellent deterrent in the war on drugs. It would make many dealers and would-be drug dealers think twice about what they are doing.

5   Some people argue that two wrongs don't make a right. This response is not going to satisfy the thousands of grieving families that have lost their loved ones due to overdoses. The politicians say they want a clear conscience. How does this come before our kids, who are getting slaughtered in the streets over crack. If the people in politics want a clear conscience then stay home. Let somebody with some backbone do the job they are unwilling to do. We as voters should send a clear message to these politicians to stop making excuses and start working on a solution.

6   Let's face it, our justice system does not work. What kind of society do we live in if the drug dealers that are

caught get sent to jail for six months only to watch cable television? That's punishment? Isn't jail supposed to be an unpleasant experience? What's to stop this scum from continuing their distribution of death once they are released? The answer, nothing. Why should they? They make $15,000 - a week, and when they get caught, they get three meals a day and a roof over their heads. And you know whats ironic? We the taxpayers are footing the bill for their holiday stay. No wonder there is overcrowding in our jails. It's a damn country club!

7   Who knows how many kids have died at the hands of drug dealers each day. What a waste of life. The only solution is to put a swift end to the problem. Catch the dealer, end his life, and he will never deal drugs again. End of problem. A death penalty for drug dealers is the only logical way to bring a quick end to a problem that will only get much worse.

Comparing Draft and Essay

In revising his draft of "Giving the Death Penalty to Drug Dealers," Kormos rearranges draft paragraph 6 to come between draft paragraphs 2 and 3. After this rearrangement, draft paragraph 3 becomes published paragraph 4, draft paragraph 4 becomes published paragraph 5, and draft paragraph 5 becomes published paragraph 6. Draft paragraphs 1, 2, and 7 are virtually unchanged from their published counterparts, with the exception of the revision of the sentence sequence of the second half of the essay's introduction.

1. What persuasive appeal or appeals is Kormos applying to his essay? How does the writer's tone alert you to his use of emotional, ethical, or logical appeal? What examples can you find to support your answer?

2. After reading the draft and published versions of the essay, why do you think that Kormos has moved draft paragraph 6 to its new place as published paragraph 3? How does this revision affect how Kormos presents his argument?

Draft Paragraphs 3 and 4
3. Compare these draft paragraphs with published paragraphs 4 and 5. How do Kormos' revisions aid his appeal to your emotions or logic?

Draft Paragraph 5

4. Which part of this paragraph appeals to your emotions and which to your intellect? How do the revisions made to published paragraph 6 support your responses to the draft paragraph?

Draft Paragraph 7

5. Often, making a change in an essay will affect portions that are not revised. Though this paragraph has not been altered, the relocation of draft paragraph 6 has a profound impact on its effectiveness. Given the momentum provided by the revisions of draft paragraph 5 that are noted above, how does this paragraph now serve as the essay's conclusion? How are you affected by it? How do you now interpret Kormos' use of the word "logical"?

Rachel L. Jones

Rachel L. Jones (b. 1961), was born in Cairo, Illinois. She attended Northwestern University and Southern Illinois University and held internships at *The New York Times* and the *Washington Post*. Originally, she wrote "What's Wrong with Black English" in a freshman composition course and revised it for publication in *Newsweek*. This is her description of her revision process:

> Because I don't have the early drafts to outline the difference in forms, I'd like to stress the importance of rewriting and careful editing. I wrote the paper in one sitting, but carefully combed through it several times to clean up grammar, punctuation and to tighten it.
>
> In rewriting it for *Newsweek,* the objective was to make the tone conversational, less formal than the paper. I read it "aloud" (in my head because I was in the library at the time!) to make sure there was a natural flow. I think good persuasive writing has a conversational quality and an underlying urgency that commands recognition.
>
> Again, it came so easily for me because I wrote for that audience of one [myself], and I simply wrote how I felt. All issues of race and understanding between races are interesting and important to me, so that also affected the tone. This made for a more "emotional" piece, as opposed to a paper, in which the main objective is substantiating a position.

What's Wrong with Black English

1   William Labov, a noted linguist, once said about the use of black English, "It is the goal of most black Americans to acquire full control of the standard language without giving up their own culture." He also suggested that there are certain advantages to having two ways to express one's feelings. I wonder if the good doctor might also consider the goals of those black Americans who have full control of standard English but who are every now and then troubled by that colorful, grammar-to-the-winds patois that is black English. Case in point—me.

2   I'm a 21-year-old black born to a family that would probably be considered the lower-middle class—which in my mind is a polite way of describing a condition only slightly better than poverty. Let's just say we rarely if ever did the winter-vacation thing in the Caribbean. I've often had to defend my humble beginnings to a most unlikely group of people for an even less likely reason. Because of the way I talk, some of my black peers look at me sideways and ask, "Why do you talk like you're white?"

3   The first time it happened to me I was nine years old. Cornered in the school bathroom by the class bully and her sidekick, I was offered the opportunity to swallow a few of my teeth unless I satisfactorily explained why I always got good grades, why I talked "proper" or "white." I had no ready answer for her, save the fact that my mother had from the time I was old enough to talk stressed the importance of reading and learning, or that L. Frank Baum and Ray

Bradbury were my closest companions. I read all my older brothers' and sisters' literature textbooks more faithfully than they did, and even lightweights like the Bobbsey Twins and Trixie Belden were allowed into my bookish inner circle. I don't remember exactly what I told those girls, but I somehow talked my way out of a beating.

4   I was reminded once again of my "white pipes" problem while apartment hunting in Evanston, Illinois, last winter. I doggedly made out lists of available places and called all around. I would immediately be invited over—and immediately turned down. The thinly concealed looks of shock when the front door opened clued me in, along with the flustered instances of "just getting off the phone with the girl who was ahead of you and she wants the rooms." When I finally found a place to live, my roommate stirred up old memories when she remarked a few months later, "You know, I was surprised when I first saw you. You sounded white over the phone." Tell me another one, sister.

5   I should've asked her a question I've wanted an answer to for years: how does one "talk white"? The silly side of me pictures a rabid white foam spewing forth when I speak. I don't use Valley Girl jargon, so that's not what's meant in my case. Actually, I've pretty much deduced what people mean when they say that to me, and the implications are really frightening.

6   It means that I'm articulate and well-versed. It means that I can talk as freely about John Steinbeck as I can about Rick James. It means that "ain't" and "he be" are not staples of my vocabulary and are only used around family and friends. (It is almost Jekyll and Hyde-ish the way I can slip out of academic abstractions into a long, lean, double-negative-filled dialogue, but I've come to terms with that aspect of my personality.) As a child, I found it hard to believe that's what people meant by "talking proper"; that would've meant that good grades and standard English were equated with white skin, and that went against everything I'd ever been taught. Running into the same type of mentality as an adult has confirmed the depressing reality that for many blacks, standard English is not only unfamiliar, it is socially unacceptable.

7   James Baldwin once defended black English by saying it had added "vitality to the language," and even went so far as to label it a language in its own right, saying, "Language [i.e., black English] is a political instrument" and a "vivid and crucial key to identity." But did Malcolm X urge blacks to take power in this country "any way y'all can"? Did Martin Luther King Jr. say to blacks, "I has been to the mountaintop, and I done seed the Promised Land"? Toni Morrison, Alice Walker and James Baldwin did not achieve their eloquence, grace and stature by using only black English in their writing. Andrew Young, Tom Bradley and Barbara Jordan did not acquire political power by saying, "Y'all crazy if you ain't gon vote for me." They all have full command of standard English, and I don't think that knowledge takes away from their blackness or commitment to black people.

8   I know from experience that it's important for black people, stripped of culture and heritage, to have something they can point to and say, "This is ours,

we can comprehend it, *we* alone can speak it with a soulful flourish." I'd be lying if I said that the rhythms of my people caught up in "some serious rap" don't sound natural and right to me sometimes. But how heartwarming is it for those same brothers when they hit the pavement searching for employment? Studies have proven that the use of ethnic dialects decreases power in the marketplace. "I be" is acceptable on the corner, but not with the boss.

9   Am I letting capitalistic, European-oriented thinking fog the issue? Am I selling out blacks to an ideal of assimilating, being as much like white as possible? I have not formed a personal political ideology, but I know this: it hurts me to hear black children use black English, knowing that they will be at yet another disadvantage in an educational system already full of stumbling blocks. It hurts me to sit in lecture halls and hear fellow black students complain that the professor "be tripping dem out using big words dey can't understand." And what hurts most is to be stripped of my own blackness simply because I know my way around the English language.

10   I would have to disagree with Labov in one respect. My goal is not so much to acquire full control of both standard and black English, but to one day see more black people less dependent on a dialect that excludes them from full participation in the world we live in. I don't think I talk white, I think I talk right.

Considering Content

1. Does Jones speak "black English"? What's the evidence?

2. Jones introduces in the first paragraph the possibility (by way of a quotation) of retaining simultaneously both a dialect and a standard language. What is Jones' attitude toward this possibility? Why? Do you share her attitude?

3. What, according to Jones' implication, would have been Martin Luther King's and Malcolm X's effectiveness if they had spoken only black English? Do you agree?

4. What is Jones' final answer to the question in her title? Do you agree?

5. Does Jones say how blacks can retain their dialect without being "dependent" on it? Does she give black English credit for what it can do for standard English, as James Baldwin does?

6. How do you think Jones would answer her own question, "Am I selling out blacks to an ideal of assimilating, being as much like whites as possible?" How would you answer her question?

7. Assimilation is a controversial idea for many groups and individuals in America. How do you feel about it? What does it mean? What does it involve besides language? Is it a matter of choice?

Considering Craft

1. Jones writes of her persuasive essay:

   The most amazing thing about the column, almost 5 years later, is the variety and depth of reactions it provoked. Writing it was very natural, almost effortless, and I think that must be the key to persuasive writing: choose that "audience of one," persuade only *one* person of something you believe in very strongly. Think it through carefully, locate data to support your position, and then write for that one person.

   How well does she follow her own advice? What evidence did you find most convincing?

2. Jones writes from a first-person point of view. How does that contribute to the persuasive impact of the essay? What examples from her own experience did you find most convincing?

3. What portrait of the writer emerges from the essay?

4. Jones also cites several references to white and black writers. Why is paragraph 7 particularly effective in establishing the validity of her thesis statement?

5. Jones begins and ends her essay with a reference to the linguist William Labov. How does this affect the unity of her essay?

6. What is the tone of the essay? Is it subjective, neutral, serious, bitter, humorous, or argumentative? What does her tone suggest about her attitude toward her subject? (See Jones' discussion of tone in Chapter 5, page 139.)

Martin Luther King, Jr.

Martin Luther King, Jr. (1929–1968) was born in Georgia and became an ordained minister at the age of 18. A graduate of Morehouse College, Boston University, and Chicago Theological Seminary, King became a national figure in 1955 when he led a boycott leading to the end of the segregated bus system in Montgomery, Alabama. He was awarded the Nobel Peace Prize in 1964. In 1968 he was assassinated. As you read "I Have a Dream," which King delivered in 1963, note how he appeals to the idealism of Americans of all races.

I Have a Dream

1   I am happy to join with you today in what will go down in history as the greatest demonstration for freedom in the history of our nation.

2   Five score years ago, a great American, in whose symbolic shadow we stand today, signed the Emancipation Proclamation. This momentous decree came as a great beacon light of hope to millions of Negro slaves who had been seared in the flames of withering injustice. It came as a joyous daybreak to end the long night of their captivity. But one hundred years later, the Negro still is not free. One hundred years later, the life of the Negro is still sadly crippled by the manacles of segregation and the chains of discrimination. One hundred years later, the Negro lives on a lonely island of poverty in the midst of a vast ocean of material prosperity. One hundred years later, the Negro is still anguished in the corners of American society and finds himself in exile in his own land. And so we have come here today to dramatize a shameful condition.

3   In a sense we have come to our nation's capital to cash a check. When the architects of our republic wrote the magnificent words of the Constitution and the Declaration of Independence, they were signing a promissory note to which every American was to fall heir. This note was the promise that all men—yes, Black men as well as white men—would be guaranteed the inalienable rights of life, liberty, and the pursuit of happiness.

4   It is obvious today that America has defaulted on this promissory note insofar as her citizens of color are concerned. Instead of honoring this sacred obligation, America has given the Negro people a bad check, a check which has come back marked "insufficient funds." But we refuse to believe that the bank of justice is bankrupt. We refuse to believe that there are insufficient funds in the great vaults of opportunity of this nation; and so we have come to cash this check, a check that will give us upon demand the riches of freedom and the security of justice.

5   We have also come to this hallowed spot to remind America of the fierce urgency of *now*. This is no time to engage in the luxury of cooling off or to take the tranquilizing drug of gradualism. *Now* is the time to make real the promises of democracy. *Now* is the time to rise from the dark and desolate valley of segregation to the sunlit path of racial justice. *Now* is the time to lift our nation from the quicksands of racial injustice to the solid rock of brotherhood. *Now* is the time to make justice a reality for all of God's children.

6   It would be fatal for the nation to overlook the urgency of the moment. This sweltering summer of the Negro's legitimate discontent will not pass until there is an invigorating autumn of freedom and equality. Nineteen Sixty-three is not an end, but a beginning. And those who hope that the Negro needed to blow off steam and will now be content will have a rude awakening if the nation returns to business as usual. There will be neither rest nor tranquility in America until the Negro is granted his citizenship rights. The whirlwinds of revolt will continue to shake the foundations of our nation until the bright day of justice emerges.

7   But there is something that I must say to my people who stand on the warm threshold which leads into the palace of justice. In the process of gaining our rightful place, we must not be guilty of wrongful deeds. Let us not seek to satisfy our thirst for freedom by drinking from the cup of bitterness and hatred. We

must forever conduct our struggle on the high plane of dignity and discipline. We must not allow our creative protest to degenerate into physical violence. Again and again we must rise to the majestic heights of meeting physical force with soul force. And the marvelous new militancy which has engulfed the Negro community must not lead us to a distrust of all white people; for many of our white brothers, as evidenced by their presence here today, have come to realize that their destiny is tied up with our destiny, and they have come to realize that their freedom is inextricably bound to our freedom.

8   We cannot walk alone. And as we walk we must make the pledge that we shall always march ahead. We cannot turn back. There are those who are asking the devotees of civil rights, "When will you be satisfied?" We can never be satisfied as long as the Negro is the victim of the unspeakable horrors of police brutality. We can never be satisfied as long as our bodies, heavy with the fatigue of travel, cannot gain lodging in the motels of the highways and the hotels of the cities. We cannot be satisfied as long as the Negro's basic mobility is from a smaller ghetto to a larger one. We can never be satisfied as long as our children are stripped of their selfhood and robbed of their dignity by signs stating "For Whites Only." We cannot be satisfied as long as the Negro in Mississippi cannot vote and a Negro in New York believes he has nothing for which to vote. No, no, we are not satisfied, and we will not be satisfied until justice rolls down like waters and righteousness like a mighty stream.

9   I am not unmindful that some of you have come here out of great trials and tribulations. Some of you have come fresh from narrow jail cells. Some of you have come from areas where your quest for freedom left you battered by the storms of persecution and staggered by the winds of police brutality. You have been the veterans of creative suffering. Continue to work with the faith that unearned suffering is redemptive.

10   Go back to Mississippi, and go back to Alabama. Go back to South Carolina. Go back to Georgia. Go back to Louisiana. Go back to the slums and ghettos of our Northern cities, knowing that somehow this situation can and will be changed. Let us not wallow in the valley of despair.

11   I say to you today, my friends, even though we face the difficulties of today and tomorrow, I still have a dream. It is a dream deeply rooted in the American dream. I have a dream that one day this nation will rise up and live out the true meaning of its creed: "We hold these truths to be self-evident, that all men are created equal." I have a dream that one day, on the red hills of Georgia, sons of former slaves and the sons of former slave owners will be able to sit down together at the table of brotherhood. I have a dream that one day even the state of Mississippi, a state sweltering with the heat of injustice, sweltering with the heat of oppression, will be transformed into an oasis of freedom and justice. I have a dream that my four children will one day live in a nation where they will not be judged by the color of their skin, but by the content of their character.

12   I have a dream today. I have a dream that one day down in Alabama—with its vicious racists, with its governor's lips dripping with the words of

interposition and nullification—one day right there in Alabama, little Black boys and Black girls will be able to join hands with little white boys and white girls as sisters and brothers.

13   I have a dream today. I have a dream that one day every valley shall be exalted and every hill and mountain shall be made low, the rough places will be made plain and the crooked places will be made straight, and the glory of the Lord shall be revealed, and all flesh shall see it together.

14   This is our hope. This is the faith that I go back to the South with. And with this faith we will be able to hew out of the mountain of despair a stone of hope. With this faith we will be able to transform the jangling discords of our nation into a beautiful symphony of brotherhood. With this faith we will be able to work together, to play together, to struggle together, to go to jail together, to stand up for freedom together, knowing that we will be free one day.

15   And this will be the day—this will be the day when all God's children will be able to sing with new meaning:

> My country, 'tis of thee,
>   Sweet land of liberty;
>   Of thee I sing;
>   Land where my fathers died,
>   Land of the Pilgrims' pride,
>   From every mountainside
>   Let freedom ring.

And if America is to be a great nation, this must become true.

16   And so let freedom ring from the prodigious hilltops of New Hampshire. Let freedom ring from the mighty mountains of New York. Let freedom ring from the heightening Alleghenies of Pennsylvania. Let freedom ring from the snowcapped Rockies of Colorado. Let freedom ring from the curvaceous slopes of California.

17   But not only that. Let freedom ring from Stone Mountain of Georgia. Let freedom ring from Lookout Mountain of Tennessee. Let freedom ring from every hill and molehill of Mississippi. "From every mountainside let freedom ring."

18   And when this happens—when we allow freedom to ring, when we let it ring from every village and every hamlet, from every state and every city—we will be able to speed up that day when all of God's children, Black men and white men, Jews and Gentiles, Protestants and Catholics, will be able to join hands and sing in the words of the old Negro spiritual: "Free at last! Free at last! Thank God Almighty. We are free at last!"

Considering Content

1. Ask yourself, as you read this twenty-nine-year-old speech, what, if anything, King would have to change were he making the speech today.

2. Why is the phrase "five score years ago" more appropriate than "a hundred years ago" or "in 1863"? Why does he later repeat the phrase "one hundred years later" so often?

3. When King speaks of "cashing a check" or "insufficient funds," is he talking about money? Explain.

4. What is the evidence that King is writing for an audience that includes whites?

5. King praises "marvelous new militancy" but warns against "physical force." Is this consistent? What is "soul force"? From what Indian religio-political leader does the phrase come? Would you call King "militant"?

6. "You have been the veterans of creative suffering." Can suffering be creative? When?

7. King says that his dream is "rooted in the American dream." What is that? King's quotation connects it with the Declaration of Independence. Is the American dream more than the hopes and rights expressed in that document? If so, in what way?

8. What events in Mississippi in the early 1960s might have caused King to single out that state? Why would he specifically mention Georgia? Why Alabama?

9. One of King's longest quotations is from Isaiah: "Every valley shall be exalted and every hill and mountain shall be made low." Why is it appropriate? What does it mean?

10. The heavily used word *freedom* is certainly one of the key words of this speech. Does King succeed in restoring new life to this word? What do you think he means by it? Consider the different possible meanings of *freedom* to the various members of his audience. What does it mean to *you*?

11. What is King's main point?

Considering Craft

1. Two primary techniques that King used to develop and organize his speech are cause and effect and repetition. Cite examples of both techniques in at least three paragraphs of the speech.

2. One characteristic of persuasion is that it uses connotative diction and figurative language to appeal to the reader's emotions. What words or expressions do you find that make you react emotionally?

3. Who do you think is King's intended audience? Can you define its characteristics?

4. Although our discussion of pacing was limited to narration (see Chapter 7), pacing also plays an important part in persuasive writing, as you can see in King's speech. Explain how King's control of pacing affects the speech.

5. According to King's vision of the civil rights movement, what is its ultimate effect? How is persuasion used to convey this dream? To what extent do you think King's training as a minister influenced his control of persuasion?

6. Characterize the tone of the speech. Is it objective, angry, neutral? Explain your answer.

Joseph Wood Krutch

Joseph Wood Krutch (1893–1970) was a professor of dramatic literature, drama critic for *The Nation* (1937–1952), and prolific author. In addition to writing books on Henry David Thoreau and Samuel Johnson, he contributed to *Atlantic Monthly, Harper's,* and *Natural History.* In his later years, he shifted his focus from drama to nature and conservation. As you read "The Vandal and the Sportsman," note how he appeals to both logic and emotion in presenting his point of view.

The Vandal and the Sportsman

1   It would not be quite true to say that "some of my best friends are hunters." Nevertheless, I do number among my respected acquaintances some who not only kill for the sake of killing but count it among their keenest pleasures. I can think of no better illustration of the fact that men may be separated at some point by a fathomless abyss yet share elsewhere much common ground.

2   To me it is inconceivable how anyone should think an animal more interesting dead than alive. I can also easily prove to my own satisfaction that killing "for sport" is the perfect type of that pure evil for which metaphysicians have sometimes sought.

3   Most wicked deeds are done because the doer proposes some good to himself. The liar lies to gain some end, the swindler and thief want things which, if honestly got, might be good in themselves. Even the murderer may be removing an impediment to normal desires or gaining possession of something which his victim keeps from him. None of these usually does evil for evil's sake. They are selfish or unscrupulous, but their deeds are not gratuitously evil. The killer for sport has no such comprehensible motive. He prefers death to life, darkness to light. He gets nothing except the satisfaction of saying, "Something which wanted to live is dead. There is that much less vitality, consciousness, and, perhaps, joy in the universe. I am the Spirit that Denies." When a man wantonly destroys one of the works of man we call him Vandal. When he wantonly destroys one of the works of God we call him Sportsman.

4   The hunter-for-food may be as wicked and as misguided as vegetarians sometimes say; but he does not kill for the sake of killing. The rancher and the

farmer who exterminate all living things not immediately profitable to them may sometimes be working against their own best interests; but whether they are or are not, they hope to achieve some supposed good by their exterminations. If to do evil not in the hope of gain but for evil's sake involves the deepest guilt by which man can be stained, then killing for killing's sake is a terrifying phenomenon and as strong a proof as we could have of that "reality of evil" with which present-day theologians are again concerned.

5   Despite all this I know that sportsmen are not necessarily monsters. Even if the logic of my position is unassailable, the fact still remains that men are not logical creatures; that most if not all are blind to much they might be expected to see and are habitually inconsistent; that both the blind spots and the inconsistencies vary from person to person.

6   To say as we all do: "Any man who would do A would do B," is to state a proposition mercifully proved false almost as often as it is stated. The murderer is not necessarily a liar any more than the liar is necessarily a murderer, and few men feel that if they break one commandment there is little use in keeping the others. Many have been known to say that they considered adultery worse than homicide but not all adulterers are potential murderers and there are even murderers to whom incontinence would be unthinkable. So the sportsman may exhibit any of the virtues—including compassion and respect for life— everywhere except in connection with his "sporting" activities. It may even be often enough true that, as "antisentimentalists" are fond of pointing out, those tenderest toward animals are not necessarily most philanthropic. They no more than sportsmen are always consistent.

7   When the Winchester gun company makes a propaganda movie concluding with a scene in which a "typical American boy" shoots a number of quail and when it then ends with the slogan "Go hunting with your boy and you'll never have to go hunting for him," I may suspect that the gun company is moved by a desire to sell more guns at least as much as by a determination to do what it can toward reducing the incidence of delinquency. I will certainly add also my belief that there are even better ways of diminishing the likelihood that a boy will grow up to do even worse things. Though it seems to me that he is being taught a pure evil I know that he will not necessarily cultivate a taste for all or, for that matter, any one of the innumerable other forms under which evil may be loved.

Considering Content

1. To Krutch the distinction between "the killer for sport" and "the hunter-for-food" is important. Do you accept this distinction? Does the sports hunter kill, as Krutch says, only to kill?

2. Krutch reaches a kind of climax in the statement that "killing for killing's sake is a terrifying phenomenon and as strong a proof as we could have of that reality of evil with which present-day theologians are again concerned." The logical next

step would be to call sports hunters "monsters," but he backs away from this step. Why?

3. Having introduced the term "monsters," Krutch goes to some lengths to protect sports hunters from the label. What is the proposition at the basis of paragraph 6? Do you agree with it?

4. Would you agree that if sports hunters are not necessarily evil, they are at least illogical?

5. Which is worse, the "vandal" or the "sportsman"? Why?

Considering Craft

1. "Most wicked deeds are done because the doer proposes some good to himself" (paragraph 3). What persuasive evidence does Krutch offer in support of this thesis?

2. "To say as we all do: Any man who would do A would do B, is to state a proposition mercifully proved false as often as it is stated" (paragraph 6). Does Krutch prove his point? What examples did you find convincing?

3. For what audience is Krutch writing? What's the evidence? Is he making an appeal primarily to their intellect, their emotions, or both? Explain your answer. Did he convince you? Why or why not?

4. What is the tone of Krutch's essay? Is it appropriate to his subject matter? Is it consistent throughout?

5. Read over Krutch's first and last paragraphs. Did he begin and conclude his essay effectively? What techniques did he use in each case?

Barbara Lazear Ascher

Barbara Lazear Ascher (b. 1946) is a graduate of Bennington College and the Cardoza School of Law. After working as a lawyer for two years, she decided to leave her practice and pursue a career in writing. She has subsequently published two collections of essays: *Playing After Dark* (1987) and *The Habit of Loving* (1989). After reading this essay from the *The Habit of Loving,* freewrite on your associations with the title.

On Compassion

1   The man's grin is less the result of circumstance than dreams or madness. His buttonless shirt, with one sleeve missing, hangs outside the waist of his

baggy trousers. Carefully plaited dreadlocks bespeak a better time, long ago. As he crosses Manhattan's Seventy-ninth Street, his gait is the shuffle of the forgotten ones held in place by gravity rather than plans. On the corner of Madison Avenue, he stops before a blond baby in an Aprica stroller. The baby's mother waits for the light to change and her hands close tighter on the stroller's handle as she sees the man approach.

2   The others on the corner, five men and women waiting for the crosstown bus, look away. They daydream a bit and gaze into the weak rays of November light. A man with a briefcase lifts and lowers the shiny toe of his right shoe, watching the light reflect, trying to catch and balance it, as if he could hold and make it his, to ease the heavy gray of coming January, February, and March. The winter months that will send snow around the feet, calves, and knees of the grinning man as he heads for the shelter of Grand Central or Pennsylvania Station.

3   But for now, in this last gasp of autumn warmth, he is still. His eyes fix on the baby. The mother removes her purse from her shoulder and rummages through its contents: lipstick, a lace handkerchief, an address book. She finds what she's looking for and passes a folded dollar over her child's head to the man who stands and stares, even though the light has changed and traffic navigates about his hips.

4   His hands continue to dangle at his sides. He does not know his part. He does not know that acceptance of the gift and gratitude are what make this transaction complete. The baby, weary of the unwavering stare, pulls its blanket over its head. The man does not look away. Like a bridegroom waiting at the altar, his eyes pierce the white veil.

5   The mother grows impatient and pushes the stroller before her, bearing the dollar like a cross. Finally, a black hand rises and closes around green.

6   Was it fear or compassion that motivated the gift?

7   Up the avenue, at Ninety-first Street, there is a small French bread shop where you can sit and eat a buttery, overpriced croissant and wash it down with rich cappuccino. Twice when I have stopped here to stave hunger or stay the cold, twice as I have sat and read and felt the warm rush of hot coffee and milk, an old man has wandered in and stood inside the entrance. He wears a stained blanket pulled up to his chin, and a woolen hood pulled down to his gray, bushy eyebrows. As he stands, the scent of stale cigarettes and urine fills the small, overheated room.

8   The owner of the shop, a moody French woman, emerges from the kitchen with steaming coffee in a Styrofoam cup, and a small paper bag of . . . of what? Yesterday's bread? Today's croissant? He accepts the offering as silently as he came, and is gone.

9   Twice I have witnessed this, and twice I have wondered, what compels this woman to feed this man? Pity? Care? Compassion? Or does she simply want to rid her shop of his troublesome presence? If expulsion were her motivation she would not reward his arrival with gifts of food. Most proprietors do not. They chase the homeless from their midst with expletives and threats.

10   As winter approaches, the mayor of New York City is moving the homeless off the streets and into Bellevue Hospital. The New York Civil Liberties Union is watchful. They question whether the rights of these people who live in our parks and doorways are being violated by involuntary hospitalization.

11   I think the mayor's notion is humane, but I fear it is something else as well. Raw humanity offends our sensibilities. We want to protect ourselves from an awareness of rags with voices that make no sense and scream forth in inarticulate rage. We do not wish to be reminded of the tentative state of our own well-being and sanity. And so, the troublesome presence is removed from the awareness of the electorate.

12   Like other cities, there is much about Manhattan now that resembles Dickensian London. Ladies in high-heeled shoes pick their way through poverty and madness. You hear more cocktail party complaints than usual, "I just can't take New York anymore." Our citizens dream of the open spaces of Wyoming, the manicured exclusivity of Hobe Sound.

13   And yet, it may be that these are the conditions that finally give birth to empathy, the mother of compassion. We cannot deny the existence of the helpless as their presence grows. It is impossible to insulate ourselves against what is at our very doorstep. I don't believe that one is born compassionate. Compassion is not a character trait like a sunny disposition. It must be learned, and it is learned by having adversity at our windows, coming through the gates of our yards, the walls of our towns, adversity that becomes so familiar that we begin to identify and empathize with it.

14   For the ancient Greeks, drama taught and reinforced compassion within a society. The object of Greek tragedy was to inspire empathy in the audience so that the common response to the hero's fall was: "There, but for the grace of God, go I." Could it be that this was the response of the mother who offered the dollar, the French woman who gave the food? Could it be that the homeless, like those ancients, are reminding us of our common humanity? Of course, there is a difference. This play doesn't end—and the players can't go home.

Considering Content

1. Consider the two homeless men Ascher presents in her essay. Do they fit your profile of homeless persons? Did you anticipate the responses of the baby's mother and the bakery owner? What motivated their responses?

2. Review paragraph 10. Is this a good "solution" to the problem of homelessness? Can you think of a better way of dealing with this situation?

3. "Compassion is not a trait like a sunny disposition." Do you agree that "compassion must be learned"? Is compassion a quality that you value? Why or why not?

4. Write a journal entry responding to the last paragraph of the essay.

Considering Craft

1. Explain Ascher's purpose in writing this essay. Is she seeking mainly to inform or does she also want to persuade her readers?

2. What is Ascher's attitude toward the two homeless men? Are her descriptions objective? Emotional?

3. Prepare a profile of the audience most likely to respond sympathetically to Ascher's essay. Might men have more empathy than women? Explain.

4. Ascher uses causes and effects in exploring her subject. Which examples did you find most and least effective?

Sydney H. Schanberg

Sydney H. Schanberg (b. 1934) is currently a reporter at *Newsday* in Melville, Long Island. He is also the author of the autobiographical essay "The Death and Life of Dith Pran," which appeared in *The New York Times Magazine* (January 20, 1980). That story is the basis for the award-winning movie "The Killing Fields." Here are his comments on his revision process:

> I spend a lot of time—sometimes days—rolling around in my head the ideas, phrases, paragraphs for a column before I scribble them on paper. Then I usually write smack on deadline, which is another phase in the revision process, the urgency focusing the mind and forcing one to compress and clarify on the typewriter. Finally, I polish the result and hope for the best, because by now it's too late for any major overhaul.

As you read "How Should Reporters Cover Death?" originally published in *Newsday*, make a list of the points you find most convincing.

How Should Reporters Cover Death?

1   It's an old question about journalism, one that will never be neatly resolved: Does the public's (read press') so-called right to know override an individual's right to privacy? It's an issue that's always been worth debating if only to make journalists think a little harder about the consequences of what we do.

2   A symposium this past week at the Columbia Presbyterian Medical Center probed usefully at this subject through the prism of how the press covers death and bereavement, particularly death that is unusual or violent.

3   A child is murdered or dies in a tragic accident, and the press descends on the child's home to get the parents' reaction. A plane crashes and the press descends on the airport where waiting relatives are just beginning to learn of the tragedy.

4   Journalism by its nature is always going to be intrusive. Reporters are supposed to find out things, explain what happened, transport the reader and the viewer to the scene of the event, be a lens through which the audience can see a story.

5   We cannot do any of these things by staying at home. We have to ring doorbells, we have to inject ourselves into emotional and volatile situations. But the question, of course, is can we not do our work more sensitively, less intrusively, with greater concern for those who are traumatized and grieving?

6   The honest answer is that we can do better, but at the same time we will probably never satisfy those who are the subjects of tragic stories. By definition, no matter how delicately we proceed, their privacy has been invaded the moment their story appears in a newspaper, but especially when it appears in living color on television.

7   Television indeed has heightened the privacy question. The swift growth of television, its world ubiquitousness and the fact that its intimacy and visual power have an impact far beyond any possible intrusion of the print press make the discussion of our role in covering grief more necessary now than it was even five years ago.

8   For example, the Columbia-Presbyterian symposium focused for a time on the television coverage of people who arrived at Kennedy Airport on the night of Dec. 21 to learn that the children and other relatives they had come to greet had all died in the crash of Pan Am Flight 103 en route from London to New York.

9   One image in particular became the symbol of that grief-torn passenger lounge. A husband and wife in a happy Christmas mood walked into the terminal, unknowing, on their way to meet their 20-year-old daughter, a Syracuse student returning from a semester of foreign studies in Europe.

10   A ticket agent said something quietly to the man. His face turned grim. Then he put his hands on his wife's shoulders and said a few words. She screamed, "Oh, my God! My baby!" She broke away from her husband and fell to the floor, spread-eagled, thrashing on her back and shrieking over and over: "Oh no! Oh no! Not my baby!"

11   It lasted maybe only 30 seconds or so but it seemed like an entire funeral. The television cameras never stopped running, and 30 seconds is a very long time on television.

12   Matthew Schwartz, a reporter for WWOR-TV/Ch. 9, was there with his crew that night, and at the symposium he talked of how bad he felt about standing and watching this woman's personal hell, but knowing that professionally he had to keep the cameras going.

13   He did the best thing he could. He urged his editors to run no more than five seconds of the scene and that's all they ran. But at least one other local channel drooled and ran a great deal more.

14   The five-second solution may not be perfect, but it's the right way, and in any event there is no perfect answer. I would argue that as intrusive as the picture of that traumatized woman was, there was community value in running

it—briefly, not at length, not ghoulishly. All of us related to that woman. We identified and empathized with her.

15   Her grief—and this is true of other tragedies if handled by the press with care—served to affirm the grief and loss that many viewers and readers had suffered in their own lives.

16   I'm not suggesting that every time we cover a tragedy or violent incident we have some lofty purpose in mind—only that if we are not unfeeling and do not succumb to the instinct to pander to what some think is a public fascination with death and pain, we can serve a purpose beyond selling newspapers or selling ads on television.

17   In other words, we will always be intrusive to a degree, but if we think before we write or air, we can do it with balance and taste.

18   It's right for people to berate us when we lapse into neanderthal microphone-in-face techniques, but my experience tells me there are darned few reporters who find it enjoyable to approach families after a death. They are there largely because of the motive force known as competition. And there is no easy solution to that, either, other than the same individual application of standards of dignity.

19   Sometimes, too, it is the absence of dignity that the story should be about. At some venues of death, as in war when innocents die from random bombs or shells, I believe reporters should write about how dignity was denied these people. We should record in detail how they died. Not grisly detail, but detail nonetheless, because this might prod people reading it far away into grappling with thoughts that would not otherwise have interrupted their peaceful existences.

20   And then there are other questions that have nothing to do with dignity or privacy. Such as whose deaths we cover and whose we ignore. Five murders are committed every day in New York City; the "cheap" ones get very little ink. Too often the socio-economic class of the victim determines the degree of coverage.

21   So there are many thoughts to wrestle with—and few simple answers—as we contemplate the consequences of how we cover death and bereavement.

Considering Content

1. Schanberg begins his essay with a question. What answers does he provide? What is your response to his question?

2. Characterize Schanberg's attitude toward his profession. Should journalists think "a little harder about the consequences" of their news coverage? Explain your answer.

3. How has television coverage "heightened the privacy question"? Do you agree that tasteful coverage of the grief-stricken can have "community value"? What examples can you cite based on your television viewing?

Considering Craft

1. Characterize Schanberg's purpose. Is it consistent with his attitude toward his audience? Explain your answer.

2. Is the tone of the essay objective? Serious? Distant? What does Schanberg's tone suggest about his attitude toward his subject?

3. "Journalism by its nature is always going to be intrusive." What evidence does Schanberg supply to support his thesis? Is it convincing? Why or why not?

4. Read over the first and last paragraphs of the essay as well as the Guidelines for Introductions and Conclusions in Chapter 6, and write a specific evaluation of both paragraphs.

Louise Montague

Louise Montague (b. 1931) has written on a variety of subjects that range from entertaining to divorce. She also published a novel, *Sand Castles,* in 1975. Her thoughts about unmarried couples living together are certain to provoke your response. The essay was first published in *Reader's Digest* in 1977, a monthly magazine with one of the largest nation-wide circulations. As you read the essay, prepare a profile of the audience Montague is most likely to convince.

Straight Talk About the Living-Together Arrangement

1   As the author of two books on divorce, I try to accept as many speaking engagements in high-school and college classes as I can. For it is my feeling that one answer to the soaring divorce rate is "preventive thinking"—the time to face many of the problems of divorce is *before* marriage. Lately, however, I find that at every session someone will stand up and state that marriage is outmoded and that the answer to the divorce problem is to live with a partner without the legal commitment of marriage.

2   Unhappily, "living together" is a modern phenomenon, a national trend today. Between 1960 and 1970, according to the U.S. Department of the Census, there was an eightfold increase in the Living-Together Arrangement (LTA). Why are so many people opting for this arrangement? And how do they get into it?

3   Certainly it's a very attractive idea sexually. But many young people also say it's a good way to "test" marriage. Others claim it's a terrific financial boon. And some don't even know how they ended up together. He started staying over or

"Straight Talk About the Living-Together Arrangement," by Louise Montague. Reprinted with permission from the April 1977 *Reader's Digest.* Copyright © 1977 by the Reader's Digest Assn., Inc.

she began to leave clothes in his closet. These young people feel that by not making their relationship permanent they can maintain the spontaneous atmosphere of new love. By eliminating the legal commitment, they feel they have eliminated the "bad" part of marriage.

4   But the phenomenon is not limited to young people. Many divorced persons burned in marriage are trying it. Some have religious convictions forbidding a second marriage. Divorced men who are financially strapped feel they can't take on the responsibility of a new wife. Or the divorced woman may be reluctant to give up the alimony which would stop with her remarriage.

5   With all these "pluses" why do so many people engaged in an LTA write to me about the problems they have encountered? Why is the Living-Together Arrangement a detriment to those involved? Let's first consider the college students who decide on or slide into an LTA. You'd be surprised, once the subject comes up for discussion in a classroom, how many youngsters tell unhappy stories about themselves or their best friends.

6   Take the case of the young couple at Stanford. After they moved in together, the boy lost his scholarship and was not able to meet the high tuition costs from his part-time job. The girl quit school in order to work and let him finish his education. When he graduated, he applied for—and received—a scholarship to do graduate work in England. The girl was extremely hurt and angry; she felt he owed it to her to stay and help her finish *her* education. They argued bitterly for a day, and then the young man packed and left!

7   This situation is typical of dozens I have heard. The LTA simply can't work when it breeds the mutual dependency of marriage without the mutual responsibility.

8   Another example is a young couple at Georgetown University who moved into an apartment together. The girl's parents, shocked and hurt, cut off all their daughter's funds. The boy suggested they split up and go back to their dorms, but the girl, having had a terrible row with her family, insisted that it was now his responsibility to take care of her! Both got jobs, and the young man, not a strong student, fell behind and was unable to graduate.

9   Certainly it's difficult to think in realistic terms when a couple imagine themselves in love. But it is unfair to expect parental values to be dropped at a whim. The censure of family and friends is one of the greatest burdens the LTA carries. Young people who need the support of family are very foolish to chuck their long-term goals for short-term pleasures.

10   To be sure, intimate relationships are widely accepted today, but any resourceful couple can find ways of being together without moving in together. Moreover, living alone at times and developing individuality should be a prime concern of young people. For few can handle the LTA until they have learned to live with themselves.

11   Some of the most heartbreaking stories I hear about LTA's concern children. Whatever life-style a single male or female chooses is that individual's responsibility. But to bring a child into this atmosphere is to involve an innocent

third party in an experiment that can leave all parties damaged. Although the law generally requires a father to support his children, it is often difficult to enforce these laws. Women are frequently left with the burden of support while the air of illegitimacy hangs heavy on the child.

12   A divorced or widowed woman who involves her children in an LTA may also be subjecting them to undue stress. Children experience great pressures to conform. What the mother and her companion view as a marvelous, free life-style, a child could see as a freaky embarrassment. The man in question, not being either father or stepfather, has no social definition as to the role he should play in the child's life. In some states, a divorced mother in an LTA stands a good chance of losing not only support payments but custody of her children.

13   Even a highly motivated working couple should be aware of the consequences of their actions. How you present yourself to the world is how you will be judged. A young petroleum engineer, living with a dental hygienist, applied for a much-wanted overseas job with an oil company. When the company conducted its routine investigation, and found that the young woman with whom he was living was not his wife, he was turned down; the firm felt that his LTA smacked of indecisiveness, instability, and failure on his part to accept responsibility. Who is to say if the oil company made the right decision? But, judging from a great many instances, it happens to be the way things are. What a couple may view as a sophisticated way to live, the business community may see as a career impediment.

14   Heartbreak and setback are also in the cards for a woman who moves in with a man in the hope of getting married. My advice is to avoid this strategy. When you demand nothing of a relationship, that's often exactly what you get. The very impermanence of the LTA suggests that that is what each partner has settled for. If marriage is what you want, marriage is what you should have. So why commit yourself to a shaky arrangement that keeps you out of the mainstream of life where you quite possibly will meet someone who shares your views?

15   Many divorced women with a great need for a little security, and with little faith in themselves, seek an LTA as a temporary answer to help them get on their feet. All this does is prolong their adjustment and reinforce their self-doubts. I'm reminded of one such woman who told me she had been living with a man for four years and wanted out but was afraid to leave. "Why?" I asked. Because, she said, she feared to give up the free rent and all that "security" she had with him. "Wrong," I said. "You have no security of any kind. You stand a good chance of being replaced by a younger version of yourself. And as for free rent, that's no security either. Security is owning the building."

16   Probably the greatest single hazard of the LTA is that it can actually spoil a good relationship between two people who should eventually marry. Because it is entered into out of weakness rather than strength, doubt rather than conviction, drift rather than decision, if offers unnecessary obstacles. Knowing this, you shouldn't casually toss aside those inherited institutions that have had a history of success.

17 If I were asked to give one reason why I am opposed to the LTA, I would state quite simply that I am morally against it. As Barbara Tuchman wrote in *McCall's:* "Standards of taste, as well as morality, need continued reaffirmation to stay alive, as liberty needs eternal vigilance." There are valid standards of judgment which come from confidence in yourself and your values. To accept a living pattern that goes against your better judgment is to chip away at your personal freedom.

18 And what of love? You cannot hope to find love by experimenting biologically. You don't build love by creating a living situation designed to test it. You don't create love by setting up a forced proximity. Love *is*. And when you love you commit to it—for better or for worse. When we finally realize that all our experiments in alternate life-styles, communal marriage and open-ended covenants are simply a means of running *from* responsibility and love, not *to* them, we will have reached the beginning of maturity.

Considering Content

1. In what paragraph does Montague first reveal her own position on the Living-Together Arrangement (LTA)? Is this a good idea? Why or why not?

2. Montague asks why so many people choose the LTA. What are her answers? Can you add others?

3. Montague says, "The censure of family and friends is one of the greatest burdens the LTA carries." Do you find this still to be true? What examples can you mention?

4. In what ways, according to Montague, can the LTA be unfair to children? Do you agree?

5. Montague distinguishes between the "moral" disapproval of the LTA and the arguments she has been listing up to that point. Do you accept this distinction? What would you label the earlier arguments? Practical? Nonmoral? Amoral? What does the word *moral* mean to you? Do you think many people would label the LTA immoral without considering its practical effects? Does Montague define what she means by "moral"?

6. According to Montague, what benefits are available to someone who chooses marriage over the LTA?

Considering Craft

1. Why does Montague begin the essay by telling us she is the author of two books on divorce and a frequent lecturer on the subject? Why does she list some of the advantages of the LTA before she details her objections?

2. What tone does Montague adopt to criticize the LTA? How reasonable does she sound? To what extent does she make effective use of induction, deduction, or cause-and-effect analysis to convince us that her argument is sensible? How effective is her final appeal to ethics in paragraph 17?

3. In paragraph 16 Montague says that people adopt the LTA out of "weakness rather than strength, doubt rather than conviction, drift rather than decision," and she goes on to suggest that marriage is therefore preferable. How valid is her implied contrast between the LTA and marriage? How important is the validity of this contrast to the validity of Montague's overall argument?

4. In paragraph 9 Montague says that although it is difficult for a young couple to be realistic when they "imagine" themselves to be in love, nevertheless it is unfair for such a couple to abandon their parents' values in order to live together "at a whim." Is she trying to appeal to emotion rather than reason? Does Montague's use of the words "imagine" and "whim" reveal anything about her attitude toward her subject? Her audience? Explain.

Guidelines for Persuasive Essays

1. Choose the appeal or appeals that suit your purpose, audience, and subject—emotional, ethical, or logical.

2. Acknowledge and refute the opposition.

3. In a logical appeal, choose the method for reasoning that suits your purpose and subject—induction or deduction. Check the validity of deductive conclusions.

4. Provide sufficient evidence for your inductive conclusions. The burden of proof is on *you.*

5. Avoid the causal fallacies of hasty generalization: oversimplification; *non sequitur;* and *post hoc, ergo propter hoc.*

6. Use narration, description, and expository methods to support your appeal.

Warm-up Exercises

1. Find an editorial in your daily newspaper with which you disagree; then write a letter to the editor that presents your side of the issue. Is your tone objective? Have you cited evidence to support your point of view?

2. Interview three people in their teens or early twenties and ask for their reaction to Montague's point that a prime concern of young people should be "living alone at times and developing individuality." Analyze their responses. Do you have enough material on which to write an essay for or against her point of view?

3. Interview three people who differ in age and ask their reaction to the diversity of dialects in (a) different geographical sections and (b) different racial and ethnic groups of the United States. Ask if they think radio announcers, for example, should all speak the same "standard English." Do your notes provide you with enough material for an essay?

4. Interview three people who differ in age and sex and record their reactions to the statement "All professional athletes should be tested for nonprescription drug use." Analyze their responses. Are they logical? Emotional? Both? Compare their ideas and feelings with your own. Do you have enough material on which to base a persuasive essay?

5. Freewrite about the effects of your first encounter with one of the following: fear, death, success, disappointment, or prejudice. Have you included enough detail to explain the effects to your reader?

6. Brainstorm about your associations with one of the following:

hangouts	a quick fix
psychotherapy	sociability
homelessness	compassion
rock music	rock concerts

7. Fusilli says that there are two ways to review or criticize rock: the artful way and the sales–popularity–image way. Choose a particular rock concert, music video, or recording of your favorite rock group. Brainstorm about the differences between these two ways of criticizing by making two lists, one containing the points that a sales–popularity–image critic would include and the other containing the points an artful critic would include. Do you have enough material to write an essay on this subject?

Writing/Revising Topics

1. Write a letter to your son or daughter or to a male or female friend who has just told you that he or she plans to move in with a girlfriend or boyfriend. Explain your reasons for disapproving. Then write a letter to your mother or to your friend's mother explaining her grandchild's or child's decision to enter a living-together arrangement, and try to convince her not to break off communication with her grandchild or child as she has threatened to do in the past when

this topic has been discussed. In which letter did you have to be more persuasive? What are the differences in tone and style?

2. Rachel L. Jones is committed to the belief that "black Americans should have full command of standard English," and in this essay she cites specific evidence to support her point of view. For a specific audience write an essay on a subject about which you feel strongly. When revising, ask yourself if you have presented evidence that will be convincing to your intended reader.

3. Write an essay analyzing how and why one of your dreams or aspirations has had an important effect on your life. When revising, ask yourself if you have presented enough detail to convince your reader of its significance to you.

4. Using Warm-up Exercise 2 as the basis, write an essay that supports or refutes Montague, using the evidence you have gathered from your interviews and your own reading. Before revising your essay, review the Guidelines for Introductions and Conclusions (Chapter 6). Have you introduced your subject in an appealing way? Is your reader likely to remember your conclusion?

5. Using Warm-up Exercise 4 as the basis, write a persuasive essay using deduction that supports or refutes the statement concerning professional athletes and drugs. Before revising your essay, review the Guidelines for Persuasive Essays, paying particular attention to 3, 5, and 6.

6. Write an essay about *one* of the following topics. In your paper, argue *for* or *against* the issue—do not take both sides!

   dissemination of birth control information in high schools
   censorship of books in school libraries
   allowing children with AIDS to attend public schools
   giving the death penalty to drug dealers
   outlawing hunting
   mandatory testing for AIDS
   educating children in their native language

   Try to base your case on an ethical appeal. To persuade your audience you might write from the perspective of a lawyer, doctor, teacher, or clergyman; in other words, create a persona (see Glossary) who uses ethical appeal.

7. Using Warm-up Exercise 7 as a starter, write an essay reviewing a rock concert, music video, or recording you know well. Decide whether and why you will emphasize the artistic aspect or the sales–popularity–image aspect of the occasion.

8. After your favorite rock star makes a controversial statement, a local journalist urges readers to attend a rally to destroy copies of the star's recordings and videos. Write a letter to the editor of the newspaper supporting or not supporting

the journalist's action. Try to apply Fusilli's concepts of "art" and "entertainment" in your argument.

9. Ascher and Orwell (Chapter 8) write about two significant social issues: homelessness and poverty. Although both intended to persuade their audience, their rhetorical techniques differ greatly. Compare and contrast their essays. Which techniques did you find more convincing?

*P*olishing for Presentation

In the previous chapters, you have studied writers who describe revising as shaping, molding, or polishing their writing. These writers use the fundamental revising techniques—adding, deleting, substituting, and rearranging—to make their writing express what they want to say. As you have applied these same techniques to your drafts, you have noticed how revision can affect aspects of writing such as purpose, meaning, audience, and tone. Yet before writers release their work to readers, they carefully examine the final drafts for minor changes that need to be made. This final revision, called editing and proofreading, consists of checking the mechanics of the work and making modifications to words or sentences that add a high gloss to the finished copy.

When you edit your writing, you will be examining discrete aspects of the work. You should carefully check the words you have chosen and make any changes that will enhance your writing. Sometimes a seemingly minor change in diction can have a great impact on how a reader perceives an essay. Most writers also check their sentences for rhythm and flow. They make sure that they have used a variety of sentence types and lengths so that their readers will not become bored by monotonous writing. Last, writers proofread their work for errors in grammar, mechanics, and spelling. This final effort is difficult, for few writers know every rule of the written word. A good grammar book and dictionary will help here, and the results will pay off because simple errors distract readers from what you are saying.

As you polish your draft for presentation, keep in mind the following considerations regarding editing and proofreading.

Editing for Language

Your choice of words should be a deliberate attempt to express exactly what you want to say. Two essential tools for selecting the right word are a *dictionary* and a *thesaurus*. A dictionary gives a word's definition, origins, parts of speech, and special usage labels, and sometimes discussions of its various synonyms; while a thesaurus usually lists only a word's synonyms and related words. These tools will both teach you new words and remind you of words you may have forgotten. Get to know both: no writer, no matter how experienced, can function without a good dictionary, and many professional writers testify to the help a thesaurus provides them. (For a strong testimonial to the value of *Roget's Thesaurus,* see William Zinsser's essay in this chapter.)

In order to select the right word you will find that you must pay attention not only to the word's meaning but also to its *level of formality,* its *concreteness,* its *specificity,* and its *connotations.*

Level of Formality.   The level of formality refers to the propriety of a word, its appropriateness to a certain context or audience, ranging from slang and dialect to the standard, general words that can be used in almost any setting. A good dictionary will tell you if a word is *not* formal or general by using such a designation as *slang* or *nonstandard;* these are the words you should probably avoid in your essays—colloquialisms (words used almost exclusively in conversation, such as *kids* for *children, into* jogging for *enjoying* jogging) and slang (highly informal, faddish words like *cop out, wimp, yuppies, spaced out, vibes*).

Concreteness.   A second language grouping classifies words as abstract or concrete. An abstract word signifies a general concept, something one's senses cannot detect. A concrete word, conversely, stands for something that can be seen, touched, tasted, heard, or smelled. Justice, anger, and happiness are abstract; bicycle, chocolate, and radio are concrete. Sometimes only an abstract word will do, but if you have a choice, use the word that appeals to the senses and your writing will gain in effectiveness.

Specificity.   A closely related classification divides words into general and specific. General words refer to groups or collections, while specific words stand for a particular item. Thus, of the two concrete descriptions chocolate and Nestle's chocolate almond bar, the latter is more specific. Again, both types have their place, but if you have a choice, choose the specific. Instead of writing that your car is "new," call it a "red 1992 Camaro." Saying that you were served a "bad" steak conveys less than if you had said it was raw, overcooked, tough, gristly, or tainted.

Connotation.   Another word grouping, one you have encountered previously (see page 134), is based on denotation and connotation. Denotation is a word's dictionary definition, and connotation refers to its implied meaning. You need to be alert to different connotations of synonyms: instead of using the word *dog*, select the word that evokes the connotation you require—*cur, hound, pooch, mongrel,* or *mutt.* Instead of *automobile* choose the more connotative word *jalopy, wheels, hotrod, wreck, station wagon, taxicab,* or *limousine.* A thesaurus can provide you with a ready list from which to choose. Connotative words express the exact shade of meaning you wish to convey. In addition to being more specific, they also get your reader to respond to your work. Concrete, specific words that convey the connotations you want will sharpen your diction and perk up your writing.

Diction Errors

Searching for the exact word you need will add power to your writing and make it more interesting and attractive for your readers. But while you search for the right word or phrase you want to use, be on guard against *jargon, pomposity, deadwood,* and *clichés.*

Jargon, the specialized language of insiders, serves a valid function within a particular profession, industry, or activity but should be avoided when you write for a general audience. Doctors, sailors, psychologists, computer programmers, and sports enthusiasts, for example, have created specialized vocabularies that cannot be understood by outsiders but help them to communicate among themselves. If you are writing a paper for your course in computers, you will be expected to use words like *input, byte, debug,* and *RAM,* but you should use specialized vocabulary only when you are writing for an audience who will understand it.

Also try to avoid *pomposity.* The use of pretentious, overblown diction will make your tone irritating and your meaning inaccessible. Make your vocabulary as simple as your subject allows. Consider the differences between "she arose and descended to breakfast" and "she got up and went down to breakfast." Compare "Are you experiencing pain?" and "Does it hurt?" Nobody likes a show-off, in person or on paper.

Check your writing for *deadwood,* words or sentences that add nothing to your meaning. You have seen in this book how often revision consists of deleting. Written communication should usually be more concise and economical than conversation. Eliminate redundant expressions such as "the truth of the matter is," "at this point in time," "it goes without saying," "the reason is because." If you read your drafts with an eye for the unnecessary word or phrase, you will be surprised how much can be jettisoned and how much neater and stronger the residue will be. As Zinsser urges in his essay, get rid of clutter.

Avoid *clichés,* expressions that were once new, fresh, and clever, but now have become overused and trite. When you find yourself using phrases like "last but not least," "few and far between," "tired but happy," "from every walk of life," stop, think, and use your own creativity to put together an expression that really says what you want to say.

Editing for Clarity

Searching for exact language and avoiding diction errors will help to make your writing more appealing and readable, but remember that well-selected words must find their places in well-made sentences. You must arrange your words in sentences that fit your purpose, meaning, audience, and tone. Just as you take care when selecting a particular word, seek out the kind of sentence that expresses exactly what you want to convey. Using questions, commands, and/or exclamations will make your sentences more lively. Even if you write only declarative sentences, you can vary the length. Sometimes you will want the impact of a very short sentence, while another passage will benefit from an unusually long one. As a rule, a mixture of long and short sentences is agreeable.

Final Editing: Proofreading

As mentioned earlier, proofreading is the *last* stage of revising. Chances are, however, that you have been proofreading throughout the drafting and revising stages as you corrected a spelling error here and there or added an occasional comma. This kind of casual proofreading should not interfere with composing. However, when writers make a more determined effort to correct their writing too early in the process, they sometimes become self-conscious about their abilities and have difficulty continuing. Or, if they generate ideas as they compose, they might get sidetracked from discovering important thoughts by proofreading at that critical moment. Yet as you approach publication of your writing—as either a submission to your school newspaper or a special interest magazine, or as an essay for your instructor or peers—you need to eliminate any remaining rough edges. Simple errors in grammar, punctuation, or spelling will rarely hide your meaning, but a reader might become confused or distracted by these mistakes. Even worse, a reader might make a value judgment on the quality of your ideas that is based on the final presentation of your work. Proofreading allows you to polish up your essay so that you can present it with greater confidence to any audience.

The essays you have studied, as well as the ones to follow, illustrate various writers' sensitivity to words and sentences as conveyors of thoughts and feelings. In the following paragraph, which explains how he first decided to become a poet, Robert Bly uses editing techniques to make final changes in his manuscript. Again, editing and proofreading come only after much substantial work has been done on a number of drafts and are not alternatives to more extensive revision. These final touches, however, have a noticeable impact on overall effectiveness—Bly's sentences become more clear and precise.

One day while studying a Yeats poem I decided to write poetry the rest of
my life. What helped me decide was the recognition that a single short poem
has room for history, psychology, music, religious thought, occult speculation,
~~mood~~ character, and events of one's own life. I still feel surprised that
such various substances can find shelter and nourishment in a poem. A poem
in fact may be a sort ~~of nourishment, the~~ nourishing liquid ~~that~~ one uses
to keep ameeba alive, which, if ~~it is~~ prepared right, can keep ~~######~~ an
image or a thought alive for ~~many~~ years, and keep insights on history
or psyche alive ~~for many years,~~ as well as our own desires and airy impulses.

By now you understand that good writers have to work hard at their craft.
Writing is a craft involving at least three complex processes: prewriting, composing,
and revising. Your new awareness of these processes should help you to apply the
techniques suggested throughout this text. Your knowledge of revision strategies
should enable you to create essays that demonstrate the benefits of rethinking,
rereading, and rewriting. And with this new ability should come the confidence to
discover yourself as a writer.

E. B. White

E. B. White (1899–1985) published several successful children's books including *Stuart Little* (1945) and *Charlotte's Web* (1952), but he primarily chose to write essays. Perhaps his foreword to *The Essays of E. B. White* (1947) explains why:

> The essayist is a self-liberated man, sustained by the childish belief that everything he thinks about, everything that happens to him, is of general interest. He is a fellow who thoroughly enjoys his work, just as people who take bird walks enjoy theirs. Each new excursion of the essayist, each new "attempt," differs from the last and takes him into new country. This delights him.

As you read "Death of a Pig," jot down any impressions you form of White as a person.

Death of a Pig

Introduction to the Essay and Draft

The simplicity that marks White's work with such distinction is difficult to achieve. The ease of the storytelling, the unobtrusive merging of purpose, meaning, and tone, and the fluidity of the prose deceive an audience into believing that White's essays are effortlessly created. However, as you have learned by examining previous drafts, most works that look simple or flawless are the result of careful, extensive, and substantive revision.

"Death of a Pig" has gone through at least four or five complete revisions. From beginning to end, the essay has been shaped and reshaped until it has achieved the form that the author is willing to call final. The selection of concrete, specific, and connotative words and the avoidance of wordiness, pomposity, and cliché help White to present his ideas and assure that his thoughts will be understood. In a similar fashion, diverse sentence constructions not only convey meaning but retain reader interest.

Perhaps the best explanation for the seeming simplicity of White's work is his creation of a writing style that is both fluid and natural. He creates a style unique to himself—his choice of diction and sentence construction represents his identity as a writer. Following White's example, you should be conscious of who you are as you write your essays. Perhaps the best advice to follow is to be yourself! Avoid using language that is not your own. While a dictionary and a thesaurus are fine tools, if you refer to them too frequently your diction might appear pretentious.

As you read the entire published version of "Death of a Pig" as well as the portion of the draft reproduced, concentrate on how the author controls diction and sentence structures. By carefully selecting and revising words and constructions, White is able to meet the requirements of an essay and also create an authentic, stylistic voice.

Published Essay

1   I spent several days and nights in mid-September with an ailing pig and I feel driven to account for this stretch of time, more particularly since the pig died at last, and I lived, and things might easily have gone the other way round and none left to do the accounting. Even now, so close to the event, I cannot recall the hours sharply and am not ready to say whether death came on the third night or the fourth night. This uncertainty afflicts me with a sense of personal deterioration; if I were in decent health I would know how many nights I had sat up with a pig.

2   The scheme of buying a spring pig in blossomtime, feeding it through summer and fall, and butchering it when the solid cold weather arrives, is a familiar scheme to me and follows an antique pattern. It is a tragedy enacted on most farms with perfect fidelity to the original script. The murder, being premeditated, is in the first degree but is quick and skillful, and the smoked bacon and ham provide a ceremonial ending whose fitness is seldom questioned.

3   Once in a while something slips—one of the actors goes up in his lines and the whole performance stumbles and halts. My pig simply failed to show up for a meal. The alarm spread rapidly. The classic outline of the tragedy was lost. I found myself cast suddenly in the role of pig's friend and physician—a farcical character with an enema bag for a prop. I had a presentiment, the very first afternoon, that the play would never regain its balance and that my sympathies were now wholly with the pig. This was slapstick—the sort of dramatic treatment that instantly appealed to my old dachshund, Fred, who joined the vigil, held the bag, and when all was over, presided at the interment. When we slid the body into the grave, we both were shaken to the core. The loss we felt was not the loss of ham but the loss of pig. He had evidently become precious to me, not that he represented a distant nourishment in a hungry time, but that he had suffered in a suffering world. But I'm running ahead of my story and shall have to go back.

4   My pigpen is at the bottom of an old orchard below the house. The pigs I have raised have lived in a faded building that once was an icehouse. There is a pleasant yard to move about in, shaded by an apple tree that overhangs the low rail fence. A pig couldn't ask for anything better—or none has, at any rate. The sawdust in the icehouse makes a comfortable bottom in which to root, and a warm bed. This sawdust, however, came under suspicion when the pig took sick. One of my neighbors said he thought the pig would have done better on new ground—the same principle that applies in planting potatoes. He said there might be something unhealthy about that sawdust, that he never thought well of sawdust.

5   It was about four o'clock in the afternoon when I first noticed that there was something wrong with the pig. He failed to appear at the trough for his supper, and when a pig (or a child) refuses supper a chill wave of fear runs through any household, or ice-household. After examining my pig, who was stretched out in the sawdust inside the building, I went to the phone and cranked it four times.

Mr. Dameron answered. "What's good for a sick pig?" I asked. (There is never any identification needed on a country phone; the person on the other end knows who is talking by the sound of the voice and by the character of the question.)

6   "I don't know, I never had a sick pig," said Mr. Dameron, "but I can find out quick enough. You hang up and I'll call Henry."

7   Mr. Dameron was back on the line again in five minutes. "Henry says roll him over on his back and give him two ounces of castor oil or sweet oil, and if that doesn't do the trick give him an injection of soapy water. He says he's almost sure the pig's plugged up, and even if he's wrong, it can't do any harm."

8   I thanked Mr. Dameron. I didn't go right down to the pig, though I sank into a chair and sat still for a few minutes to think about my troubles, and then I got up and went to the barn, catching up on some odds and ends that needed tending to. Unconsciously I held off, for an hour, the deed by which I would officially recognize the collapse of the performance of raising a pig; I wanted no interruption in the regularity of feeding, the steadiness of growth, the even succession of days. I wanted no interruption, wanted no oil, no deviation. I just wanted to keep on raising a pig, full meal after full meal, spring into summer into fall. I didn't even know whether there were two ounces of castor oil on the place.

9   Shortly after five o'clock, I remembered that we had been invited out to dinner that night and realized that if I were to dose a pig there was no time to lose. The dinner date seemed a familiar conflict: I move in a desultory society and often a week or two will roll by without my going to anybody's house to dinner or anyone's coming to mine, but when an occasion does arise, and I am summoned, something usually turns up (an hour or two in advance) to make all human intercourse seem vastly inappropriate. I have come to believe that there is in hostesses a special power of divination, and that they deliberately arrange dinners to coincide with pig failure or some other sort of failure. At any rate, it was after five o'clock and I knew I could put off no longer the evil hour.

10   When my son and I arrived at the pigyard, armed with a small bottle of castor oil and a length of clothesline, the pig had emerged from his house and was standing in the middle of his yard, listlessly. He gave us a slim greeting. I could see that he felt uncomfortable and uncertain. I had brought the clothesline thinking I'd have to tie him (the pig weighed more than a hundred pounds) but we never used it. My son reached down, grabbed both front legs, upset him quickly, and when he opened his mouth to scream I turned the oil into his throat—a pink, corrugated area I had never seen before. I had just time to read the label while the neck of the bottle was in his mouth. It said Puretest. The screams, slightly muffled by oil, were pitched in the hysterically high range of pig-sound, as though torture were being carried out, but they didn't last long: it was all over rather suddenly, and, his legs released, the pig righted himself.

11   In the upset position the corners of his mouth had been turned down, giving him a frowning expression. Back on his feet again, he regained the set smile that a pig wears even in sickness. He stood his ground, sucking lightly at the residue

of oil; a few drops leaked out of his lips while his wicked eyes, shaded by their coy little lashes, turned on me in disgust and hatred. I scratched him gently with oily fingers and he remained quiet, as though trying to recall the satisfaction of being scratched when in health, and seeming to rehearse in his mind the indignity to which he had just been subjected. I noticed, as I stood there, four or five small dark spots on his back near the tail end, reddish brown in color, each about the size of a housefly. I could not make out what they were. They did not look troublesome but at the same time they did not look like mere surface bruises or chafe marks. Rather they seemed blemishes of internal origin. His stiff white bristles almost completely hid them and I had to part the bristles with my fingers to get a good look.

12   Several hours later, a few minutes before midnight, having dined well and at someone else's expense, I returned to the pighouse with a flashlight. The patient was asleep. Kneeling, I felt his ears (as you might put your hand on the forehead of a child) and they seemed cool, and then with the light made a careful examination of the yard and the house for sign that the oil had worked. I found none and went to bed.

13   We had been having an unseasonable spell of weather—hot, close days, with the fog shutting in every night, scaling for a few hours in midday, then creeping back again at dark, drifting in first over the trees on the point, then suddenly blowing across the fields, blotting out the world and taking possession of houses, men, and animals. Everyone kept hoping for a break, but the break failed to come. Next day was another hot one. I visited the pig before breakfast and tried to tempt him with a little milk in his trough. He just stared at it, while I made a sucking sound through my teeth to remind him of past pleasures of the feast. With very small, timid pigs, weanlings, this ruse is often quite successful and will encourage them to eat; but with a large, sick pig the ruse is senseless and the sound I made must have made him feel, if anything, more miserable. He not only did not crave food, he felt a positive revulsion to it. I found a place under the apple tree where he had vomited in the night.

14   At this point, although a depression had settled over me, I didn't suppose that I was going to lose my pig. From the lustiness of a healthy pig a man derives a feeling of personal lustiness; the stuff that goes into the trough and is received with such enthusiasm is an earnest of some later feast of his own, and when this suddenly comes to an end and the food lies stale and untouched, souring in the sun, the pig's imbalance becomes the man's vicariously, and life seems insecure, displaced, transitory.

15   As my own spirits declined, along with the pig's, the spirits of my vile old dachshund rose. The frequency of our trips down the footpath through the orchard to the pigyard delighted him, although he suffers greatly from arthritis, moves with difficulty, and would be bedridden if he could find anyone willing to serve him meals on a tray.

16   He never missed a chance to visit the pig with me, and he made many professional calls on his own. You could see him down there at all hours, his white face parting the grass along the fence as he wobbled and stumbled about,

his stethoscope dangling—a happy quack, writing his villainous prescriptions and grinning his corrosive grin. When the enema bag appeared, and the bucket of warm suds, his happiness was complete, and he managed to squeeze his enormous body between the two lowest rails of the yard and then assumed full charge of the irrigation. Once, when I lowered the bag to check the flow, he reached in and hurriedly drank a few mouthfuls of the suds to test their potency. I have noticed that Fred will feverishly consume any substance that is associated with trouble—the bitter flavor is to his liking. When the bag was above reach, he concentrated on the pig and was everywhere at once, a tower of strength and inconvenience. The pig, curiously enough, stood rather quietly through this colonic carnival, and the enema, though ineffective, was not as difficult as I had anticipated.

17   I discovered, though, that once having given a pig an enema there is no turning back, no chance of resuming one of life's more stereotyped roles. The pig's lot and mine were inextricably bound now, as though the rubber tube were the silver cord. From then until the time of his death I held the pig steadily in the bowl of my mind; the task of trying to deliver him from his misery became a strong obsession. His suffering soon became the embodiment of all earthly wretchedness. Along toward the end of the afternoon, defeated in physicking, I phoned the veterinary twenty miles away and placed the case formally in his hands. He was full of questions, and when I casually mentioned the dark spots on the pig's back, his voice changed its tone.

18   "I don't want to scare you," he said, "but when there are spots, erysipelas has to be considered."

19   Together we considered erysipelas, with frequent interruptions from the telephone operator, who wasn't sure the connection had been established.

20   "If a pig has erysipelas can he give it to a person?" I asked.

21   "Yes, he can," replied the vet.

22   "Have they answered?" asked the operator.

23   "Yes, they have," I said. Then I addressed the vet again. "You better come over here and examine this pig right away."

24   "I can't come myself," said the vet, "but McFarland can come this evening if that's all right. Mac knows more about pigs than I do anyway. You needn't worry too much about the spots. To indicate erysipelas they would have to be deep hemorrhagic infarcts."

25   "Deep hemorrhagic what?" I asked.

26   "Infarcts," said the vet.

27   "Have they answered?" asked the operator.

28   "Well," I said, "I don't know what you'd call these spots, except they're about the size of a housefly. If the pig has erysipelas I guess I have it, too, by this time, because we've been very close lately."

29   "McFarland will be over," said the vet.

30   I hung up. My throat felt dry and I went to the cupboard and got a bottle of whiskey. Deep hemorrhagic infarcts—the phrase began fastening its hooks in my head. I had assumed that there could be nothing much wrong with a pig during

the months it was being groomed for murder; my confidence in the essential health and endurance of pigs had been strong and deep, particularly in the health of pigs that belonged to me and that were part of my proud scheme. The awakening had been violent and I minded it all the more because I knew that what could be true of my pig could be true also of the rest of my tidy world. I tried to put this distasteful idea from me, but it kept recurring. I took a short drink of the whiskey and then, although I wanted to go down to the yard and look for fresh signs, I was scared to. I was certain I had erysipelas.

31　　It was long after dark and the supper dishes had been put away when a car drove in and McFarland got out. He had a girl with him. I could just make her out in the darkness—she seemed young and pretty. "This is Miss Owen," he said "We've been having a picnic supper on the shore, that's why I'm late."

32　　McFarland stood in the driveway and stripped off his jacket, then his shirt. His stocky arms and capable hands showed up in my flashlight's gleam as I helped him find his coverall and get zipped up. The rear seat of his car contained an astonishing amount of paraphernalia, which he soon overhauled, selecting a chain, a syringe, a bottle of oil, a rubber tube, and some other things I couldn't identify. Miss Owen said she'd go along with us and see the pig. I led the way down the warm slope of the orchard, my light picking out the path for them, and we all three climbed the fence, entered the pighouse, and squatted by the pig while McFarland took a rectal reading. My flashlight picked up the glitter of an engagement ring on the girl's hand.

33　　"No elevation," said McFarland, twisting the thermometer in the light. "You needn't worry about erysipelas." He ran his hand slowly over the pig's stomach and at one point the pig cried out in pain.

34　　"Poor piggledy-wiggledy!" said Miss Owen.

35　　The treatment I had been giving the pig for two days was then repeated, somewhat more expertly, by the doctor. Miss Owen and I handed him things as he needed them—holding the chain that he had looped around the pig's upper jaw, holding the syringe, holding the bottle stopper, the end of the tube, all of us working in darkness and in comfort, working with the instinctive teamwork induced by emergency conditions, the pig unprotesting, the house shadowy, protecting, intimate. I went to bed tired but with a feeling of relief that I had turned over part of the responsibility of the case to a licensed doctor. I was beginning to think, though, that the pig was not going to live.

36　　He died twenty-four hours later, or it might have been forty-eight—there is a blur in time here, and I may have lost or picked up a day in the telling and the pig one in the dying. At intervals during the last day I took cool fresh water down to him and at such times as he found the strength to get to his feet he would stand with head in the pail and snuffle his snout around. He drank a few sips but no more; yet it seemed to comfort him to dip his nose in water and bobble it about, sucking in and blowing out through his teeth. Much of the time, now, he lay indoors half buried in sawdust. Once, near the last, while I was attending him I saw him try to make a bed for himself but he lacked the strength, and when he set his snout into the dust he was unable to plow even the little furrow he needed to lie down in.

37   He came out of the house to die. When I went down, before going to bed, he lay stretched in the yard a few feet from the door. I knelt, saw that he was dead, and left him there: his face had a mild look, expressive neither of deep peace nor of deep suffering, although I think he had suffered a good deal. I went back up to the house and to bed, and cried internally—deep hemorrhagic intears. I didn't wake till nearly eight the next morning, and when I looked out the open window the grave was already being dug, down beyond the dump under a wild apple. I could hear the spade strike against the small rocks that blocked the way. Never send to know for whom the grave is dug, I said to myself, it's dug for thee. Fred, I well knew, was supervising the work of digging, so I ate breakfast slowly.

38   It was a Saturday morning. The thicket in which I found the gravediggers at work was dark and warm, the sky overcast. Here, among alders and young hackmatacks, at the foot of the apple tree, Lennie had dug a beautiful hole, five feet long, three feet wide, three feet deep. He was standing in it, removing the last spadefuls of earth, while Fred patrolled the brink in simple but impressive circles, disturbing the loose earth of the mound so that it trickled back in. There had been no rain in weeks and the soil, even three feet down, was dry and powdery. As I stood and stared, an enormous earthworm which had been partially exposed by the spade at the bottom dug itself deeper and made a slow withdrawal, seeking even remoter moistures at even lonelier depths. And just as Lennie stepped out and rested his spade against the tree and lit a cigarette, a small green apple separated itself from a branch overhead and fell into the hole. Everything about this last scene seemed overwritten—the dismal sky, the shabby woods, the imminence of rain, the worm (legendary bedfellow of the dead), the apple (conventional garnish of a pig).

39   But even so, there was a directness and dispatch about animal burial, I thought, that made it a more decent affair than human burial: there was no stopover in the undertaker's foul parlor, no wreath nor spray; and when we hitched a line to the pig's hind legs and dragged him swiftly from his yard, throwing our weight into the harness and leaving a wake of crushed grass and smoothed rubble over the dump, ours was a businesslike procession, with Fred, the dishonorable pallbearer, staggering along in the rear, his perverse bereavement showing in every seam in his face; and the post-mortem performed handily and swiftly right at the edge of the grave, so that the inwards that had caused the pig's death preceded him into the ground and he lay at last resting squarely on the cause of his own undoing.

40   I threw in the first shovelful, and then we worked rapidly and without talk, until the job was complete. I picked up the rope, made it fast to Fred's collar (he is a notorious ghoul), and we all three filed back up the path to the house, Fred bringing up the rear and holding back every inch of the way, feigning unusual stiffness. I noticed that although he weighed far less than the pig, he was harder to drag, being possessed of the vital spark.

41   The news of the death of my pig traveled fast and far, and I received many expressions of sympathy from friends and neighbors, for no one took the event lightly and the premature expiration of a pig is, I soon discovered, a departure

which the community marks solemnly on its calendar, a sorrow in which it feels fully involved. I have written this account in penitence and in grief, as a man who failed to raise his pig, and to explain my deviation from the classic course of so many raised pigs. The grave in the woods is unmarked, but Fred can direct the mourner to it unerringly and with immense good will, and I know he and I shall often revisit it, singly and together, in seasons of reflection and despair, on flagless memorial days of our own choosing.

Draft

1   I spent several days and nights in mid-September with
an ailing pig, and I feel driven to account for this stretch of
time, more particularly since the pig died at last, and I lived,
and things might easily have gone the other way round and none left
to do the accounting. Even now, so close to the event, I cannot
recall the hours sharply and am not ready to say for sure whether
death came on the third night or the fourth night. This uncertainty
[fills me with a sense of personal deterioration; if I were in
decent health I should *would* know how many nights I had sat up with a pig.

2   The scheme of buying a spring pig in blossom time, feeding
it through summer and fall, and butchering it when the solid cold
weather arrives, is a familiar scheme to me and simply follows a
pattern centuries old. It is a tragedy enacted on most farms with
perfect devotion *fidelity* to the original script. The murder *being premeditated* is in the first
degree but is quick and skilful; and the smoked bacon and ham provide
a ceremonial ending whose fitness is seldom questioned. Once in a
while something goes wrong---one of the actors *goes up in his lines* drops a line and the
whole performance stumbles and halts. My pig failed to show up for a *one day*
meal. The alarm spread rapidly. *at line* The classic form of the tragedy was
lost; I found myself_suddenly_cast in the role of a pig's friend and
physician, a farcical business *character* with an enema bag for a prop. I had a
presentiment hunch, the very first afternoon, that the play would never regain its
balance and that my sympathies were now wholly with the pig. This was
slapstick---the sort of *dramatic* treatment which instantly appealed to my old
dachshund, who joined the vigil, held the bag, and, when all was over,
presided at the interment. When we slid the body into the grave, we

both ~~xxxxxxxxxxxx~~ were shaken to the core. ~~and not from~~

~~xxxx~~ *The loss we felt was not the loss of ham — but the*

to me, not that he represented a distant involvement in
~~He had become precious because he had~~ *a hungry time.*
flopped in a Suffery world.

loss of pig. But I'm running ahead of my ~~story~~ *and shall* ~~I have to go back.~~

3   My pig pen is at the bottom of an old orchard below
~~where the xxxxxxxxxxxxxxxxxxxxxxxxx~~ ~~this ax ice-house~~
the house. The pigs I have raised have lived in ~~an abandoned ice~~
~~xxxxxxxxxxxxx the xxxxxxxxxxxxxx~~ *a little building*
house. They have a ~~xxxxxx~~ pleasant yard to move about in, shaded
which used to be an ice-house.
by an apple tree which overhangs the ~~xxxxx~~ low rail fence. A pig
or, none has (at any rate)
couldn't ask for anything better. The sawdust in the ice house makes

a comfortable bottom for rooting around in, and a warm bed. **This**

sawdust, hoever, became under suspicion when the pig~~xxxx~~ took

sick. One of my neighbors said he thought the ~~xxxxxx~~ pig would

have done better on new ground---some~~thing xxxxx poin xxx xxx xxxxx~~
in planting
the sme principle that applies ~~to~~ potatoes---and he said he
He found   *might the*
thought ~~xxxxxxxxxxxxxxxxxxxxxxxxxx~~ there ~~was~~ something about *that*
— that he never thought well of sawdust.
sawdust.

4
knew there was something
~~I noticed something~~ rong with the pig ~~an~~ about

~~four o'clock in the afternoon, when he failed to show up at the~~

~~trough, bursting with enthusiasm.~~

5   It was about four o'clock in the a fternoon when
that there was
I first noticed so~~mething~~ Wrong ith the pig. He failed to show
or a child
up at the trough for his supper, and when a pig doesn't ant supper

~~nothing xxxxx good xxxxxx anything xxxx happen~~ a chill wave of fear
After examing my pig, who was
runs through any household, or icehousehold. I went to the phone
stretched out in the sawdust inside the building.
right away and cranked it four times. r. Henderson answered.

"What's good for a sick pig?" I asked. (There is never any

~~xxxxx~~ identification needed on a country phone -- the persn on the

other end knows who is talking by the ~~xxxxxxxx~~ sound of the voice
by
and the character of the quetion.)

6   "I ~~dunno~~ *don't know;* I never had a sick pig," said Mr.
N
Hederson, "but I can find out ~~q~~uick enough. You hang up~~xx~~ and

I'll call Irving."

by which I should officially accept the

7 Mr. Henderson was back on the line again in five minutes.
"Irving says roll him ~~right~~ over on his back and give him
~~two ounces~~ two ounces of castor oil, or sweet oil, and if
bring him round
that doesn't open him up, give him an injection of soapy water.
He says he's almost sure the pig's ~~is~~ plugged up, and even if
he's wrong, it can't do any harm."

8   I thanked Mr. Henderson. I didn't go right down
still   *think about my truth.*
to the pig, though. I sat ~~down~~ for a few minutes to ~~brood~~ , and
then I got up and went around the place, ~~doing~~ catching up on
some odds and ends that need tending to. I unconsciously held off,
~~mark the end of freedom~~
for an hour, the ~~last~~ act, which would ~~interfere with~~ the smooth
performance of raising a pig (from spring to late fall)---the
regularity of feeding, the ~~regularity~~ steadiness of growth, the
procession
even tenor of days. I wanted no interruption, wanted no oil,
no deviation, no soapy water. I just wanted to keep on raising a
pig, full meal after full meal. I didn't even know whether I
had two ounces of castor oil on the place.

9   Shortly after five o'clock I remembered that we
~~was~~ had been invited out to dinner that night, and that if I
before dark,   *dinner*
were to dose a pig, it would have to be soon. The ~~sinister inner~~
date seemed ~~strangely appropriate~~ a natural, ~~human thing~~
~~its~~ conflict, a familiar one. I move in a desultory society
to anybody's house
and often a week or two will go by without my going ~~anywhere~~ to
have psychic powers (sic)
dinner, but my friends ~~are a gifted bunch~~, and can almost always
manage to ~~anticipate~~ anticipate, by a few
and is accepted,
hours, a crisis, so that their invitation arrives a few hours
or till myself full at their board
in advance of a   pig's stoppage, ~~invariably~~ At any rate
it was after 5 o'clock
I knew that I couldn't put off any longer the evil hour.

Comparing Draft and Essay

Like other writers you have studied, E. B. White revises both during and after the composing stage of the writing process. (Note typewritten revisions such as strike-overs and retyping and handwritten changes such as cross-outs and additions.) Also note changes in wording and sentence structure that appear between typed lines and in margins.

Draft Paragraph 2

1. Which words of the following word pairs have been included in the published version of "Death of a Pig": devotion, fidelity; outline, form; character, business; presentiment, hunch; story, play. How can you explain White's selections? How does context help to guide diction choice?

2. Study the length of the sentences in this paragraph. Are all sentences the same length? If not, why would the author vary them? How are you affected as a reader?

3. The sentence "The loss we felt was not the loss of ham but the loss of pig" might be interpreted as offhand or flippant. How do you know that the author's distinction is deliberate and at least partially serious?

Draft Paragraph 5

After comparing this paragraph to published paragraph 5, note the kinds of revisions that White makes. Additions and deletions are readily apparent, but substitution and rearrangement may also be found. These revising techniques serve mostly to focus diction and strengthen sentences. The first sentence is a recasting of the previous one (deleted draft paragraph 4); the third sentence simultaneously adds explanatory information and deletes deadwood ("right away"). Also, the word "appear" is substituted for "show up" and "sound" replaces "quality"—two diction changes that help to convey the author's exact meaning.

4. Why does White include the typewritten, between-line-insertion "or a child"? Why does he use the pronoun "who" (usually reserved for people) instead of "which" (usually applied to things or animals)? How do these word selections convey meaning, and what meaning is expressed?

Draft Paragraph 7

5. Because this paragraph is written as dialogue, diction requirements are strict. That is, when an author creates spoken language, it is essential that he make the sentences *sound* authentic. One way to give dialogue a natural sound is to include informal language or colloquialisms that are representative of speech. What words or expressions can you find that White uses to present the illusion of talking?

Draft Paragraphs 8 and 9

6. Note the substitution of the words "sank into a chair" for "sat down" and "went to the barn" for "went around the place." Which phrases contain exact language? Which phrases are more expressive?

7. Compare these paragraphs to published paragraphs 8 and 9. What information has been added? Do these insertions affect meaning or are they revisions of style? What modifications are made to sentence structures to accommodate these revisions?

Russell Baker

Russell Baker (b. 1925) is a regular columnist for *The New York Times*. He has written several books including his autobiography *Growing Up* (1982) for which he won the Pulitzer Prize. His second volume of memoirs, *The Good Times,* was published in 1989. Baker makes an interesting distinction between revisions for his daily newspaper columns like "Here to Stay" and revising for his books:

> I have always thought journalism ought to be at least slightly imperfect, so my first drafts are almost always the final drafts. After a few minutes of pencil revision, the first draft goes to the printer. If it's not so hot I say, "It's only daily journalism." In the next forty-eight hours, I'll have another chance to do better. Books are different. My last book has passages I rewrote fifty times.

As you study his changes, speculate as to why they were necessary to clarify his meaning.

Here to Stay

Introduction to the Essay and Draft

Russell Baker's revisions are an example of *editing*. The author's alteration of a word here and a sentence there bears the earmarks of the final stage of revision. As you read "Here to Stay," try to concentrate on the author's initial choice of diction and sentence structure as well as the editing changes that are made. The effectiveness of Baker's selections should help you to understand the importance of adequate revising in the prewriting, composing, and rewriting stages of the writing process.

Published Essay

1   He was a grim man and he stared grimly out of the television screen with what he obviously thought was a grim message. "Like it or not," he said, "the computer is here to stay."

2   He reminded me of certain teachers who threaten indolent schoolchildren. I once had such a teacher. She was exasperated because I wasn't interested in the difference between an adjective and adverb. "Like it or not, the adverb is here to stay," she said.

3   Her obvious anger seemed to come out of suspicion that I disliked the adverb. Clearly she was devoted to the adverb and resented all who weren't. I had nothing against the adverb at the time. Later, I even came to understand that the adverb was useful if applied, like aspirin, in small doses.

4   At the time, though, I was indifferent to the adverb. Not hostile. Just indifferent. In the same way I was indifferent to the secant, to which my mathematics teacher was passionately attached. ("Like it or not, sonny, the secant is here to stay.")

5   Why teachers should mistake my indifference for hostility was puzzling. I happened to be deeply interested at the time in playing marbles. Marbles didn't visibly interest teachers, and I didn't expect them to. It never occurred to me to go red in the face and tell a teacher, "Like it or not, marbles are here to stay."

6   What was wrong with these teachers?

7   Thanks to the grim man on television, I think the question can now be answered. They were trying to sell me the adverb and the secant and were angered by my sales resistance.

8   This of course was precisely what the grim man on television was up to. He was a salesman working hard territory. The manager had assigned him all the pinchpennies who had resisted spiels about joining the glorious computer revolution, about the joy of being the first on the block to see all their bills neatly displayed on their personal video screens.

9   So there he was, menacing and glowering with what he thought was news that would make us shudder. "Like it or not . . . here to stay."

10   This must be basically the same message the Nazis spoke to the sulking masses of German-occupied Europe: no use resisting destiny, better make the best of it, et cetera.

11   Behind this argument I detect a queasy sense of uncertainty in the computer business. I have noticed it in persons who work in the computer industry and even among those who don't but have bought new machines. When they meet somebody who still hasn't taken the plunge, they cannot resist warning you that you will soon be obsolete if you don't buy fast, because, like it or not, the computer is here to stay.

12   I don't recall that anybody had to be bullied into buying a television set back in the pioneering age of Morey Amsterdam, Dagmar and Gorgeous George. A lot of people remained indifferent to television, but the mass public descent on Madman Muntz's TV store was such that Mrs. Muntz never had time to go into the street and browbeat the passing crowd with warnings that they were as out-of-date as the horse collar.

13   Quickly, even the indifferent realized that television was here to stay, like it or not, and bought. When something is here to stay, nobody has to announce it.

When a salesman starts telling me his merchandise is here to stay, I don't necessarily doubt him; instead, I ask myself, "Do I really care?"

14   The math teacher who pronounced the secant "here to stay" was correct but that still hasn't made me buy. I just never felt a need for the secant. Some people do, and those people bought, and that seems sensible. As life unfolded, I felt a need for the adverb, and fortunately the teacher who'd said it was here to stay had been correct. As a result, I have had it right here at my disposal for the past several hundred words.

15   Many Americans don't need the adverb even though it is here to stay. Very few need the secant. I don't need the secant myself, but I wouldn't want to see it abolished. The people who do need it probably need it for good, sound public purposes.

16   So far, the computer strikes me as much more like the adverb and the secant than like television, if we are talking about things that are here to stay.

17   As with the adverb, I may someday feel a need for the computer and rejoice in its existence. At present, though, feeling nothing but revulsion at the prospect of seeing all my debts lit up on a video screen at the touch of a button, I feel as personally uninterested in it as I am in the secant.

18   I am grateful nevertheless that the computer is here to stay. When it can help me get to the office on a rainy day without being drenched at a bus stop, I shall certainly want to buy one.

Draft

```
advance for sunday magazine

copy to klein and news service

bakers sunday observer for december 3



1            New York, Nov. 8--⌐He was a grim man and he stared

grimly out of the television screen with what he obviously

thought was a grim message. "Like it or not," he said, "the

computer is here to stay."

2            ⌐He reminded me of certain teachers who threaten
      INDOLENT _____
slow-witted pupils pupils. I once had such a teacher. She
```

was exasperated because I wasn't interested in the difference

between ~~the~~ and adjective and an adverb. "Like it or not, the

adverb is here to stay," she said.

3   Her obvious anger seemed to come out of suspicion that

I ~~had something against~~ DISLIKED the adverb. Clearly she was devoted to

the adverb and resented all who weren't. I had nothing against

the adverb at the time. Later I even came to understand that

the adverb was useful if ~~taken~~ applied, like aspirin, in small doses.

4   At the time though, I was indifferent to the adverb.

Not hostile. Just indifferent. In the same way I was indifferent

to the secant, to which ~~the~~ MY mathematics teacher was ~~profoundly~~ PASSIONATELY

attached. ("Like it or not, sonny, the secant is here to stay.")

5   Why teachers should mistake my indifference for

hostility ~~baffl~~ was ~~sim~~ puzzling. I happened to be ~~very~~ DEEPLY

INTERESTED   PLAYING
~~interest~~ at the time in ~~shooting~~ marbles. Marbles didn't

visibly interest teachers, ~~though~~, and I didn't expect them

to. It never occurred to me to go red in the face and tell a

teacher, "Like it or not, marbles are here to stay."

6   What was wrong with these teachers?

7   Thanks to the grim man on television, I THINK the question

can now be answered~~,~~ ~~I think.~~ They were trying to sell me the

adverb and the secant and were angered by my sales resistance.

8   This of course was precisely what the grim man on

television was up to. He was a salesman working hard territory.

The manager had assigned him all the pinchpennies who had

resisted spiels about joining the glorious computer revolution,

about the joys of being the first on their block to see all

their bills neatly ~~totaled up~~ DISPLAYED on their personal video screens.

9   So there he was, ~~mass~~ menacing and glowering with

what he thought ~~was~~ was news that would make us shudder.

"Like it or not....here to stay."

10   This must be basically the same message the Nazis

spoke to ~~smiting~~ the sulking masses of German-occupied Europe:

no use resisting destiny, better make the best of it, etcetera.

11   Behind this argument there ~~lies~~ I DETECT a queasy sense of

uncertainty (IN THE COMPUTER BUSINESS). I have noticed it often in persons who ~~are~~ WORK

~~devoted~~ IN to the computer industry and even among those who ~~aren't~~ DON'T

but have bought ~~their~~ NEW machines anyhow. When they meet somebody

who still hasn't taken the plunge they ~~can't~~ CANNOT resist ~~telling~~ WARNING

you that you ~~are going to~~ WILL SOON be obsolete if you don't buy ~~in~~ FAST,

because, like it or not, ~~the~~ the computer is here to stay.

12   I don't recall that anybody had to be bullied into

buying a television set back int the pioneering age of

Morey Amsterdam, Dagmar and Gorgeous George. A lot of people remained indifferent to television, but the mass public descent

on Madman Muntz's TV store was such that Mrs. Muntz never

had to go into the street and browbeat a crowd with ~~threats~~ TIME the passing warnings ~~denunciations~~

that they were as out-of-date as the horse collar.

13   Quickly, even the indifferent ~~grasped~~ REALIZED that television

was here to stay, like it or not, and bought. When something

is here to stay, nobody has to ~~tell you~~ so. ANNOUNCE IT. When ~~somebody~~ a

salesman ~~starts~~ telling ~~you~~ me his merchandise is here to

stay, I don't necessarily doubt him; instead, I ask myself,

"Do I really care?"

14   The math teacher who pronounced the secant "here to

stay" was correct," but ~~indubitably~~ that still hasn't made

me buy because I just never felt a ~~vital~~ need for the secant. Some

people do, and those people bought, and that ~~seems~~ sensible.

As life ~~unfolds~~ unfolded, I felt a need for the adverb, and

fortunately the teacher who'd said it was here to stay had been

correct. As a result I have ~~had~~ had it at my ~~disposal dispos~~ RIGHT HERE
disposal for the past ~~everal hun~~ several hundred words. ~~right here.~~

15   Many Americans don't need the adverb even though it

is here to stay. Very few need the secant. I don't need the

secant myself, but I wouldn't want to see it abolished. The

people who DO need it ~~are~~ probably need it for good sound public

purposes.

16   So far, the computer strikes me as much more like

the adverb and the secant than like television, if we are

talking about things that are here to stay. As with the adverb,

THE COMPUTER

I may some day feel a need for it and rejoice in its existence.

THOUGH;

17   At present, feeling nothing but revulsion at the

prospect of seeing all my debts lit up on a video screen at

the touch of a button, I feel as personally uninterested in it

as I am in the secant.

THE COMPUTER

18   I am grateful nevertheless that it is here to stay.

When it can help me get to the office on a rainy day without

being drenched at a bus stop, I shall certainly want to buy one.

Comparing Draft and Essay

Draft Paragraphs 2 through 5

1. Examine the following word pairs: indolent, slow-witted; applied, taken; passionately, profoundly; my, the; very, deeply. Which word of each pair is more descriptive? Which one captures your attention? Which one is more to the point?

2. Baker substitutes the word "playing" for "shooting" in draft paragraph 5. Why has he made this change?

Draft Paragraph 8

3. Jargon and cliché are two types of diction that writers try to avoid. Yet these diction errors are present in draft paragraph 8. Identify them and explain why you think Baker has retained them.

Draft Paragraphs 11 through 13

4. How do the revisions of the first sentence of draft paragraph 11 change the voice from passive to active? How do the diction changes affect tone? Why do you think Baker makes these revisions?

5. Look over the word choices that Baker makes in these paragraphs. Does he consistently choose words that are specific and concrete? Explain your answer, supporting it with examples.

Draft Paragraphs 14 through 18

6. Compare these sentences to those in previous paragraphs. Is there a difference in sentence length or style? To what extent can the emphatic nature of these sentences be attributed to the choice of diction?

7. Evaluate the diction changes of these paragraphs. Are they simple or complicated, formal or informal, concrete or abstract, specific or general? How does the choice of words reflect the author's purpose? How does diction selection help to set tone?

William Zinsser

William Zinsser (b. 1922) was born in New York City and educated at Princeton. After a successful career as a journalist, he began teaching writing at Yale University in 1970. He has published several books, including *On Writing Well* (1976), *Writing to Learn* (1988), and *Inventing the Truth: The Art and Craft of Memoir* (1989). As you read "Words," from *On Writing Well,* reflect on Zinsser's comment that "clutter is the disease of American writing" and make some notes on the points you find most helpful.

Words

1   There is a kind of writing that might be called journalese, and it is the death of freshness in anybody's style. It is the common currency of newspapers and of magazines like *Time*—a mixture of cheap words, made-up words and clichés which have become so pervasive that a writer can hardly help using them automatically. You must fight these phrases off or you will sound like every hack who sits down at a typewriter. In fact, you will never make your mark as a writer unless you develop a respect for words and a curiosity about their shades of meaning that is almost obsessive. The English language is rich in strong and supple words. Take the time to root around and find the ones you want.

2   What is "journalese"? It is a quilt of instant words patched together out of other parts of speech. Adjectives are used as nouns ("greats," "notables"). Nouns are used as adjectives ("top officials," "health reasons") or extended into adjectives ("insightful"). Nouns are used as verbs ("to host"), or they are chopped off to form verbs ("enthuse," "emote"), or they are padded to form verbs ("beef up," "put teeth into").

3   This is a world where eminent people are "framed" and their associates are "staffers," where the future is always "upcoming" and someone is forever "firing off" a note. Nobody in *Time* has merely sent a note or a memo or a telegram in years. Famed Diplomat Henry Kissinger, who hosts foreign notables to beef up the morale of top State Department staffers, sits down and fires off a lot of notes. Notes that are fired off are always fired in anger and from a sitting position.

4   Here, for example, is a *Time* article of several years ago that is hard to match for sheer fatigue:

> *Last February, Plainclothes Patrolman Frank Serpico and two other New York City policemen knocked at the door of a suspected Brooklyn heroin pusher. When the door opened a crack, Serpico shouldered his way in only to be met by a .22-cal. pistol slug crashing into his face. Somehow he survived, although there are still buzzing fragments in his head, causing dizziness and permanent deafness in his left ear. Almost as painful is the suspicion that he may well have been set up for the shooting by other policemen. For Serpico, 35, has been waging a lonely, four-year war against the routine and endemic corruption that he and others claim is rife in the New York City police department. His efforts are now sending*

shock waves through the ranks of New York's finest. . . . Though the impact of the commission's upcoming report has yet to be felt, Serpico has little hope that anything will really change. . .

5   The upcoming report has yet to be felt because it is still upcoming, and as for the "permanent deafness," it is still a little early to tell. And what makes those buzzing fragments buzz? I would have thought that by now only the head would be buzzing.

6   But apart from these lazinesses of logic, what makes the story so infinitely tired is the failure of the writer to reach for anything but the nearest cliché. "Shouldered his way," "only to be met," "crashing into his face," "waging a lonely war," "corruption that is rife," "sending shock waves"—these dreary phrases constitute journalese at its worst and writing at its most banal. We know just what to expect. No surprise awaits us in the form of a bizarre word, an oblique look. We are in the hands of a hack and we know it right away.

7   Don't let yourself get in this position. The only way to fight it is to care deeply about words. If you find yourself writing that someone recently "enjoyed" a spell of illness or that a business has been "enjoying" a slump, stop and think how much they really enjoyed it. Notice the decisions that other writers make in their choice of words and be finicky about the ones that you select from the vast supply. The race in writing is not to the swift but to the original.

8   In contrast to the lonely Serpico, here is how *Life* led its issue November 1, 1968, which went to press only forty-eight hours after the surprise announcement that Mrs. Kennedy would marry Mr. Onassis. The magazine assigned the article to its best writer, Paul O'Neil, who began his story—adjacent to a color photograph of Skorpios—like this:

> *But look carefully at this island in its indigo sea; observe the yacht with the golden bathtub spigots and 42 telephones; see the swimming pool; see the scarred hill where the castle will be built and while doing so think of the money piled up by the little fellow in dark glasses who owns it—one thousand million dollars. Ladies . . . ladies . . . you've had a week to be scandalized, but now we must insist that you cease sputtering and be serious—those of you over 30, at any rate, who know husbands are to be endured. And gentlemen . . . we're all carnivores here although you need not say so aloud. Are there any of us who really suspect that Jackie is not capable of enormous satisfaction at a union so rich in drama, creature comfort, power, sudden independence of social constraint—and the sweet knowledge of breast-heaving by a million indignant and defeated females—or that Onassis is not bursting with pride at his bauble of baubles?*

9   If the story contains almost no substance (and it doesn't), it is because O'Neil had to write it in little more than a day, only with fragmentary cables from Greece and with old clippings about the new bridegroom. Nevertheless he gave the reader a touch of elegance and a sense that, whatever the next sentence might bring, it wouldn't be like anyone else's.

10　So in learning to write nonfiction, make a habit of reading what is being written today and what has been written before. But cultivate the best writers. Don't assume that because an article is in a newspaper or a magazine it must be good. Lazy editing is endemic to our papers, and writers who use clichés by reflex are likely to work for editors who have seen so many clichés that they no longer even recognize them as they go limping by.

11　Also get in the habit of using dictionaries. My favorite for handy use is *Webster's New Collegiate,* based on the Second Edition of *Webster's New International Dictionary,* though, like all word freaks, I own many bigger dictionaries which will reward me in their own fashion when I am on some more specialized search.

12　If you have any doubt of what a word means, look it up. Learn its etymology and notice what curious branches its original root has put forth. See if it has any other meanings that you didn't know it had. Master the small gradations between words that seem to be synonyms. What is the difference between "cajole," "wheedle," "blandish" and "coax"? An excellent guide to these nuances is *Webster's Dictionary of Synonyms.*

13　And don't scorn that bulging grab-bag, *Roget's Thesaurus.* It's easy to regard the book as hilarious. Look up "villain," for example, and you will be awash in such rascality as only a lexicographer could conjure back from centuries of iniquity, obliquity, depravity, knavery, profligacy, frailty, flagrancy, infamy, immorality, corruption, wickedness, wrongdoing, backsliding and sin. You will find rogues and wretches, ruffians and riffraff, miscreants and malefactors, reprobates and rapscallions, hooligans and hoodlums, scamps and scapegraces, scoundrels and scalawags, jezebels and jades. You will find adjectives to fit them all (foul and fiendish, devilish and diabolical), and adverbs, and verbs to describe how the wrongdoers do their wrong, and cross-references leading to still other thickets of venality and vice. Still, there is no better friend to have around to nudge the memory than Roget. It saves you the time of rummaging in your own memory—that network of overloaded grooves—to find the word that is right on the tip of your tongue, where it doesn't do you any good. The *Thesaurus* is to the writer what a rhyming dictionary is to a songwriter—a reminder of all the choices—and you should use it with gratitude. If, having found the scalawag and the scapegrace, you want to know how they differ, *then* go to the dictionary.

14　Also bear in mind, when you are choosing words and stringing them together, how they sound. This may seem absurd: readers read with their eyes. But actually they hear what they are reading—in their inner ear—far more than you realize. Therefore such matters as rhythm and alliteration are vital to every sentence. A typical example—maybe not the best, but undeniably the nearest— is the preceding paragraph. Obviously I enjoyed making a certain arrangement of my ruffians and riffraff, my hooligans and hoodlums, and the reader enjoyed it, too—far more than if I had given him a mere list. He enjoyed not only the arrangement but the effort to entertain him. He wasn't enjoying it, however, with his eyes. He was enjoying it mainly in his ear.

15   E. B. White makes the case cogently in *The Elements of Style* (the best book on writing that I know) when he suggests trying to rearrange any phrase that has survived for a century or two, such as Thomas Paine's "These are the times that try men's souls":

> *Times like these try men's souls.*
> *How trying it is to live in these times!*
> *These are trying times for men's souls.*
> *Soulwise, these are trying times.*

16   Paine's phrase is like poetry and the other four are like oatmeal, which, of course, is the divine mystery of the creative process. Yet the good writer of prose must be part poet, always listening to what he writes. E. B. White continues across the years to be my favorite stylist because I am so conscious of being with a man who cares in his bones about the cadences and sonorities of the language. I relish (in my ear) the pattern that his words make as they fall into a sentence. I try to surmise how in rewriting the sentence he reassembled it to end with a phrase that will momentarily linger, or how he chose one word over another because he was after a certain emotional weight. It is the difference between, say, "serene" and "tranquil"—one so soft, the other strangely disturbing because of the unusual "n" and "q."

17   Listen to how White begins his book *Here Is New York:*

> *On any person who desires such queer prizes, New York will bestow the gift of loneliness and the gift of privacy. It is this largess that accounts for the presence within the city's walls of a considerable section of the population; for the residents of Manhattan are to a large extent strangers who have pulled up stakes somewhere and come to town, seeking sanctuary or fulfillment or some greater or lesser grail. The capacity to make such dubious gifts is a mysterious quality of New York. It can destroy an individual, or it can fulfill him, depending a good deal on luck. No one should come to New York to live unless he is willing to be lucky.*

18   Don't be deceived by the simplicity of the paragraph. I wouldn't be surprised if White took a week to write and rewrite it. The first sentence is a gem; so is the last. The mingling of long Latin words like "population" and "sanctuary" with such colloquialisms as "pulled up stakes" and a "a good deal" is a deliberate balancing act—the writer wants to use graceful words and still be himself, talking to the reader naturally. The phrase "some greater or lesser grail" is positively lyrical and its position at the end of a sentence no accident.

19   Such considerations of sound and rhythm should be woven through every aspect of what you write. If all your sentences move at the same plodding gait, which even you recognize as deadly but don't know how to cure, read them aloud. You will begin to hear where the trouble lies. See if you can gain variety

by reversing the order of a sentence, by substituting a word that has freshness or oddity, by altering the length of your sentences so that they don't all sound as if they came out of the same computer. An occasional short sentence can carry a tremendous punch. It stays in the reader's ear.

20   Remember, then, that words are the only tools that you will be given. Learn to use them with originality and care. Value them for their strength and their infinite diversity. And also remember: somebody out there is listening.

Considering Content

1. What is Zinsser's main point about words?

2. What function does a thesaurus serve? What difficulty in using a thesaurus does Zinsser fail to mention?

3. What aspect of words, in addition to meaning, should you consider? Zinsser says his reader enjoyed his list of synonyms because of their arrangement. What is that enjoyable arrangement?

Considering Craft

1. How effective is Zinsser's introductory paragraph? Why does he use "root around" instead of "look around"?

2. What makes paragraph 4 interesting and informative? How does it reinforce Zinsser's point that a writer must be curious about words and their shades of meaning?

3. Zinsser praises White for "the mingling of long Latin words . . . with . . . colloquialisms." Do you think it is always appropriate to mingle formal vocabulary with colloquialisms? If not, when is it appropriate and when should it be avoided?

4. What are the colloquialisms in the following excerpts?

   like all words freaks, I own many bigger dictionaries which will reward me in their own fashion

   awash in such rascality as only a lexicographer could conjure

   a man who cares in his bones about the cadences and sonorities of the language

   An occasional short sentence can carry a tremendous punch

5. How does his concluding paragraph reemphasize the points made in his opening paragraph? What does the paragraph add to the essay?

6. How, according to Zinsser, can you improve the sound and rhythm of your writing? Does Zinsser practice what he preaches? How does the sentence "It stays in the reader's ear" illustrate his point? Can you find other examples like this one?

Joan Didion

Joan Didion (b. 1934) is a graduate of the University of California at Berkeley. Her published works of fiction and nonfiction include *Slouching Towards Bethlehem* (1969), *The White Album* (1979), *Salvador* (1983), *Democracy* (1984), and *Miami* (1987). As you read "Marrying Absurd," from *Slouching Towards Bethlehem,* compare your ideas about wedding ceremonies with those that Didion describes.

Marrying Absurd

1   To be married in Las Vegas, Clark County, Nevada, a bride must swear that she is eighteen or has parental permission and a bridegroom that he is twenty-one or has parental permission. Someone must put up five dollars for the license. (On Sundays and holidays, fifteen dollars. The Clark County Courthouse issues marriage licenses at any time of the day or night except between noon and one in the afternoon, between eight and nine in the evening, and between four and five in the morning.) Nothing else is required. The State of Nevada, alone among these United States, demands neither a premarital blood test nor a waiting period before or after the issuance of a marriage license. Driving in across the Mojave from Los Angeles, one sees the signs way out on the desert, looming up from that moonscape of rattlesnakes and mesquite, even before the Las Vegas lights appear like a mirage on the horizon: "GETTING MARRIED? Free License Information First Strip Exit." Perhaps the Las Vegas wedding industry achieved its peak operational efficiency between 9:00 p.m. and midnight of August 26, 1965, an otherwise unremarkable Thursday which happened to be, by Presidential order, the last day on which anyone could improve his draft status merely by getting married. One hundred and seventy-one couples were pronounced man and wife in the name of Clark County and the State of Nevada that night, sixty-seven of them by a single justice of the peace, Mr. James A. Brennan. Mr. Brennan did one wedding at the Dunes and the other sixty-six in his office, and charged each couple eight dollars. One bride lent her veil to six others: "I got it down from five to three minutes," Mr. Brennan said later of his feat. "I could've married them *en masse,* but they're people, not cattle. People expect more when they get married."

2   What people who get married in Las Vegas actually do expect—what, in the largest sense, their "expectations" are—strikes one as a curious and self-contradictory business. Las Vegas is the most extreme and allegorical of

American settlements, bizarre and beautiful in its venality and in its devotion to immediate gratification, a place the tone of which is set by mobsters and call girls and ladies' room attendants with amyl nitrite poppers in their uniform pockets. Almost everyone notes that there is no "time" in Las Vegas, no night and no day and no past and no future (no Las Vegas casino, however, has taken the obliteration of the ordinary time sense quite so far as Harold's Club in Reno, which for a while issued, at odd intervals in the day and night, mimeographed "bulletins" carrying news from the world outside); neither is there any logical sense of where one is. One is standing on a highway in the middle of a vast hostile desert looking at an eight-foot sign which blinks "STARDUST" or "CAESAR'S PALACE." Yes, but what does that explain? This geographical implausibility reinforces the sense that what happens there has no connection with "real" life; Nevada cities like Reno and Carson are ranch towns, Western towns, places behind which there is some historical imperative. But Las Vegas seems to exist only in the eye of the beholder. All of which makes it an extraordinarily stimulating and interesting place, but an odd one in which to want to wear a candlelight satin Priscilla of Boston wedding dress with Chantilly lace insets, tapered sleeves and a detachable modified train.

3   And yet the Las Vegas wedding business seems to appeal to precisely that impulse. "Sincere and Dignified Since 1954," one wedding chapel advertises. There are nineteen such wedding chapels in Las Vegas, intensely competitive, each offering better, faster, and, by implication, more sincere services than the next: Our Photos Best Anywhere, Your Wedding on a Phonograph Record, Candlelight with Your Ceremony, Honeymoon Accommodations, Free Transportation from Your Motel to Courthouse to Chapel and Return to Motel, Religious or Civil Ceremonies, Dressing Rooms, Flowers, Rings, Announcements, Witnesses Available, and Ample Parking. All of these services, like most others in Las Vegas (sauna baths, payroll-check cashing, chinchilla coats for sale or rent) are offered twenty-four hours a day, seven days a week, presumably on the premise that marriage, like craps, is a game to be played when the table seems hot.

4   But what strikes one most about the Strip chapels, with their wishing wells and stained-glass paper windows and their artificial bouvardia, is that so much of their business is by no means a matter of simple convenience, of late-night liaisons between show girls and baby Crosbys. Of course there is some of that. (One night about eleven o'clock in Las Vegas I watched a bride in an orange minidress and masses of flamecolored hair stumble from a Strip chapel on the arm of her bridegroom, who looked the part of the expendable nephew in movies like *Miami Syndicate*. "I gotta get the kids," the bride whimpered. "I gotta pick up the sitter, I gotta get to the midnight show." "What you gotta get," the bridegroom said, opening the door of a Cadillac Coupe de Ville and watching her crumple on the seat, "is sober.") But Las Vegas seems to offer something other than "convenience"; it is merchandising "niceness," the facsimile of proper ritual, to children who do not know how else to find it, how to make the

arrangements, how to do it "right." All day and evening long on the Strip, one sees actual wedding parties, waiting under the harsh lights at a crosswalk, standing uneasily in the parking lot of the Frontier while the photographer hired by The Little Church of the West ("Wedding Place of the Stars") certifies the occasion, takes the picture: the bride in a veil and white satin pumps, the bridegroom usually in a white dinner jacket, and even an attendant or two, a sister or a best friend in hot-pink *peau de soie,* a flirtation veil, a carnation nosegay. "When I Fall in Love It Will Be Forever," the organist plays, and then a few bars of Lohengrin. The mother cries; the stepfather, awkward in his role, invites the chapel hostess to join them for a drink at the Sands. The hostess declines with a professional smile; she has already transferred her interest to the group waiting outside. One bride out, another in, and again the sign goes up on the chapel door: "One moment please — Wedding."

5   I sat next to one such wedding party in a Strip restaurant the last time I was in Las Vegas. The marriage had just taken place; the bride still wore her dress, the mother her corsage. A bored waiter poured out a few swallows of pink champagne ("on the house") for everyone but the bride, who was too young to be served. "You'll need something with more kick than that," the bride's father said with heavy jocularity to his new son-in-law; the ritual jokes about the wedding night had a certain Panglossian character, since the bride was clearly several months pregnant. Another round of pink champagne, this time not on the house, and the bride began to cry. "It was just as nice," she sobbed, "as I hoped and dreamed it would be."

Considering Content

1. Was it pure chance ("which happened to be") that the largest number of couples ever married on one day in Las Vegas were married on August 26, 1965? Is "operational efficiency" important to "the Las Vegas wedding industry"? Is this efficiency measured in quantity or in quality?

2. Is Mr. James A. Brennan aware that numbers are secondary to other considerations where marriage is concerned? Do his words fit his deeds?

3. Note the detailed description of the wedding dress at the end of paragraph 2. Why is such a dress "odd" for a person to wear in Las Vegas? Why does it "seem to appeal" anyway?

4. According to Didion, how is marriage, "presumably," like craps?

5. What is the effect of tucking into a parenthesis the story of the redheaded bride? What does the last word in the story ("sober") tell us about the bride? About the bridegroom? Does the story indicate that theirs was a "late-night liaison"? A sudden decision?

6. Why does Didion call those who use the Las Vegas wedding industry "children"?

7. What is your reaction to these three items from the story told in the last paragraph: (a) bride too young to be served liquor, (b) bride already pregnant, and (c) bride crying with happiness over her dream wedding?

Considering Craft

1. Didion's first paragraph is longer than most introductions. What effect does she achieve by including so much detail?

2. Look up "absurd" in a dictionary or a thesaurus. Is it an appropriate choice for the essay's title? What would you have chosen instead?

3. Study Didion's sentence arrangement. Does it vary in length and complexity? How does the sentence diversity contribute to the essay's meaning?

4. Characterize her tone. Is it satirical, serious, condescending, humorous? Is it appropriate for her subject? Why or why not?

5. What is the thesis of Didion's essay and where is it expressed?

6. Point out examples of irony in the essay. What is the effect of using this technique?

7. Read over Didion's conclusion. Does it contribute to the essay's unity? What nuance does it add to meaning?

8. What is Didion's purpose in "Marrying Absurd"? Is she only informing or is she also trying to persuade? Explain your answer.

Anne Morrow Lindbergh

Anne Morrow Lindbergh (b. 1906) is an American writer. She is also the widow of Charles A. Lindbergh, best known for his solo flight across the Atlantic Ocean in 1927. She has described their flights together in *North to the Orient* (1935) and *Listen! The Wind* (1938). In 1955 she published *Gift from the Sea,* a collection of essays addressed especially to women. As you read "A Few Shells" from *Gift from the Sea,* ask yourself if Lindbergh also has something to say to a male audience.

A Few Shells

1   I am packing to leave my island. What have I for my efforts, for my ruminations on the beach? What answers or solutions have I found for my life? I have a few shells in my pocket, a few clues, only a few.

2   When I think back to my first days here, I realize how greedily I collected. My pockets bulged with wet shells, the damp sand clinging to their crevices. The beach was covered with beautiful shells and I could not let one go by unnoticed. I couldn't even walk head up looking out to sea, for fear of missing something precious at my feet. The collector walks with blinders on; he sees nothing but the prize. In fact, the acquisitive instinct is incompatible with true appreciation of beauty. But after all the pockets were stretched and damp, and the bookcase shelves filled and the window ledges covered, I began to drop my acquisitiveness. I began to discard from my possessions, to select.

3   One cannot collect all the beautiful shells on the beach. One can collect only a few, and they are more beautiful if they are few. One moon shell is more impressive than three. There is only one moon in the sky. One double-sunrise is an event; six are a succession, like a week of schooldays. Gradually one discards and keeps just the perfect specimen; not necessarily a rare shell, but a perfect one of its kind. One sets it apart by itself, ringed around by space—like the island.

4   For it is only framed in space that beauty blooms. Only in space are events and objects and people unique and significant—and therefore beautiful. A tree has significance if one sees it against the empty face of sky. A note in music gains significance from the silences on either side. A candle flowers in the space of night. Even small and casual things take on significance if they are washed in space, like a few autumn grasses in one corner of an Oriental painting, the rest of the page bare.

5   My life in Connecticut, I begin to realize, lacks this quality of significance and therefore of beauty, because there is so little empty space. The space is scribbled on; the time has been filled. There are so few empty pages in my engagement pad, or empty hours in the day, or empty rooms in my life in which to stand alone and find myself. Too many activities, and people, and things. Too many worthy activities, valuable things, and interesting people. For it is not merely the trivial which clutters our lives but the important as well. We can have a surfeit of treasures—an excess of shells, where one or two would be significant.

6   Here on this island I have had space. Paradoxically, in this limited area, space has been forced upon me. The geographical boundaries, the physical limitations, the restrictions on communication, have enforced a natural selectivity. There are not too many activities or things or people, and each one, I find, is significant, set apart in the frame of sufficient time and space. Here there is time; time to be quiet; time to work without pressure; time to think; time to watch the heron, watching with frozen patience for his prey. Time to look at the stars or to study a shell; time to see friends, to gossip, to laugh, to talk. Time, even, *not* to talk. At home, when I meet my friends in those cubby-holed hours, time is so precious we feel we must cram every available instant with conversation. We cannot afford the luxury of silence. Here on the island I find I can sit with a friend without talking, sharing the day's last sliver of pale green light on the horizon, or the whorls in a small white shell, or the dark scar left in

a dazzling night sky by a shooting star. Then communication becomes communion and one is nourished as one never is by words.

7   Island living selects for me, but it is a natural, not an artificial selection. It selects numerically but not in kind. There are all kinds of experiences on this island, but not too many. There are all kinds of people, but not too many. The simplicity of life forces me into physical as well as intellectual or social activity. I have no car, so I bicycle for my supplies and my mail. When it is cold, I collect driftwood for my fireplace and chop it up, too. I swim instead of taking hot baths. I bury my garbage instead of having it removed by a truck. And when I cannot write a poem, I bake biscuits and feel just as pleased. Most of these physical chores would be burdens at home, where my life is crowded and schedules are tight. There I have a house full of children and I am responsible for many people's lives. Here, where there is time and space, the physical tasks are a welcome change. They balance my life in a way I find refreshing and in which I seldom feel refreshed at home. Making beds or driving to market is not as refreshing as swimming or bicycling or digging in the earth. I cannot go on burying the garbage when I get home, but I can dig in a garden; I can bicycle to the cabin where I work; and I can remember to bake biscuits on bad days.

8   My island selects for me socially too. Its small circumference cannot hold too many people. I see people here that I would not see at home, people who are removed from me by age or occupation. In the suburbs of a large city we tend to see people of the same general age and interests. That is why we chose the suburbs, because we have similar needs and pursuits. My island selects for me people who are very different from me—the stranger who turns out to be, in the frame of sufficient time and space, invariably interesting and enriching. I discover here what everyone has experienced on an ocean voyage or a long train ride or a temporary seclusion in a small village. Out of the welter of life, a few people are selected for us by the accident of temporary confinement in the same circle. We never would have chosen these neighbors; life chose them for us. But thrown together on this island of living, we stretch to understand each other and are invigorated by the stretching. The difficulty with big city environment is that if we select—and we must in order to live and breathe and work in such crowded conditions—we tend to select people like ourselves, a very monotonous diet. All hors d'oeuvres and no meat; or all sweets and no vegetables, depending on the kind of people we are. But however much the diet may differ between us, one thing is fairly certain: we usually select the known, seldom the strange. We tend not to choose the unknown which might be a shock or a disappointment or simply a little difficult to cope with. And yet it is the unknown with all its disappointments and surprises that is the most enriching.

9   In so many ways this island selects for me better than I do myself at home. When I go back will I be submerged again, not only by centrifugal activities, but by too many centripetal ones? Not only by distractions but by too many opportunities? Not only by dull people but by too many interesting ones? The multiplicity of the world will crowd in on me again with its false sense of values. Values weighed in quantity, not quality; in speed, not stillness; in noise, not

silence; in words, not in thoughts; in acquisitiveness, not beauty. How shall I resist the onslaught? How shall I remain whole against the strains and stresses of "Zerrissenheit"?

10   For the natural selectivity of the island I will have to substitute a conscious selectivity based on another sense of values—a sense of values I have become more aware of here. Island-precepts, I might call them if I could define them, signposts toward another way of living. Simplicity of living, as much as possible, to retain a true awareness of life. Balance of physical, intellectual, and spiritual life. Work without pressure. Space for significance and beauty. Time for solitude and sharing. Closeness to nature to strengthen understanding and faith in the intermittency of life: life of the spirit, creative life, and the life of human relationships. A few shells.

11   Island living has been a lens through which to examine my own life in the North. I must keep my lens when I go back. Little by little one's holiday vision tends to fade. I must remember to see with island eyes. The shells will remind me; they must be my island eyes.

Considering Content

1. What activity prompts these "ruminations"?

2. How is the single, perfect specimen one selects from a collection like an island? Is this an important idea in the essay? What other comparisons does Lindbergh use to make the point?

3. Note that Lindbergh uses her own—not a biologist's or naturalist's—names for her shells ("moon," "double-sunrise"). Why do you suppose she uses these more private names?

4. How does "this island select for [Lindbergh] better than [she does] herself at home"? What "physical chores" does it "select"? What people?

5. Lindbergh says that suburbanites are more alike than city dwellers. Do you agree? Do you prefer the diversity of the city or the homogeneity of the suburbs? But even in the city, says Lindbergh, "we tend to select people like ourselves." Is a small island more like a city or the suburbs?

6. Lindbergh fears that she will return to her old ways with their "too many opportunities" and "too many interesting [people]." Do you understand her fear? How do you think Lindbergh deals with uninteresting people?

7. "The multiplicity of the world will crowd in on me again with its false sense of values." How do you think Lindbergh would react to the people of "Marrying Absurd"?

8. What "island-precepts" does Lindbergh hope to carry with her? Does one of them sum up the others? Do the "few shells" symbolize them? Would you also like to be able to follow these precepts? What would be the first step?

Considering Craft

1. How effective is Lindbergh's introduction? Does it make you curious about "solutions" she may have found for her life?

2. Lindbergh's main expository technique is contrast and comparison. Find two or three examples. Which did you find most effective?

3. Select three or four topic sentences and evaluate Lindbergh's techniques for supporting them. Does she include specific examples, anecdotes, and information?

4. Lindbergh is writing about simplifying life. Does the vocabulary also reflect this concept? Is the shell an effective symbol in the essay? Why or why not?

5. What is Lindbergh's purpose in writing "A Few Shells"? Is she only recounting a personal experience or does she want to persuade her reader?

6. Characterize Lindbergh's tone. Is it consistent and appropriate for her subject? Explain your answer.

7. How does her conclusion reinforce her introduction? What object does she use in both to contribute to the essay's unity?

Guidelines for Polishing for Presentation

1. Use a dictionary and a thesaurus to assist you in finding the *exact* word you want to use.

2. Choose concrete and specific words with the appropriate connotations.

3. Avoid diction errors such as *jargon, pomposity, deadwood,* and *clichés.* Use deletion and substitution to sharpen your selection of words and phrases.

4. Vary sentence patterns to make your writing more effective. A grammar book may help you to become more aware of the varieties of sentence structures available.

5. Proofread your paper thoroughly. Eliminate errors in grammar, punctuation, and spelling.

Warm-up Exercises

1. Go through a magazine and select four advertisements that attract your attention. Analyze the language of each. Can you find any examples of clichés?

2. Interview three people who work with computers. What do they think of computers? Do they enjoy working with them? What functions can these

computers perform? Did the interviews influence your ideas about computers? How? What specialized words or phrases did you learn during your interviews? Was jargon a problem?

3. Read through the sports section of your favorite newspaper and select an article that supports Zinsser's point that journalists often use clichés. Make a list of the clichés the columnist used and then suggest an alternative expression for each.

4. Slang expressions tend to change rapidly and thus become dated. Conduct an experimental test of this thesis by interviewing five people at least ten years apart in age and ask them what terms they used as adolescents for being attractive, popular, up-to-date, masculine, feminine, and any other categories you can think of. How are their slang expressions similar to or different from yours? What did you learn about slang in relation to audience?

5. Revise these sentences replacing slang and jargon with language understandable by a general audience.

   a. Virginia is very foxy but she is really hung up on clothes.
   b. I met James after his sociology test, and he told me he was blown away by the exam.
   c. To develop good communications skills, you have to interface with people.
   d. Students should study financial aid guidelines to understand how the guidelines impact on them.
   e. To achieve success, you must prioritize your goals and maximize your potential.
   f. BMW advertisements are geared to upscale customers.
   g. Our psychology professor told us that research into phobias is an important ongoing study.
   h. The dean of students asked for our feedback on the new catering service.
   i. Our psychology professor asked for our input in class discussions.

6. Eliminate deadwood from the following sentences.

   a. It is interesting to note that sales of foreign cars are increasing.
   b. At the outset let me say that my entire family will all attend my graduation.
   c. The consensus of opinion is that Dr. Glass is an excellent teacher.
   d. You should be familiar with the different varieties of personal computers.
   e. In the paper which I am about to write I will prove that in my opinion a college education is necessary.
   f. In our present society today young college students have not had enough experience in making decisions.
   g. Let me repeat again that it is absolutely necessary and essential to work hard in college.

h. When I returned my English book back to the library I had to pay one dollar in past overdue fines.

7. Write a paragraph comparing the meaning—denotation, connotation, or both—of one of the following pairs of closely related words.

    a. shame/guilt

    b. knowledge/wisdom

    c. liberty/license

    d. caste/class

    e. solitude/loneliness

    f. propaganda/public relations

8. Combine the following groups of short sentences into one sentence. Use compound elements, appositives, subordinate clauses, and phrases of all kinds, such as participal and prepositional phrases.

    a. I like to swim.
       I like to water-ski.
       I like to fish.
       Lake Crystal is my favorite lake.
       Lake Crystal is clear.
       Lake Crystal is in the mountains.

    b. The jury requested more information.
       The information was about the slope of the driveway.
       They requested it from the judge.
       The judge's name was McMahan.
       The jury reached a verdict.
       The verdict was not guilty.

    c. I graduated from college.
       I was twenty-two years old.
       My alma mater is Union College.
       My degree was a B.A.
       My major was history.

    d. The water shortage was severe.
       The shortage caused hardship.
       People were not allowed to wash their cars.
       They were not allowed to water the grass.
       They were not allowed to open fire hydrants.
       The police enforced these bans.

    e. He was a sergeant.
       He was in the Marine Corps.
       He was stationed in San Diego, California.
       He was attached to a special unit.
       The unit was trained to recover parts from the Pacific.
       The parts came from the space shuttle.

9. Brainstorm about your association with *one* of the following:

genius	marriage	simplicity
creativity	death	solitude
individuality		

Read over what you have written. Have you hit on something you can expand into an essay? What person or group of persons that you know would be interested in this subject?

Writing/Revising Topics

1. We all come into contact with computers every day: cash registers, the telephone system, cable television programming, and pocket calculators, for example. Write an essay about your experience with a computer, for instance, during registration. In revising your essay, focus on the clarity and conciseness of your sentences, and replace vocabulary that might not be accessible to a general audience.

2. Zinsser is excited about words but you may be creative in another medium such as photography, music, art, or dance. Write an essay in which you first describe your creative process and then the emotions it evokes. Revise your essay, making sure that you vary sentence patterns and explain any vocabulary that may be particular to your subject.

3. Write two advertisements for *one* of the following products gearing one toward your parents and the other toward your peers: perfume, cologne, toothpaste, sunglasses. Read over what you have written. Is your choice of words in each advertisement appropriate for your audience? How has your awareness of audience affected your diction? Have you avoided clichés?

4. Cover a sports event for your local or college paper. Try to capture the color and action in your story. Revise to appeal to a visitor from another country who knows nothing about this sport. What changes do you need to make in diction?

5. Some sociologists think that the language we use reveals a good deal about the values by which we live. Write an essay in which you discuss what the specialized language of a particular cultural activity in America reveals about American values in general. What, for example, does the language of American sportscasters, disc jockeys, or movie heroes reveal about our present-day values? In revising your essay, make sure that you have explained fully any terms that may not be immediately accessible to a general audience.

6. Some of the world's greatest works were written in prison or confinement—for example, *Don Quixote, The Autobiography of Malcolm X,* and "Letters from a Birmingham Jail." Do you see any similarities between Lindbergh's situation and that of a creative prisoner? Any differences? Do you find that enforced solitude

brings out creative impulses in you? If your response is affirmative, write for your peers an essay about your experiences. Read over what you have written. How has awareness of audience affected your diction and tone? Have you avoided clichés?

7. Using Warm-up Exercise 9 as the basis, write an essay for your intended audience. In revising your essay, focus on the clarity and conciseness of your sentences.

8. Write a persuasive essay presenting reasons for purchasing *one* of the following: word processor, VCR, microwave oven, compact disk player, Sony Walkman, or video camera. When revising your paper, focus on editing. How many unnecessary words can you eliminate? Have you varied sentence patterns sufficiently to maintain your reader's interest?

9. Recall an experience that caused you to feel a singularly strong emotion. Pick one word that denotes this emotion, then make use of as many synonyms for this word as you can think of in the course of describing the experience and its effect on you. Once the experience is written, replace those synonyms that seem repetitious with whatever concrete details of your description better symbolize the emotion.

Glossary

Addition   A revising technique that enables you to add information to your draft. Words, phrases, or paragraphs may be inserted to clarify or enhance what you have written.

Allegory   *See* **Symbol.**

Allusion   An indirect reference to a person, place, historical event, or work of art. Because writers make assumptions about their audiences' knowledge when using allusions, references should be made with care.

Analogy   A type of comparison that points out a resemblance between two things that are otherwise quite different. Analogy is usually used to explain something complex by showing how it resembles something simpler or easier to understand.

Anecdote   A brief narrative.

Argument   In persuasive essays, a unit of discourse meant to prove your point or convince your reader.

Argumentation   *See* **Logical Appeal.**

Audience   Your answer to the question "*Who* will read what I write?" will define your audience. Audiences may vary in size from few to many readers—sometimes you will write only for yourself while other times you may write for as many people as you can possibly reach.

Audience Profile   A careful, objective assessment of your audience. Such variables as age, sex, religion, attitudes, amount of knowledge, morals, and politics may be factors that you need to consider when writing for a specific audience.

Body   The part of an easy that develops your thesis and fully explains your ideas.

Brainstorming   A prewriting technique in which you rapidly write down ideas in list form. Each idea is usually represented by only one or two words.

Cause and Effect   A kind of exposition used primarily to answer the questions "Why did this occur?" and "What will happen next?" The structure of a cause-and-effect essay is a series of events or conditions, the last of which (the effect) could not occur without the preceding ones (causes). When you write a cause-and-effect essay, it might be helpful to keep chronology clearly in mind: remember that causes always create effects and that effects are derived from causes.

Chronological Order   In description, arranging details through time. Most descriptions use a straightforward chronological order, presenting details as they occur from the beginning to the end.

Chronology   The time sequence of a narrative or description. The two most popular ones are straight chronology (from beginning to middle to end) and flashback (end to beginning to middle to end). By withholding information and manipulating chronology, writers are able to create suspense.

Cliché   A trite, overused expression. Whenever you write, pass over timeworn phrases for those that are fresh and original.

Colloquialism   A word used almost exclusively in conversation and best reserved for informal writing.

Combining   A rearrangement strategy that helps you to concentrate information in a draft by taking ideas expressed in two or more locations and placing them together. Such a change can improve essay organization and the logical presentation of main ideas.

Comparison and Contrast   A type of exposition that notes similarities and differences between two or more things. Two types of organization for comparison and contrast essays are point by point and subject by subject.

Conclusion   The final part of an essay which restates the thesis and makes the essay memorable. A conclusion might contain a summary of your main points but should not present a new argument or viewpoint.

Connotation   A word's implied meaning. Some words are charged with meanings that go beyond their dictionary definitions; such additional responses are connotative meanings.

Deduction   A logical or argumentative appeal in persuasive essays, deductive reasoning elicits a specific conclusion from a generalization. Deduction as a logical approach proceeds from the general to the particular.

Definition   A type of exposition that explains the meaning of a word by bringing its characteristics into sharp focus. *See* **Extended Definition** and **Dictionary Definition**.

Deletion   The revising strategy that enables you to remove unnecessary information from your draft. Words, phrases, or paragraphs may have to be dropped if you find they clutter or digress.

Denotation   A word's exact dictionary definition.

Description   A method of paragraph development that conveys sensory experience through the five senses: sight, hearing, touch, taste, and smell.

Diction   A writer's choice of words. Some major word groups that writers need to become familiar with are: *formal* words—standard words that can be used in almost any work; *nonstandard* words—informal or slang words that should be avoided in most writing; *abstract* words—words that signify general concepts, things one's senses cannot detect; *concrete* words—that stand for things that can be seen, touched, tasted, heard, or smelled; *general* words—words that refer to groups or collections; *specific* words—words that refer to particular items.

Dictionary Definition (lexical definition)   The kind of precise, direct definition found in a dictionary. It places a word into a class with similar items but also differentiates from other members of the same class.

Division/Classification   A type of exposition that divides something large into its constituent parts. This method is useful when clarifying and explaining the relationship of parts to the whole and to one another.

Dominant Impression   In a subjective description, the primary mood or feeling you want to create about the person, place, or thing you are describing.

Draft   A draft is any work in progress, from first to final versions. Since all works can be improved, drafts of essays benefit from thorough, thoughtful revision.

Dramatic Order   In description or narration, building up to the most important details as the essay progresses.

Editing   The final stage of revising, not to be substituted for careful revision. Changes in punctuation, spelling, and word choice are all editing changes.

Emotional Appeal   Caters to your reader's emotions in a persuasive essay. By carefully choosing language and sentence rhythms, you can elicit an emotional reaction from your audience.

Ethical Appeal   Establishes a writer's credibility in a persuasive essay. Credentials, ethics, fairness, knowledge, honesty, and trustworthiness all contribute to establishing a writer's ethical appeal.

Exposition   A type of writing that explains. An expository essay is one that shows the meaning of things; it carefully explains the topic under consideration.

Extended Definition   A type of definition that explores the feelings and ideas you attach to a word. Extended definitions are suited to words with complicated meanings, words that are subject to interpretation, or words that people react strongly to or form opinions about. They can be used as a basis for organizing exposition.

Fallacy   In a persuasive or cause-and-effect essay, the failure of logic. Some of the more common fallacies are: *hasty generalization*—accepting as true a premise needing further testing for validity, jumping to a conclusion; *stereotyping*—seeing a person only as a member of a group and as possessing those traits, usually exaggerated or false, attributed to the whole group; *non sequitur*—ascribing an effect to a wrong cause; *post hoc, ergo propter hoc*—wrongly assuming that a particular event is part of a series of events, presuming that causality, not coincidence, determines the relationship between events.

Figurative Language   Imaginative, vivid language that expresses more meaning than literal words or phrases do. Some common classifications of figurative language are: *simile*—compares two explicitly different things and uses the word *like* or *as* in the comparison; *metaphor*—an implied comparison in which one object is identified with another; *hyperbole*—deliberate exaggeration designed to present a memorable image; *personification*—attributing human characteristics to animals, inanimate objects, or concepts.

First-Person Narrator   A narrator who tells a story in his or her own words and knows and reveals only his or her own thoughts and feelings.

Formality   Whether or not a word is standard or nonstandard diction, its appropriateness for use with a particular audience. *See* **Diction.**

Freewriting   A prewriting activity that requires you to write down thoughts about a subject as they occur to you. Essentially, you are taking dictation from your brain.

Induction   An aspect of logical or argumentative appeal in persuasive essays, induction produces a general conclusion from a specific statement or statements. Induction as a logical approach proceeds from the particular to the general.

Introduction   The opening paragraph of an essay which captures a reader's attention and establishes the writer's purpose. An introduction also sets the tone and contains a thesis statement.

Jargon   A specialized vocabulary developed and used by insiders of a profession or interest group to help them communicate among themselves. While jargon improves communication within the group, it cannot be understood by outsiders and therefore should not be used when addressing a general audience.

Journal   A record of your ideas, memories, experiences, dreams—anything that occurs to you during the day that you write down. A journal can be used for prewriting and as a source for formal writing.

Logical Appeal   Shows a reader how logical thinking and sound evidence lead to certain conclusions in a persuasive essay. Also known as argumentative appeal.

Meaning   What a writer wants to convey in his or her essay. Your intended meaning is your answer to the question *"What* do I want to say?"

Moving   A rearrangement technique that enables you to take information from one part of an essay and place it in another. Although no information is lost or gained, moving helps to clarify and strengthen organization.

Narration   Narration is a story or the technique used to tell a story. When writing a narrative essay, you need to pay attention to point of view, pacing, chronology, and transitions.

Objective Description   Description that is factual and exact. Scientific in nature, it aims at freedom from personal and emotional bias.

Omniscient Narrator   *See* **Third-Person Narrator.**

Outline   An outline is a diagram of your essay's organization. Some outlines are *formal;* they neatly lay out your ideas according to a prescribed, schematic plan. Other outlines may be *informal* and only appear as brainstorming lists or notes about your topic.

Pacing   The rate at which a writer reveals the details of his or her narrative. Unimportant events should be glossed over; essential events need to be carefully explained.

Persona The *persona* was the mask worn by ancient Greek actors. Today the word means a role that one assumes in interpersonal relations or as a writer.

Persuasion A writing approach used to convince an audience to do or believe something.

Point by Point One method of organizing a comparison-and-contrast essay. When applying this plan, you consider how each point in turn relates to each subject.

Point of View In narration, *point of view* means the perspective from which a story is being told; it answers the question "*Who* is telling the story?" Traditionally, four points of view are available to writers: first person, third person omniscient, third person limited omniscient, and third person objective.

Pomposity The use of pretentious, overblown diction. To avoid sounding artificial, do not overuse a thesaurus or dictionary.

Prewriting One of the three main writing processes, prewriting concerns what you do before you begin drafting your essay. Prewriting can be thought of as getting started; freewriting, brainstorming, and keeping a journal are all prewriting activities.

Purpose A writer's reason for writing. A writer's purpose is clarified by his or her answer to the question "*Why* am I writing?"

Reader-Self That part of you that questions what you have written in much the same way as a person who reads your essay for the first time. The reader-self knows only what it learns from the writing—it cannot depend on knowledge available only to the writer for understanding. The reader-self guides revision by asking questions about meaning, purpose, audience, and tone.

Rearrangement The revising process that enables you to reorganize your draft by changing the placement of information. Three subsidiary rearrangement techniques are moving, combining, and redistributing.

Redistributing A rearrangement strategy that helps you to reorganize your essay by taking a block of information and breaking it up into smaller units. Such a revision might help you to explain ideas more carefully or divide main ideas into more understandable units.

Revising The writing process that enables you to change what you have written. Revising implies rethinking, rereading, and rewriting and does not necessarily come after a whole essay is created. Revising helps you bring what you have written into line with what you want to write.

Satire A form of writing that uses irony, sarcasm, wit, and ridicule to expose or denounce human follies or vices. A writer of satire needs to carefully set the tone of his or her work, a tone that might range from gentle mockery to scathing condemnation.

Slang Highly informal, often faddish words best avoided in formal writing.

Spatial Order In description, arranging your essay to conform to the physical layout of the object or scene you are describing. If you are describing a landscape, for example, you might present the scene as you look from left to right, right to left, foreground to background, or background to foreground.

Subject by Subject   One method of organizing a comparison-and-contrast essay. When using this scheme, you need to discuss completely one subject of the comparison and contrast before moving on to the other.

Subjective Description   Description that is based on personal or emotional interpretation and that creates a mood.

Subsidiary Points   The parts of a paragraph that develop and support the main idea (topic sentence).

Substitution   A revising strategy that allows you to replace unsatisfactory words, phrases, or paragraphs with ones that are more desirable. Substitution uses both addition and deletion in the same place in the draft.

Syllogism   A model in logical thinking that establishes valid conclusions by employing the mathematical theorem that things equal to the same thing are equal to each other. Usually made up of two statements, called premises, and a conclusion, the truth of each statement needs to be established before the conclusion may be considered valid.

Symbol   Something that stands for something else; any word, image, or description that has meanings or associations beyond the literal denotation. Two types of writing that depend heavily on symbols are *allegory* (in which people, things, and actions signify other people, things, and actions) and *parable* (a narrative that presents a moral or lesson).

Thesis   A thesis or thesis statement is that part of an essay that clearly and directly states a writer's meaning—it tells what the essay will be about. A thesis should be one sentence long and is usually placed in the introduction.

Third-Person Narrator   A narrator who may reveal the consciousness of varying numbers of the story's characters. Three types of third-person narrators are frequently used by writers: *third person omniscient*—thoughts and feelings of any number of characters are revealed; *third person limited omniscient*—only one character's thoughts and feelings are revealed; *third person objective*—no character's thoughts or feelings are revealed.

Tone   A writer's attitude toward his or her topic and audience, the way a writer sounds to a reader (serious, ironic, informal, and so on). An objective tone or attitude denotes a scientific approach to a topic and appeals to your reader's intellect; a subjective approach implies a personal response to a topic and appeals to your reader's emotions. Tone is expressed primarily through diction and sentence style.

Topic   The subject of your essay's discussion. Because a topic is generally broad, it usually helps to narrow it down to a more workable size.

Topic Sentence   That part of a paragraph that provides the main idea. Just as a thesis statement guides the development of an entire essay, a topic sentence guides the development of a paragraph.

Transition   A word, phrase, or sentence used to link sentences and paragraphs in an essay and to guide your reader from main idea to main idea.

Universal Audience   A general audience whose tastes and attitudes are not known and whose interest in your work cannot be taken for granted. When writing for a universal audience, you must be careful not to overestimate or underestimate their knowledge of your subject—try to keep general readers interested in what you have to say.

Writer's Block   Being unable to get started writing. If you feel blocked because of fear, anxiety, or just not knowing what to write, try using prewriting techniques to get your ideas flowing.

Writer-Self   The part of you that creates your essay by carefully prewriting, composing, and revising. The writer-self is responsible for clearly expressing purpose, meaning, and tone with respect to a specific audience. When revising, the writer-self needs to work closely with the reader-self to pinpoint the parts of a draft needing improvement.

Acknowledgments

Chapter 1

pp. 3–5   Peter Elbow, *Writing with Power*. Oxford: Oxford University Press, 1981; and *Writing Without Teachers* by Peter Elbow. Copyright © by Oxford University Press, Inc. Reprinted by permission.

pp. 6–7   William Stafford, "Writing" from *Writing the Australian Crawl*. Ann Arbor: The University of Michigan Press, 1978.

pp. 12–14   "6/6/44" by Pete Hamill, *New York Daily News Sunday Magazine,* June 24, 1984. Reprinted by permission of the New York Times Syndicate. Notes reprinted by permission of the author.

pp. 15–17   Journal entries by Miriam Vento, February 27 and March 19, 1983. Reprinted by permission of the author.

pp. 17–18   "Statement on Keeping a Journal" by Steven C. Hirschfeld. Reprinted by permission of the author.

pp. 18–20   From *Anne Frank: The Diary of a Young Girl* by Anne Frank. Copyright © 1952 by Otto H. Frank. Used by permission of Doubleday, a division of Bantam Doubleday Dell Publishing Group, Inc.

pp. 21–22   From *Blue Collar Journal: A College President's Sabbatical* by John Coleman. Copyright © 1974 by John R. Coleman. Reprinted by permission of Collier Associates.

pp. 23–25   "On Keeping a Diary" by William Safire in *The New York Times,* September 9, 1974. Copyright © 1974/86 by The New York Times Company. Reprinted by permission.

pp. 25–28   From *Dispatches* by Michael Herr. Copyright © 1977 by Michael Herr. Reprinted by permission of Alfred A. Knopf, Inc.

Chapter 2

pp. 40–43   "Snow" by Julia Alvarez. First appeared in the *Northwest Review*, Vol. 22, Nos. 1 and 2. Draft, published version, and purpose statement reprinted by permission of the author.

pp. 45–49   From "The Ambivalence of Abortion" by Linda Bird Francke in *The New York Times,* May 14, 1976. Copyright © 1976 by The New York Times Company. Reprinted by permission.

pp. 52–53   From "About Men: Playing Air Guitar" by Adam Liptak in *The New York Times,* September 1, 1985. Copyright © 1985 by The New York Times Company. Reprinted by permission.

pp. 54–57   "Hers: The Spoils of War" by Lynne Sharon Schwartz in *The New York Times,* October 9, 1980. Copyright © 1980 by The New York Times Company. Reprinted by permission.

pp. 58–59   From "My Two Countries, My Flesh and Blood" by Pham Thanh in *The New York Times,* April 19, 1991. Copyright © 1991 by The New York Times Company. Reprinted by permission.

pp. 59–60   From "War's Aftermath" by Margaret Zeman. Reprinted by permission of the author.

Chapter 3

pp. 70–78, 88–93   Notes, draft, and essay "Notes on the Writing of 'Confessions of a Working Stiff'" and "Confessions of a Working Stiff" by Patrick Fenton. Copyright © 1922 by Patrick Fenton. Reprinted by permission of the author.

pp. 81–86   "A Perilous Journey" by Joyce Maynard. Copyright © 1984 by Joyce Maynard. Draft and essay used by permission of the author.

pp. 95–96   "I Am a Catholic" by Anna Quindlen in *The New York Times,* March 6, 1986. Copyright © 1986 by The New York Times Company. Reprinted by permission.

pp. 97–98   "Losing People" by Ann Taylor Fleming. Reprinted by permission of the author.

Chapter 4

pp. 108–113 "Money and Freedom" by Marshall Glickman in *The New York Times,* April 26, 1987. Copyright © 1987 by The New York Times Company. Reprinted by permission.

pp. 117–121 "Janushinka" by Hana Wehle. Draft and final version, purpose and revision statement reprinted by permission of the author.

pp. 123–126 "Claiming an Education" is reprinted from *On Lies, Secrets, and Silence, Selected Prose 1966–1978,* by Adrienne Rich, by permission of W. W. Norton & Company, Inc. Copyright © 1979 by W. W. Norton & Company, Inc.

pp. 127–129 "About Men: One Man's Kids" by Daniel Meier in *The New York Times,* November 1, 1987. Copyright © 1987 by The New York Times Company. Reprinted by permission.

Chapter 5

pp. 136–137 Excerpt from "How to Run for Office in a Very Small Town" in *Twenty Questions for the Writer: A Rhetoric with Readings,* Fourth Edition, by Jacqueline Berke. Copyright © 1985 by Harcourt Brace Jovanovich, Inc. Reprinted by permission of the publisher.

pp. 139–145 From "Judging a Book by Its Cover" by Rachel L. Jones. Reprinted by permission of the author.

pp. 148–152 From "I Wish" by Margaret Cardello. Reprinted by permission of the author.

pp. 154–156 H. L. Mencken, "The Penalty of Death" from *A Mencken Chrestomathy.* New York: Alfred A. Knopf, 1956.

pp. 158–160 "Unfair Game" by Susan Jacoby in *The New York Times,* February 23, 1978. Copyright © 1978 by The New York Times Company. Reprinted by permission of The New York Times and Georges Borchardt, Inc.

pp. 161–163 "Going to the Gym" by Anna Quindlen in *The New York Times,* March 6, 1986. Copyright © 1986 by The New York Times Company. Reprinted by permission.

pp. 164–166 "Every 23 Minutes" by Linda Weltner in *The Boston Globe.* Reprinted by permission of the author.

Chapter 6

pp. 175–180 "Mercy" from *Letters to a Young Doctor* by Richard Selzer. Copyright © 1982 by David Goldman and Janet Selzer, trustees. Reprinted by permission of Simon & Schuster, Inc.

pp. 183–186 "Farewell to the Bird" by Myra Miller. Reprinted by permission of the author.

pp. 188–192 Excerpt from "Shades and Splashes of Light" by Maya Angelou from the book *Black Women Writers (1950–1980): A Critical Evaluation* edited by Mari Evans. Copyright © 1983 by Mari Evans. Reprinted by permission of Doubleday, a division of Bantam, Doubleday, Dell Publishing Group, Inc.: and "Step Forward in the Car Please" by Maya Angelou from *I Know Why the Caged Bird Sings.* New York: Random House, 1969.

pp. 193–197 "Noses, Naturally" by Peter Steinhart in *Audubon,* September 1983. Reprinted by permission of the author.

pp. 198–200 "A Brother's Murder" by Brent Staples in *The New York Times.* Reprinted by permission of the author.

Chapter 7

pp. 208–209 D. H. Lawrence, *St. Mawr.* New York: Vintage Books/Random House, 1925, pp. 659–660.

pp. 212–222 "Daughter of Invention" by Julia Alvarez. Reprinted by permission of the author.

pp. 224–229 "A Second Chance" by Christine Donaghy. Reprinted by permission of the author.

pp. 231–235 "A Shot at Dreams" by Louis J. Russo III. Reprinted by permission of the author.

pp. 237–240 From *Writers at Work: The Paris Review Interviews,* 4th Series, edited by George Plimpton. Copyright © 1974, 1976 by The Paris Review, Inc. All rights reserved. Reprinted by permission of Viking Penguin, Inc.; and "Miss Duling" reprinted by permission of the publishers from *One Writer's Beginnings* by Eudora Welty, Cambridge, MA: Harvard University Press. Copyright © 1983, 1984 by Eudora Welty.

pp. 241–244 "How Flowers Changed the World" from *The Immense Journey* by Loren Eiseley. Copyright © 1957 by Loren Eiseley. Reprinted by permission of Random House, Inc.

pp. 245–247 From "About Men: Man Talk" by Christopher Hallowell in *The New York Times,* September 28, 1986. Copyright © 1986 by The New York Times Company. Reprinted by permission.

pp. 248–250 "In New Mexico: A Family Lives in Its Own World" by Joan Ackerman. Reprinted by permission of the author.

Chapter 8

p. 256 Entry for "jujitsu." Copyright © 1969 by Houghton Mifflin Company. Reprinted by permission from *The American Heritage Dictionary of the English Language.*

pp. 259–262 "Hail the Anhinga" by Edward Hoagland. Copyright © 1984 by Edward Hoagland. Draft and published version and introduction reprinted by permission of Lescher & Lescher, Ltd.

pp. 265–276 "Are You Really a Failure?" by Wendy Modeste. Reprinted by permission of the author.

pp. 278–280 "Living in Two Worlds" by Marcus Mabry from *Newsweek on Campus,* April 1988. Copyright © 1988, Newsweek, Inc. All rights reserved. Reprinted by permission.

pp. 284–285 Excerpt from *Down and Out in Paris and London,* copyright © 1933 by George Orwell and renewed 1961 by Sonia Pitt-Rivers. Reprinted by permission of Harcourt Brace Jovanovich, Inc.

Chapter 9

pp. 295–302 "Criticizing Rock Music Critics" by Jim Fusilli, draft, essay, and headnote. Reprinted by permission of Pickering Associates, Inc.

pp. 305–309 "Why I Don't Read the News Anymore" by Tekla Devai, essay and draft. Reprinted by permission of the author.

pp. 311–314 "Giving the Death Penalty to Drug Dealers" by George Kormos, essay and draft. Reprinted by permission of the author.

pp. 316–318 "What's Wrong with Black English" by Rachel L. Jones, essay, headnote, and quotation. Reprinted by permission of the author.

pp. 319–322 "I Have a Dream" by Martin Luther King, Jr. Copyright © 1963 by Martin Luther King, Jr. Reprinted by permission of Joan Daves.

pp. 324–325 "The Vandal and the Sportsman" from *The Great Chain of Life* by Joseph Wood Krutch. Copyright © 1956 by Joseph Wood Krutch. Copyright renewed 1984 by Marcelle L. Krutch. Reprinted by permission of Houghton Mifflin Company.

pp. 326–328 From "The Habit of Loving" by Barbara Ascher. Copyright © 1986, 1987, 1989 by Barbara Lazear Ascher. Reprinted by permission of Random House, Inc.

pp. 329–331 "How Should Reporters Cover Death?" by Sydney Schanberg from *New York Newsday,* February 17, 1989. Reprinted by permission of the Los Angeles Times Syndicate International.

Chapter 10

p. 344 From "Being a Poet in the United States" by Robert Bly in the *The New York Times Book Review,* January 22, 1984. Copyright © 1984 by The New York Times Company. Reprinted by permission.

pp. 346–354 "Death of a Pig" from *Essays of E. B. White* by E. B. White. Copyright © 1947 by E. B. White. Originally appeared in *Atlantic Magazine.* Draft and published version reprinted by permission of Harper & Row, Publishers, Inc., Cornell University Library and the Estate of E. B. White.

pp. 356–362 "Here to Stay" by Russell Baker in *The New York Times Magazine,* December 3, 1983. Copyright © 1983 by The New York Times Company. Reprinted by permission.

pp. 364–368 "Words" by William Zinsser from *On Writing Well,* 4th edition. Copyright © 1976, 1980, 1985, 1988, 1990 by William K. Zinsser. Reprinted by permission of the author.

pp. 369–371 "Marrying Absurd" from *Slouching Towards Bethlehem* by Joan Didion. Copyright © 1967, 1968 by Joan Didion. Reprinted by permission of Farrar, Straus and Giroux, Inc.

pp. 372–375 "A Few Shells" from *Gift from the Sea* by Anne Morrow Lindbergh. Copyright © 1955 by Anne Morrow Lindbergh. Reprinted by permission of Pantheon Books, a Division of Random House, Inc.